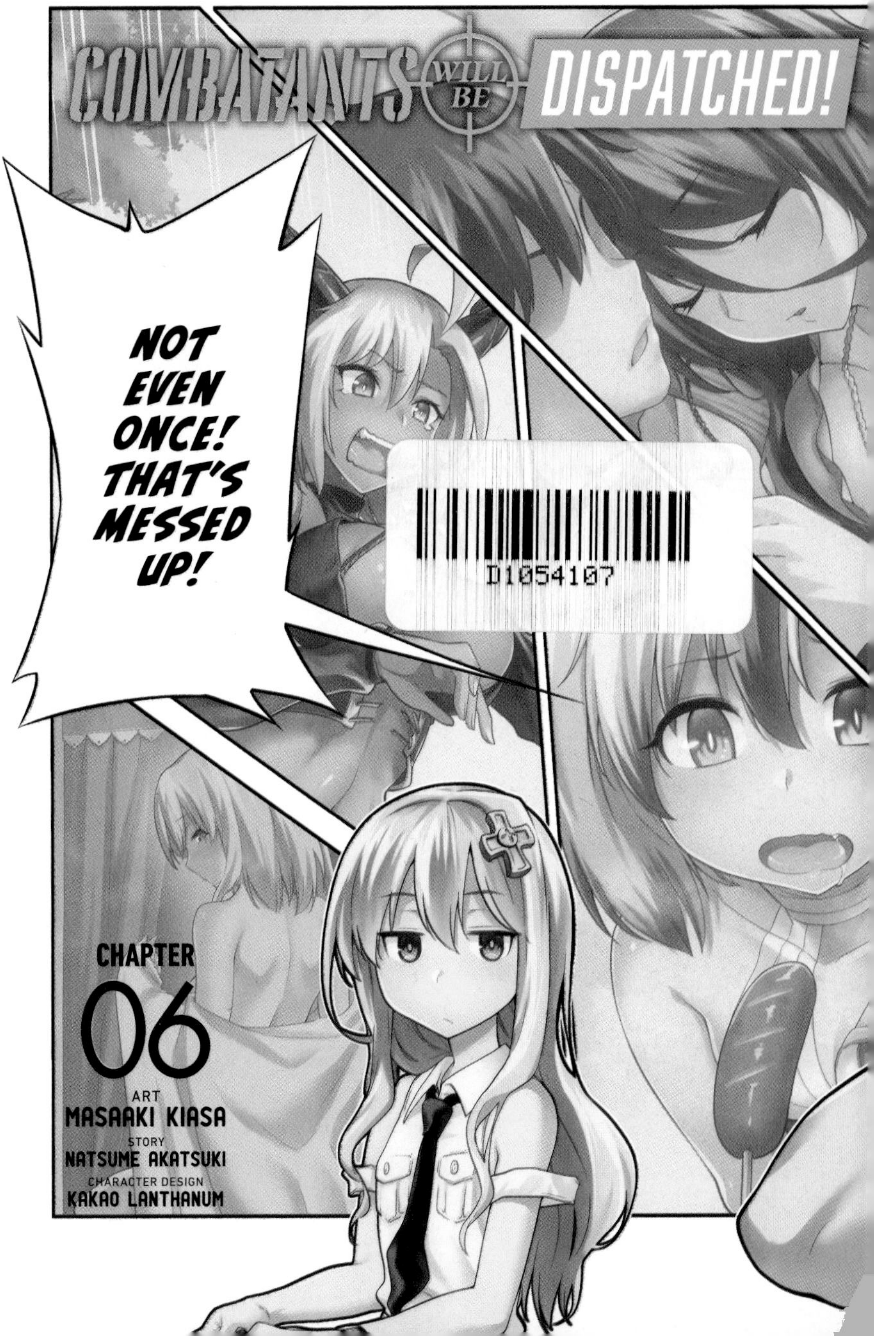
COMBATANTS WILL BE DISPATCHED!
NOT EVEN ONCE! THAT'S MESSED UP!
CHAPTER 06
ART MASAAKI KIASA
STORY NATSUME AKATSUKI
CHARACTER DESIGN KAKAO LANTHANUM

(CONTENTS)

YEN PRESS

COMBATANTS WILL BE DISPATCHED!

CHARACTERS

GRIMM

The Archbishop of Zenarith, God of Undeath and Disaster. Capable of casting curses with bizarre effects like "dizziness" or "the intense pain of stubbing your toe on a dresser." Her targets are usually monsters or happy couples.

ROSE

An always-hungry artificial Chimera who takes on the characteristics of whatever she eats. Honors the dying wish of her creator, her Grandpa, by using incredibly cringy catchphrases.

SNOW

An absolute workaholic who rose to the position of Captain of the Royal Guard despite starting out as a slum-dwelling orphan. However, she's way too much of a glory hound, and never shuts up about getting her share of the credit.

ALICE KISARAGI

A "high-spec, pretty-girl" android made by the Kisaragi Corporation. Equipped with a nuclear reactor that will go critical and self-destruct if treated too roughly.

AGENT SIX

One of the evil Kisaragi Corporation's combat agents. He's best known for his habit of making stupid, offensive comments, but he's actually among the company's top tier when it comes to getting results. Good at coming up with merciless, unorthodox tactics.

STORY SO FAR

The latest assignment for Agent Six, a shock trooper for the nefarious Kisaragi Corporation who has been thrown into more harsh battles against Heroes than he can count, is to conquer a swords-and-sorcery style fantasy world. While searching for a foothold for Kisaragi's invasion, he and his partner Alice, the "pretty-girl" android, discover the Kingdom of Grace, a country apparently populated by humans that is under attack from the armies of the Demon Lord. To keep Kisaragi's competitor from beating it to the punch, this country is going to need a Chosen One...but since it already has one, Six might as well pitch in by becoming a mercenary and leading (former) Royal Guard Captain Snow, Battle Chimera Rose, and Archbishop Grimm in the struggle against the Demon Army. It's up to them to deal with the Demon Lord's Elite Four...

Chapter 06

COMBATANTS WILL BE DISPATCHED!

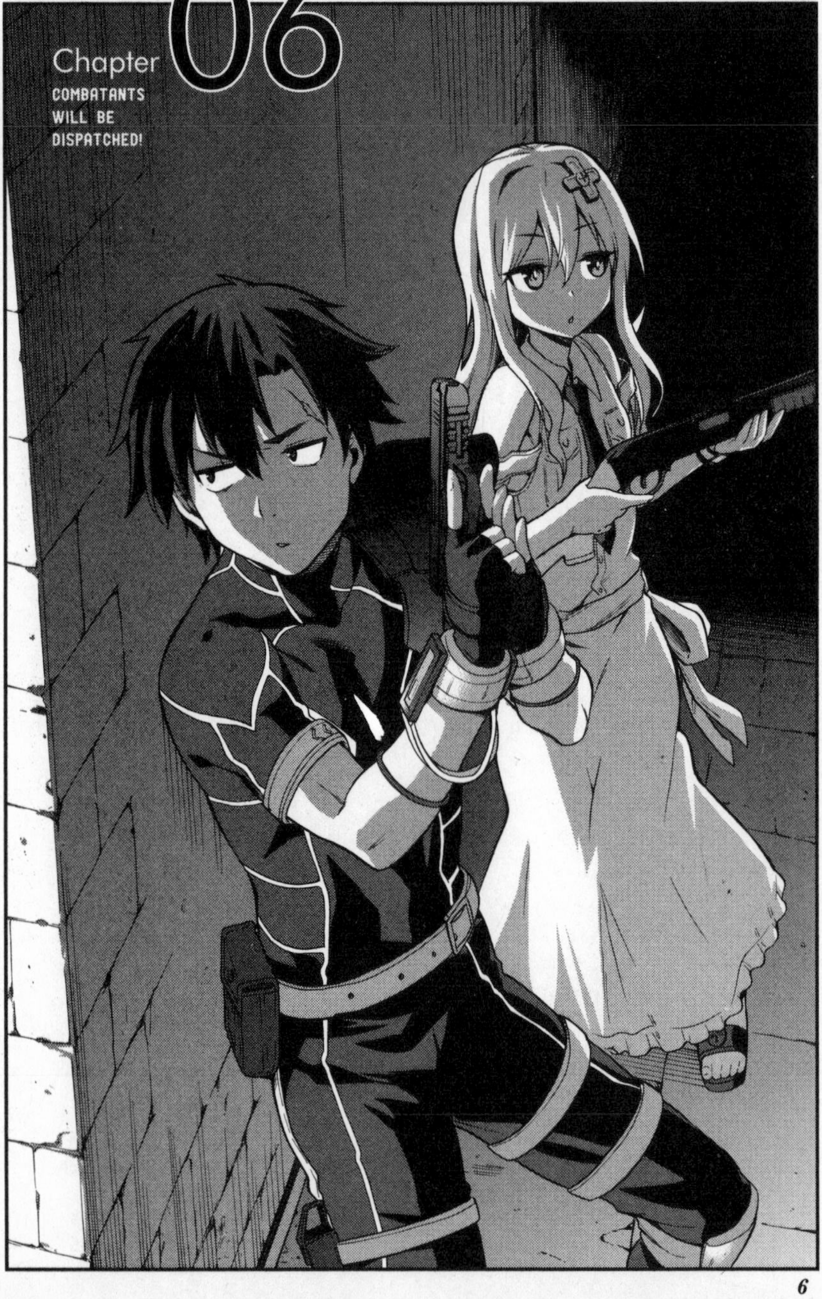

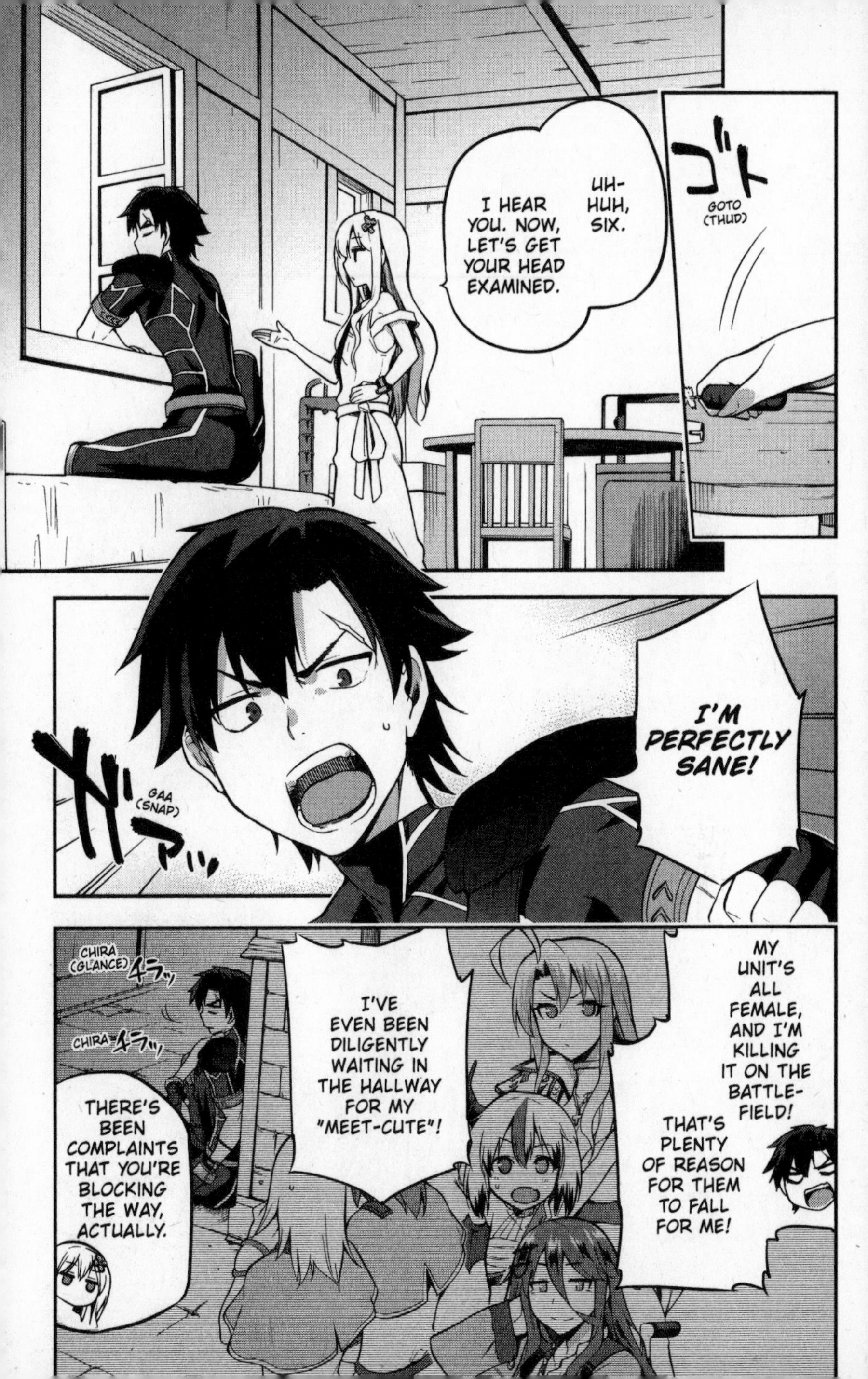
GOTO (THUD)
UH-HUH, SIX.
I HEAR YOU. NOW, LET'S GET YOUR HEAD EXAMINED.
I'M PERFECTLY SANE!
GAA (SNAP)
MY UNIT'S ALL FEMALE, AND I'M KILLING IT ON THE BATTLEFIELD!
THAT'S PLENTY OF REASON FOR THEM TO FALL FOR ME!
I'VE EVEN BEEN DILIGENTLY WAITING IN THE HALLWAY FOR MY "MEET-CUTE"!
CHIRA (GLANCE)
CHIRA
THERE'S BEEN COMPLAINTS THAT YOU'RE BLOCKING THE WAY, ACTUALLY.

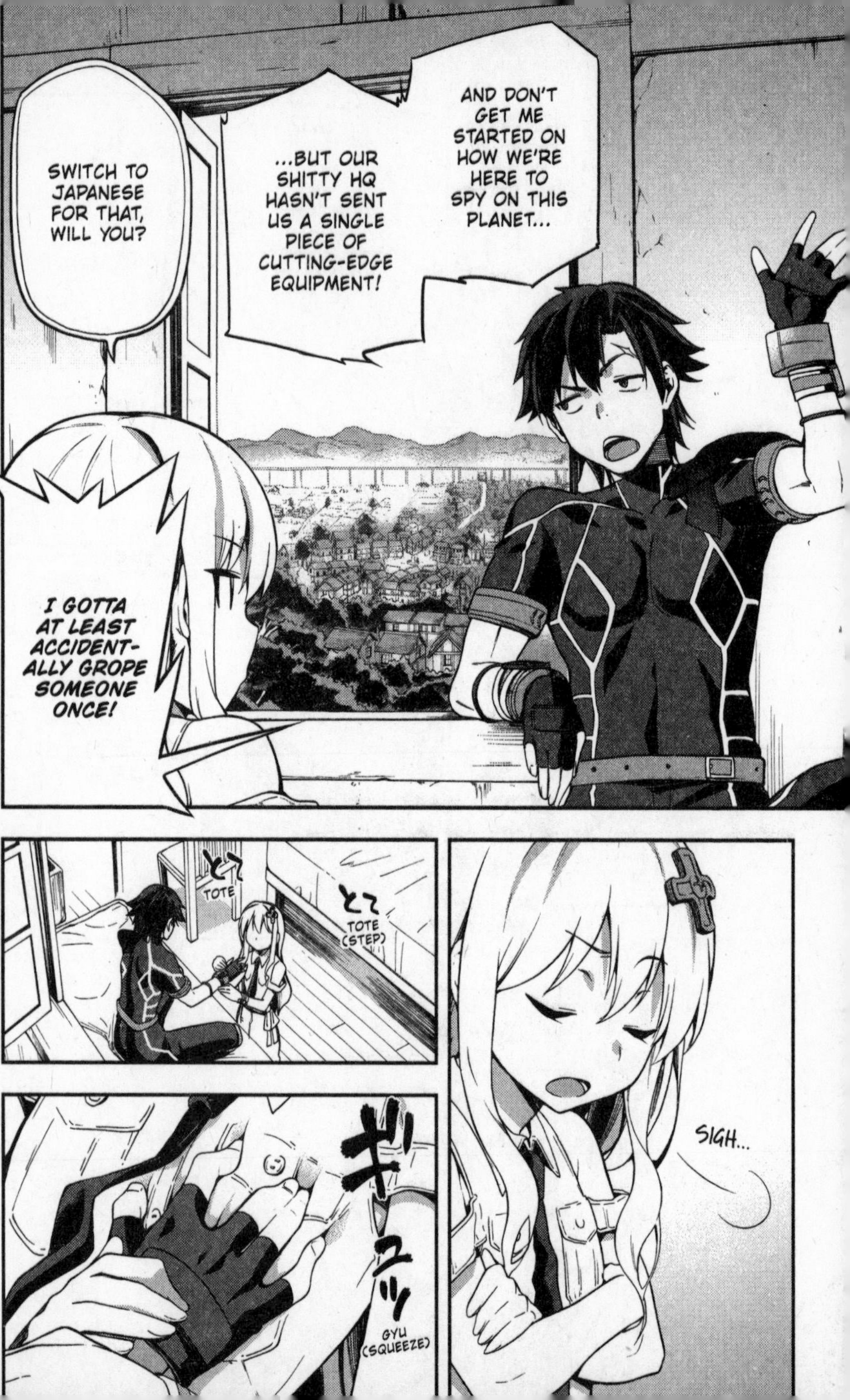
AND DON'T GET ME STARTED ON HOW WE'RE HERE TO SPY ON THIS PLANET...
...BUT OUR SHITTY HQ HASN'T SENT US A SINGLE PIECE OF CUTTING-EDGE EQUIPMENT!
SWITCH TO JAPANESE FOR THAT, WILL YOU?
I GOTTA AT LEAST ACCIDENTALLY GROPE SOMEONE ONCE!
SIGH...
とて
TOTE
とて
TOTE (STEP)
ギュッ
GYU (SQUEEZE)

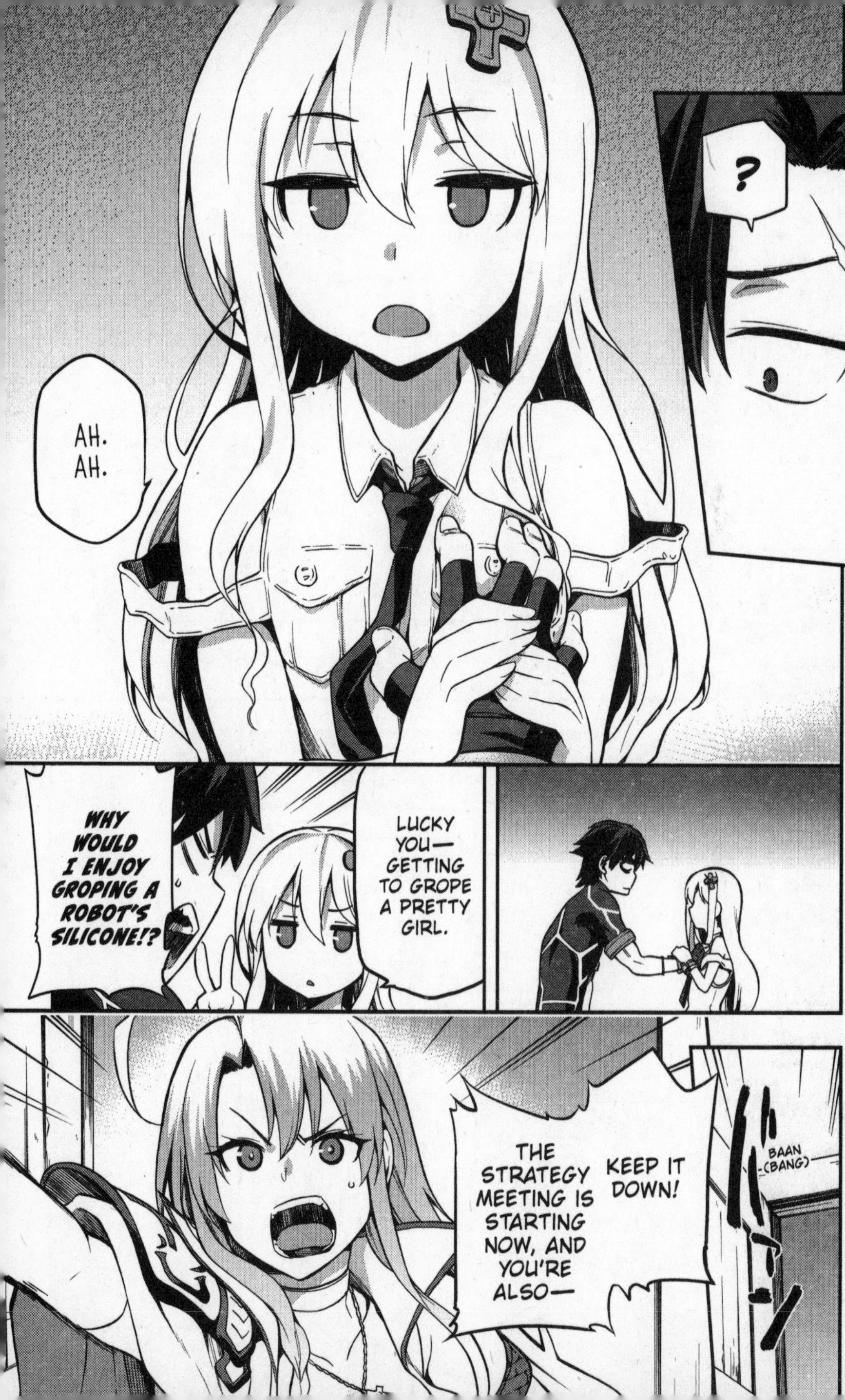
?
AH. AH.
LUCKY YOU—GETTING TO GROPE A PRETTY GIRL.
WHY WOULD I ENJOY GROPING A ROBOT'S SILICONE!?
BAAN (BANG)
KEEP IT DOWN!
THE STRATEGY MEETING IS STARTING NOW, AND YOU'RE ALSO—

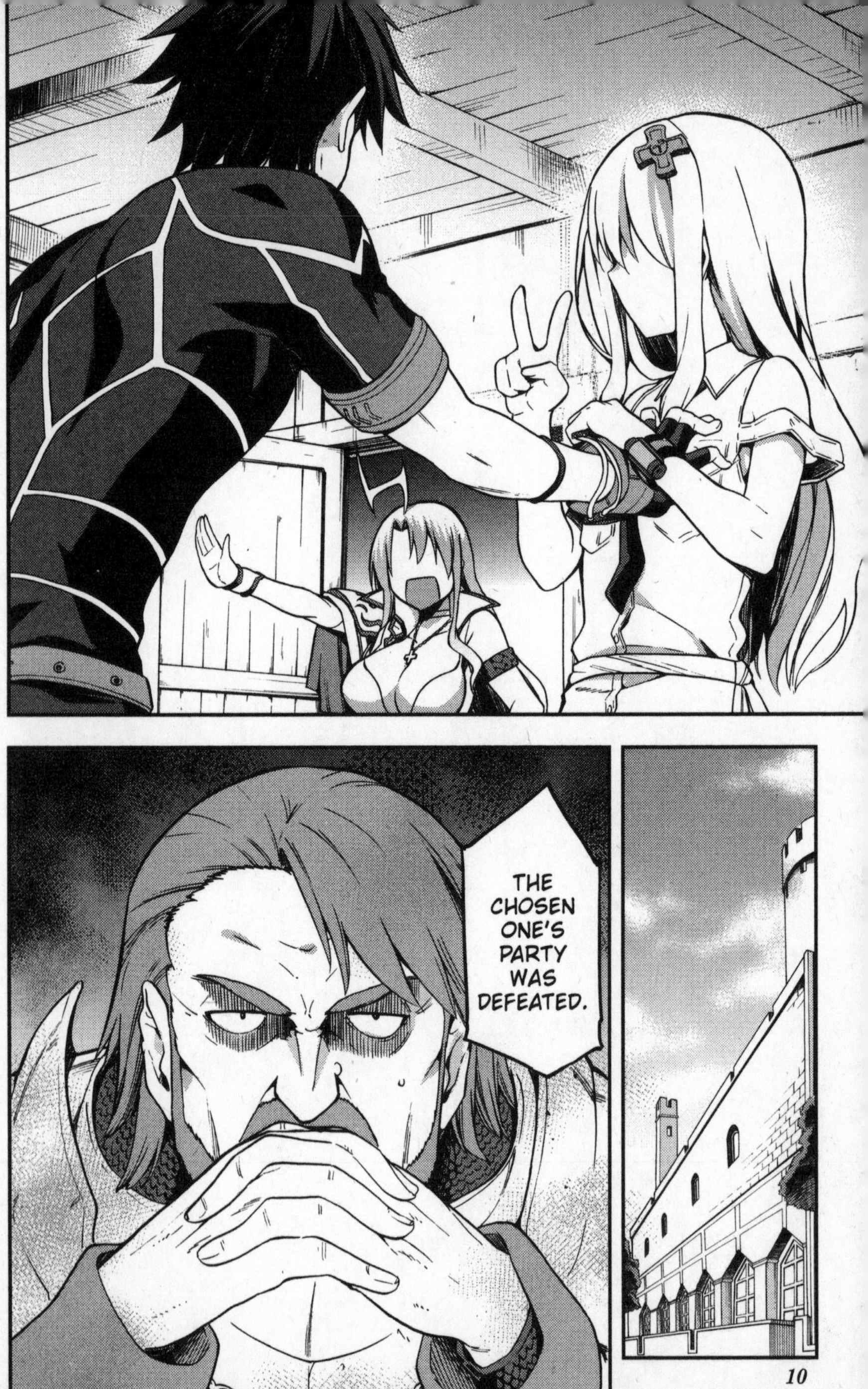
THE CHOSEN ONE'S PARTY WAS DEFEATED.

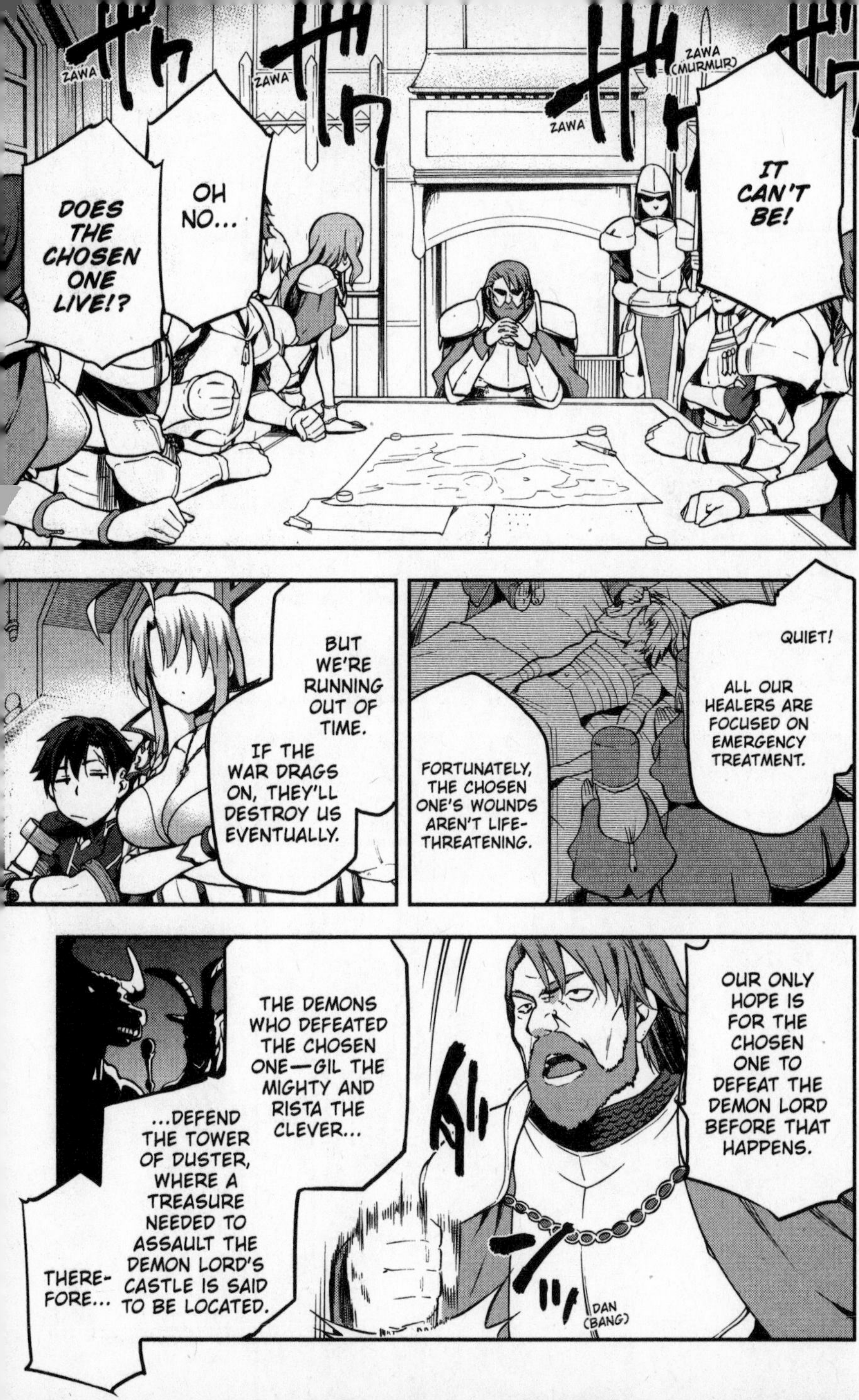
ZAWA (MURMUR)
IT CAN'T BE!
ZAWA
ZAWA
OH NO...
DOES THE CHOSEN ONE LIVE!?
ZAWA
QUIET!
ALL OUR HEALERS ARE FOCUSED ON EMERGENCY TREATMENT.
FORTUNATELY, THE CHOSEN ONE'S WOUNDS AREN'T LIFE-THREATENING.
BUT WE'RE RUNNING OUT OF TIME.
IF THE WAR DRAGS ON, THEY'LL DESTROY US EVENTUALLY.
OUR ONLY HOPE IS FOR THE CHOSEN ONE TO DEFEAT THE DEMON LORD BEFORE THAT HAPPENS.
DAN (BANG)
THE DEMONS WHO DEFEATED THE CHOSEN ONE—GIL THE MIGHTY AND RISTA THE CLEVER...
...DEFEND THE TOWER OF DUSTER, WHERE A TREASURE NEEDED TO ASSAULT THE DEMON LORD'S CASTLE IS SAID TO BE LOCATED.
THERE-FORE...

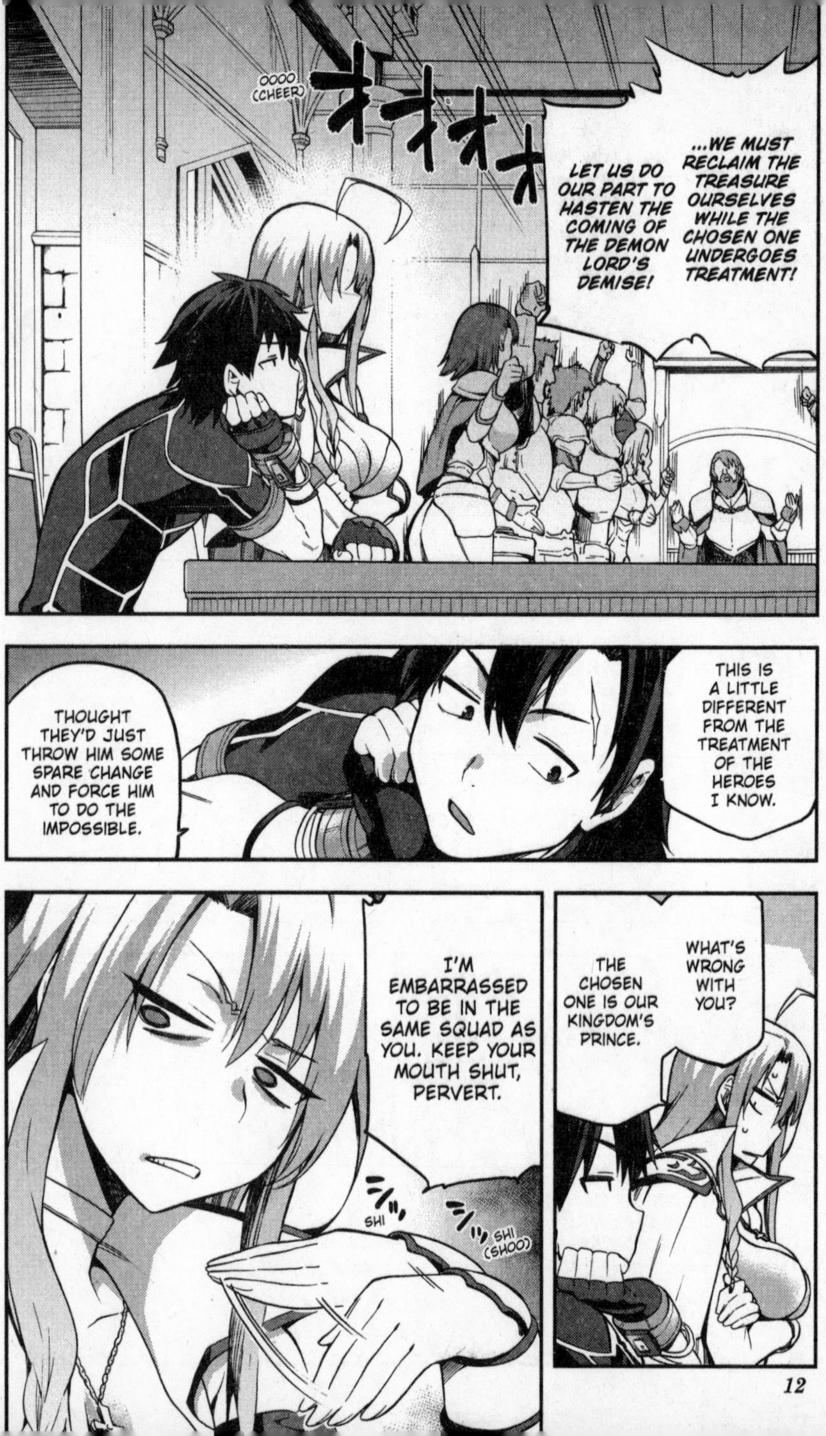
...WE MUST RECLAIM THE TREASURE OURSELVES WHILE THE CHOSEN ONE UNDERGOES TREATMENT!
LET US DO OUR PART TO HASTEN THE COMING OF THE DEMON LORD'S DEMISE!
オオオオ
OOOO (CHEER)
THIS IS A LITTLE DIFFERENT FROM THE TREATMENT OF THE HEROES I KNOW.
THOUGHT THEY'D JUST THROW HIM SOME SPARE CHANGE AND FORCE HIM TO DO THE IMPOSSIBLE.
WHAT'S WRONG WITH YOU?
THE CHOSEN ONE IS OUR KINGDOM'S PRINCE.
I'M EMBARRASSED TO BE IN THE SAME SQUAD AS YOU. KEEP YOUR MOUTH SHUT, PERVERT.
SHI
SHI (SHOO)

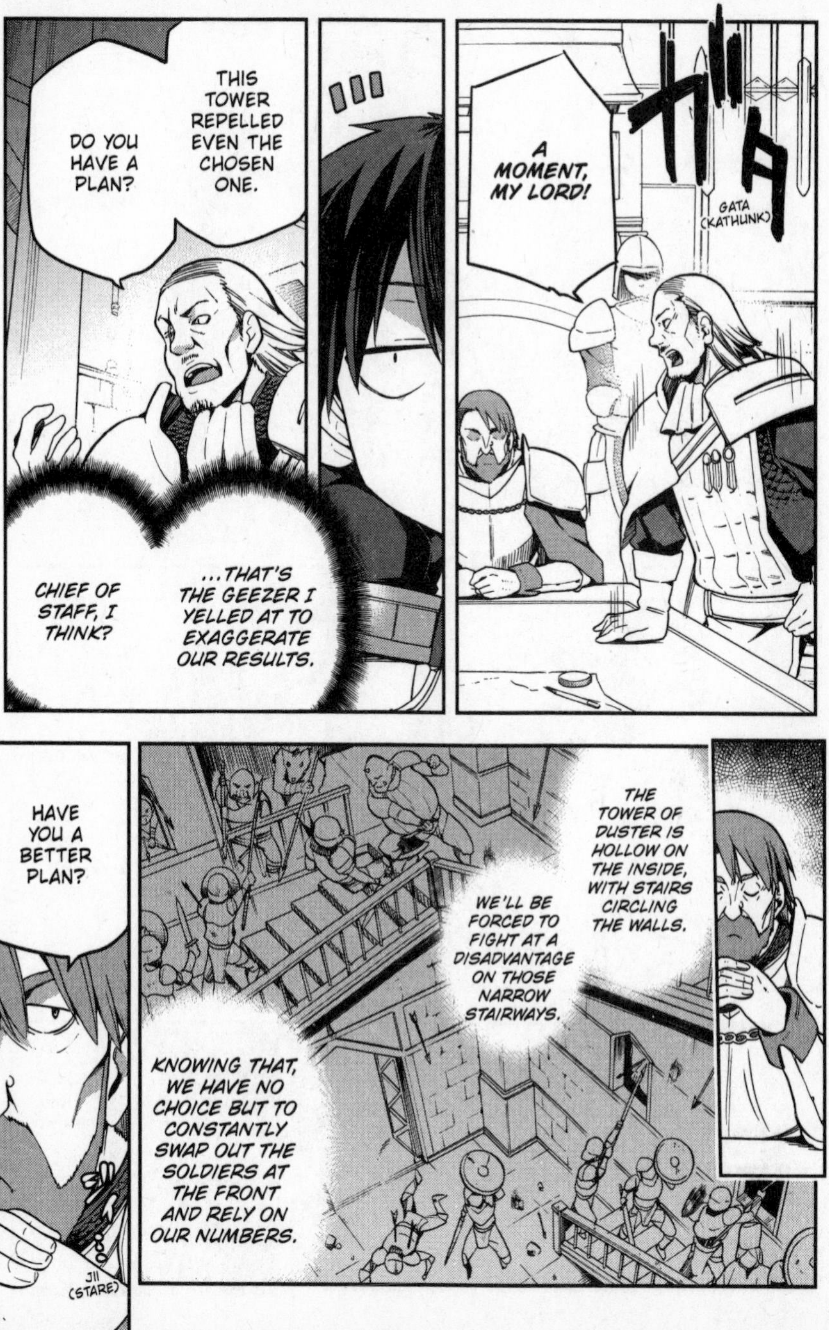
A MOMENT, MY LORD!
GATA (KATHUNK)
THIS TOWER REPELLED EVEN THE CHOSEN ONE.
DO YOU HAVE A PLAN?
...THAT'S THE GEEZER I YELLED AT TO EXAGGERATE OUR RESULTS.
CHIEF OF STAFF, I THINK?
THE TOWER OF DUSTER IS HOLLOW ON THE INSIDE, WITH STAIRS CIRCLING THE WALLS.
WE'LL BE FORCED TO FIGHT AT A DISADVANTAGE ON THOSE NARROW STAIRWAYS.
KNOWING THAT, WE HAVE NO CHOICE BUT TO CONSTANTLY SWAP OUT THE SOLDIERS AT THE FRONT AND RELY ON OUR NUMBERS.
HAVE YOU A BETTER PLAN?
JII (STARE)

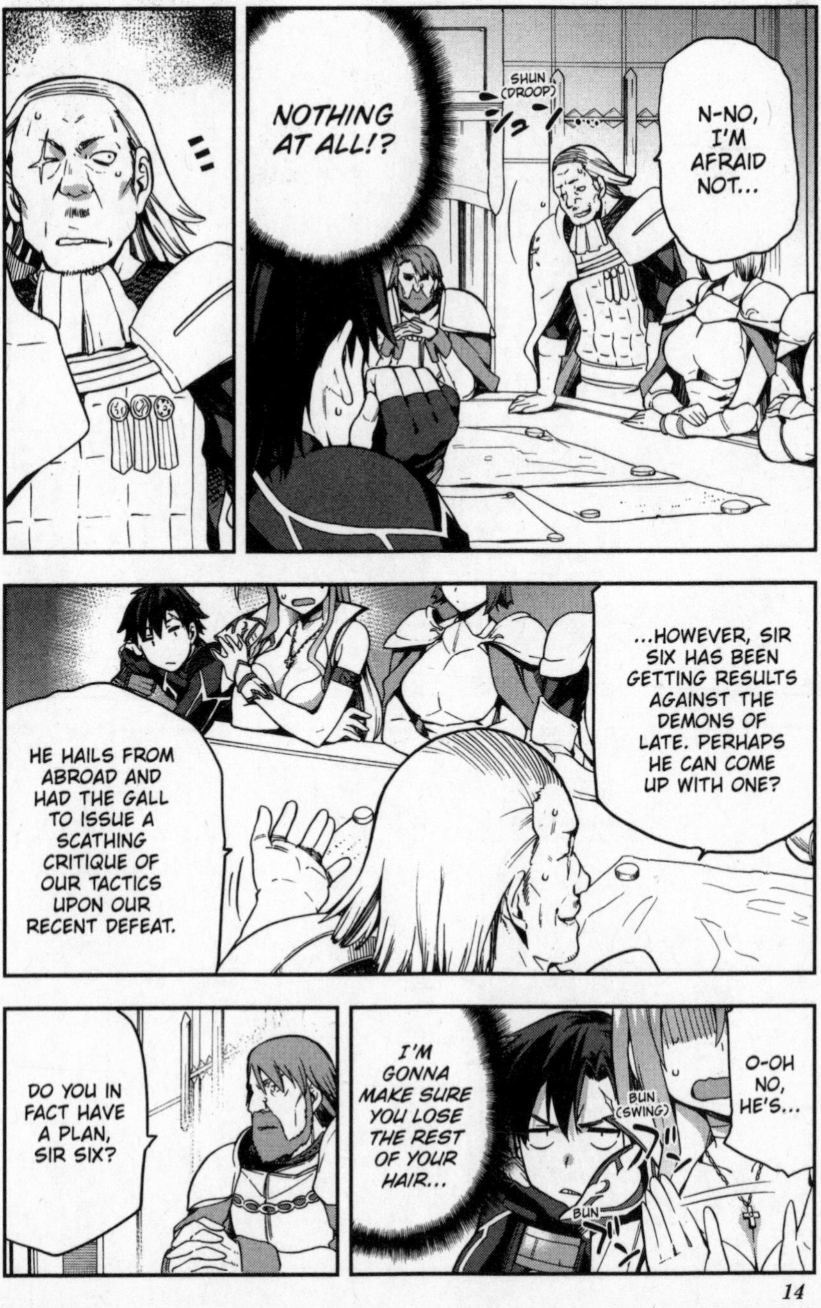
N-NO, I'M AFRAID NOT...
SHUN (DROOP)
NOTHING AT ALL!?
...HOWEVER, SIR SIX HAS BEEN GETTING RESULTS AGAINST THE DEMONS OF LATE. PERHAPS HE CAN COME UP WITH ONE?
HE HAILS FROM ABROAD AND HAD THE GALL TO ISSUE A SCATHING CRITIQUE OF OUR TACTICS UPON OUR RECENT DEFEAT.
O-OH NO, HE'S...
BUN (SWING)
I'M GONNA MAKE SURE YOU LOSE THE REST OF YOUR HAIR...
BUN
DO YOU IN FACT HAVE A PLAN, SIR SIX?

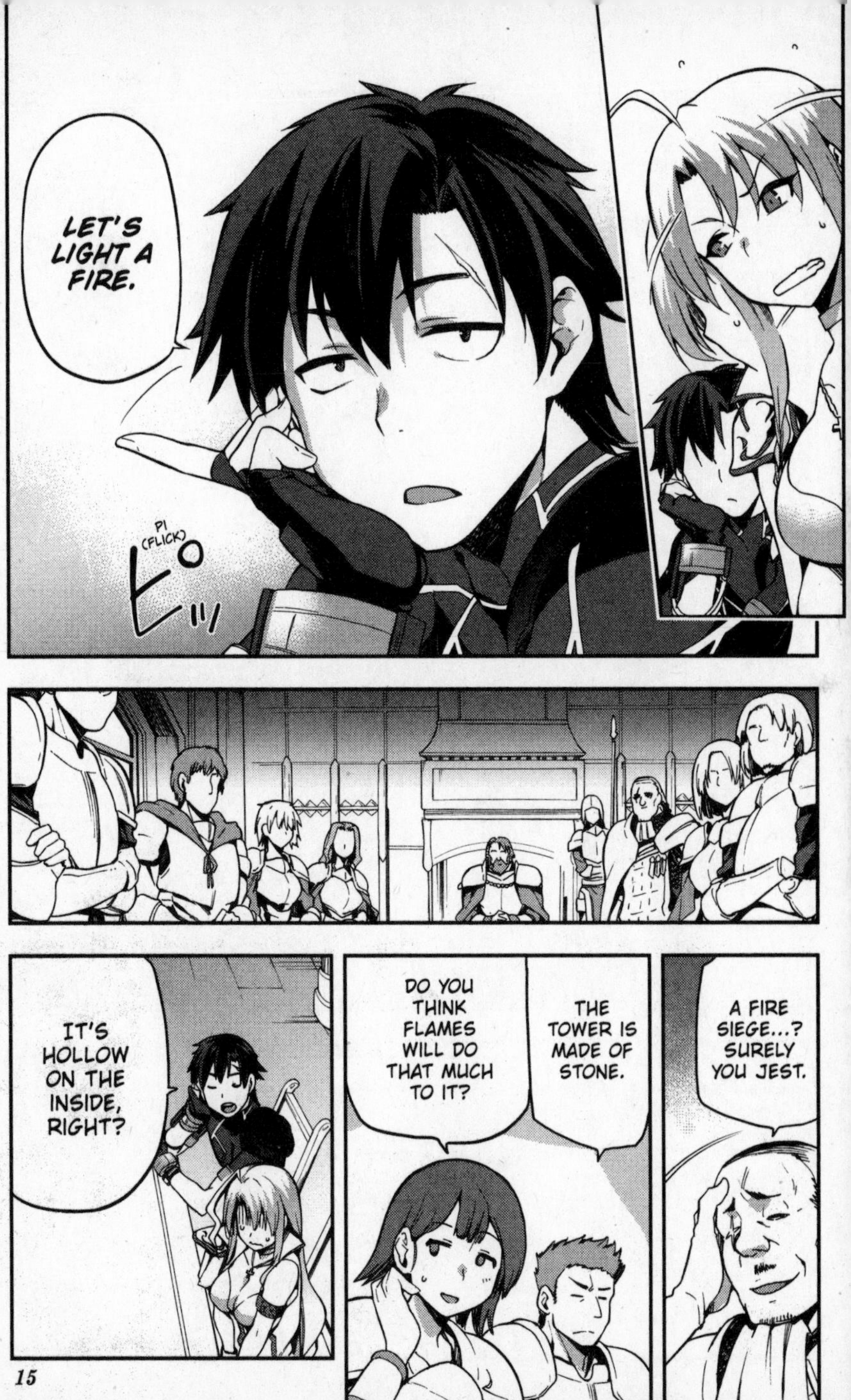
LET'S LIGHT A FIRE.
PI (FLICK)
ピッ
A FIRE SIEGE...? SURELY YOU JEST.
THE TOWER IS MADE OF STONE.
DO YOU THINK FLAMES WILL DO THAT MUCH TO IT?
IT'S HOLLOW ON THE INSIDE, RIGHT?

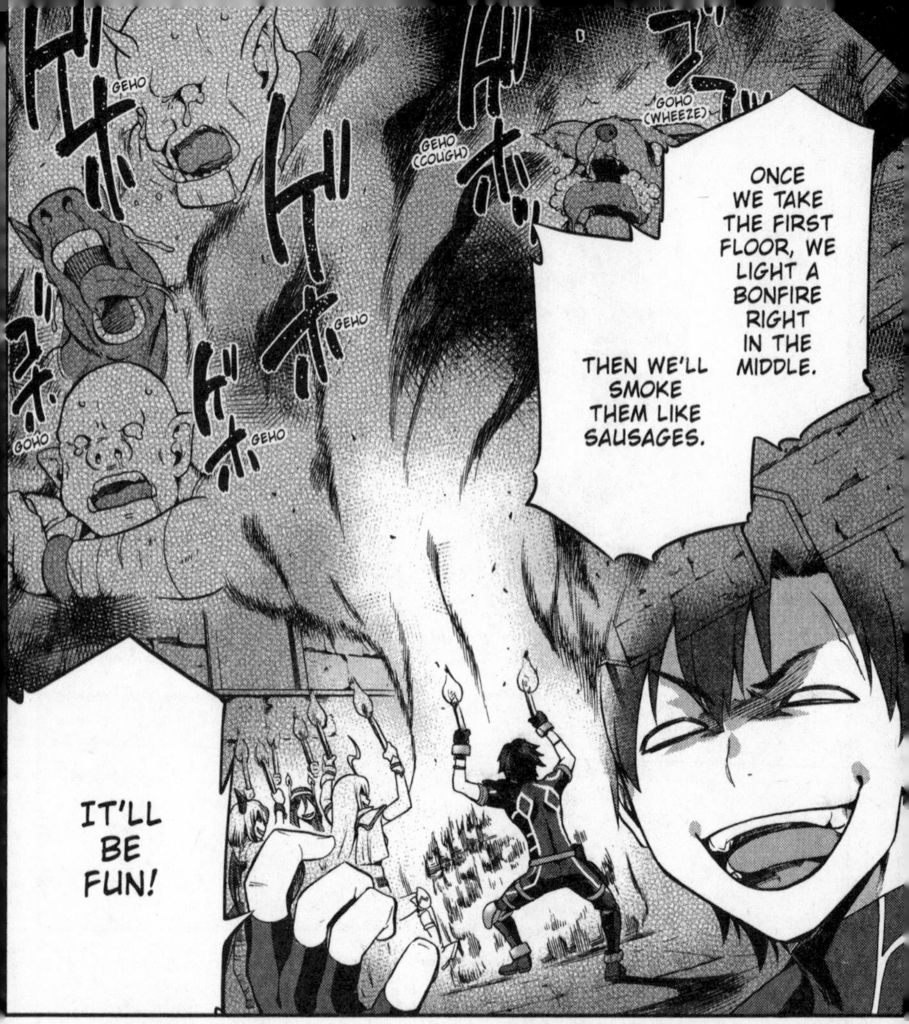
GOHO (WHEEZE)
GEHO (COUGH)
GEHO
ONCE WE TAKE THE FIRST FLOOR, WE LIGHT A BONFIRE RIGHT IN THE MIDDLE.
THEN WE'LL SMOKE THEM LIKE SAUSAGES.
GEHO
GEHO
GOHO
IT'LL BE FUN!

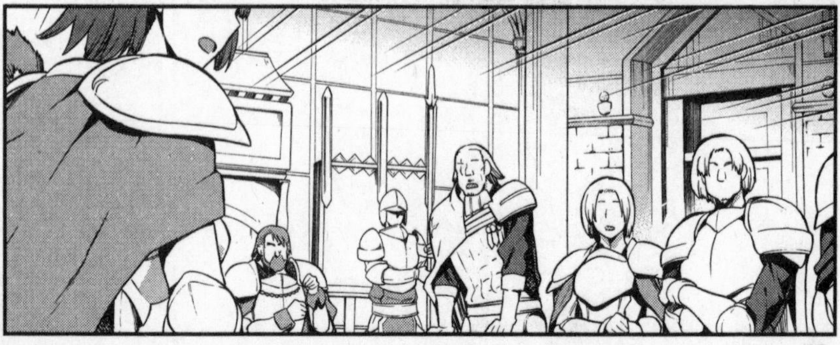

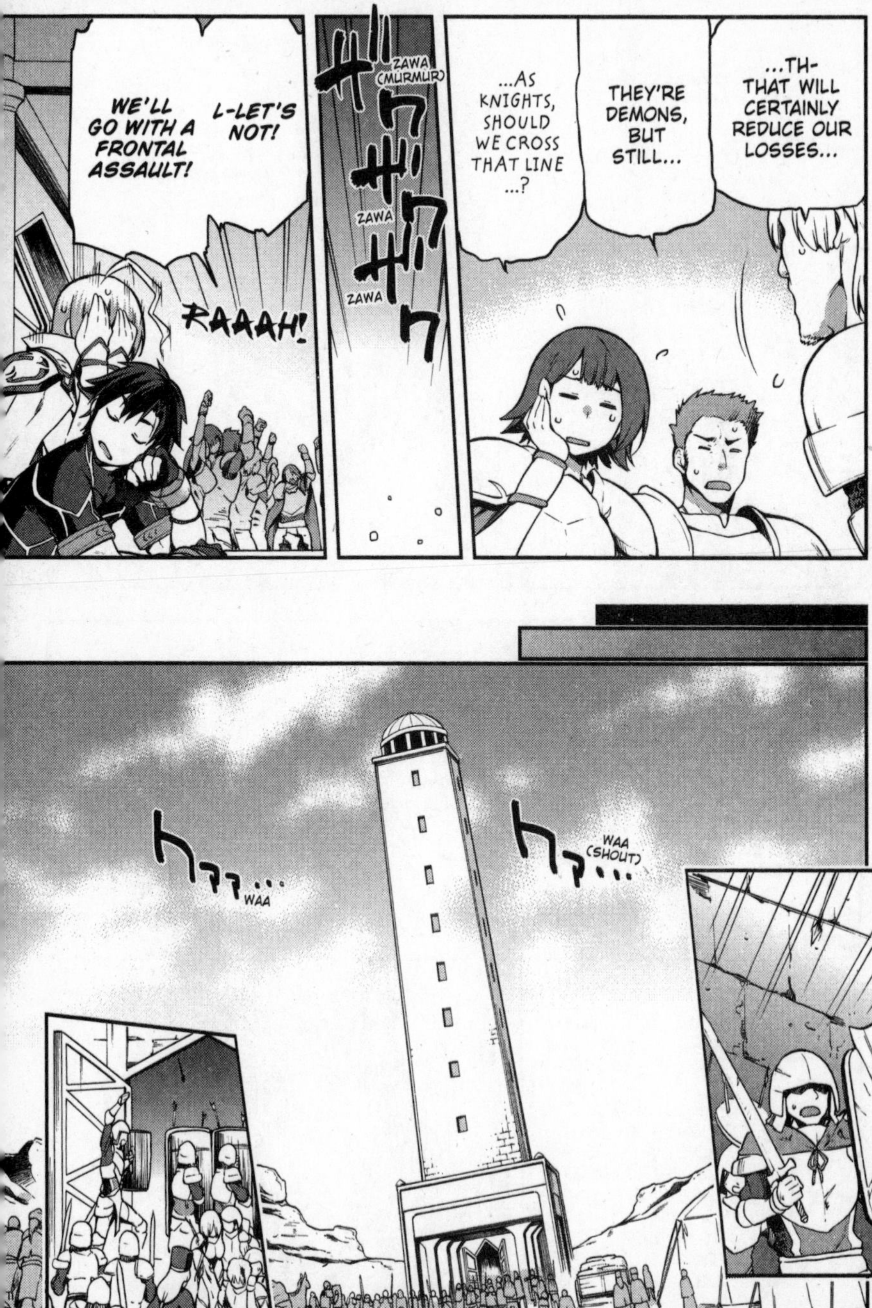
...TH- THAT WILL CERTAINLY REDUCE OUR LOSSES...
THEY'RE DEMONS, BUT STILL...
...AS KNIGHTS, SHOULD WE CROSS THAT LINE ...?
ZAWA (MURMUR)
ZAWA
ZAWA
L-LET'S NOT!
WE'LL GO WITH A FRONTAL ASSAULT!
RAAAH!
WAA (SHOUT)
WAA

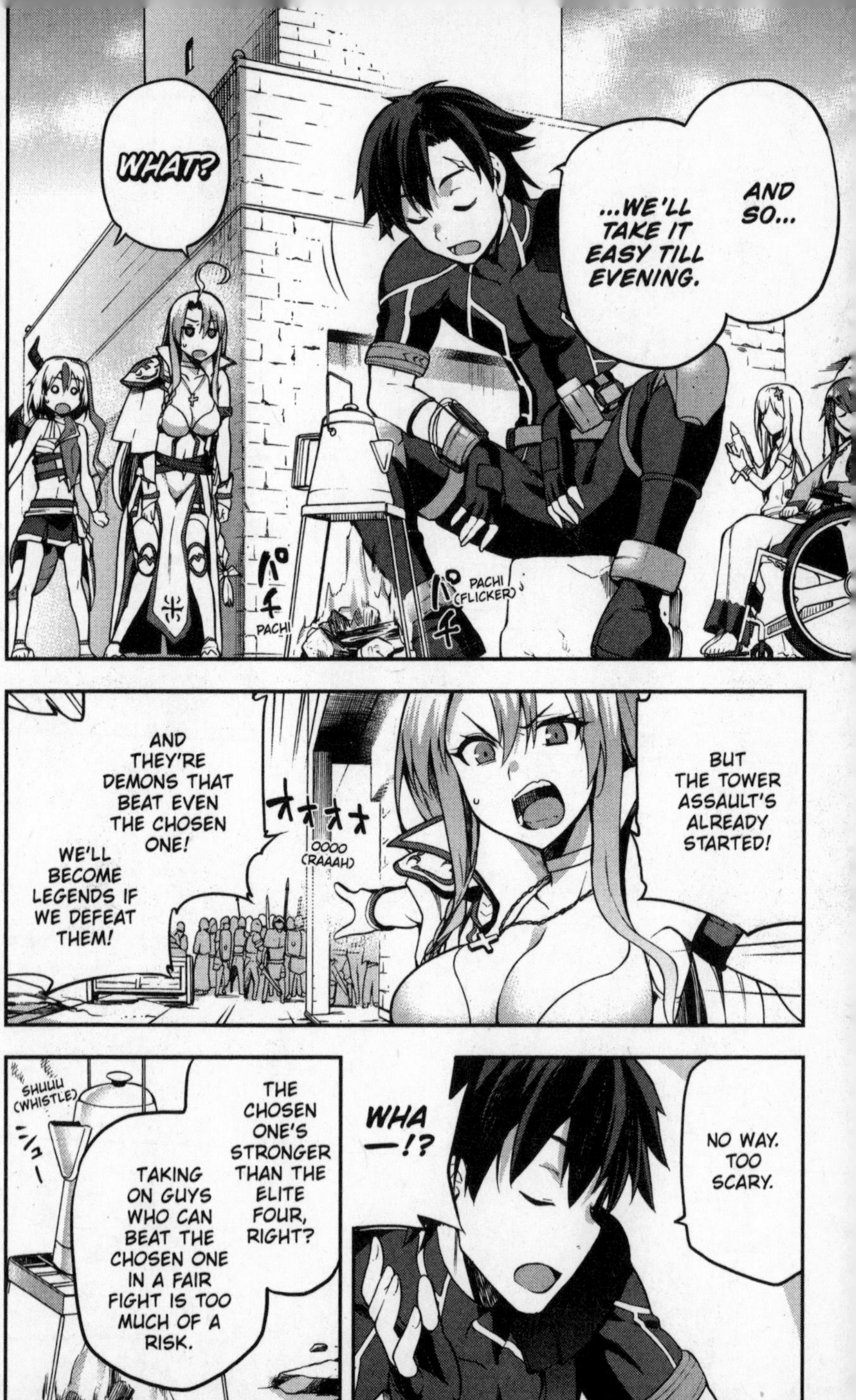
AND SO...
...WE'LL TAKE IT EASY TILL EVENING.
PACHI (FLICKER)
WHAT?
PACHI
BUT THE TOWER ASSAULT'S ALREADY STARTED!
OOOO (RAAAH)
AND THEY'RE DEMONS THAT BEAT EVEN THE CHOSEN ONE!
WE'LL BECOME LEGENDS IF WE DEFEAT THEM!
NO WAY. TOO SCARY.
WHA—!?
THE CHOSEN ONE'S STRONGER THAN THE ELITE FOUR, RIGHT?
TAKING ON GUYS WHO CAN BEAT THE CHOSEN ONE IN A FAIR FIGHT IS TOO MUCH OF A RISK.
SHUUU (WHISTLE)

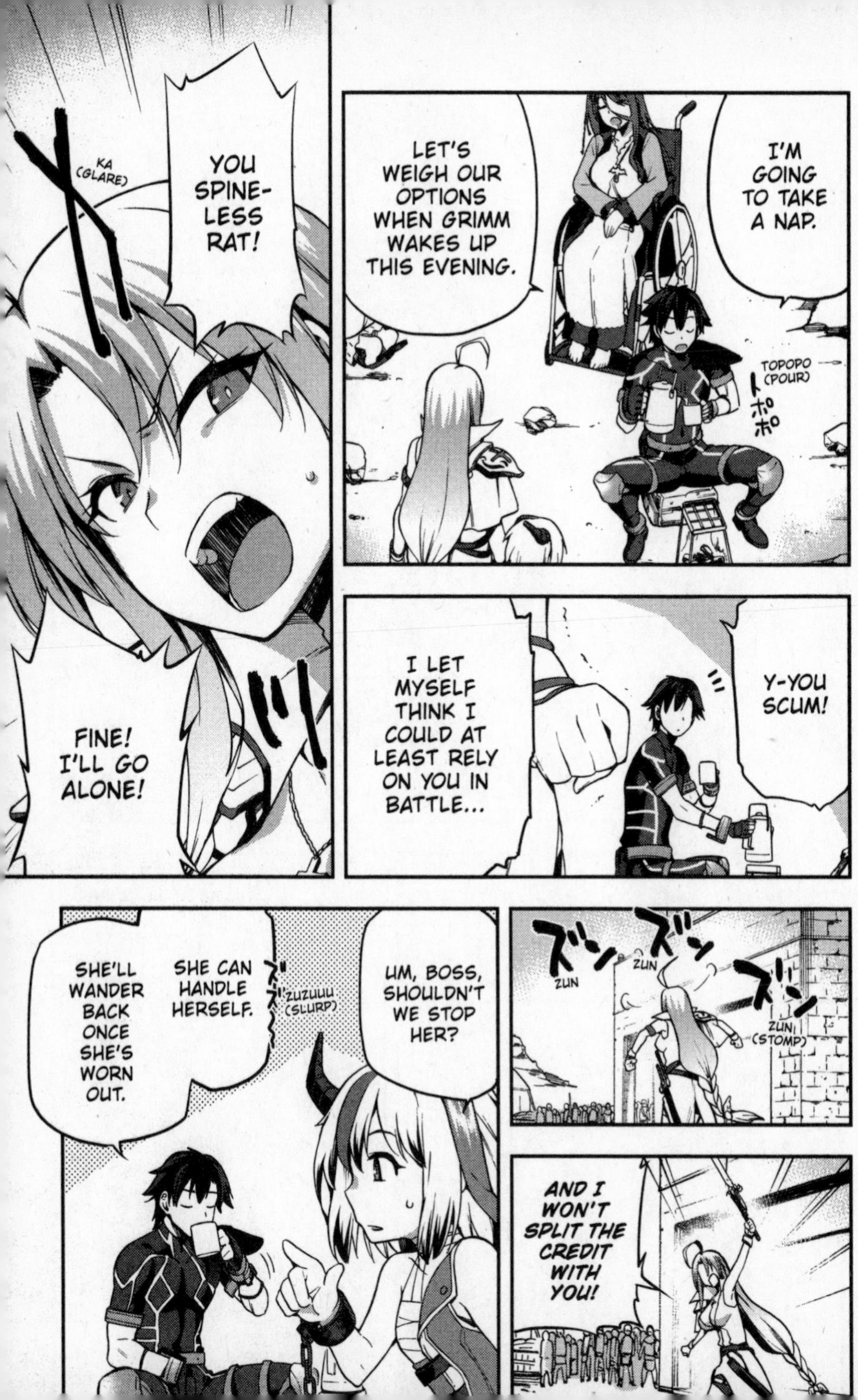
I'M GOING TO TAKE A NAP.
LET'S WEIGH OUR OPTIONS WHEN GRIMM WAKES UP THIS EVENING.
TOPOPO (POUR)
Y-YOU SCUM!
I LET MYSELF THINK I COULD AT LEAST RELY ON YOU IN BATTLE...
KA (GLARE)
YOU SPINELESS RAT!
FINE! I'LL GO ALONE!
ZUN
ZUN
ZUN (STOMP)
AND I WON'T SPLIT THE CREDIT WITH YOU!
UM, BOSS, SHOULDN'T WE STOP HER?
ZUZUUU (SLURP)
SHE CAN HANDLE HERSELF.
SHE'LL WANDER BACK ONCE SHE'S WORN OUT.

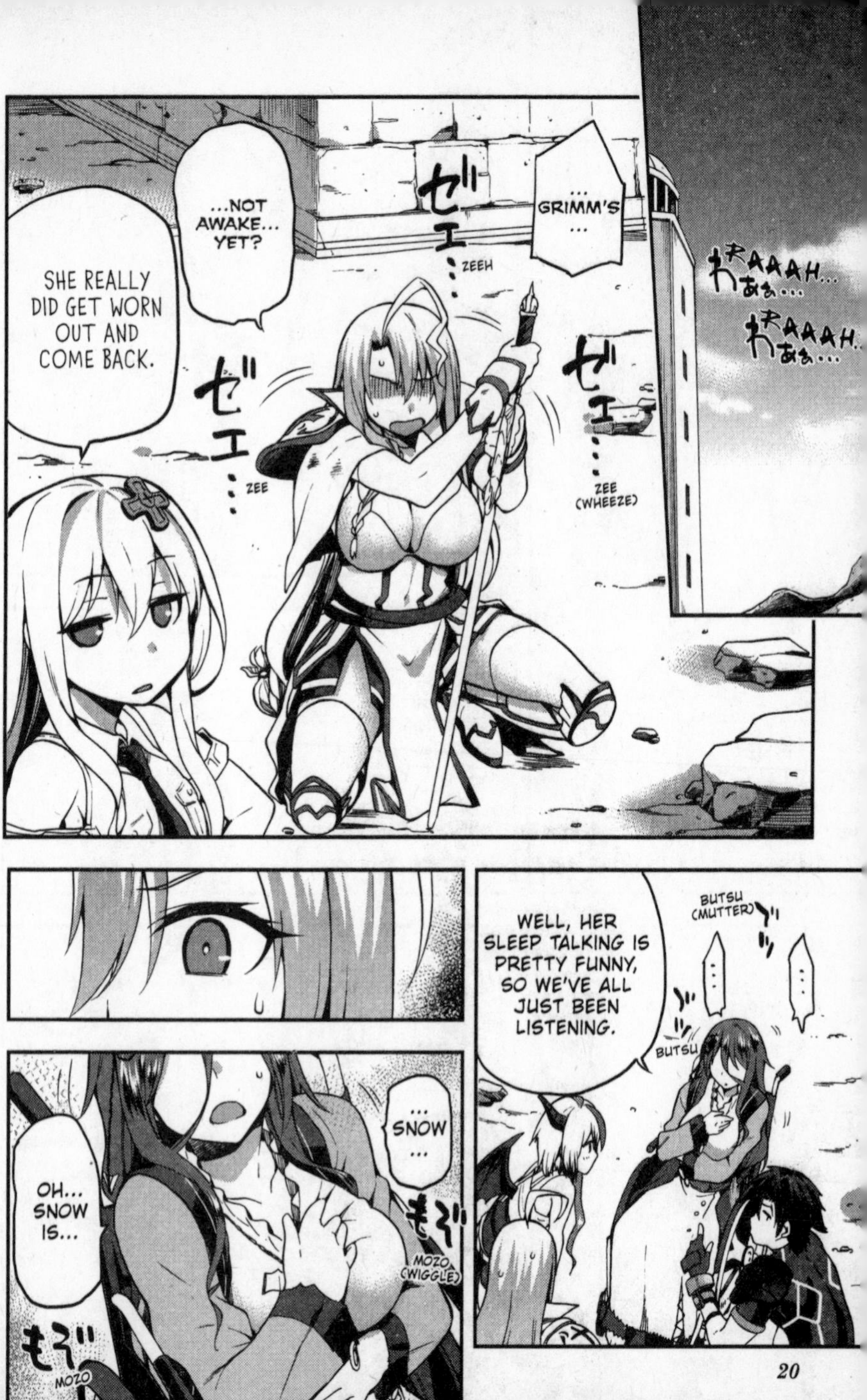

わあぁ… RAAAH...
わあぁ… RAAAH...
...GRIMM'S...
ゼェ… ZEEH
...NOT AWAKE... YET?
ゼェ… ZEE (WHEEZE)
SHE REALLY DID GET WORN OUT AND COME BACK.
ゼェ… ZEE
ブツ BUTSU (MUTTER)
ブツ BUTSU
WELL, HER SLEEP TALKING IS PRETTY FUNNY, SO WE'VE ALL JUST BEEN LISTENING.
...
...
...SNOW...
OH... SNOW IS...
もぞ MOZO (WIGGLE)
もぞ MOZO

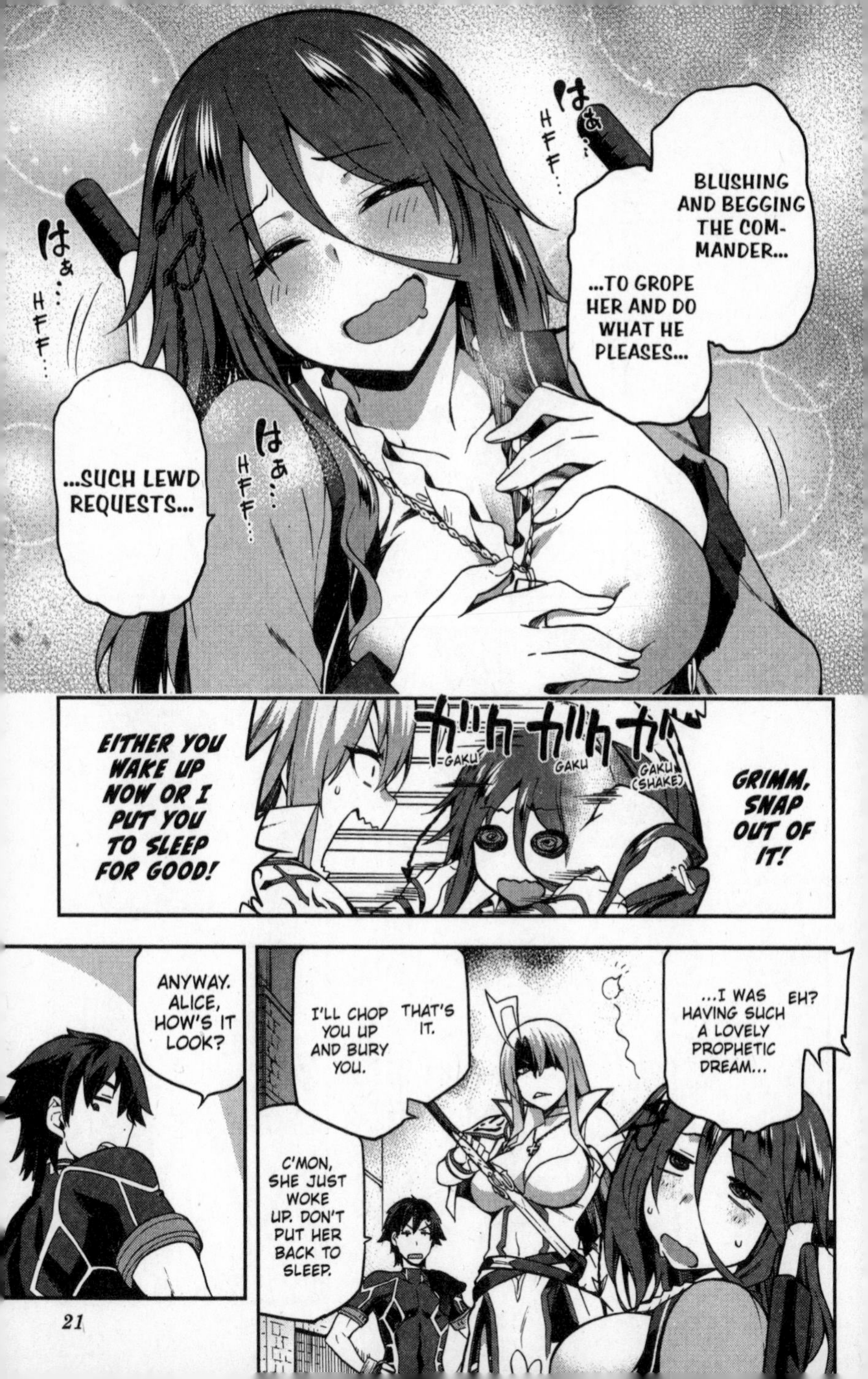

はぁ… HFF…
BLUSHING AND BEGGING THE COM-MANDER...
...TO GROPE HER AND DO WHAT HE PLEASES...
はぁ… HFF…
はぁ… HFF…
...SUCH LEWD REQUESTS...
GRIMM, SNAP OUT OF IT!
ガクガクガ GAKU GAKU GAKU (SHAKE)
EITHER YOU WAKE UP NOW OR I PUT YOU TO SLEEP FOR GOOD!
EH?
...I WAS HAVING SUCH A LOVELY PROPHETIC DREAM...
THAT'S IT.
I'LL CHOP YOU UP AND BURY YOU.
C'MON, SHE JUST WOKE UP. DON'T PUT HER BACK TO SLEEP.
ANYWAY. ALICE, HOW'S IT LOOK?

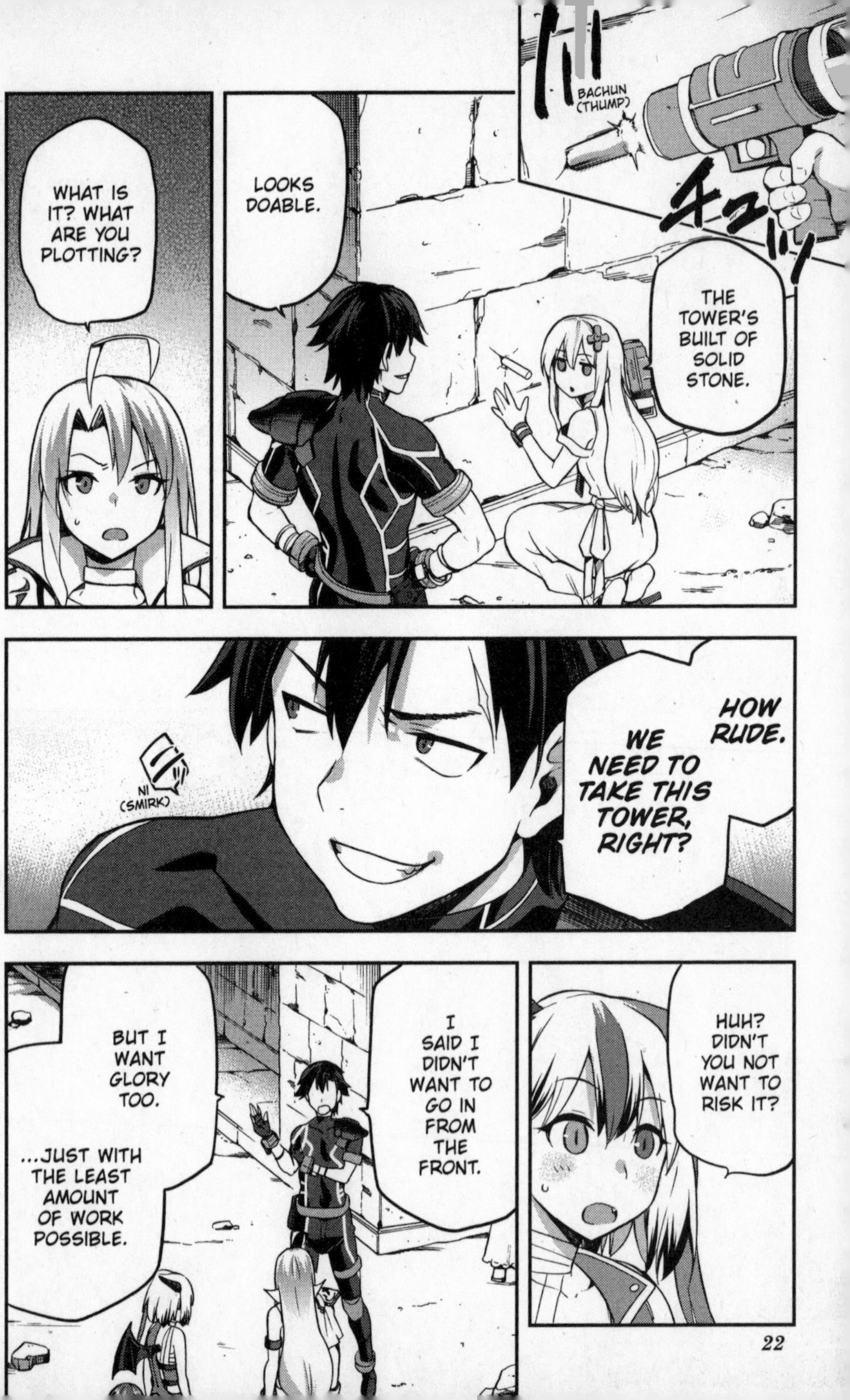
BACHUN (THUMP)
THE TOWER'S BUILT OF SOLID STONE.
LOOKS DOABLE.
WHAT IS IT? WHAT ARE YOU PLOTTING?
HOW RUDE.
WE NEED TO TAKE THIS TOWER, RIGHT?
NI (SMIRK)
HUH? DIDN'T YOU NOT WANT TO RISK IT?
I SAID I DIDN'T WANT TO GO IN FROM THE FRONT.
BUT I WANT GLORY TOO.
...JUST WITH THE LEAST AMOUNT OF WORK POSSIBLE.

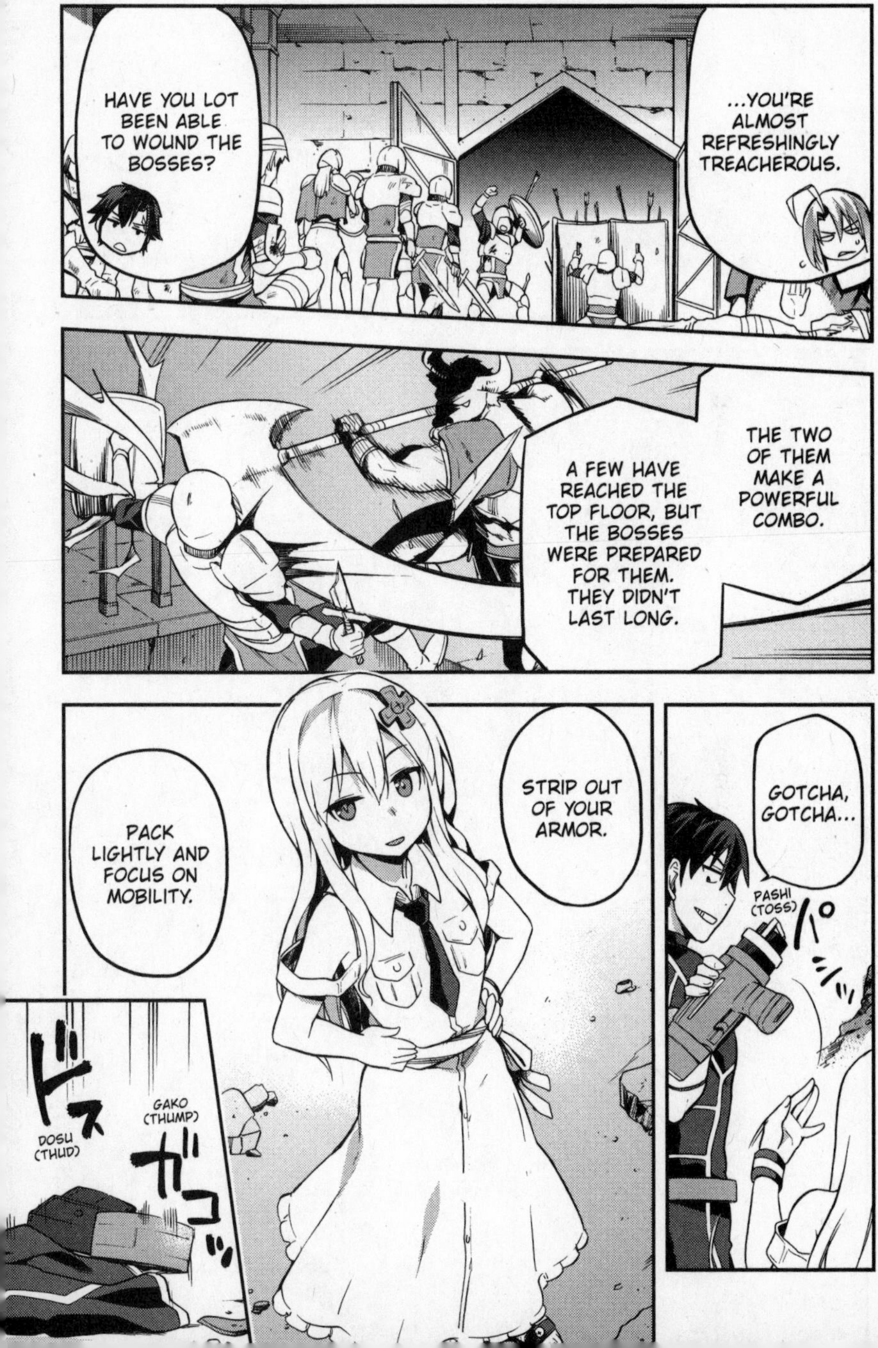
...YOU'RE ALMOST REFRESHINGLY TREACHEROUS.
HAVE YOU LOT BEEN ABLE TO WOUND THE BOSSES?
THE TWO OF THEM MAKE A POWERFUL COMBO.
A FEW HAVE REACHED THE TOP FLOOR, BUT THE BOSSES WERE PREPARED FOR THEM. THEY DIDN'T LAST LONG.
GOTCHA, GOTCHA...
PASHI (TOSS)
STRIP OUT OF YOUR ARMOR.
PACK LIGHTLY AND FOCUS ON MOBILITY.
GAKO (THUMP)
DOSU (THUD)

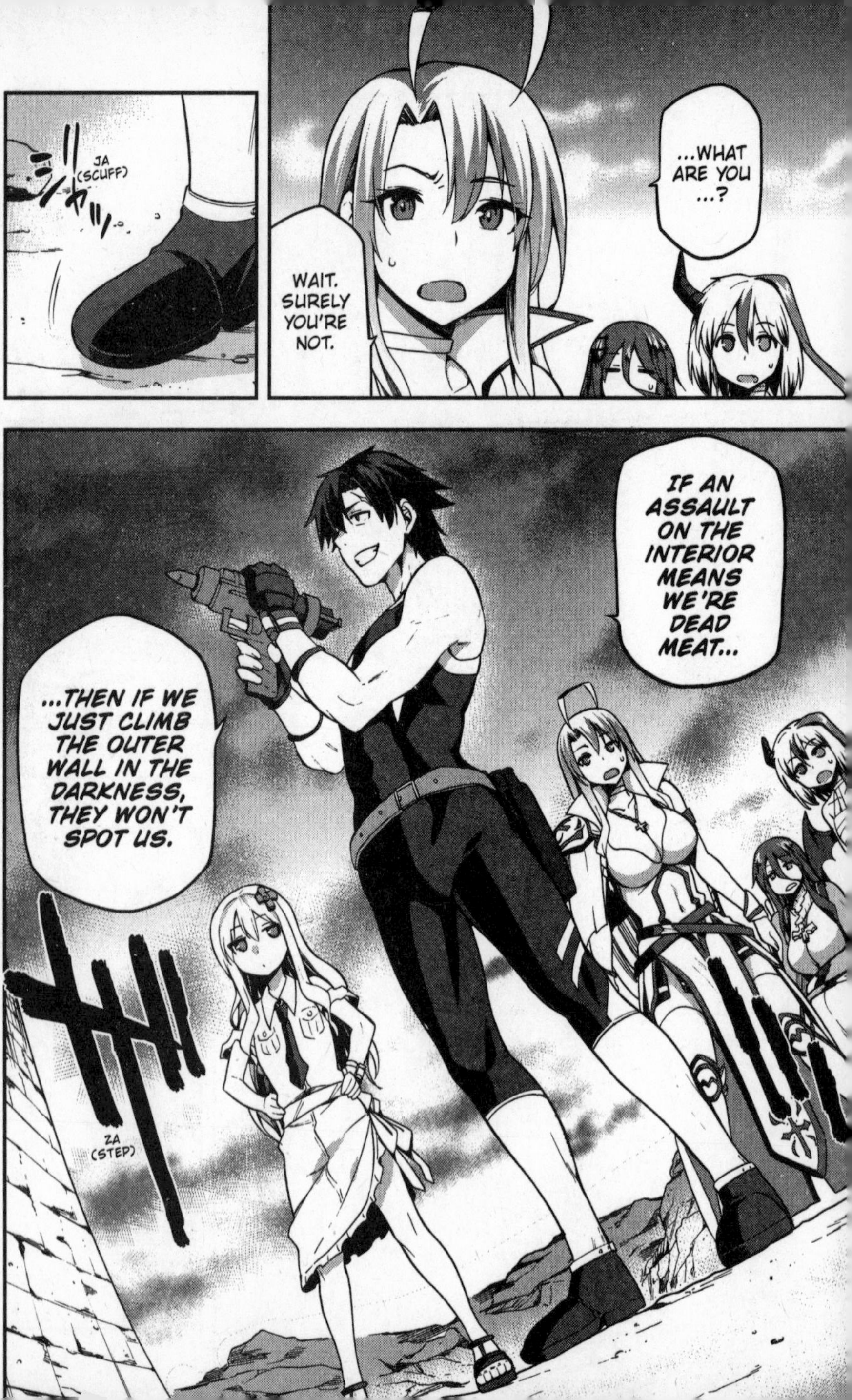
...WHAT ARE YOU ...?
WAIT. SURELY YOU'RE NOT.
JA (SCUFF)
IF AN ASSAULT ON THE INTERIOR MEANS WE'RE DEAD MEAT...
...THEN IF WE JUST CLIMB THE OUTER WALL IN THE DARKNESS, THEY WON'T SPOT US.
ZA (STEP)

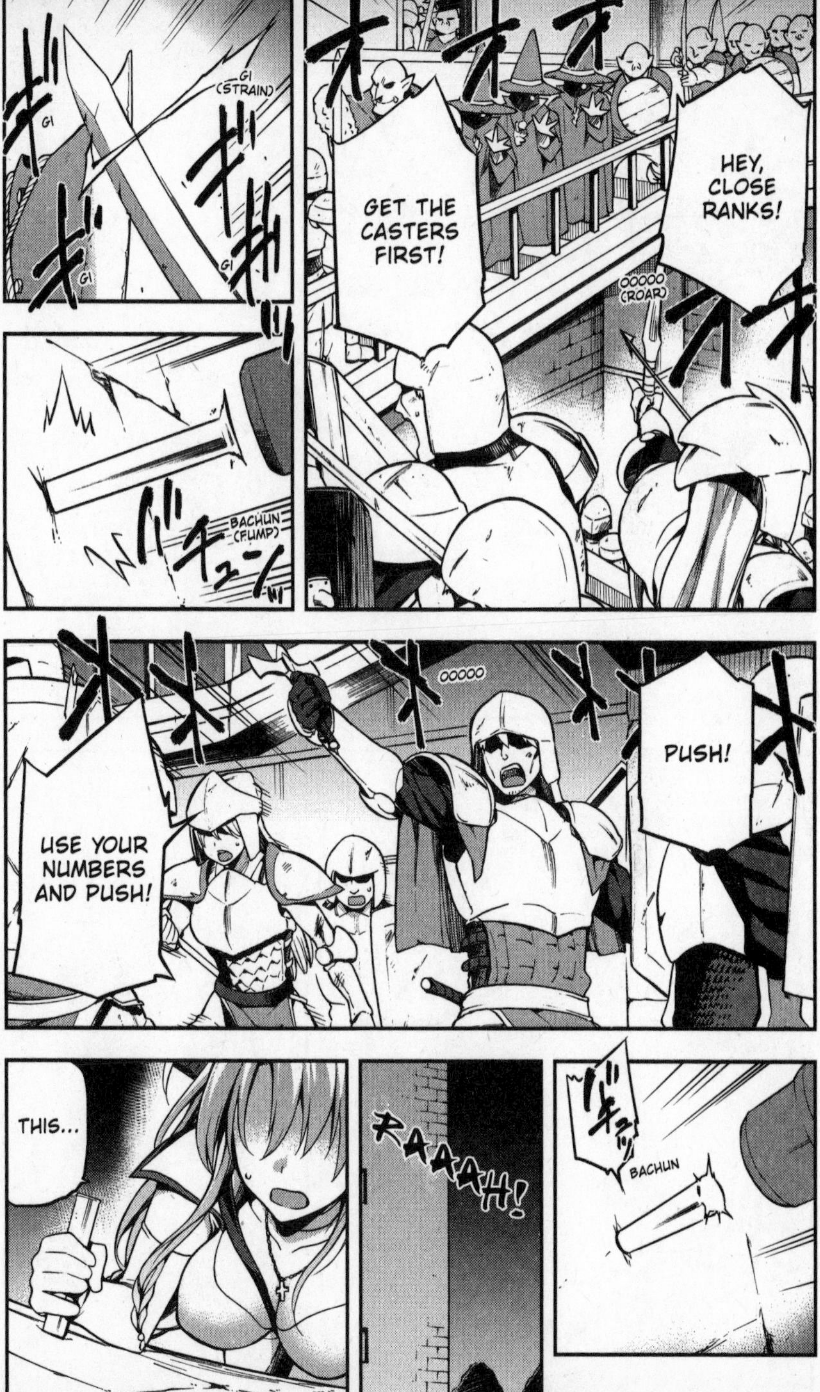
HEY, CLOSE RANKS!
OOOOO (ROAR)
GET THE CASTERS FIRST!
GI (STRAIN)
GI
GI
GI
BACHUN (FUMP)
OOOOO
PUSH!
USE YOUR NUMBERS AND PUSH!
BACHUN
RAAAAH!
THIS...

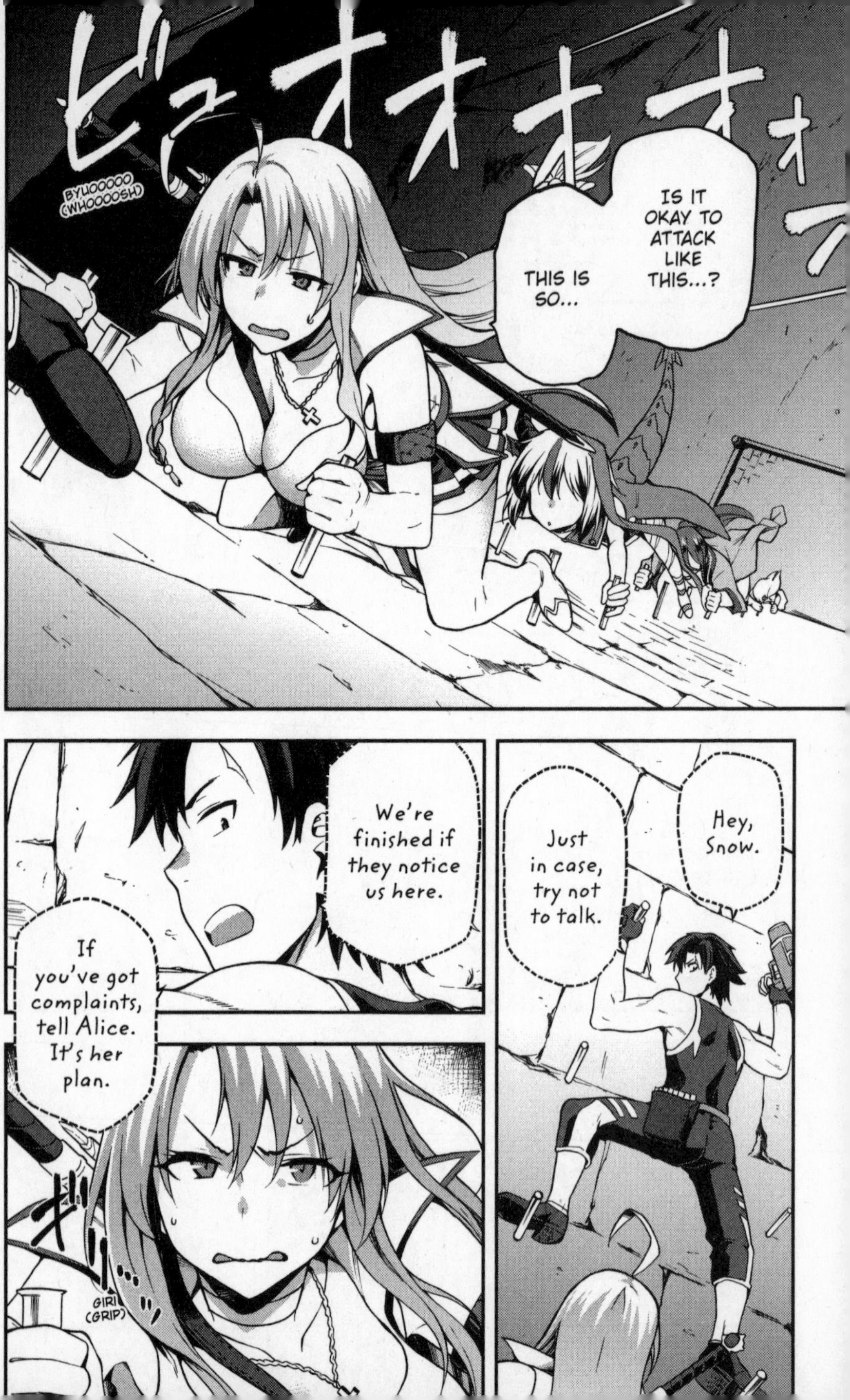
ビュオオオオオ
BYUOOOOO
(WHOOOOSH)
IS IT OKAY TO ATTACK LIKE THIS...?
THIS IS SO...
Hey, Snow.
Just in case, try not to talk.
We're finished if they notice us here.
If you've got complaints, tell Alice. It's her plan.
GIRI
(GRIP)

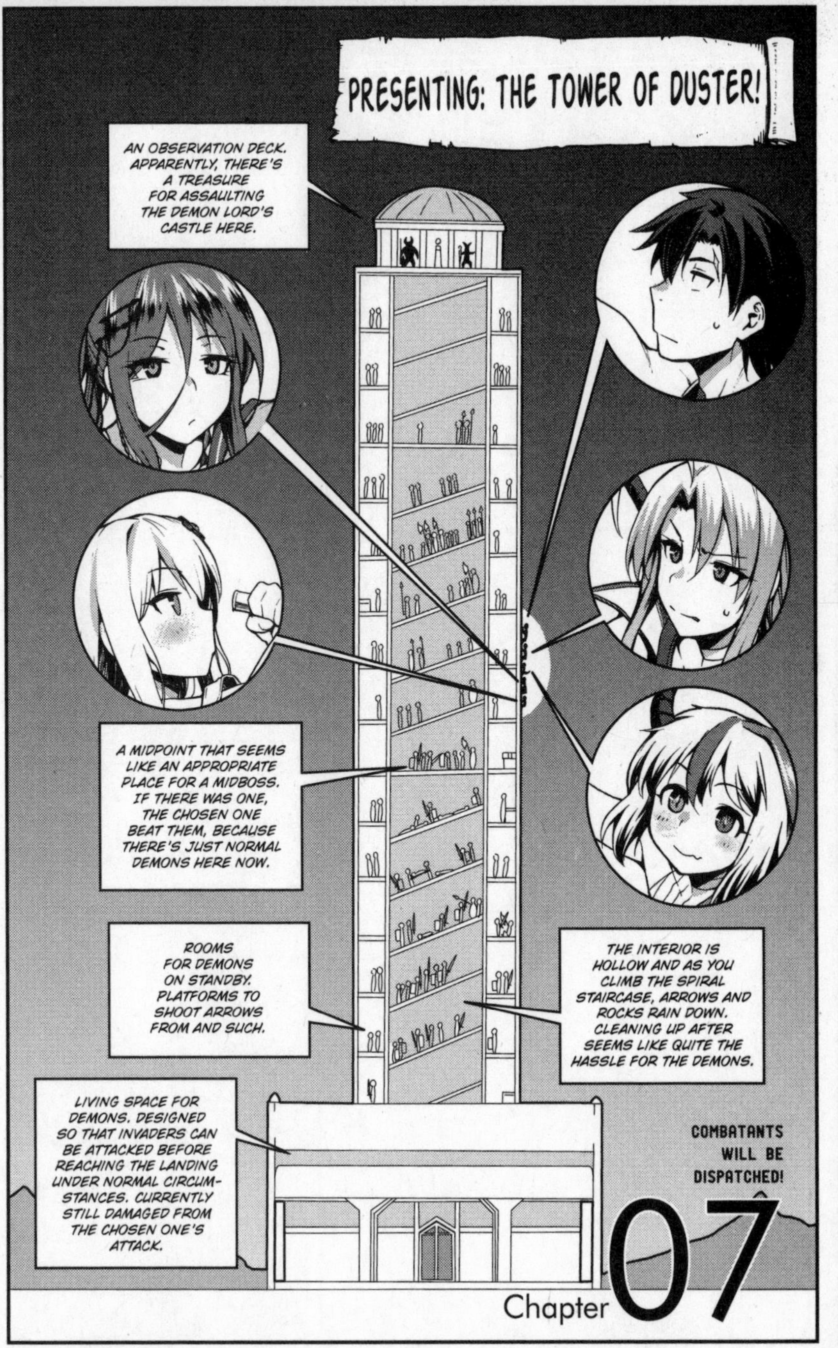
PRESENTING: THE TOWER OF DUSTER!
AN OBSERVATION DECK. APPARENTLY, THERE'S A TREASURE FOR ASSAULTING THE DEMON LORD'S CASTLE HERE.
A MIDPOINT THAT SEEMS LIKE AN APPROPRIATE PLACE FOR A MIDBOSS. IF THERE WAS ONE, THE CHOSEN ONE BEAT THEM, BECAUSE THERE'S JUST NORMAL DEMONS HERE NOW.
THE INTERIOR IS HOLLOW AND AS YOU CLIMB THE SPIRAL STAIRCASE, ARROWS AND ROCKS RAIN DOWN. CLEANING UP AFTER SEEMS LIKE QUITE THE HASSLE FOR THE DEMONS.
ROOMS FOR DEMONS ON STANDBY. PLATFORMS TO SHOOT ARROWS FROM AND SUCH.
COMBATANTS WILL BE DISPATCHED!
LIVING SPACE FOR DEMONS. DESIGNED SO THAT INVADERS CAN BE ATTACKED BEFORE REACHING THE LANDING UNDER NORMAL CIRCUM-STANCES. CURRENTLY STILL DAMAGED FROM THE CHOSEN ONE'S ATTACK.
Chapter 07

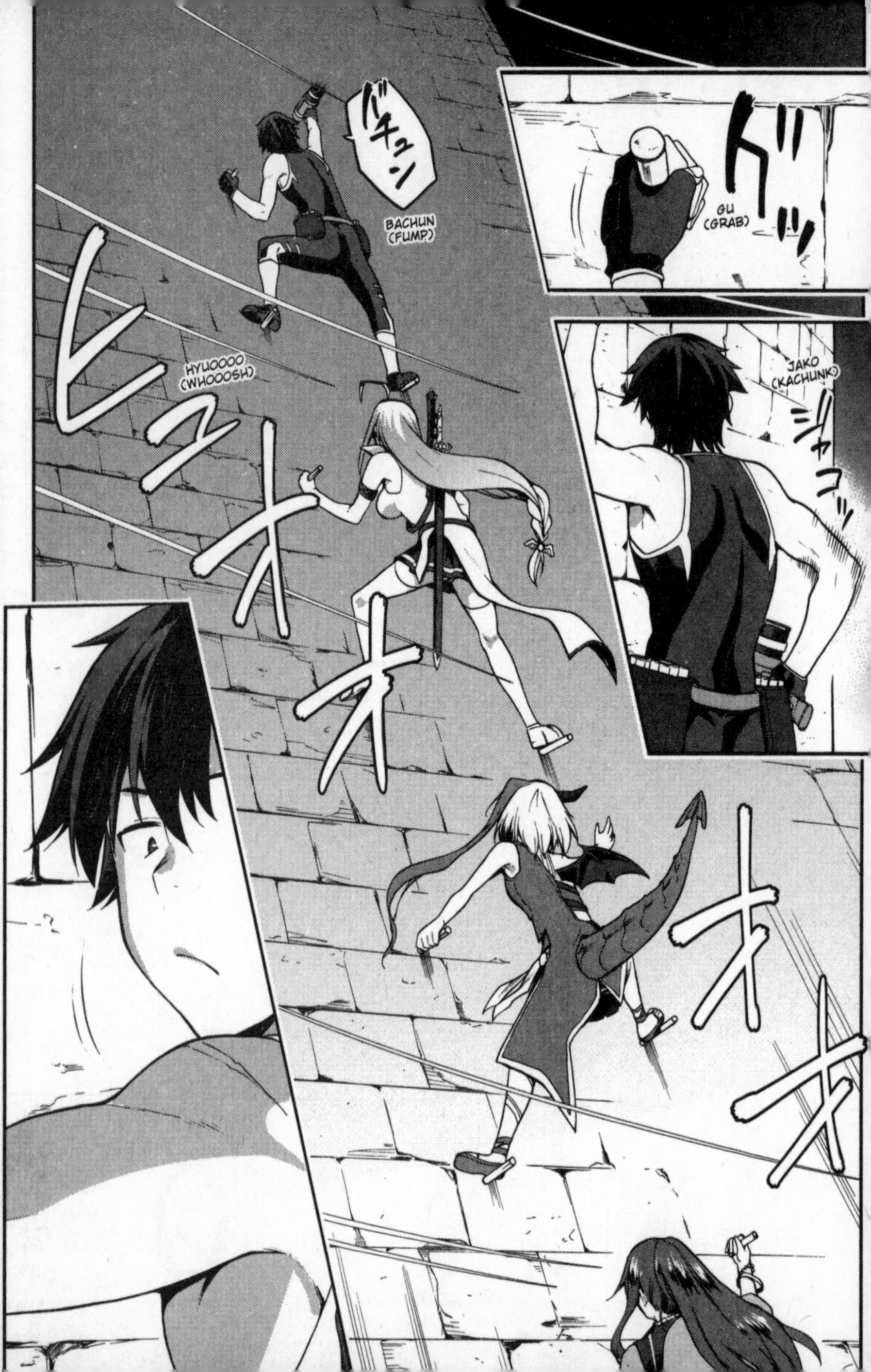
グッ
GU (GRAB)
ジャコッ
JAKO (KACHUNK)
バチュン
BACHUN (FUMP)
ヒュオオオオ
HYUOOOO (WHOOOSH)

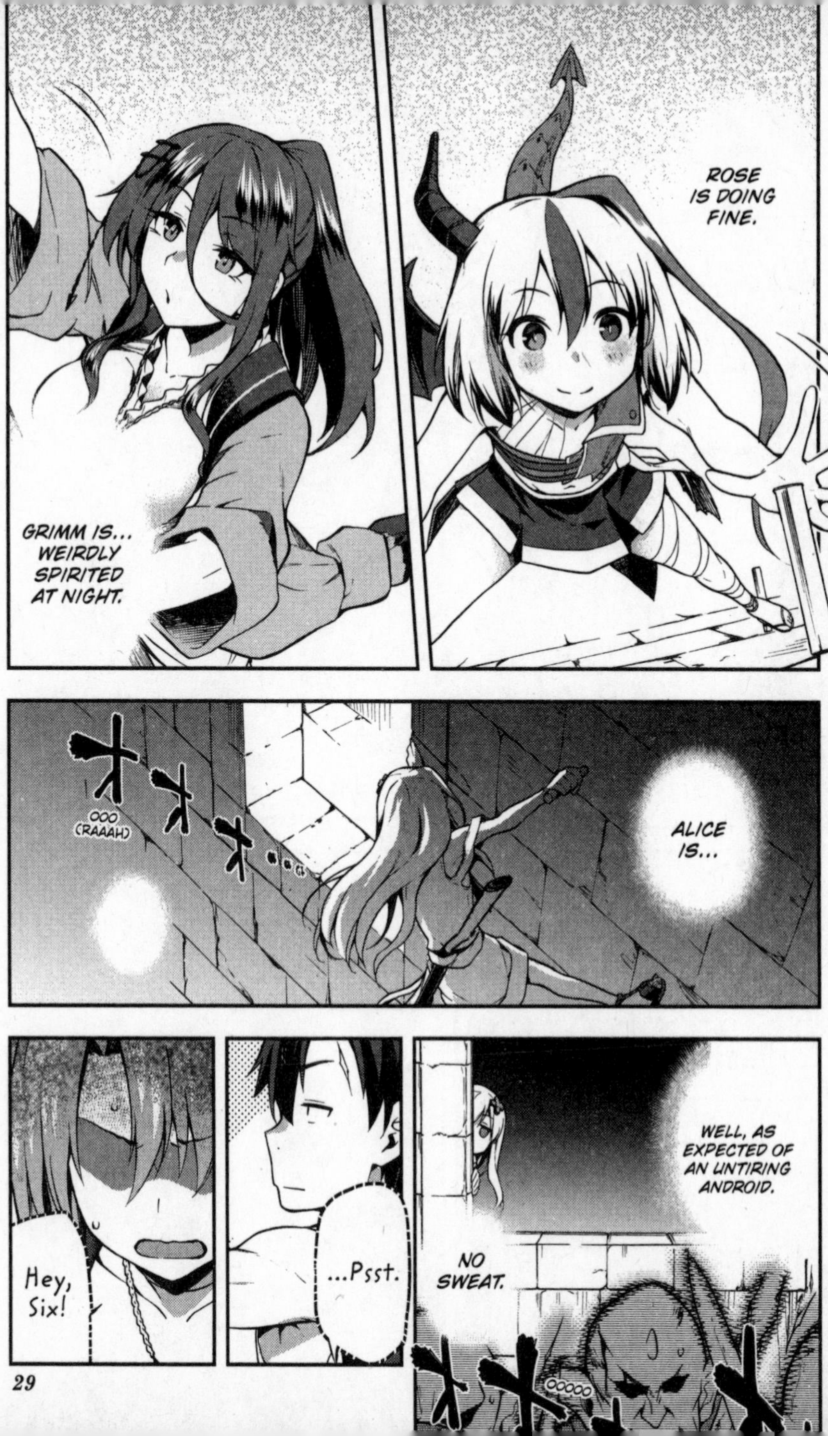
ROSE IS DOING FINE.
GRIMM IS... WEIRDLY SPIRITED AT NIGHT.
ALICE IS...
オオオ…
OOO (RAAAH)
WELL, AS EXPECTED OF AN UNTIRING ANDROID.
NO SWEAT.
OOOOO
...Psst.
Hey, Six!

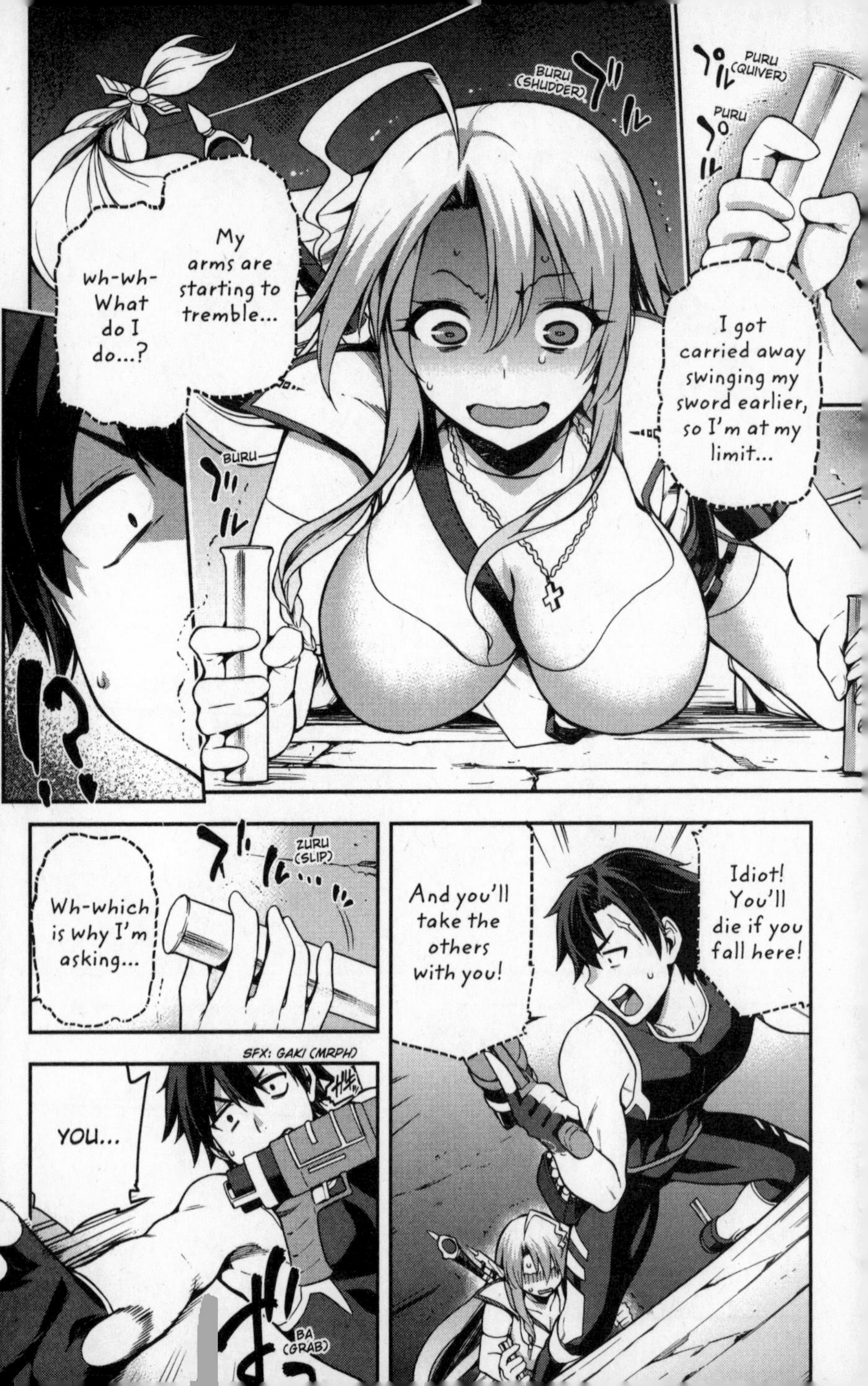
PURU (QUIVER)
PURU
I got carried away swinging my sword earlier, so I'm at my limit...
BURU (SHUDDER)
My arms are starting to tremble...
wh-wh- What do I do...?
BURU
Idiot! You'll die if you fall here!
And you'll take the others with you!
ZURU (SLIP)
Wh-which is why I'm asking...
SFX: GAKI (MRPH)
YOU...
BA (GRAB)

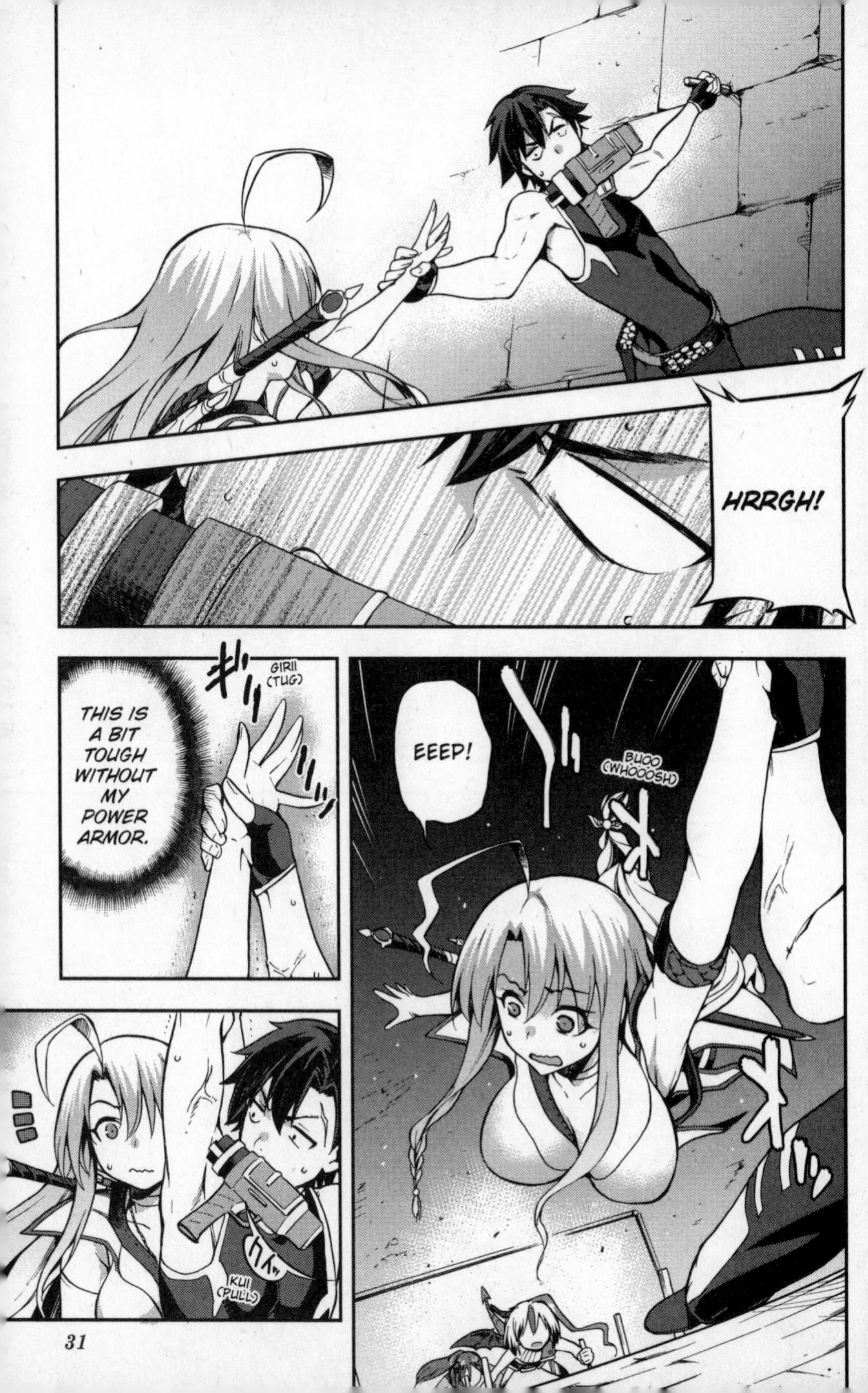
HRRGH!
EEEP!
BUOO (WHOOOSH)
GIRII (TUG)
THIS IS A BIT TOUGH WITHOUT MY POWER ARMOR.
KUI (PULL)

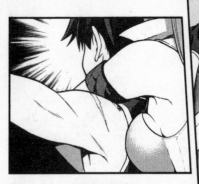

ギュ
GYU
(SQUEEZE)

Oof...

S-sorry.

Hey.

Try to avoid the wind by pressing closer.

ギゅぅ
GYUUUUU
(SQUEEZE)

Like this?

Closer!

A-all right.

ムニ
MUNI
(WIGGLE)

32

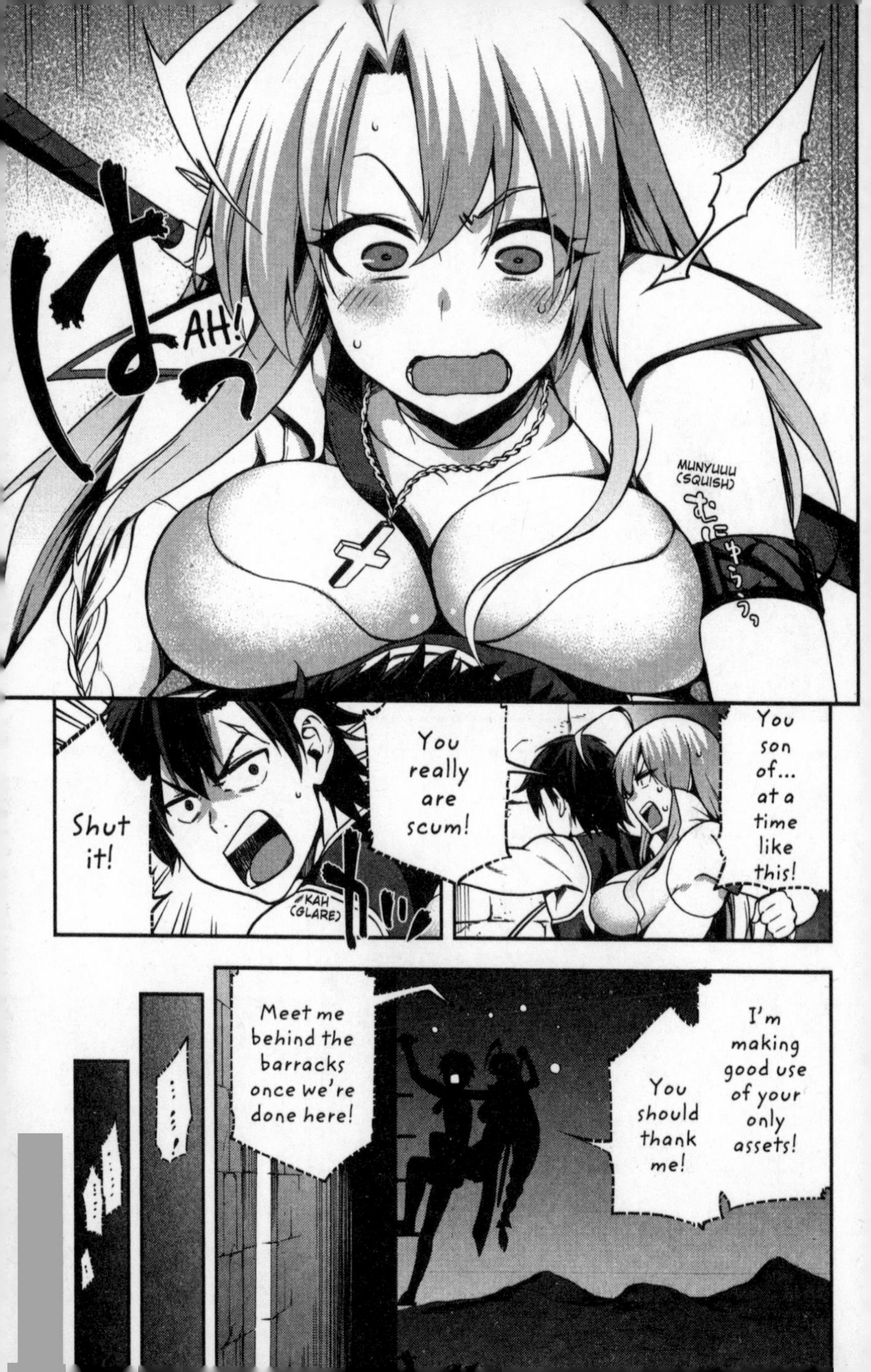
AH!
MUNYUUU (SQUISH)
You son of... at a time like this!
You really are scum!
Shut it!
KAH (GLARE)
I'm making good use of your only assets!
You should thank me!
Meet me behind the barracks once we're done here!
......!

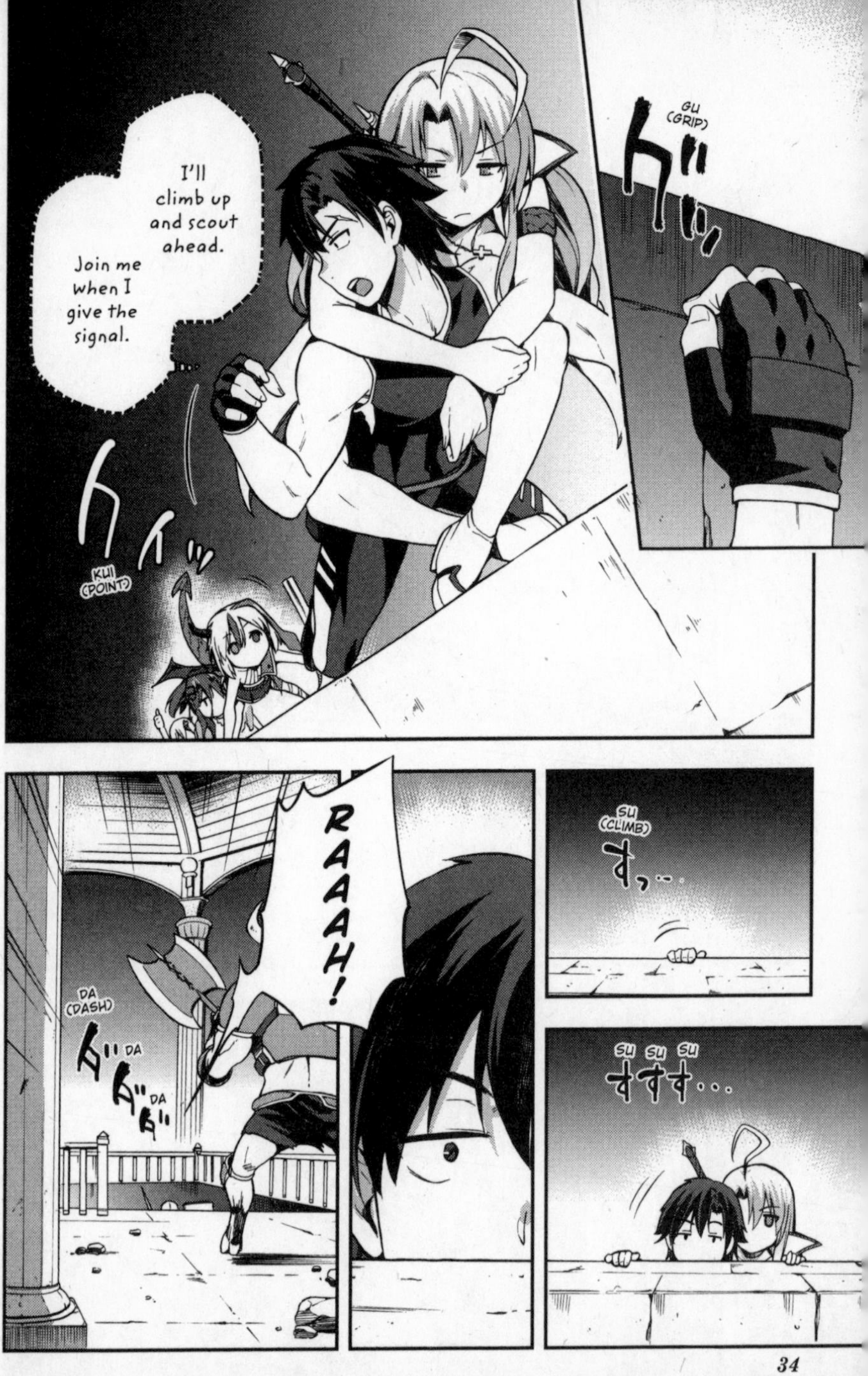
GU (GRIP)
I'll climb up and scout ahead.
Join me when I give the signal.
KUI (POINT)
SU (CLIMB)
SU SU SU
RAAAAH!
DA (DASH)
DA
DA

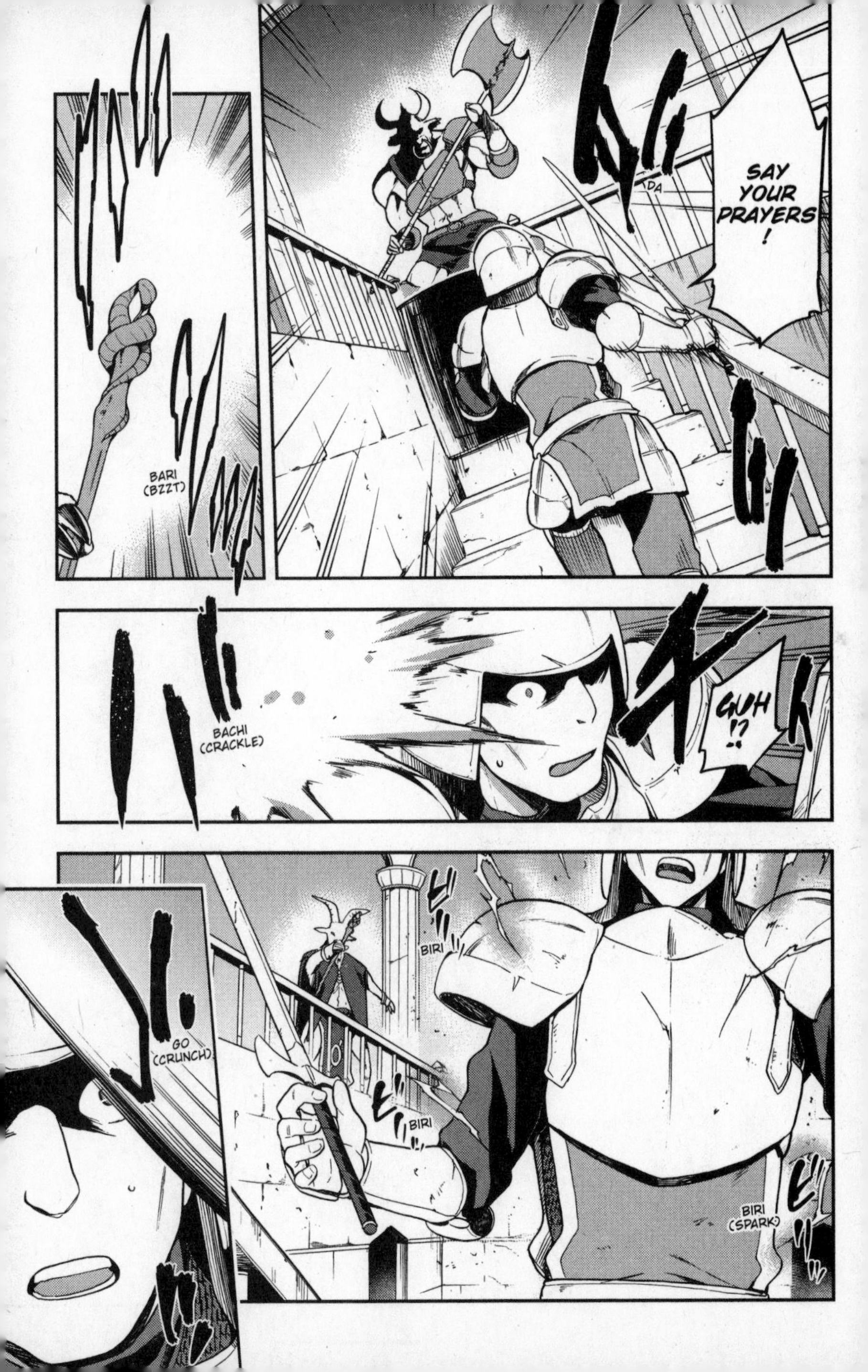
SAY YOUR PRAYERS!
DA
BARI (BZZT)
GUH!?
BACHI (CRACKLE)
BIRI
BIRI
BIRI (SPARK)
GO (CRUNCH)

GOZU
(SLASH)

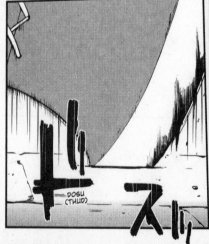
DOSU
(THUD)

GA
(THUD)

GORO
(ROLLS)

GO
(WHACK)

GORO

GORO

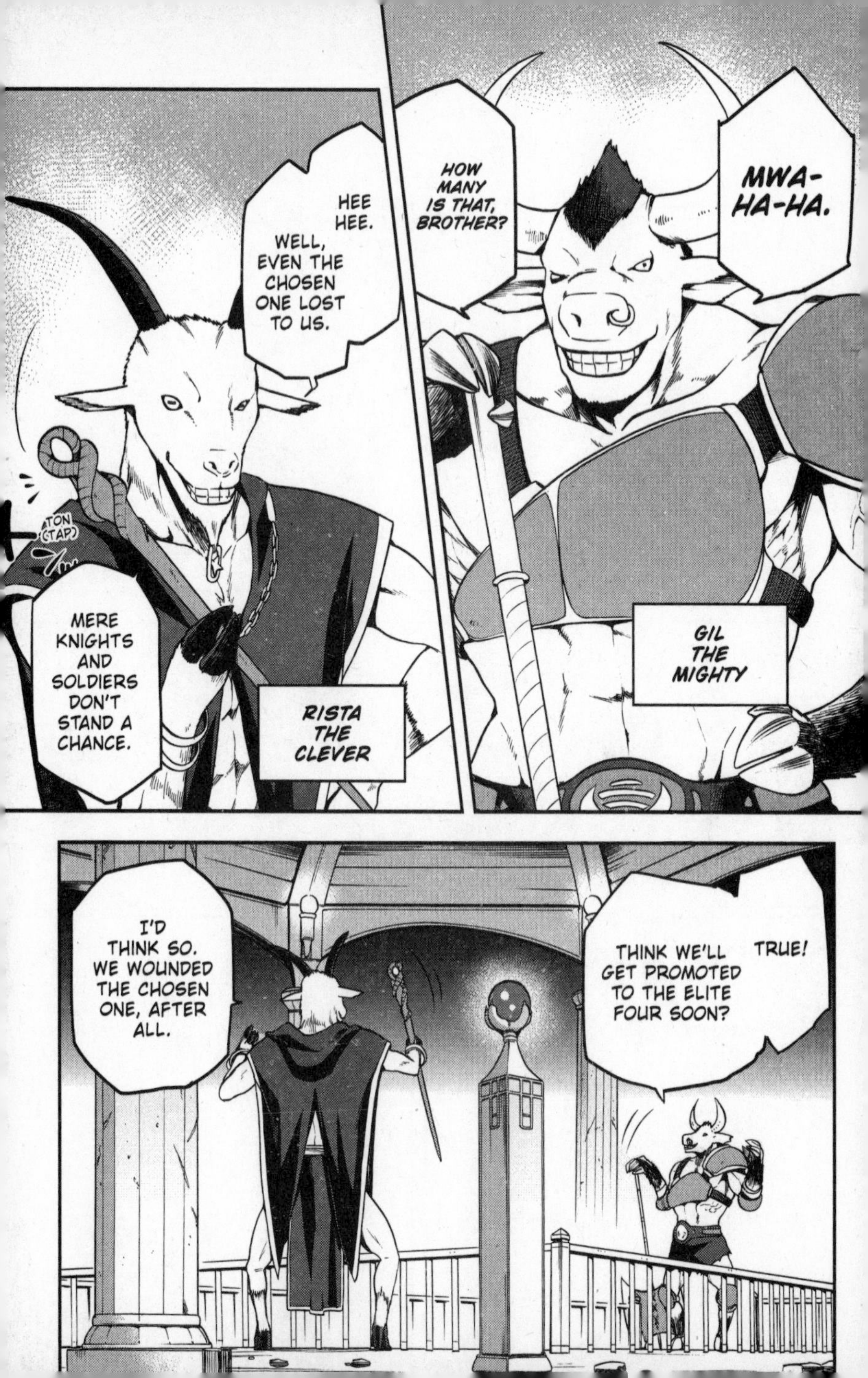
MWA-HA-HA.
HOW MANY IS THAT, BROTHER?
GIL THE MIGHTY
HEE HEE.
WELL, EVEN THE CHOSEN ONE LOST TO US.
TON (TAP)
MERE KNIGHTS AND SOLDIERS DON'T STAND A CHANCE.
RISTA THE CLEVER
TRUE!
THINK WE'LL GET PROMOTED TO THE ELITE FOUR SOON?
I'D THINK SO. WE WOUNDED THE CHOSEN ONE, AFTER ALL.

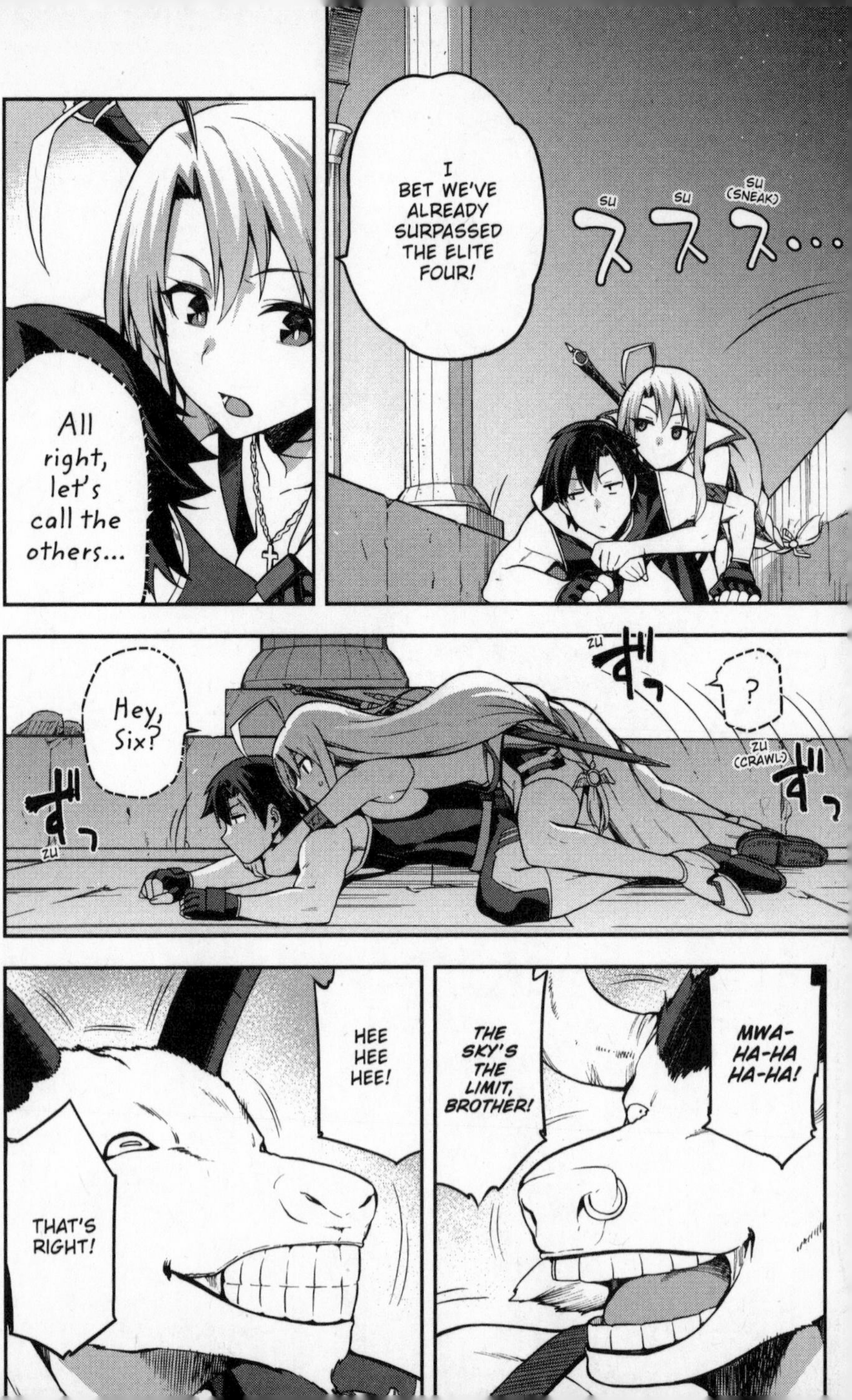
I BET WE'VE ALREADY SURPASSED THE ELITE FOUR!
SU SU SU (SNEAK)
ススス…
All right, let's call the others...
?
ZU (CRAWL)
ずっ
ZU
ずっ
Hey, Six?
ZU
ずっ
MWA-HA-HA HA-HA!
THE SKY'S THE LIMIT, BROTHER!
HEE HEE HEE!
THAT'S RIGHT!

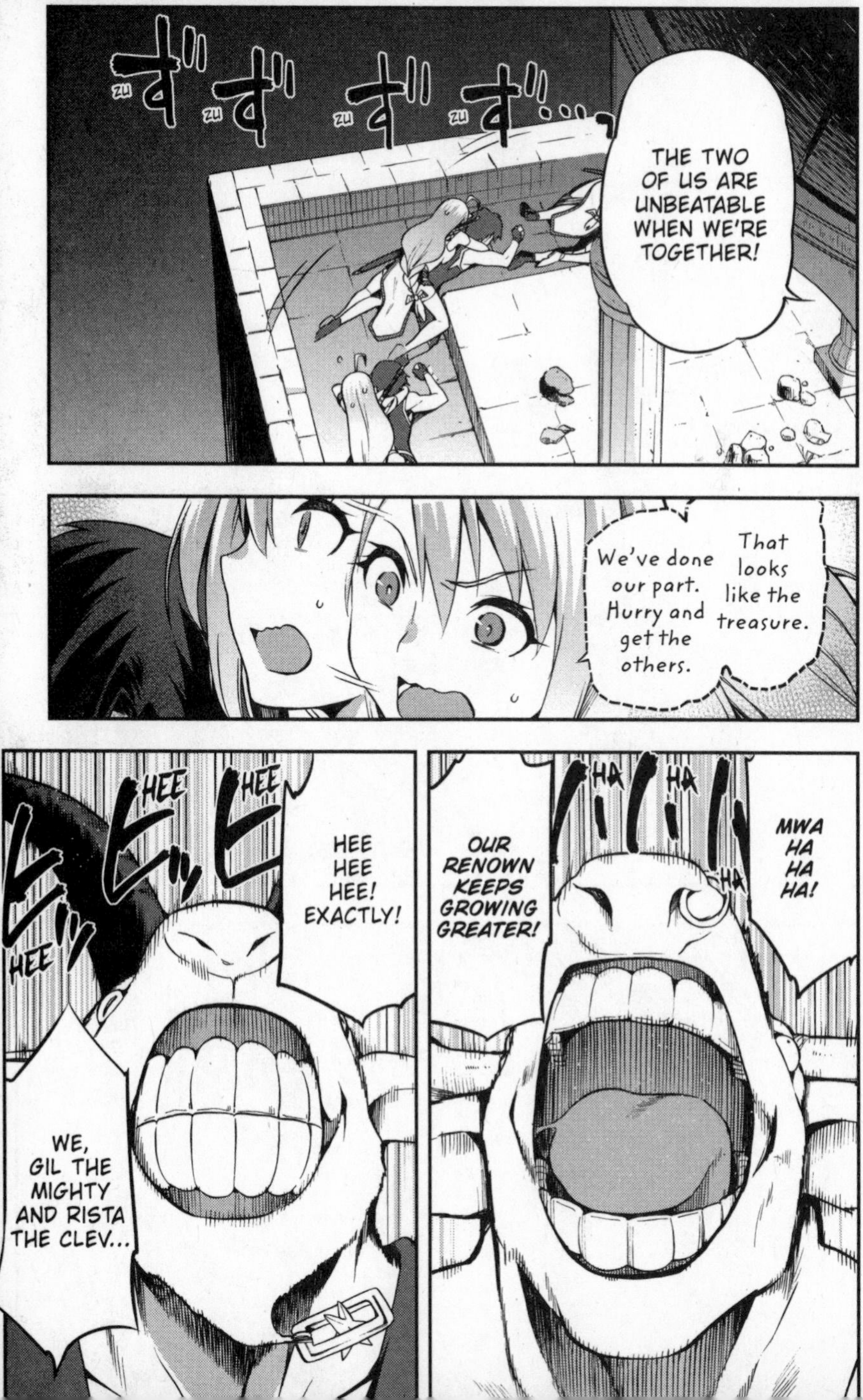
ZU ZU ZU ZU
THE TWO OF US ARE UNBEATABLE WHEN WE'RE TOGETHER!
That looks like the treasure.
We've done our part. Hurry and get the others.
MWA HA HA HA!
HA HA HA
OUR RENOWN KEEPS GROWING GREATER!
HEE HEE HEE
HEE HEE HEE! EXACTLY!
WE, GIL THE MIGHTY AND RISTA THE CLEV...

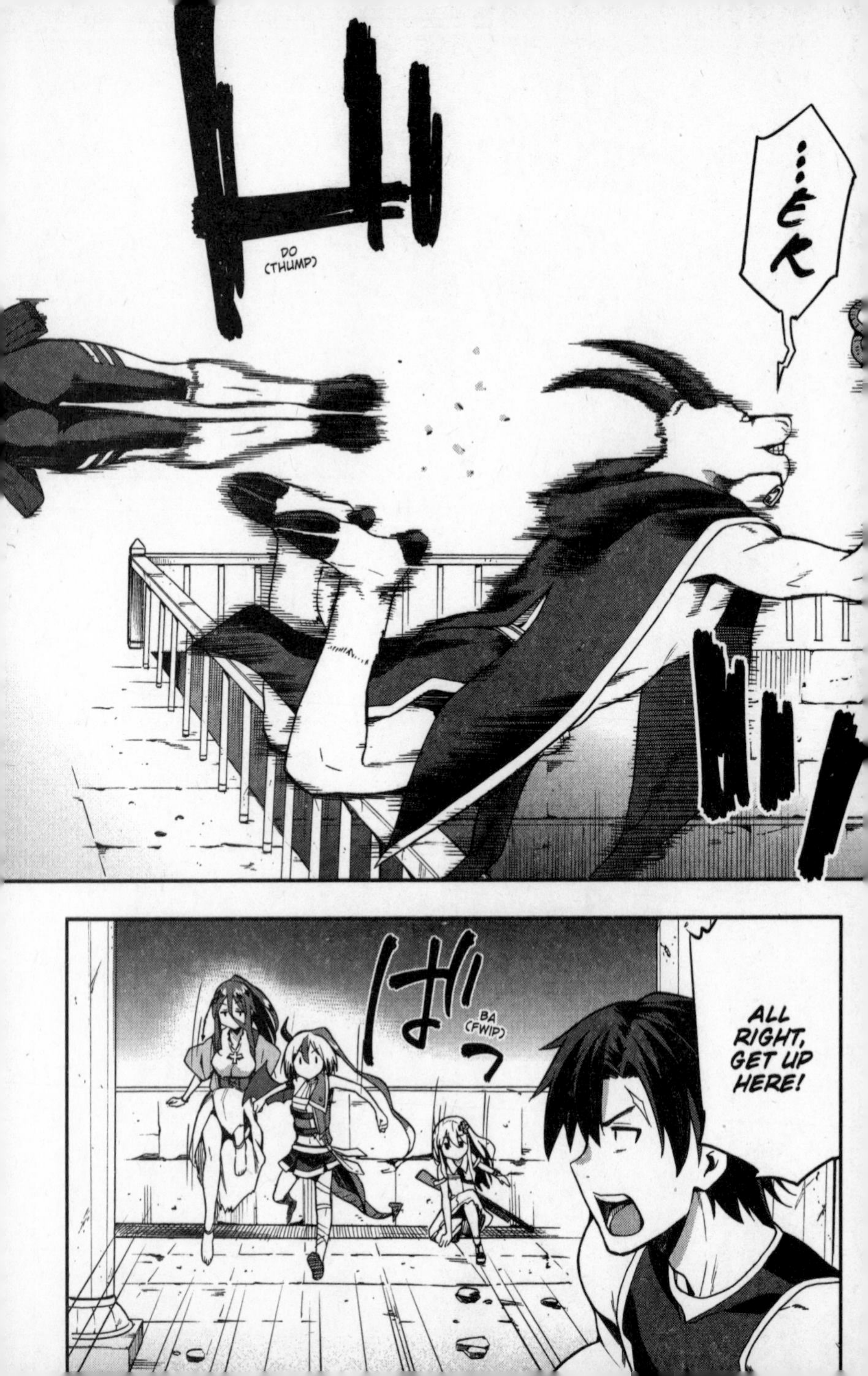
...EK
DO
(THUMP)
ALL RIGHT, GET UP HERE!
BA
(FWIP)

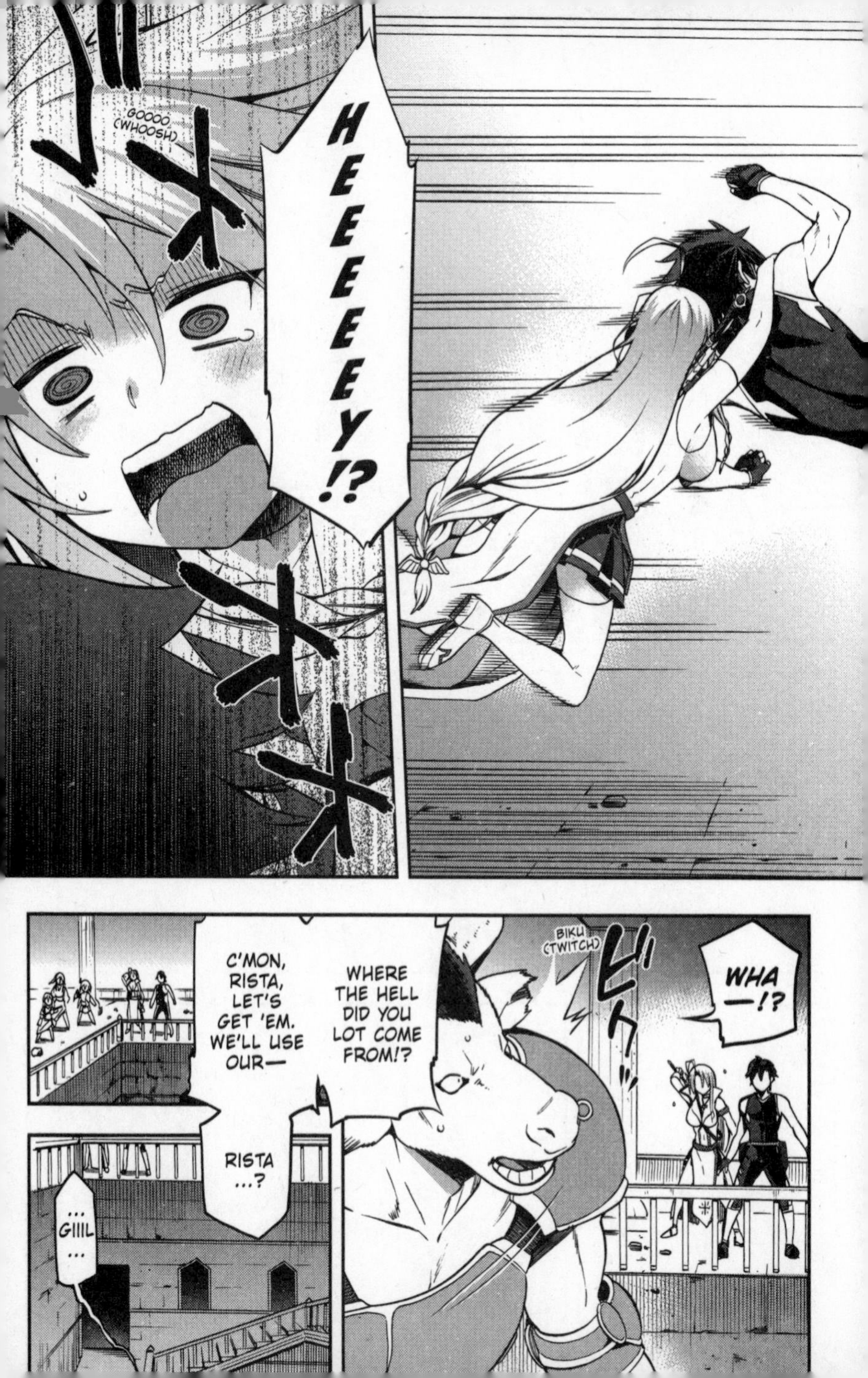
HEEEEEEY!?
GOOOO (WHOOSH)
BIKU (TWITCH)
WHA—!?
WHERE THE HELL DID YOU LOT COME FROM!?
C'MON, RISTA, LET'S GET 'EM. WE'LL USE OUR—
RISTA ...?
... GIIIL ...

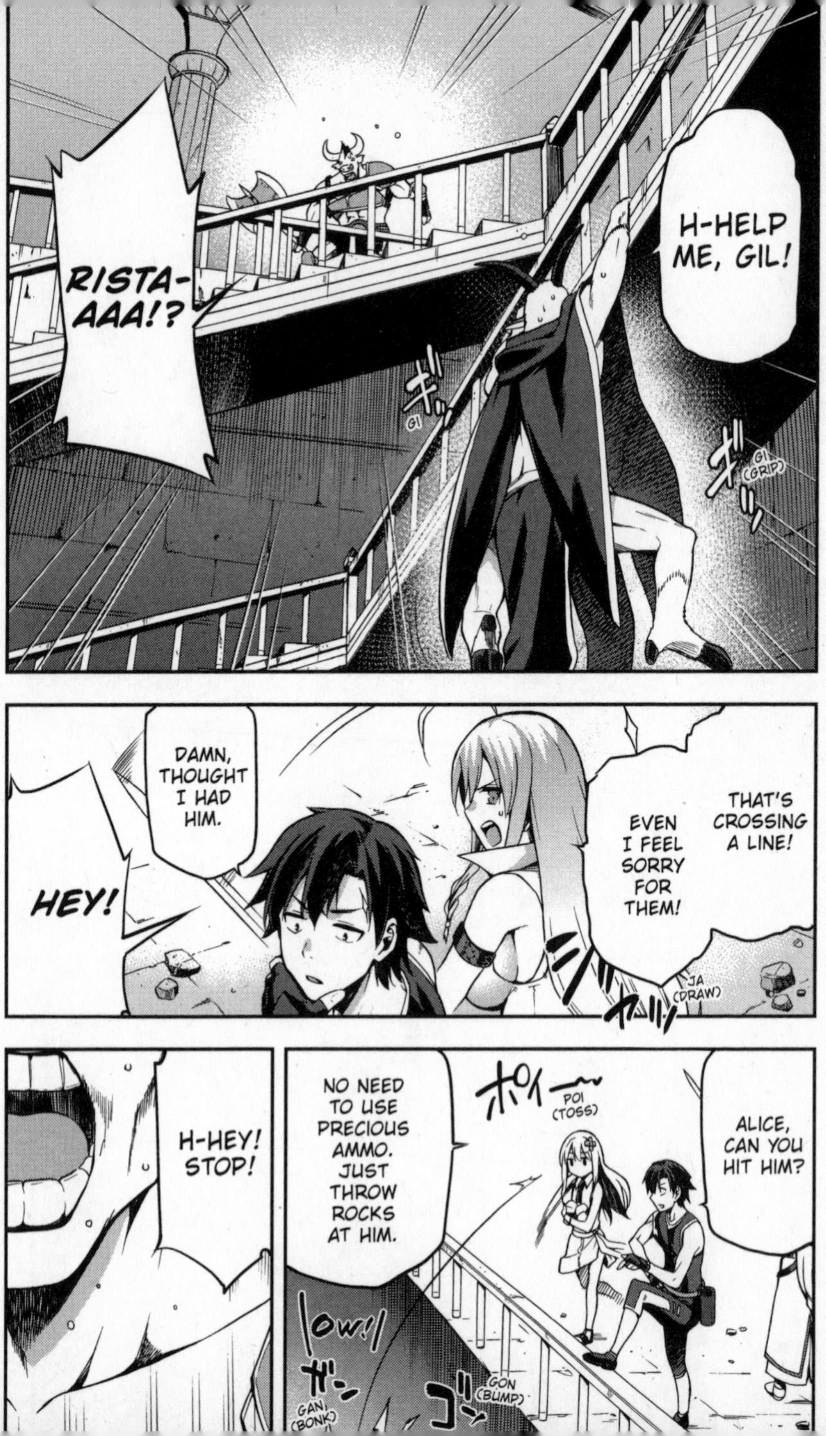
H-HELP ME, GIL!
RISTA-AAA!?
GI
GI (GRIP)
THAT'S CROSSING A LINE!
EVEN I FEEL SORRY FOR THEM!
JA (DRAW)
DAMN, THOUGHT I HAD HIM.
HEY!
ALICE, CAN YOU HIT HIM?
POI (TOSS)
NO NEED TO USE PRECIOUS AMMO. JUST THROW ROCKS AT HIM.
GON (BUMP)
OW!
GAN (BONK)
H-HEY! STOP!

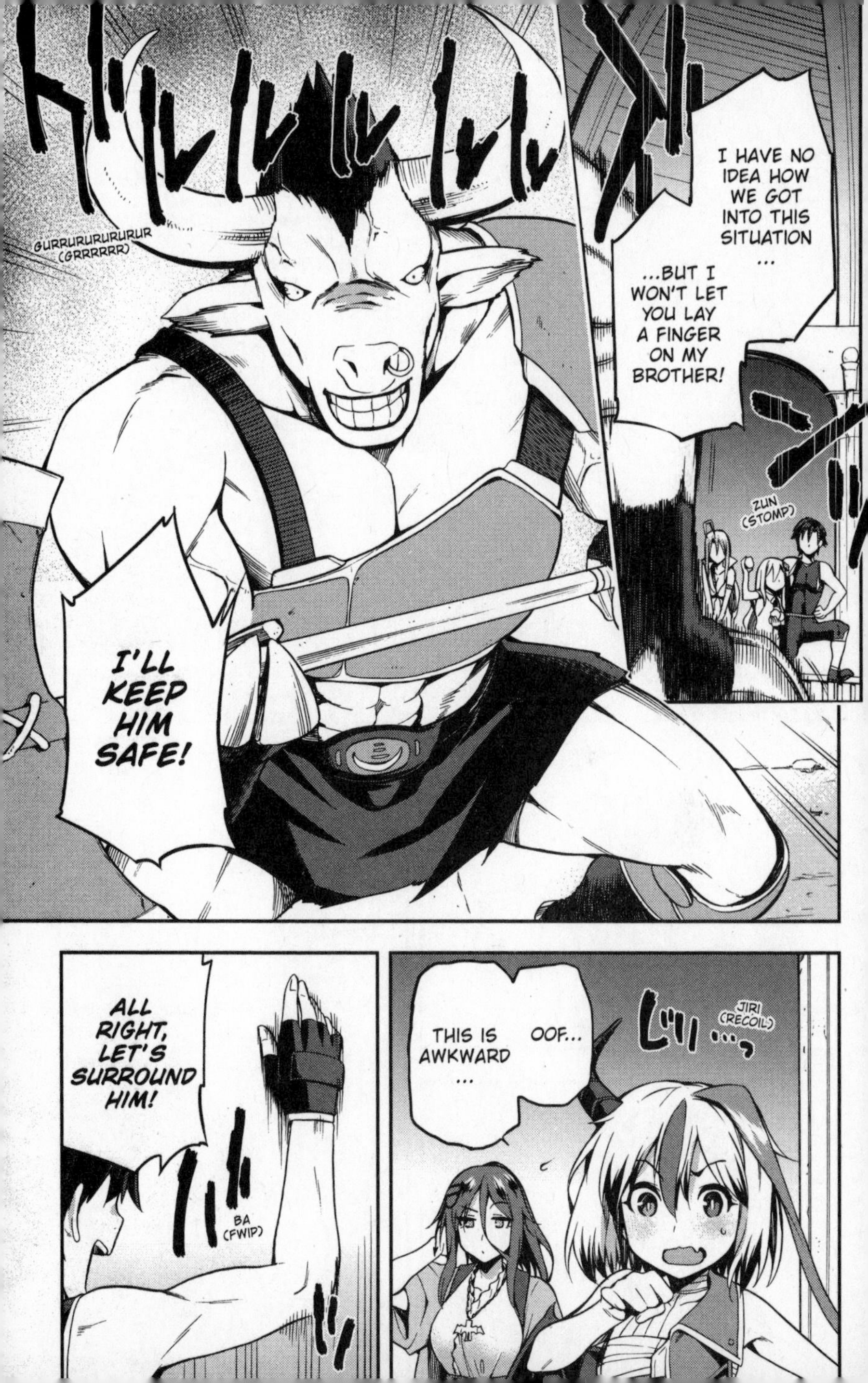
I HAVE NO IDEA HOW WE GOT INTO THIS SITUATION ...
...BUT I WON'T LET YOU LAY A FINGER ON MY BROTHER!
ZUN (STOMP)
GURRURURURURUR (GRRRRRR)
I'LL KEEP HIM SAFE!
JIRI (RECOIL)
OOF...
THIS IS AWKWARD ...
ALL RIGHT, LET'S SURROUND HIM!
BA (FWIP)

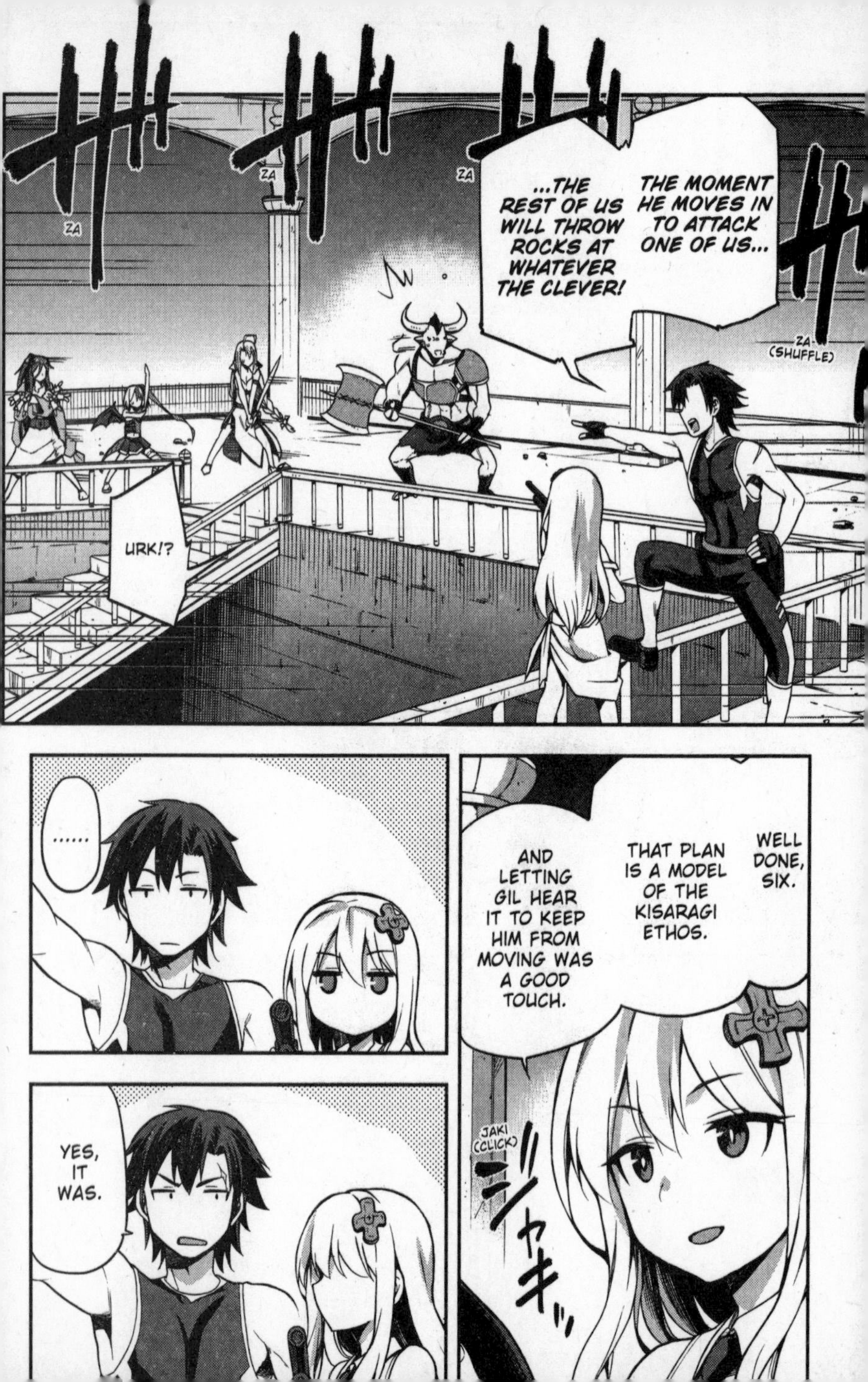
ZA
ZA
ZA
ZA (SHUFFLE)
THE MOMENT HE MOVES IN TO ATTACK ONE OF US...
...THE REST OF US WILL THROW ROCKS AT WHATEVER THE CLEVER!
URK!?
WELL DONE, SIX.
THAT PLAN IS A MODEL OF THE KISARAGI ETHOS.
AND LETTING GIL HEAR IT TO KEEP HIM FROM MOVING WAS A GOOD TOUCH.
JAKI (CLICK)
......
YES, IT WAS.

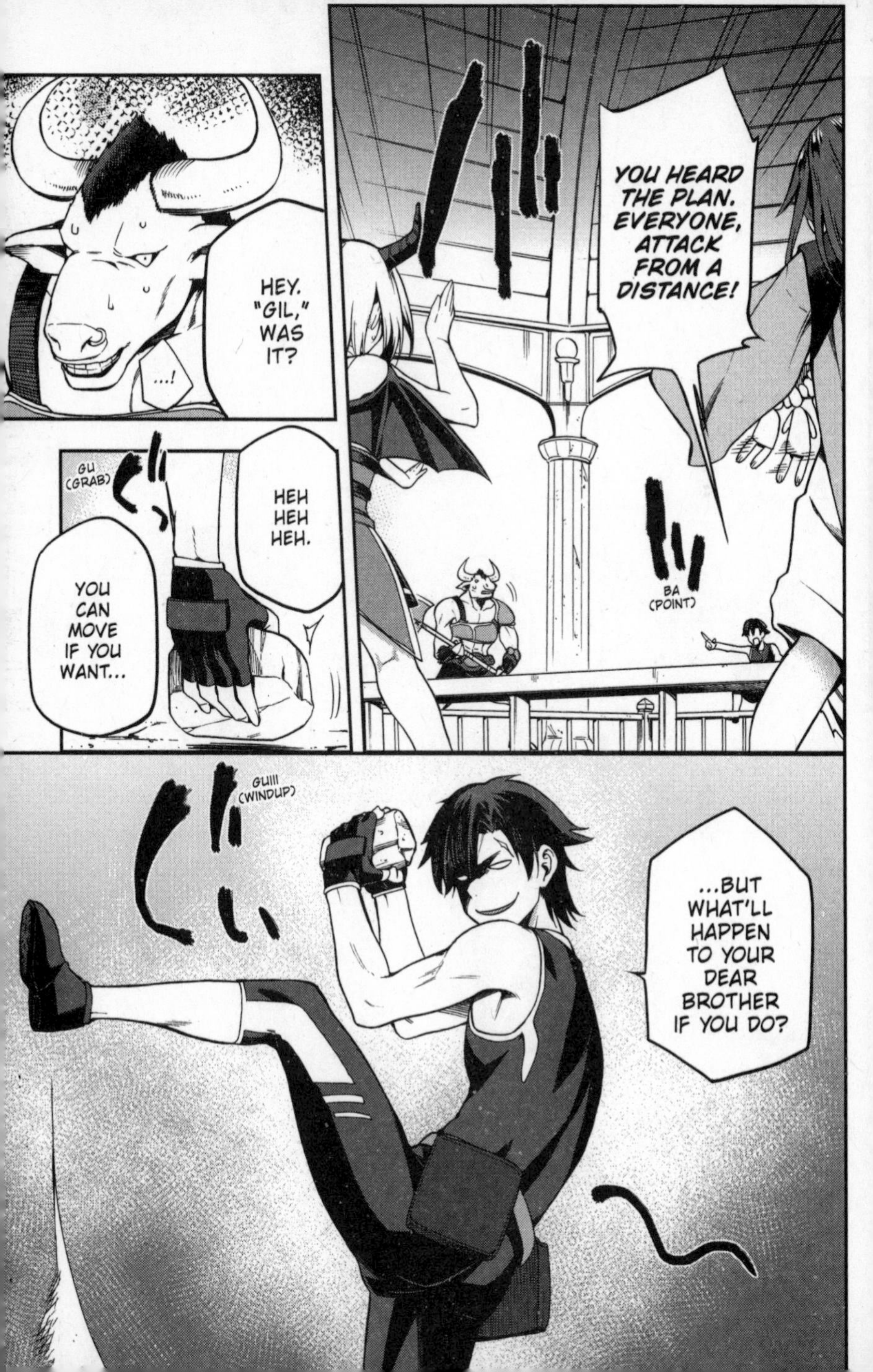
YOU HEARD THE PLAN. EVERYONE, ATTACK FROM A DISTANCE!
BA (POINT)
HEY. "GIL," WAS IT?
...!
HEH HEH HEH.
GU (GRAB)
YOU CAN MOVE IF YOU WANT...
...BUT WHAT'LL HAPPEN TO YOUR DEAR BROTHER IF YOU DO?
GUIII (WINDUP)

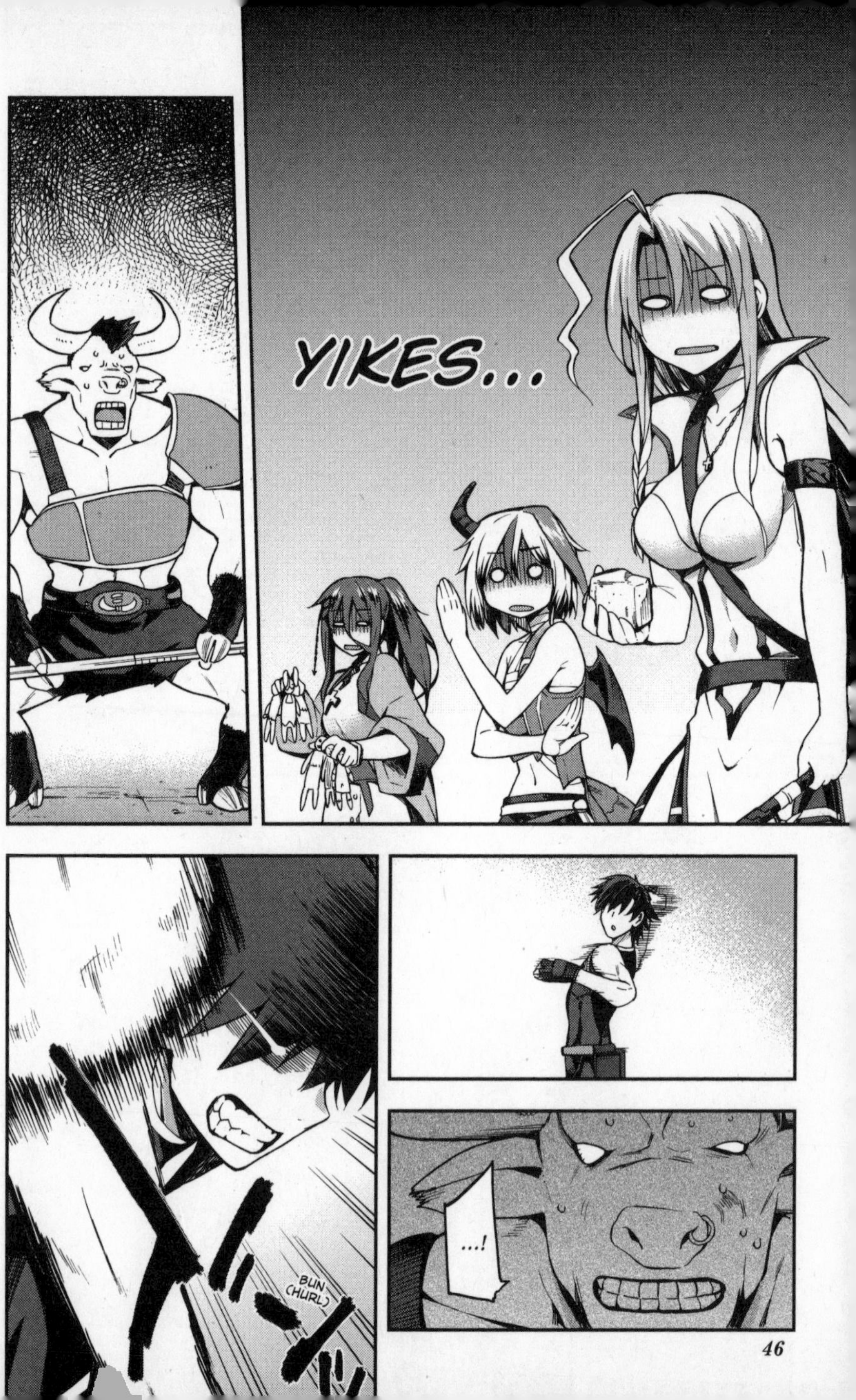
YIKES...
...!
BUN
(HURL)

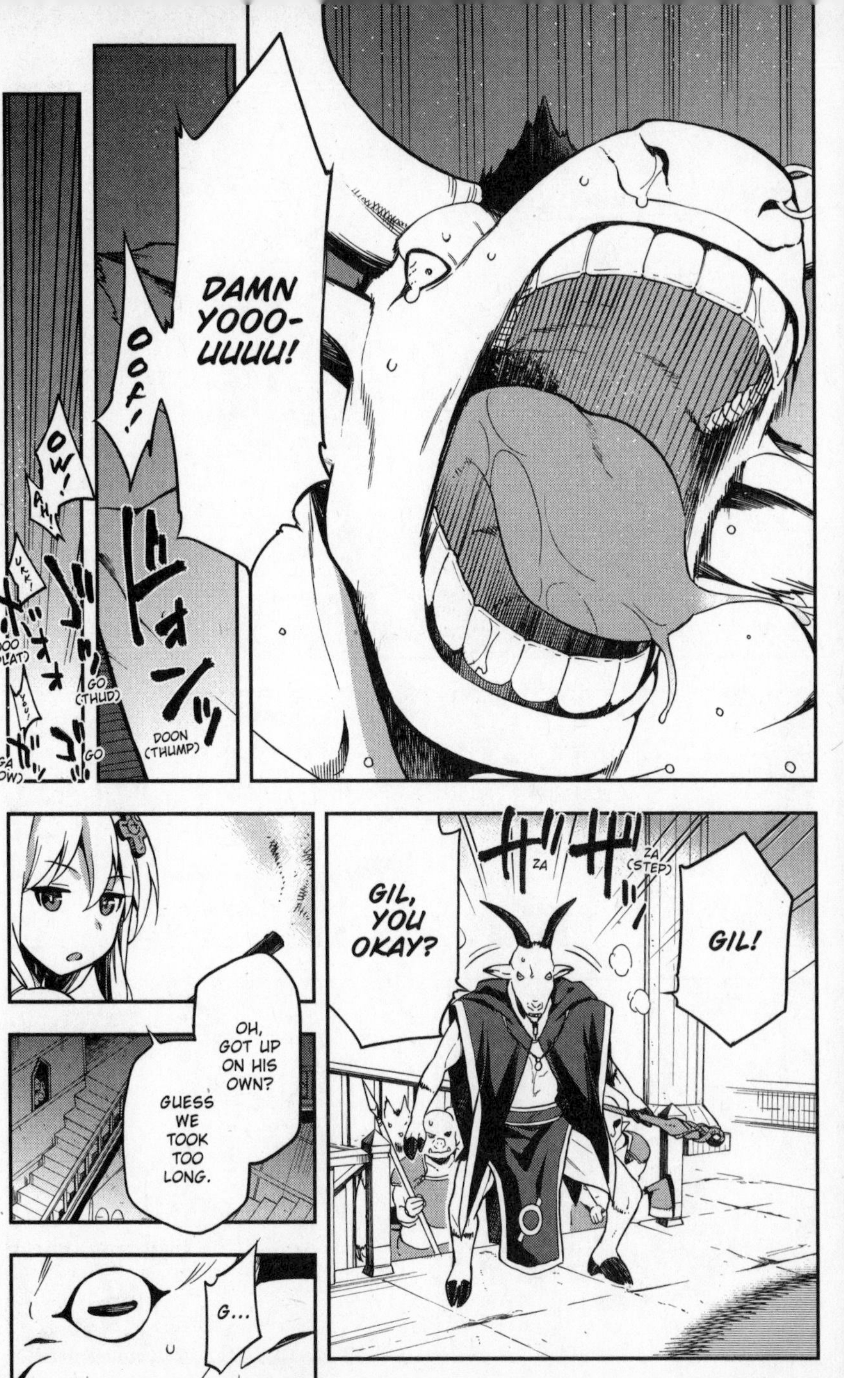
DAMN YOOO-UUUU!
OOF!
OW!
AH!
URK!
YOU!
DOON (THUMP)
GO (THUD)
GO
BOOO (SPLAT)
GA (POW)
GIL!
ZA (STEP)
ZA
GIL, YOU OKAY?
OH, GOT UP ON HIS OWN?
GUESS WE TOOK TOO LONG.
G...

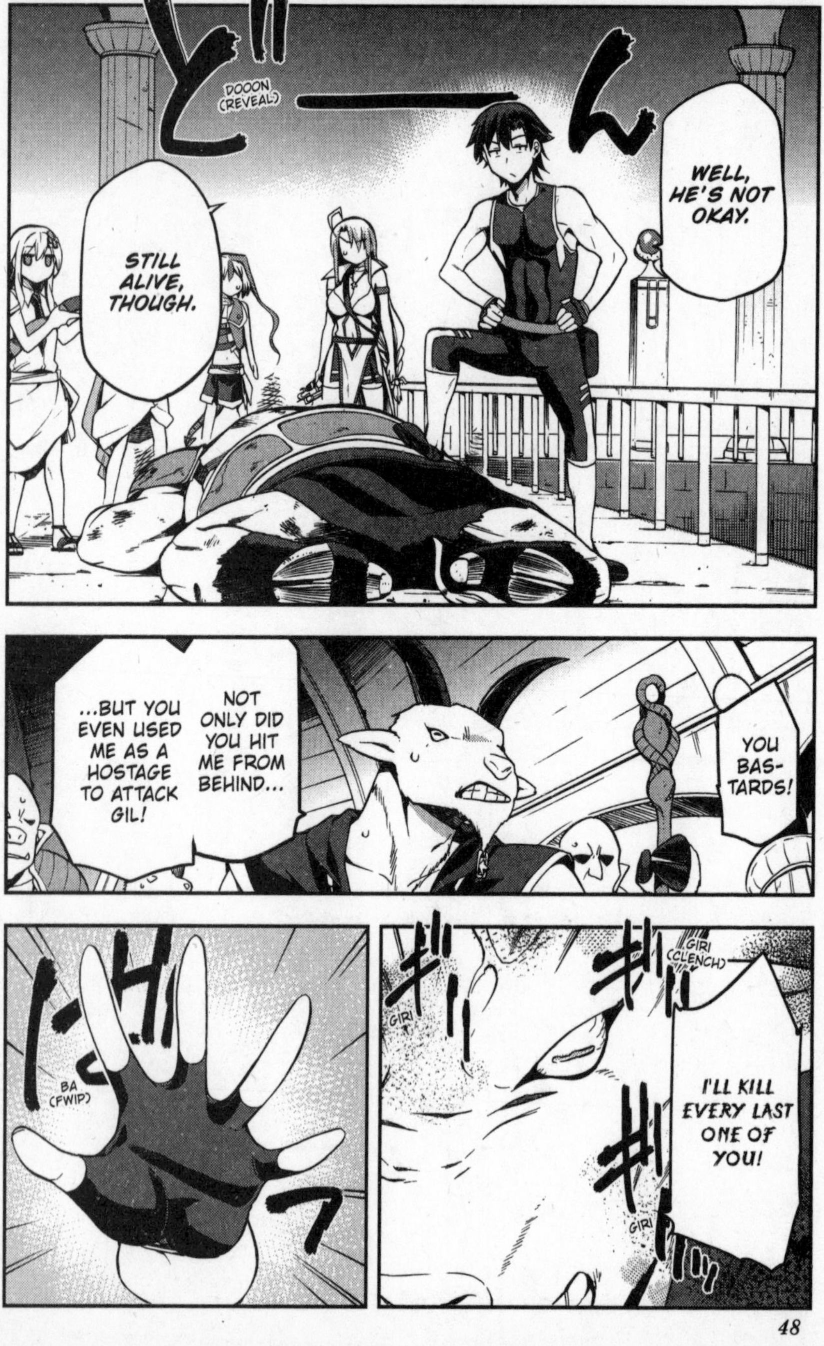
DOOON (REVEAL)
WELL, HE'S NOT OKAY.
STILL ALIVE, THOUGH.
YOU BASTARDS!
NOT ONLY DID YOU HIT ME FROM BEHIND...
...BUT YOU EVEN USED ME AS A HOSTAGE TO ATTACK GIL!
GIRI (CLENCH)
GIRI
I'LL KILL EVERY LAST ONE OF YOU!
GIRI
BA (FWIP)

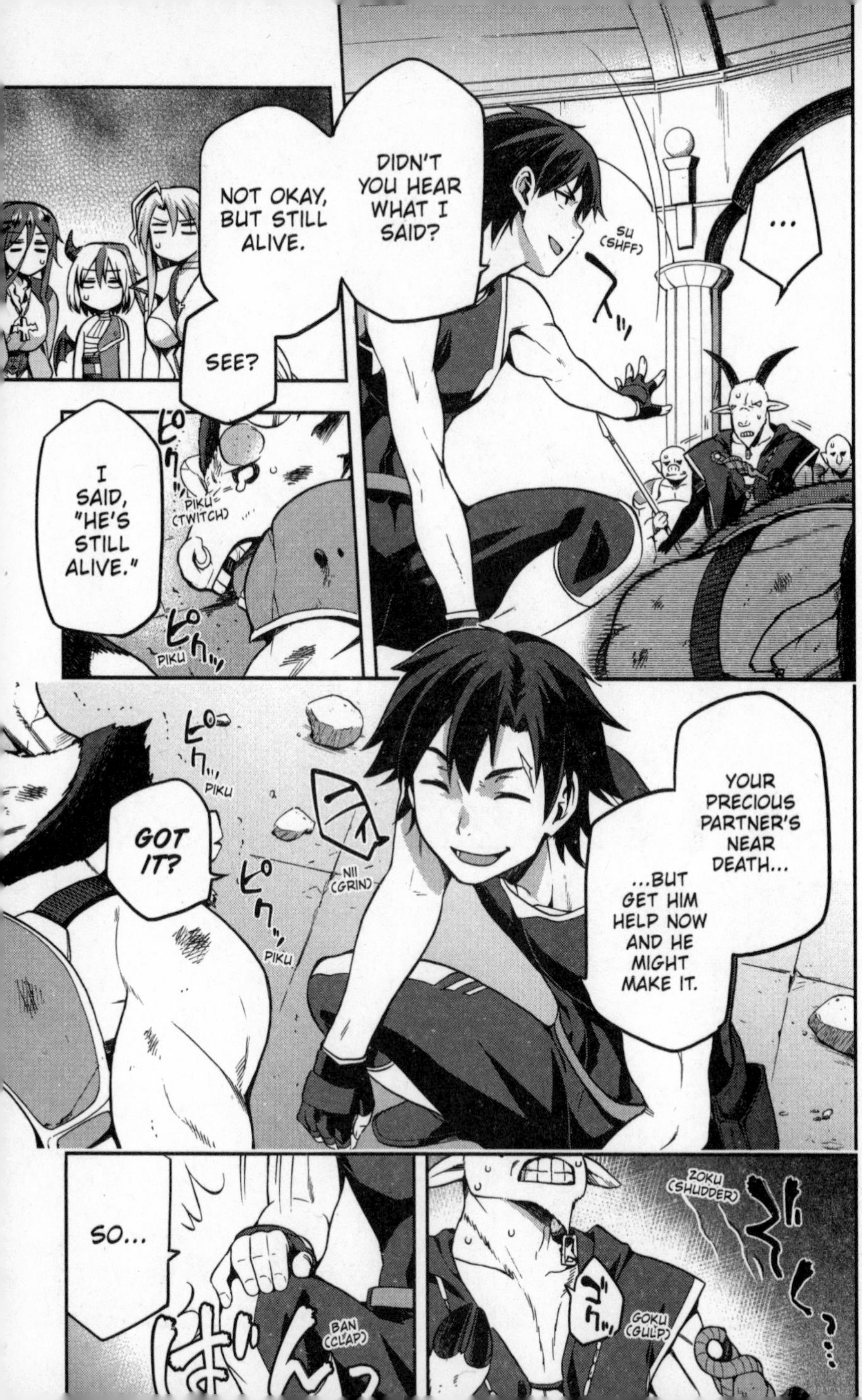
...
SU (SHFF)
DIDN'T YOU HEAR WHAT I SAID?
NOT OKAY, BUT STILL ALIVE.
SEE?
I SAID, "HE'S STILL ALIVE."
PIKU (TWITCH)
PIKU
YOUR PRECIOUS PARTNER'S NEAR DEATH...
...BUT GET HIM HELP NOW AND HE MIGHT MAKE IT.
NII (GRIN)
GOT IT?
PIKU
PIKU
ZOKU (SHUDDER)
GOKU (GULP)
SO...
BAN (CLAP)

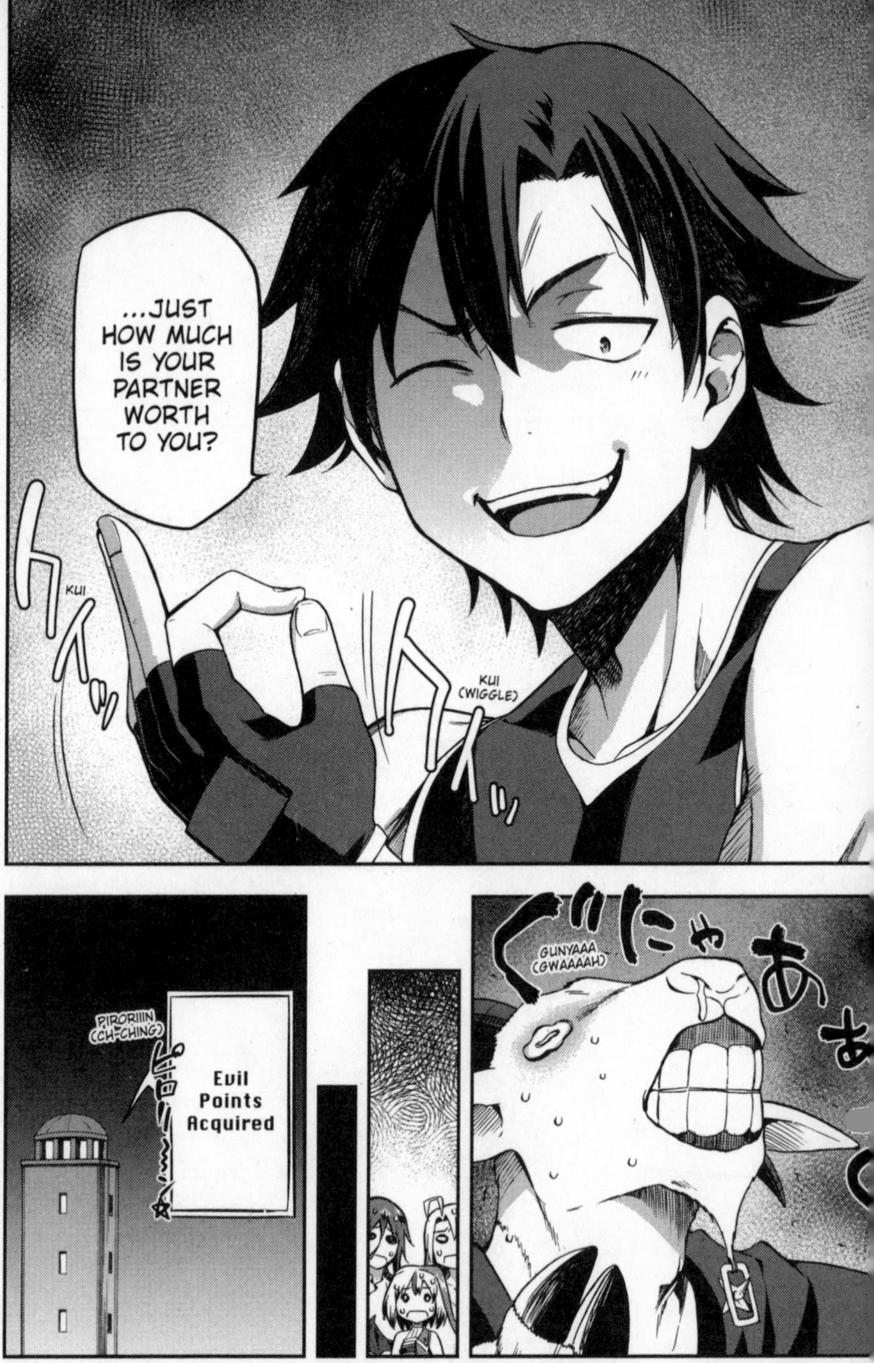
...JUST HOW MUCH IS YOUR PARTNER WORTH TO YOU?
KUI (WIGGLE)
KUI
GUNYAAA (GWAAAAH)
PIRORIIIN (CH-CHING)
Evil Points Acquired

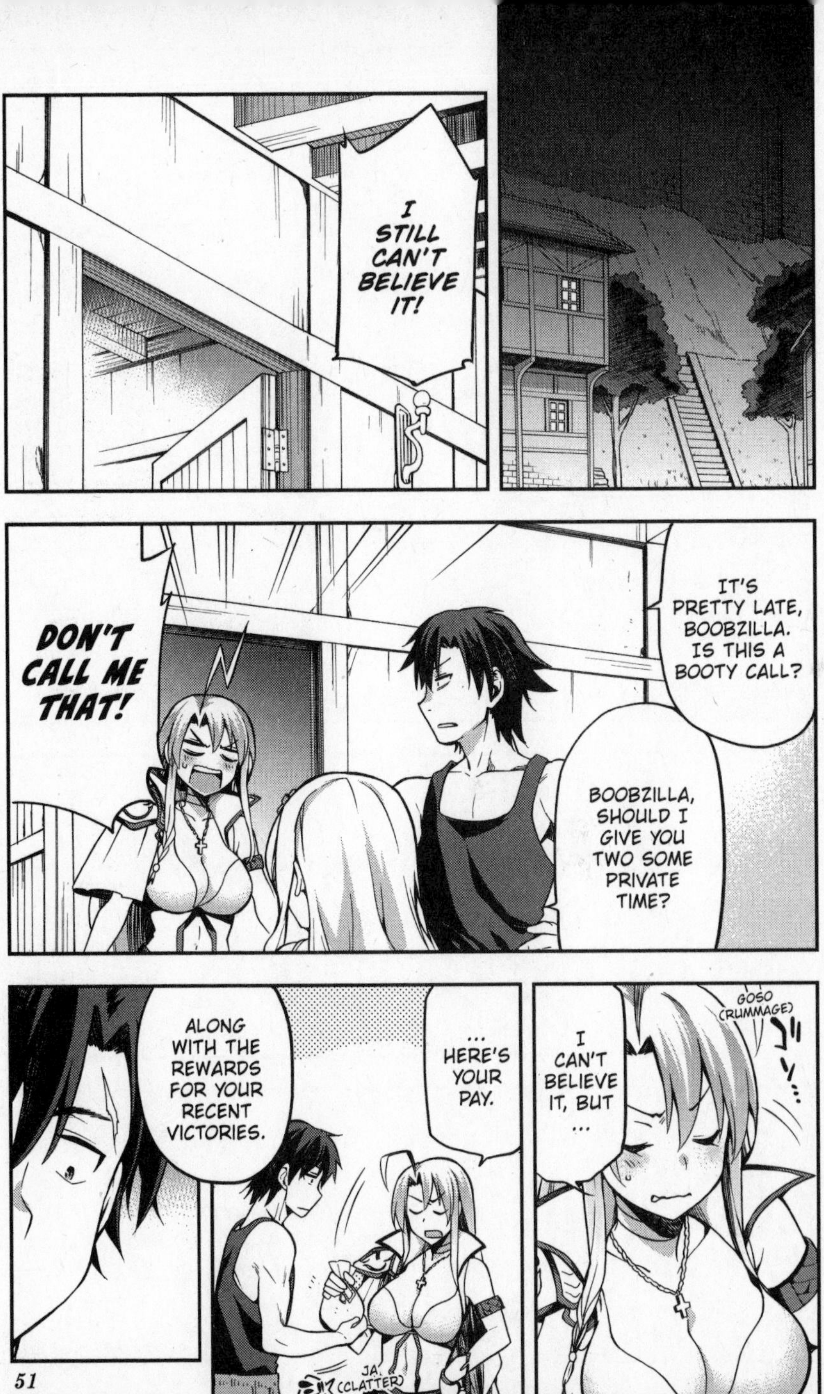
I STILL CAN'T BELIEVE IT!
IT'S PRETTY LATE, BOOBZILLA. IS THIS A BOOTY CALL?
BOOBZILLA, SHOULD I GIVE YOU TWO SOME PRIVATE TIME?
DON'T CALL ME THAT!
GOSO (RUMMAGE)
I CAN'T BELIEVE IT, BUT ...
... HERE'S YOUR PAY.
JA (CLATTER)
ALONG WITH THE REWARDS FOR YOUR RECENT VICTORIES.

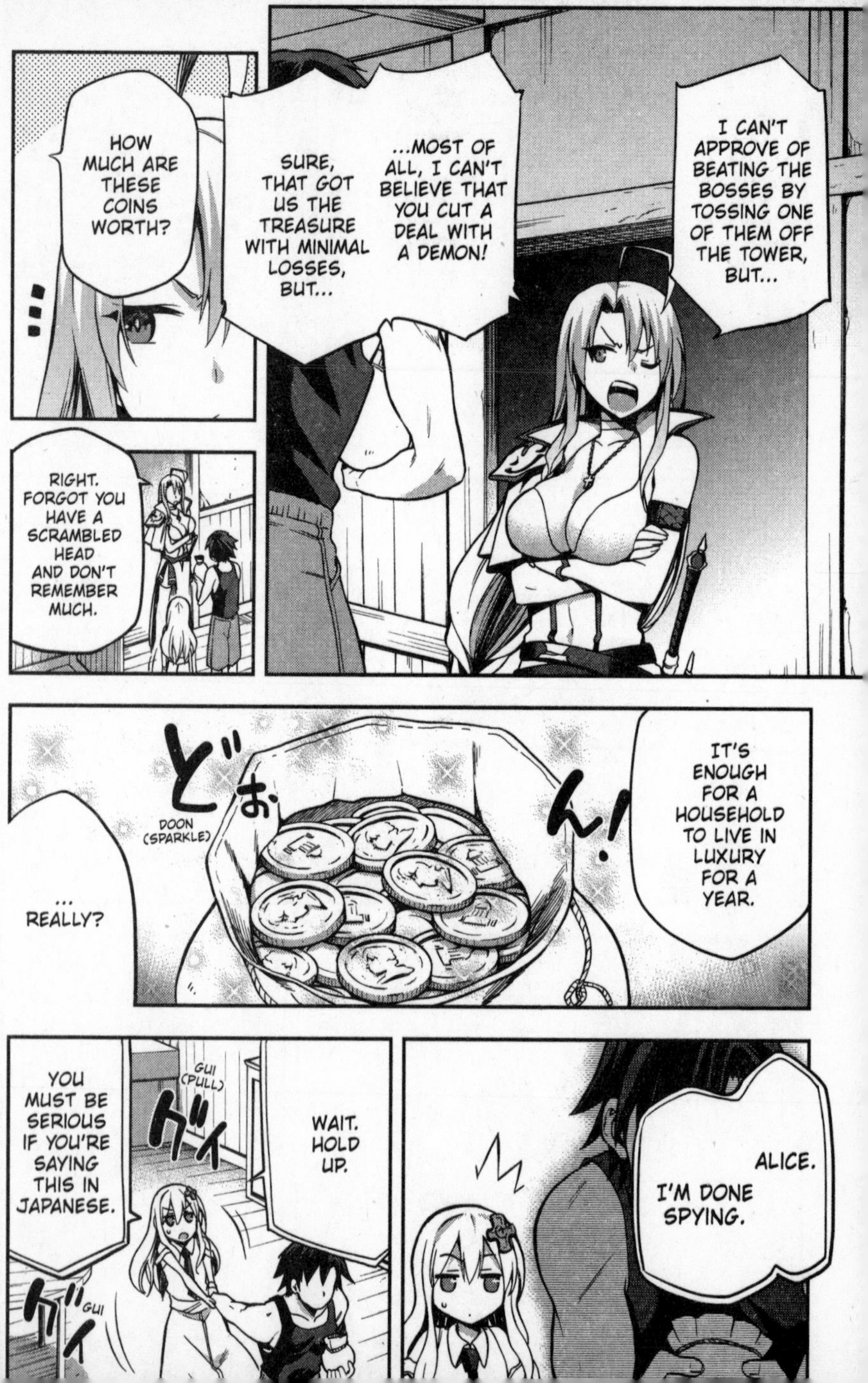
I CAN'T APPROVE OF BEATING THE BOSSES BY TOSSING ONE OF THEM OFF THE TOWER, BUT...
...MOST OF ALL, I CAN'T BELIEVE THAT YOU CUT A DEAL WITH A DEMON!
SURE, THAT GOT US THE TREASURE WITH MINIMAL LOSSES, BUT...
HOW MUCH ARE THESE COINS WORTH?
...
RIGHT. FORGOT YOU HAVE A SCRAMBLED HEAD AND DON'T REMEMBER MUCH.
IT'S ENOUGH FOR A HOUSEHOLD TO LIVE IN LUXURY FOR A YEAR.
どぉん!
DOON (SPARKLE)
... REALLY?
ALICE.
I'M DONE SPYING.
WAIT. HOLD UP.
グイ
GUI (PULL)
YOU MUST BE SERIOUS IF YOU'RE SAYING THIS IN JAPANESE.
グイ
GUI

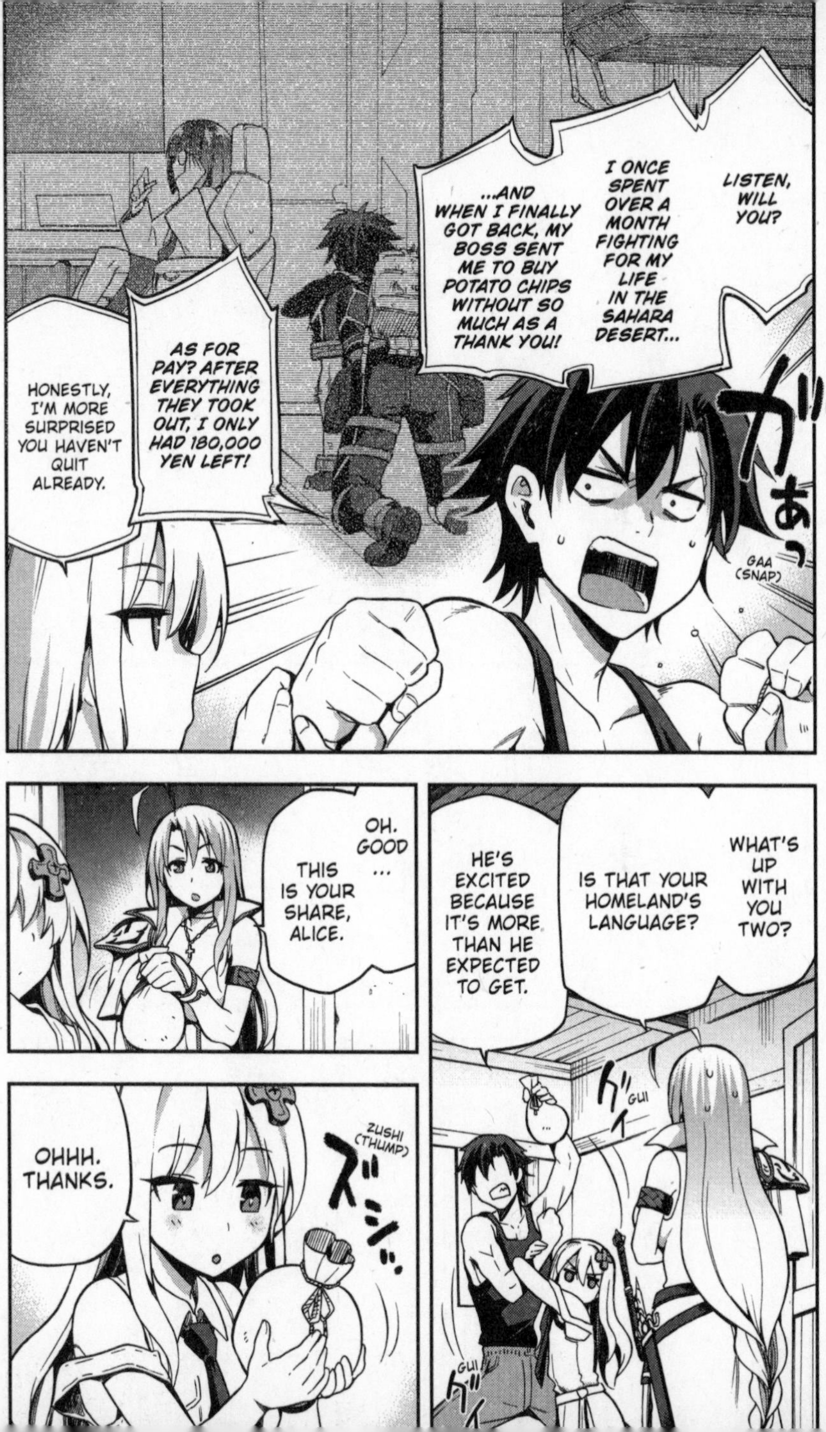
LISTEN, WILL YOU?
I ONCE SPENT OVER A MONTH FIGHTING FOR MY LIFE IN THE SAHARA DESERT...
...AND WHEN I FINALLY GOT BACK, MY BOSS SENT ME TO BUY POTATO CHIPS WITHOUT SO MUCH AS A THANK YOU!
AS FOR PAY? AFTER EVERYTHING THEY TOOK OUT, I ONLY HAD 180,000 YEN LEFT!
HONESTLY, I'M MORE SURPRISED YOU HAVEN'T QUIT ALREADY.
GAA (SNAP)
WHAT'S UP WITH YOU TWO?
IS THAT YOUR HOMELAND'S LANGUAGE?
HE'S EXCITED BECAUSE IT'S MORE THAN HE EXPECTED TO GET.
GUI
...
GUI
OH. GOOD ...
THIS IS YOUR SHARE, ALICE.
OHHH. THANKS.
ZUSHI (THUMP)

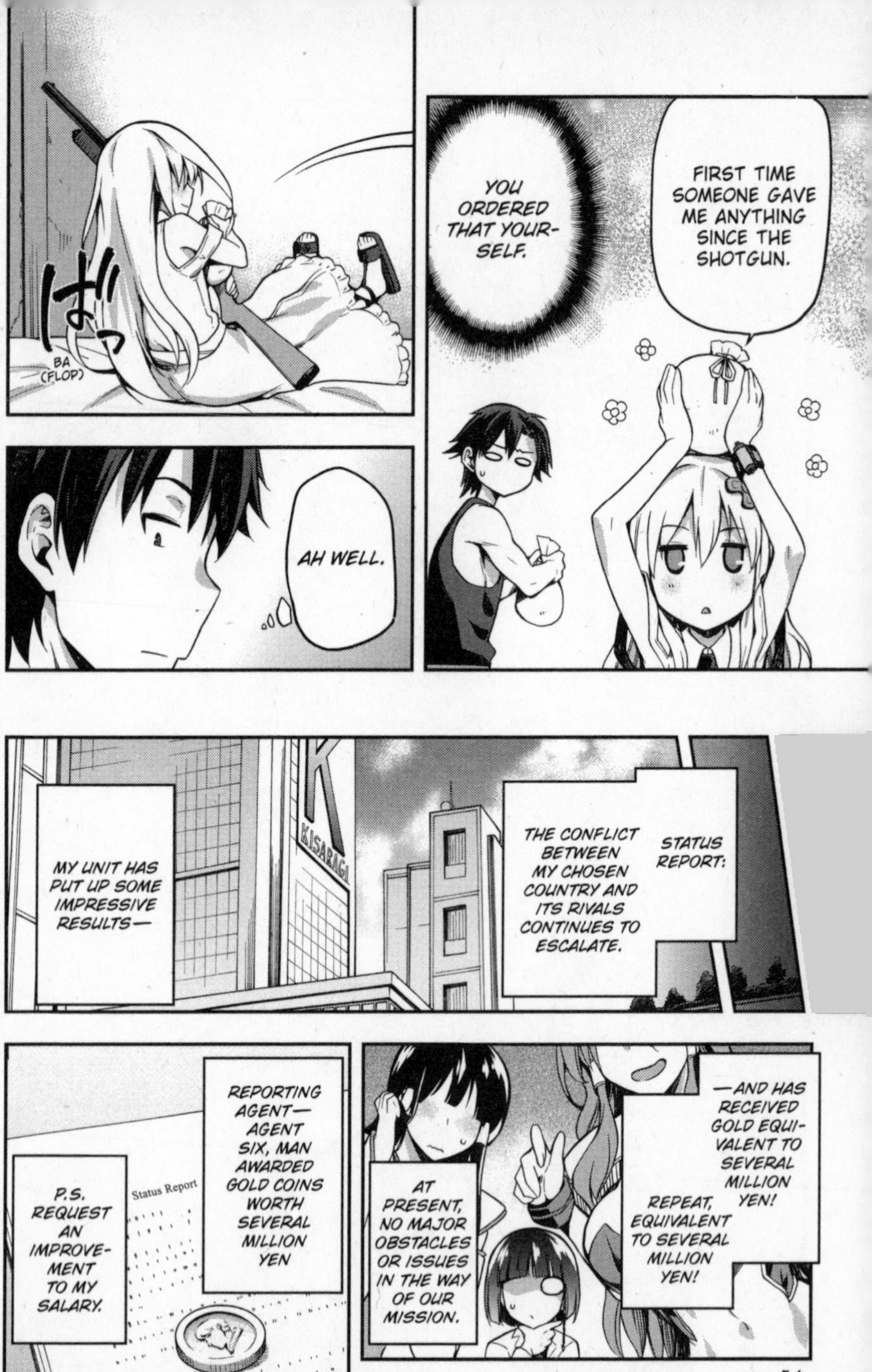
FIRST TIME SOMEONE GAVE ME ANYTHING SINCE THE SHOTGUN.
YOU ORDERED THAT YOURSELF.
ばっ
BA (FLOP)
AH WELL.
STATUS REPORT:
THE CONFLICT BETWEEN MY CHOSEN COUNTRY AND ITS RIVALS CONTINUES TO ESCALATE.
MY UNIT HAS PUT UP SOME IMPRESSIVE RESULTS—
KISARAGI
—AND HAS RECEIVED GOLD EQUIVALENT TO SEVERAL MILLION YEN!
REPEAT, EQUIVALENT TO SEVERAL MILLION YEN!
AT PRESENT, NO MAJOR OBSTACLES OR ISSUES IN THE WAY OF OUR MISSION.
REPORTING AGENT—AGENT SIX, MAN AWARDED GOLD COINS WORTH SEVERAL MILLION YEN
P.S. REQUEST AN IMPROVEMENT TO MY SALARY.
Status Report

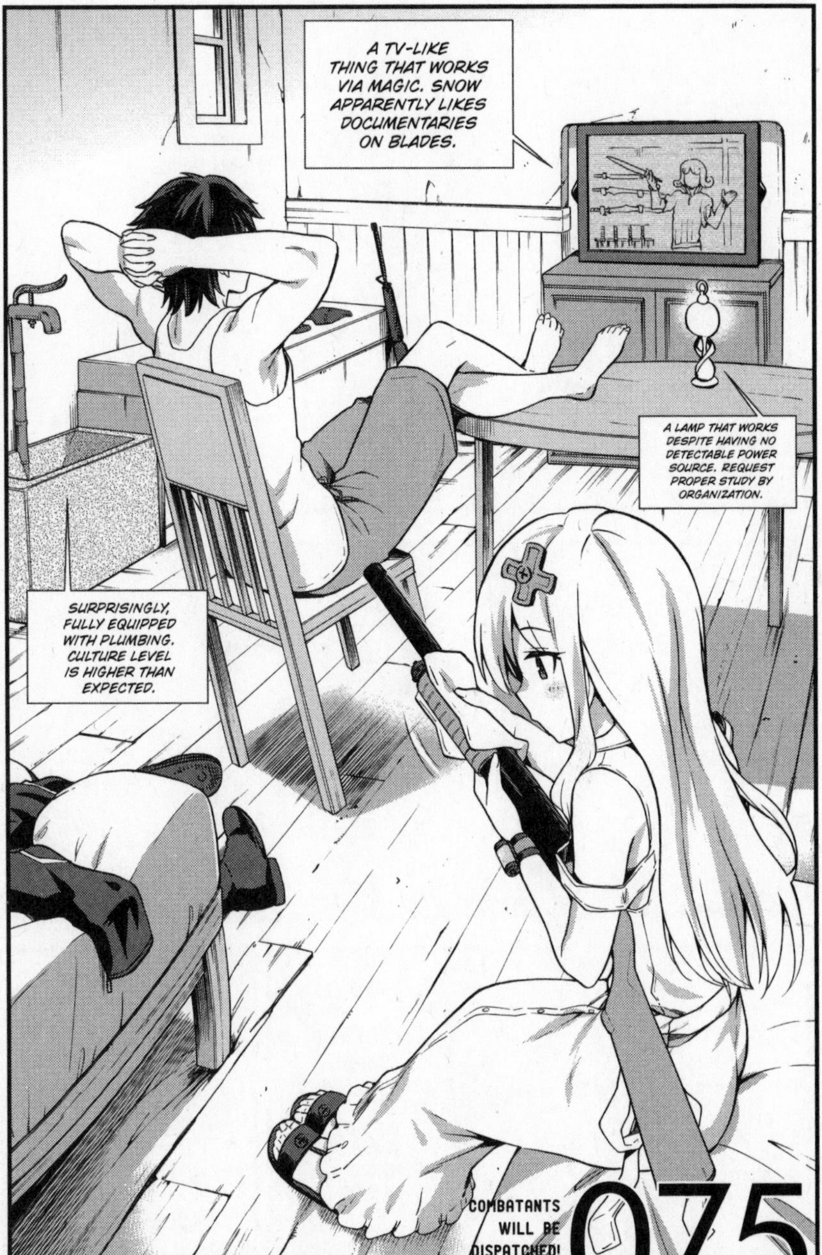
A TV-LIKE THING THAT WORKS VIA MAGIC. SNOW APPARENTLY LIKES DOCUMENTARIES ON BLADES.
A LAMP THAT WORKS DESPITE HAVING NO DETECTABLE POWER SOURCE. REQUEST PROPER STUDY BY ORGANIZATION.
SURPRISINGLY, FULLY EQUIPPED WITH PLUMBING. CULTURE LEVEL IS HIGHER THAN EXPECTED.
COMBATANTS WILL BE DISPATCHED!

Chapter 07.5

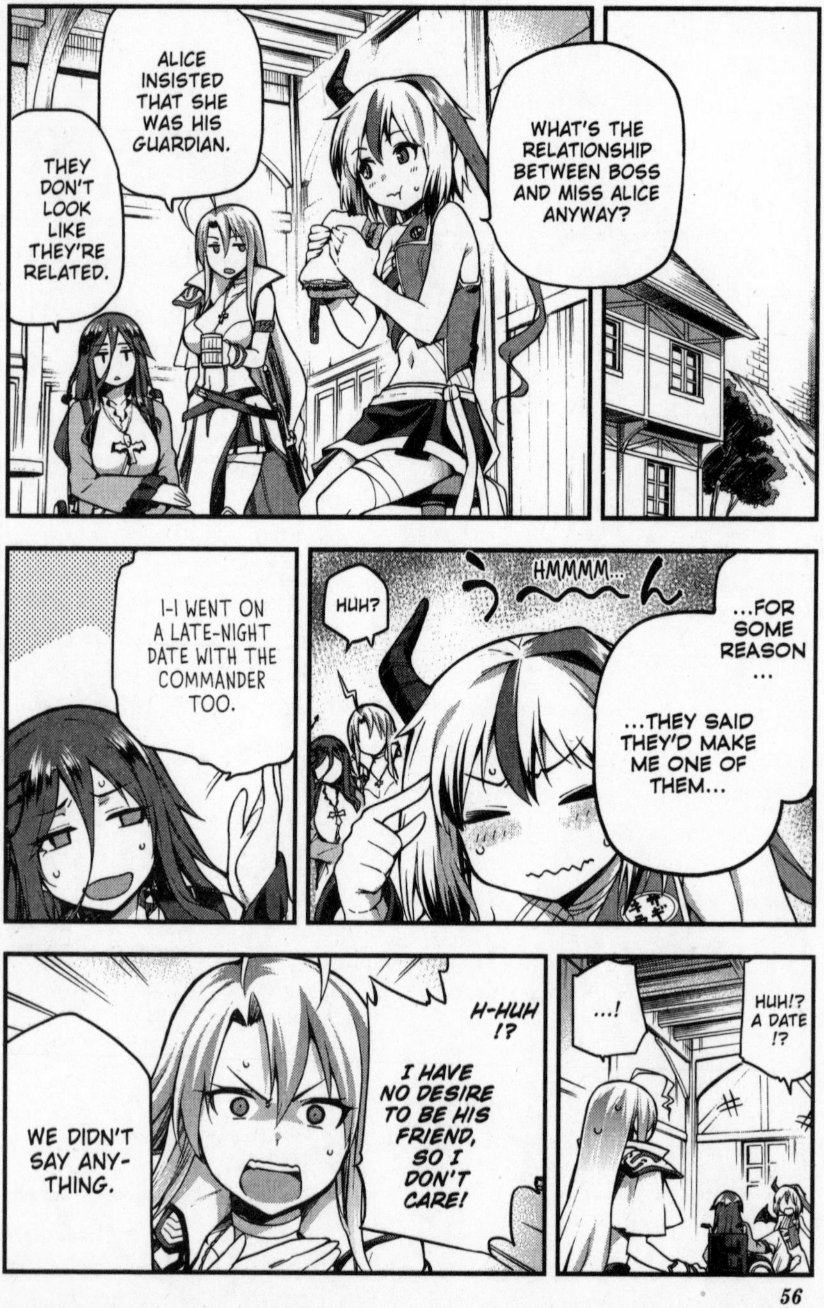
WHAT'S THE RELATIONSHIP BETWEEN BOSS AND MISS ALICE ANYWAY?
ALICE INSISTED THAT SHE WAS HIS GUARDIAN.
THEY DON'T LOOK LIKE THEY'RE RELATED.
HMMMM...
う〜〜ん
...FOR SOME REASON ...
...THEY SAID THEY'D MAKE ME ONE OF THEM...
HUH?
I-I WENT ON A LATE-NIGHT DATE WITH THE COMMANDER TOO.
HUH!? A DATE !?
...!
H-HUH !?
I HAVE NO DESIRE TO BE HIS FRIEND, SO I DON'T CARE!
WE DIDN'T SAY ANY-THING.

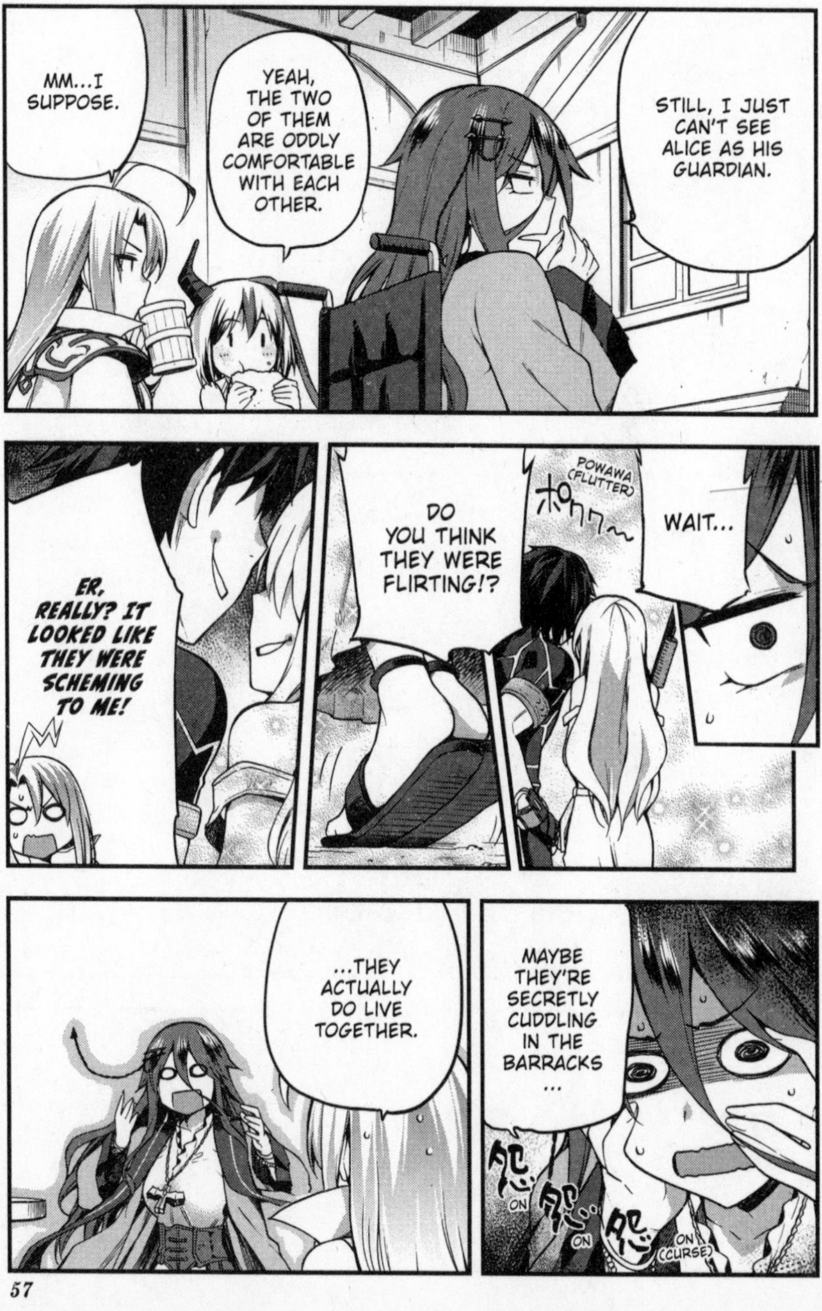
STILL, I JUST CAN'T SEE ALICE AS HIS GUARDIAN.
YEAH, THE TWO OF THEM ARE ODDLY COMFORTABLE WITH EACH OTHER.
MM...I SUPPOSE.
WAIT...
POWAWA (FLUTTER)
DO YOU THINK THEY WERE FLIRTING!?
ER, REALLY? IT LOOKED LIKE THEY WERE SCHEMING TO ME!
MAYBE THEY'RE SECRETLY CUDDLING IN THE BARRACKS...
ON
ON
ON (CURSE)
...THEY ACTUALLY DO LIVE TOGETHER.

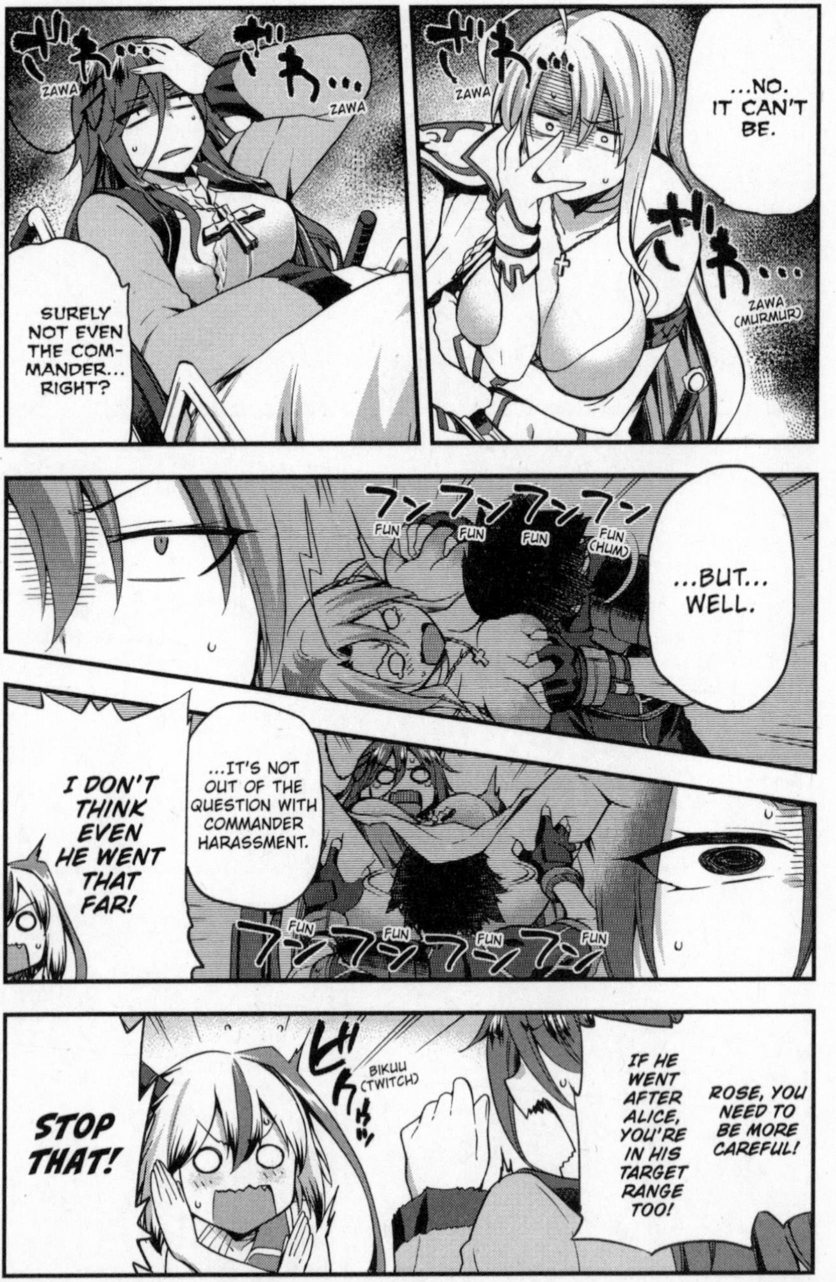
ZAWA
...NO. IT CAN'T BE.
ZAWA (MURMUR)
ZAWA
ZAWA
SURELY NOT EVEN THE COMMANDER... RIGHT?
FUN FUN FUN FUN (HUM)
...BUT... WELL.
...IT'S NOT OUT OF THE QUESTION WITH COMMANDER HARASSMENT.
I DON'T THINK EVEN HE WENT THAT FAR!
FUN FUN FUN FUN
ROSE, YOU NEED TO BE MORE CAREFUL!
IF HE WENT AFTER ALICE, YOU'RE IN HIS TARGET RANGE TOO!
BIKUU (TWITCH)
STOP THAT!

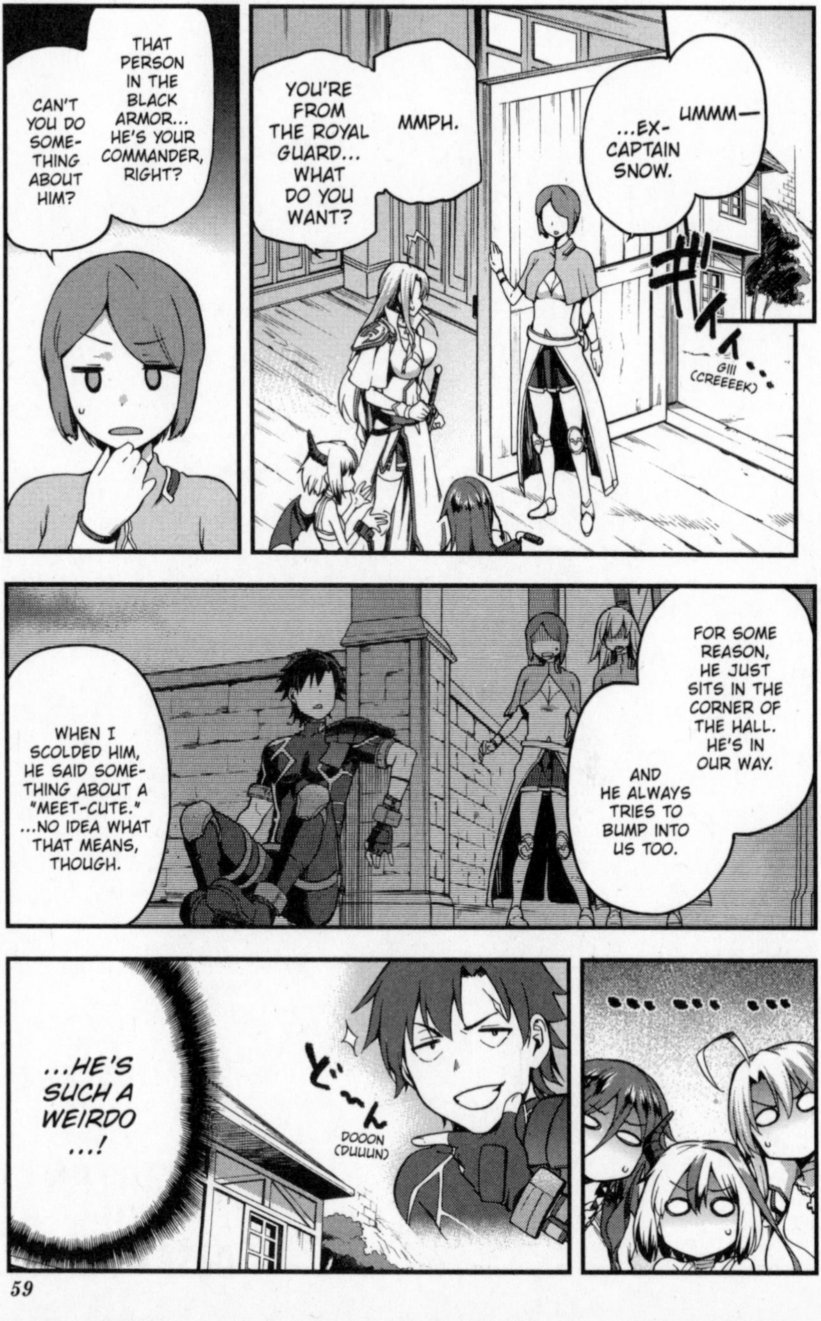
UMMM—
...EX-CAPTAIN SNOW.
ギィィ
GIII (CREEEEK)
MMPH.
YOU'RE FROM THE ROYAL GUARD... WHAT DO YOU WANT?
THAT PERSON IN THE BLACK ARMOR... HE'S YOUR COMMANDER, RIGHT?
CAN'T YOU DO SOMETHING ABOUT HIM?
FOR SOME REASON, HE JUST SITS IN THE CORNER OF THE HALL. HE'S IN OUR WAY.
AND HE ALWAYS TRIES TO BUMP INTO US TOO.
WHEN I SCOLDED HIM, HE SAID SOMETHING ABOUT A "MEET-CUTE." ...NO IDEA WHAT THAT MEANS, THOUGH.
... ...
ど〜ん
DOOON (DUUUN)
...HE'S SUCH A WEIRDO...!

COMBATANTS
WILL BE
DISPATCHED!

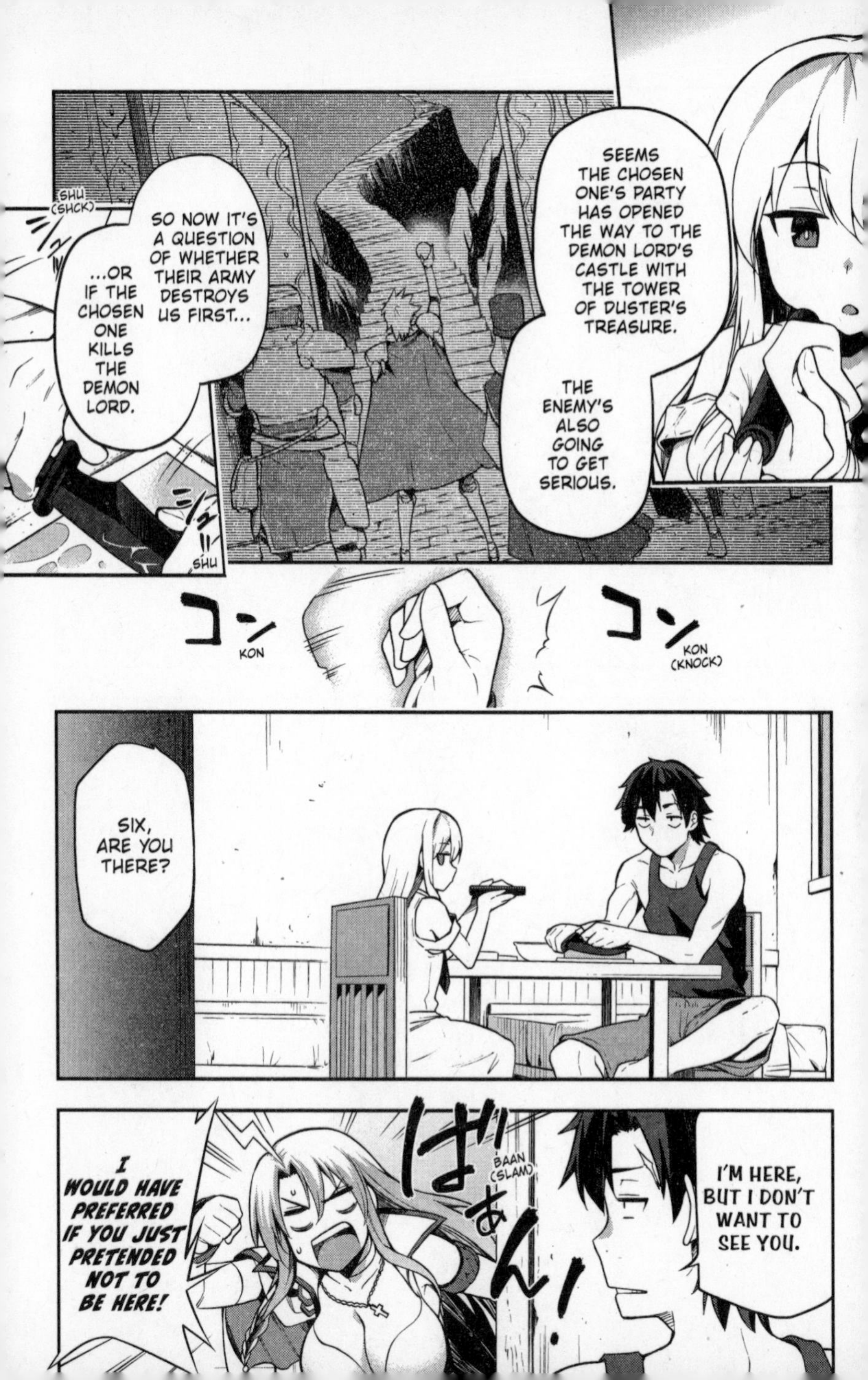
SEEMS THE CHOSEN ONE'S PARTY HAS OPENED THE WAY TO THE DEMON LORD'S CASTLE WITH THE TOWER OF DUSTER'S TREASURE.
THE ENEMY'S ALSO GOING TO GET SERIOUS.
SO NOW IT'S A QUESTION OF WHETHER THEIR ARMY DESTROYS US FIRST...
...OR IF THE CHOSEN ONE KILLS THE DEMON LORD.
SHU (SHCK)
SHU
KON (KNOCK)
KON
SIX, ARE YOU THERE?
I'M HERE, BUT I DON'T WANT TO SEE YOU.
BAAN (SLAM)
I WOULD HAVE PREFERRED IF YOU JUST PRETENDED NOT TO BE HERE!

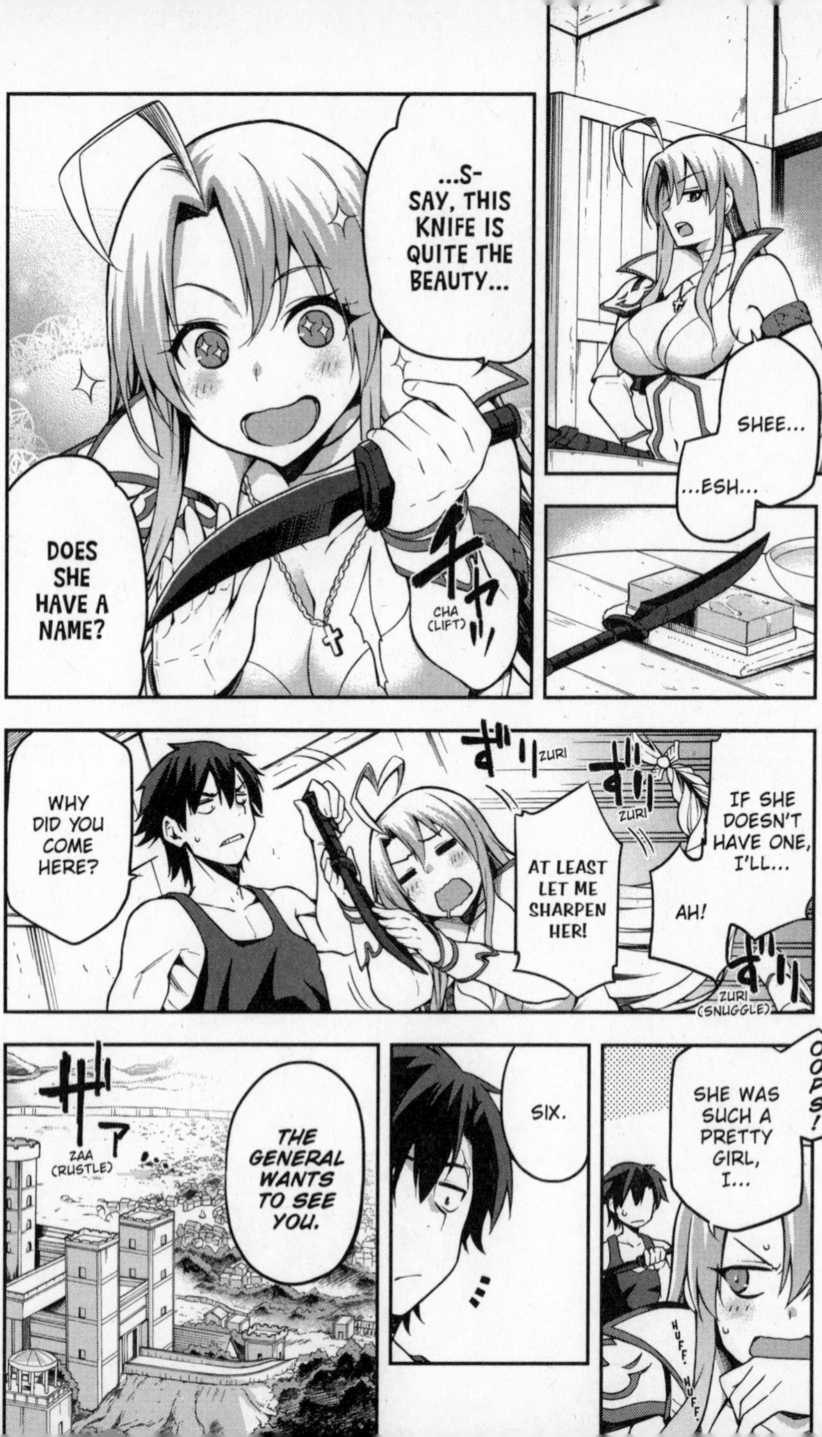
SHEE...
...ESH...
...S- SAY, THIS KNIFE IS QUITE THE BEAUTY...
CHA (LIFT)
DOES SHE HAVE A NAME?
IF SHE DOESN'T HAVE ONE, I'LL...
AH!
ZURI
ZURI
ZURI (SNUGGLE)
AT LEAST LET ME SHARPEN HER!
WHY DID YOU COME HERE?
OOPS!
SHE WAS SUCH A PRETTY GIRL, I...
HUFF. HUFF.
SIX.
THE GENERAL WANTS TO SEE YOU.
ZAA (RUSTLE)

Chapter 08

COMBATANTS
WILL BE
DISPATCHED!

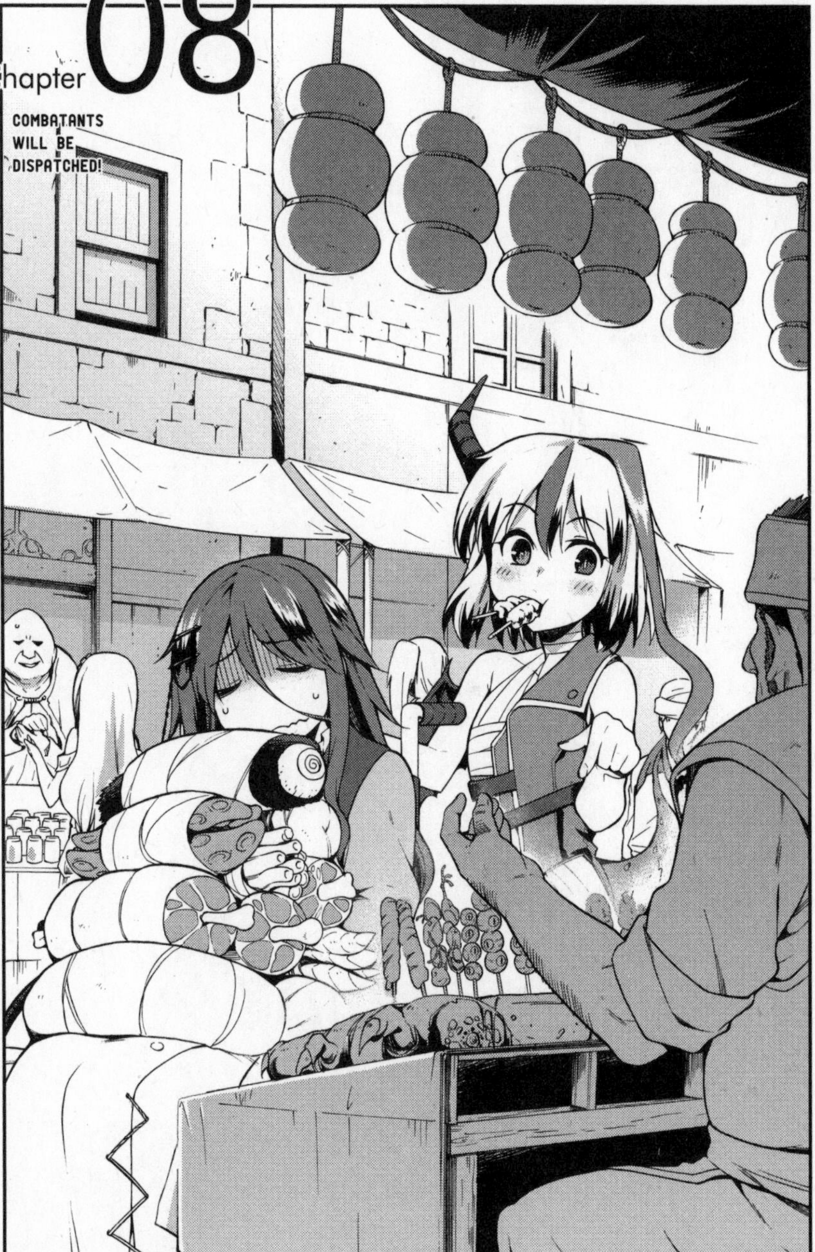

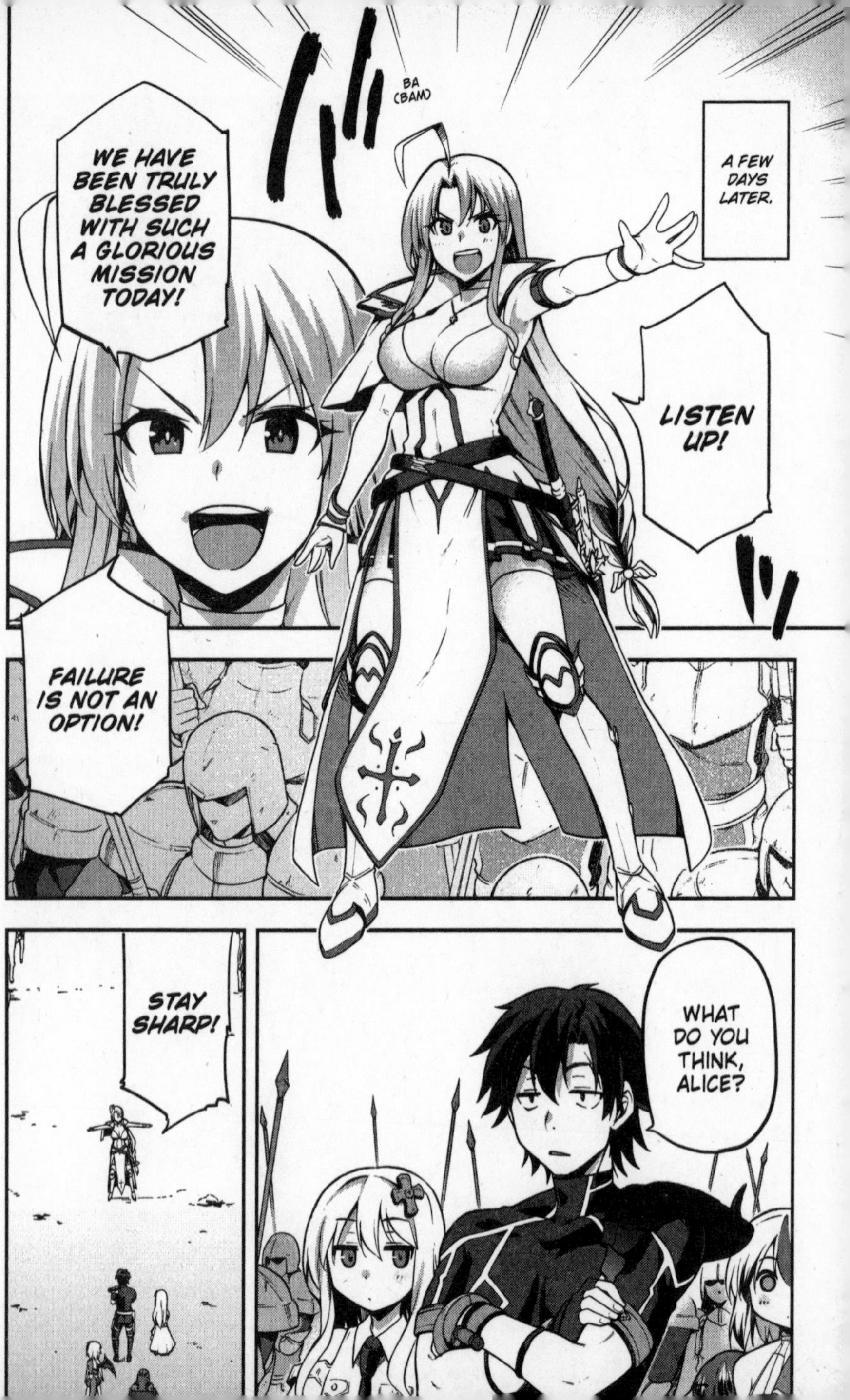
BA (BAM)
A FEW DAYS LATER.
LISTEN UP!
WE HAVE BEEN TRULY BLESSED WITH SUCH A GLORIOUS MISSION TODAY!
FAILURE IS NOT AN OPTION!
WHAT DO YOU THINK, ALICE?
STAY SHARP!

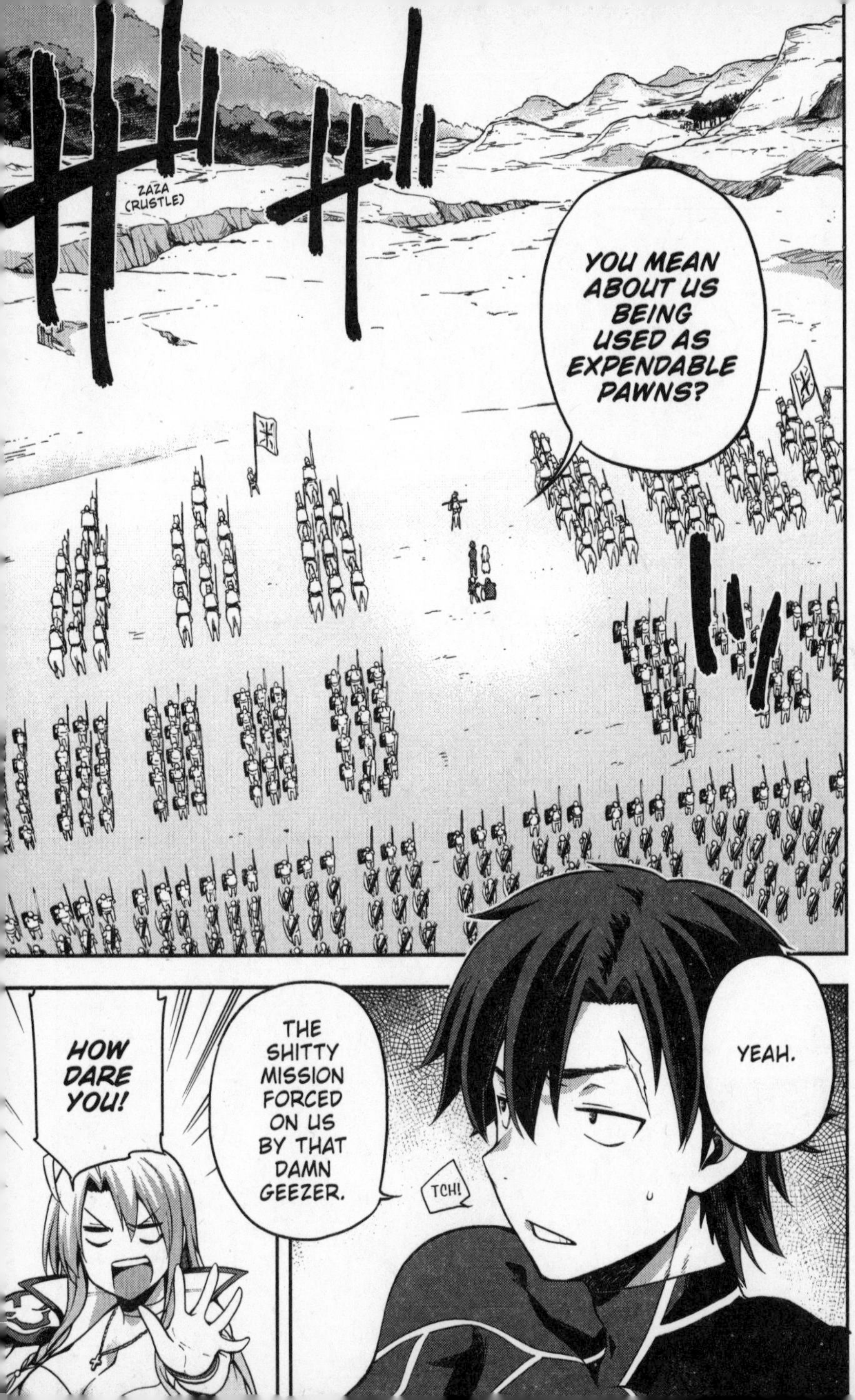

YOU MEAN ABOUT US BEING USED AS EXPENDABLE PAWNS?
ZAZA (RUSTLE)
YEAH.
THE SHITTY MISSION FORCED ON US BY THAT DAMN GEEZER.
TCH!
HOW DARE YOU!

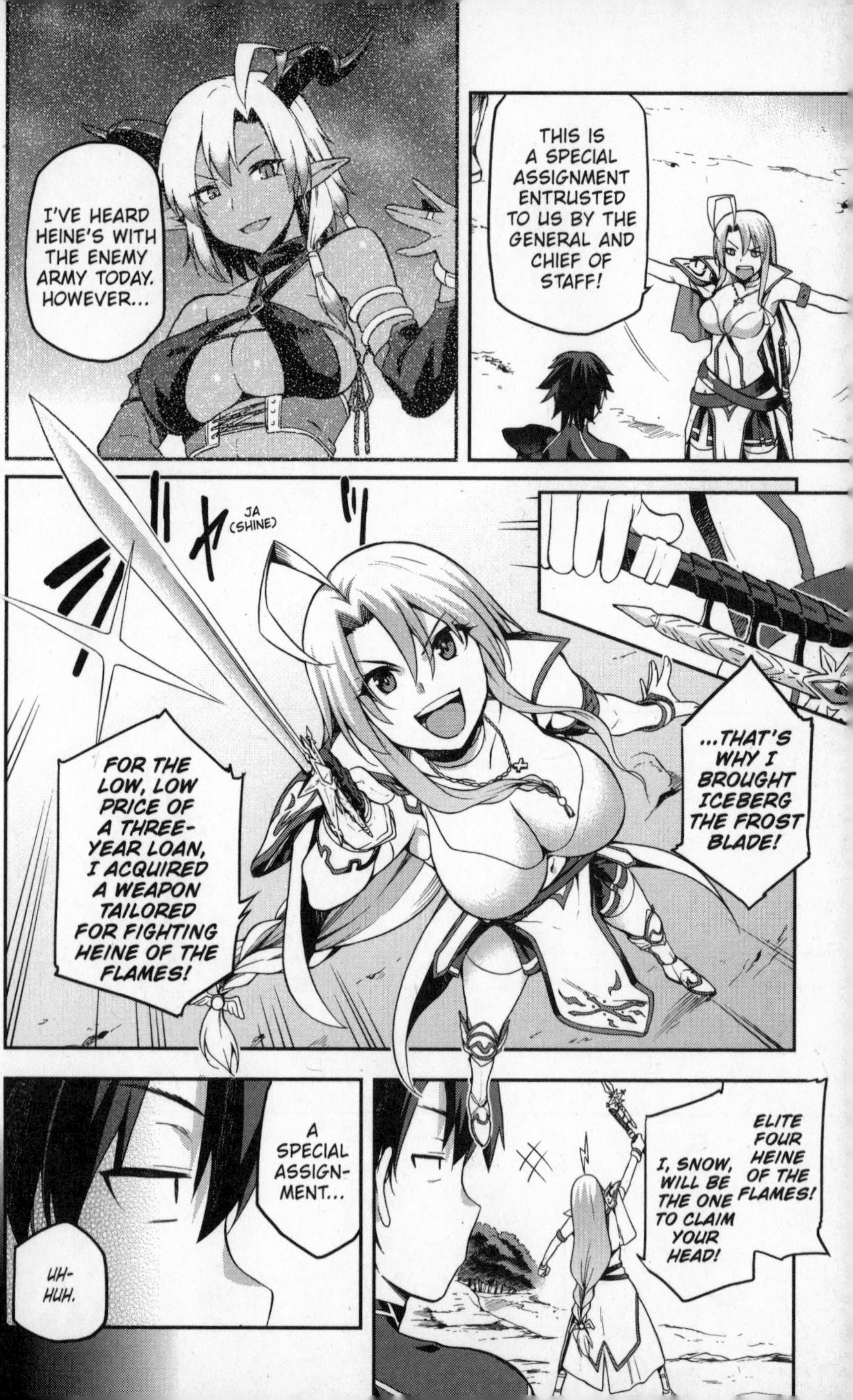
THIS IS A SPECIAL ASSIGNMENT ENTRUSTED TO US BY THE GENERAL AND CHIEF OF STAFF!
I'VE HEARD HEINE'S WITH THE ENEMY ARMY TODAY. HOWEVER...
...THAT'S WHY I BROUGHT ICEBERG THE FROST BLADE!
JA (SHINE)
FOR THE LOW, LOW PRICE OF A THREE-YEAR LOAN, I ACQUIRED A WEAPON TAILORED FOR FIGHTING HEINE OF THE FLAMES!
ELITE FOUR HEINE OF THE FLAMES!
I, SNOW, WILL BE THE ONE TO CLAIM YOUR HEAD!
A SPECIAL ASSIGNMENT...
UH-HUH.

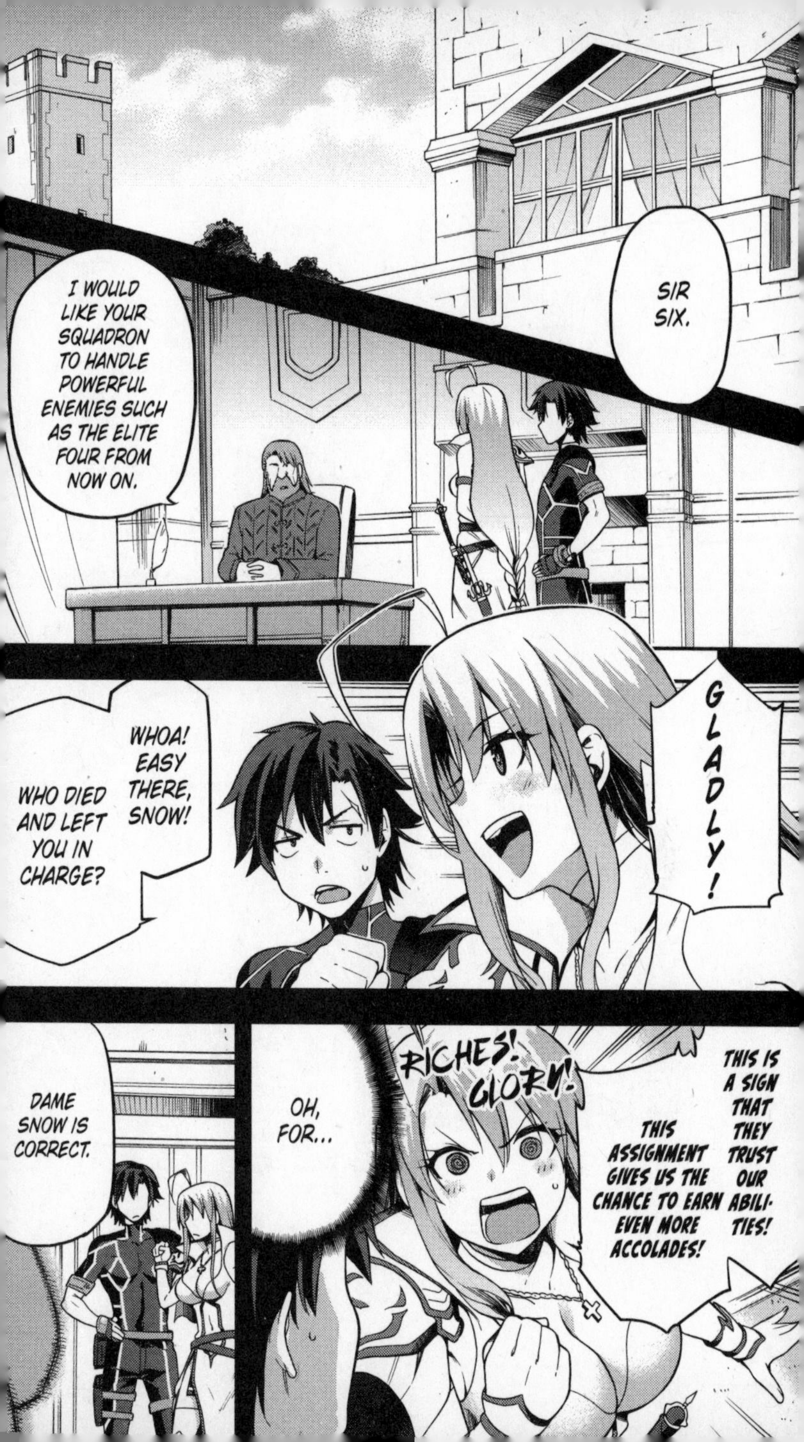
SIR SIX.
I WOULD LIKE YOUR SQUADRON TO HANDLE POWERFUL ENEMIES SUCH AS THE ELITE FOUR FROM NOW ON.
GLADLY!
WHOA! EASY THERE, SNOW!
WHO DIED AND LEFT YOU IN CHARGE?
THIS IS A SIGN THAT THEY TRUST OUR ABILITIES!
THIS ASSIGNMENT GIVES US THE CHANCE TO EARN EVEN MORE ACCOLADES!
RICHES! GLORY!
OH, FOR...
DAME SNOW IS CORRECT.

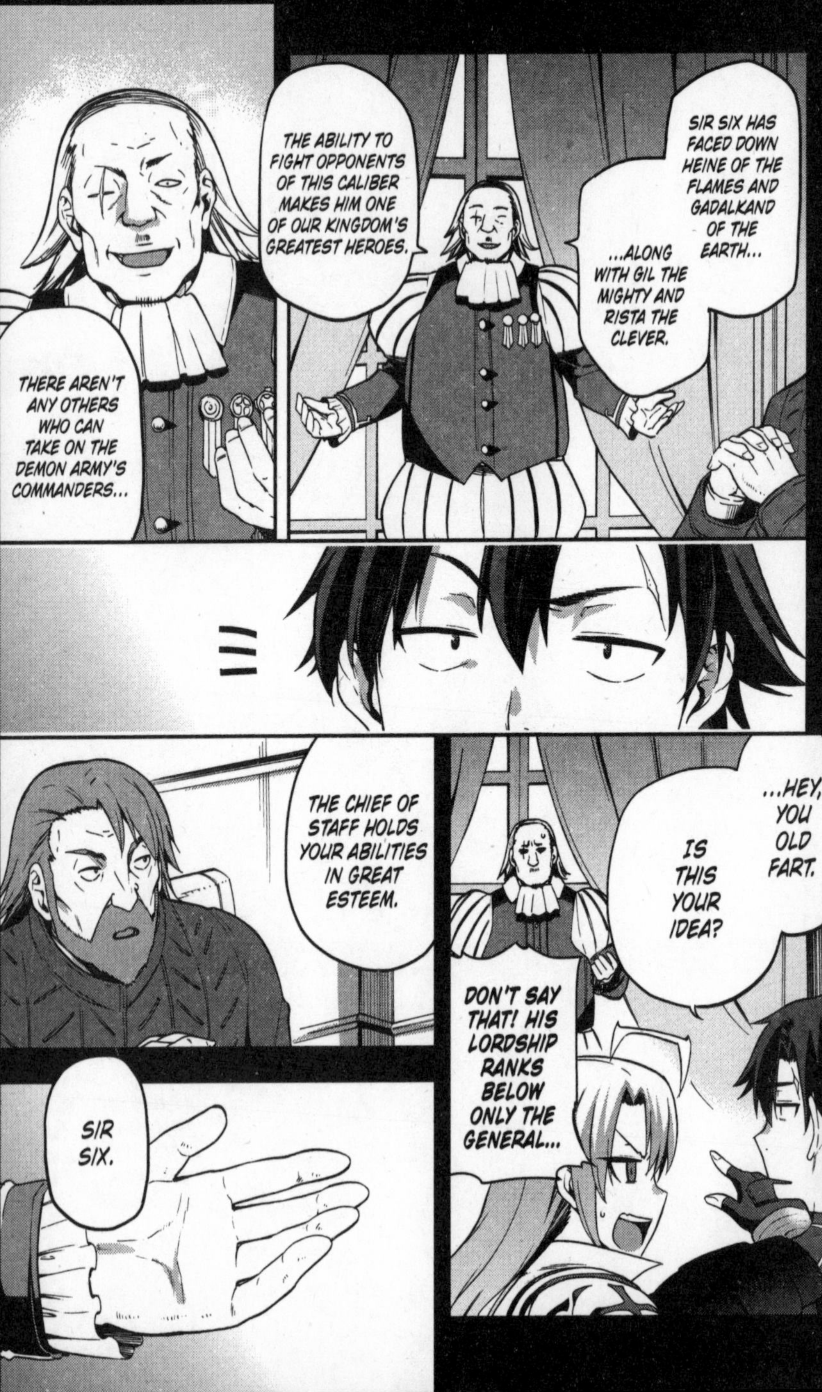
SIR SIX HAS FACED DOWN HEINE OF THE FLAMES AND GADALKAND OF THE EARTH...
...ALONG WITH GIL THE MIGHTY AND RISTA THE CLEVER.
THE ABILITY TO FIGHT OPPONENTS OF THIS CALIBER MAKES HIM ONE OF OUR KINGDOM'S GREATEST HEROES.
THERE AREN'T ANY OTHERS WHO CAN TAKE ON THE DEMON ARMY'S COMMANDERS...
...HEY, YOU OLD FART.
IS THIS YOUR IDEA?
DON'T SAY THAT! HIS LORDSHIP RANKS BELOW ONLY THE GENERAL...
THE CHIEF OF STAFF HOLDS YOUR ABILITIES IN GREAT ESTEEM.
SIR SIX.

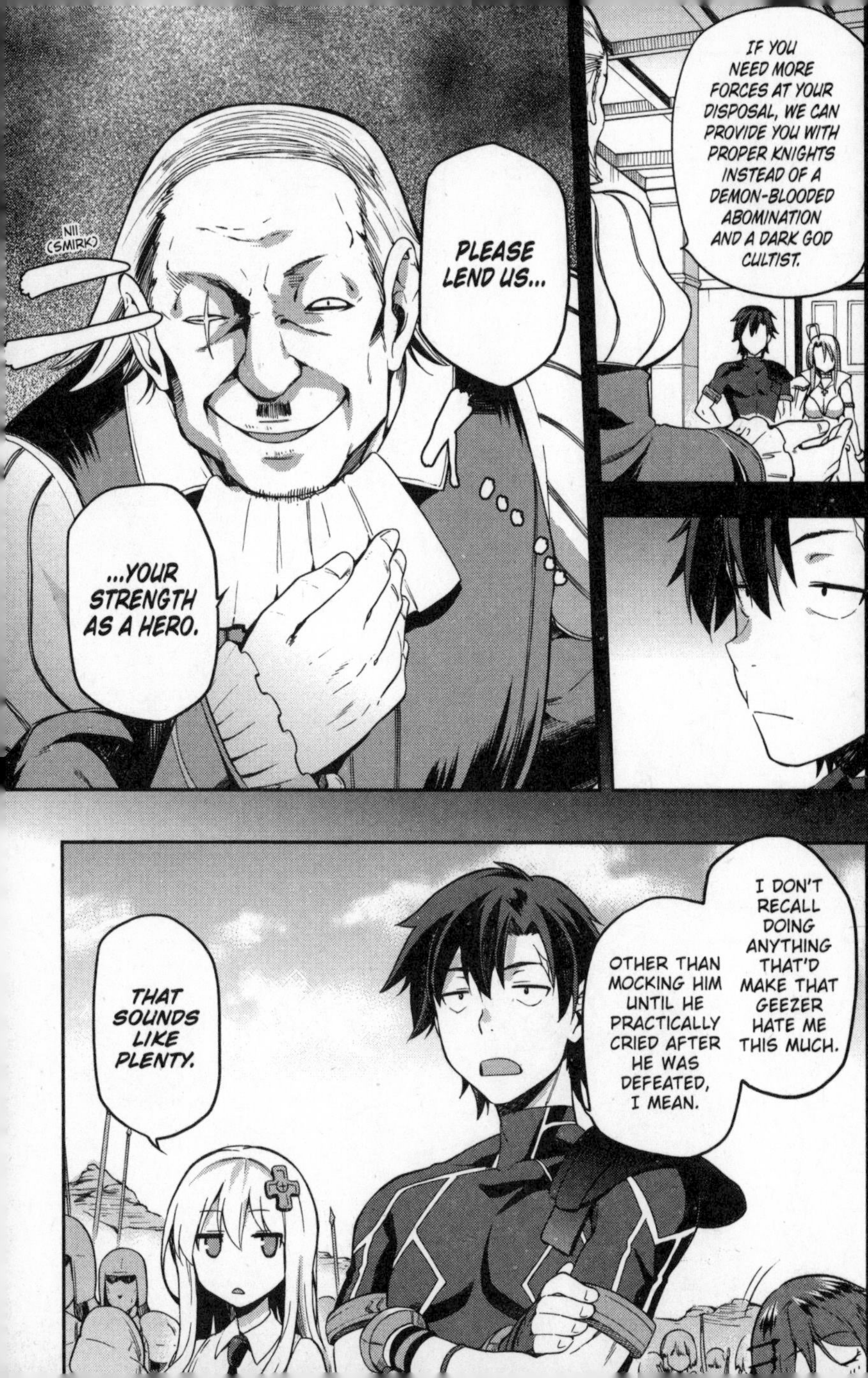
IF YOU NEED MORE FORCES AT YOUR DISPOSAL, WE CAN PROVIDE YOU WITH PROPER KNIGHTS INSTEAD OF A DEMON-BLOODED ABOMINATION AND A DARK GOD CULTIST.
NII (SMIRK)
PLEASE LEND US...
...YOUR STRENGTH AS A HERO.
I DON'T RECALL DOING ANYTHING THAT'D MAKE THAT GEEZER HATE ME THIS MUCH.
OTHER THAN MOCKING HIM UNTIL HE PRACTICALLY CRIED AFTER HE WAS DEFEATED, I MEAN.
THAT SOUNDS LIKE PLENTY.

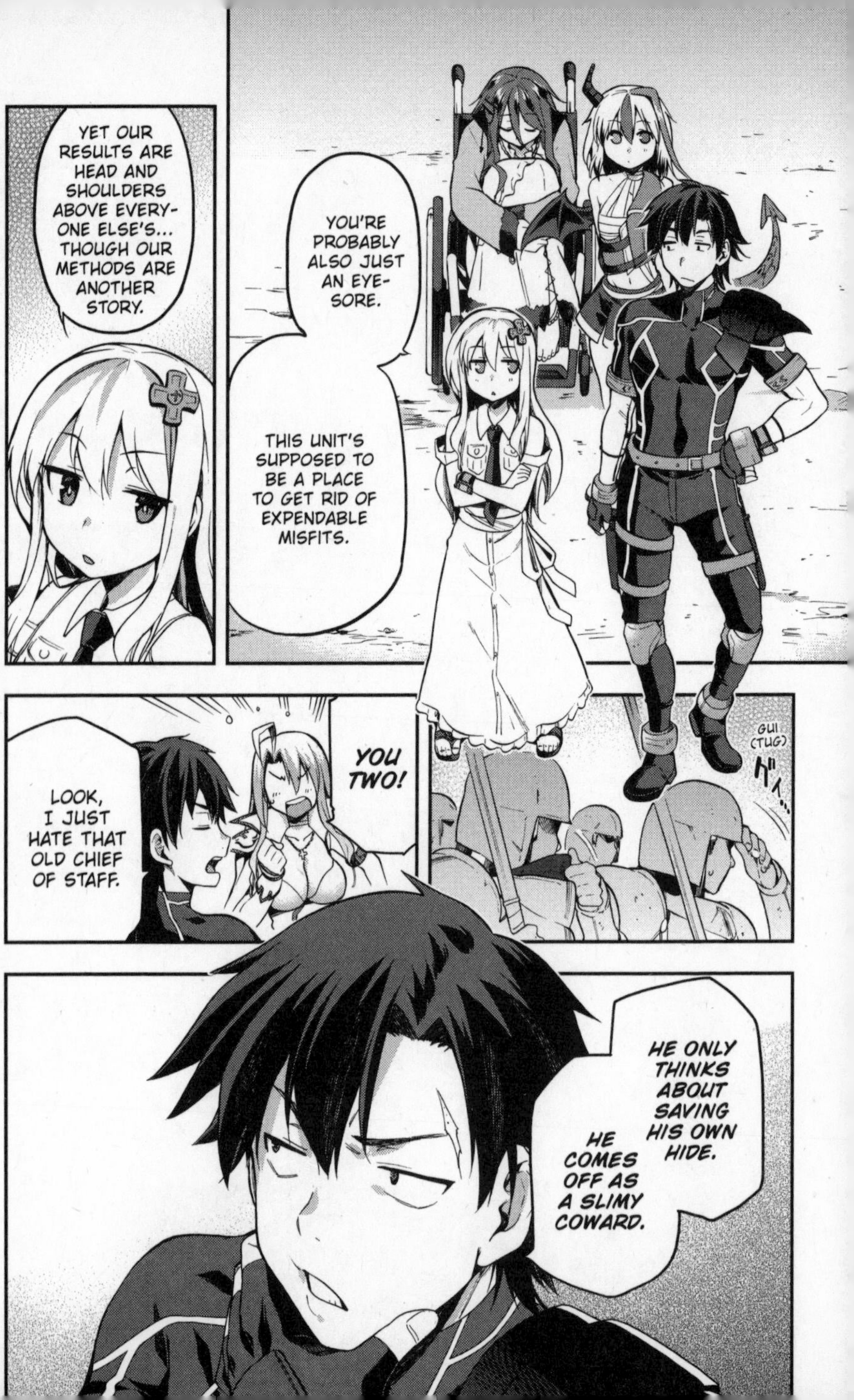
YOU'RE PROBABLY ALSO JUST AN EYE-SORE.
THIS UNIT'S SUPPOSED TO BE A PLACE TO GET RID OF EXPENDABLE MISFITS.
YET OUR RESULTS ARE HEAD AND SHOULDERS ABOVE EVERY-ONE ELSE'S... THOUGH OUR METHODS ARE ANOTHER STORY.
GUI (TUG)
グイ…
YOU TWO!
LOOK, I JUST HATE THAT OLD CHIEF OF STAFF.
HE ONLY THINKS ABOUT SAVING HIS OWN HIDE.
HE COMES OFF AS A SLIMY COWARD.

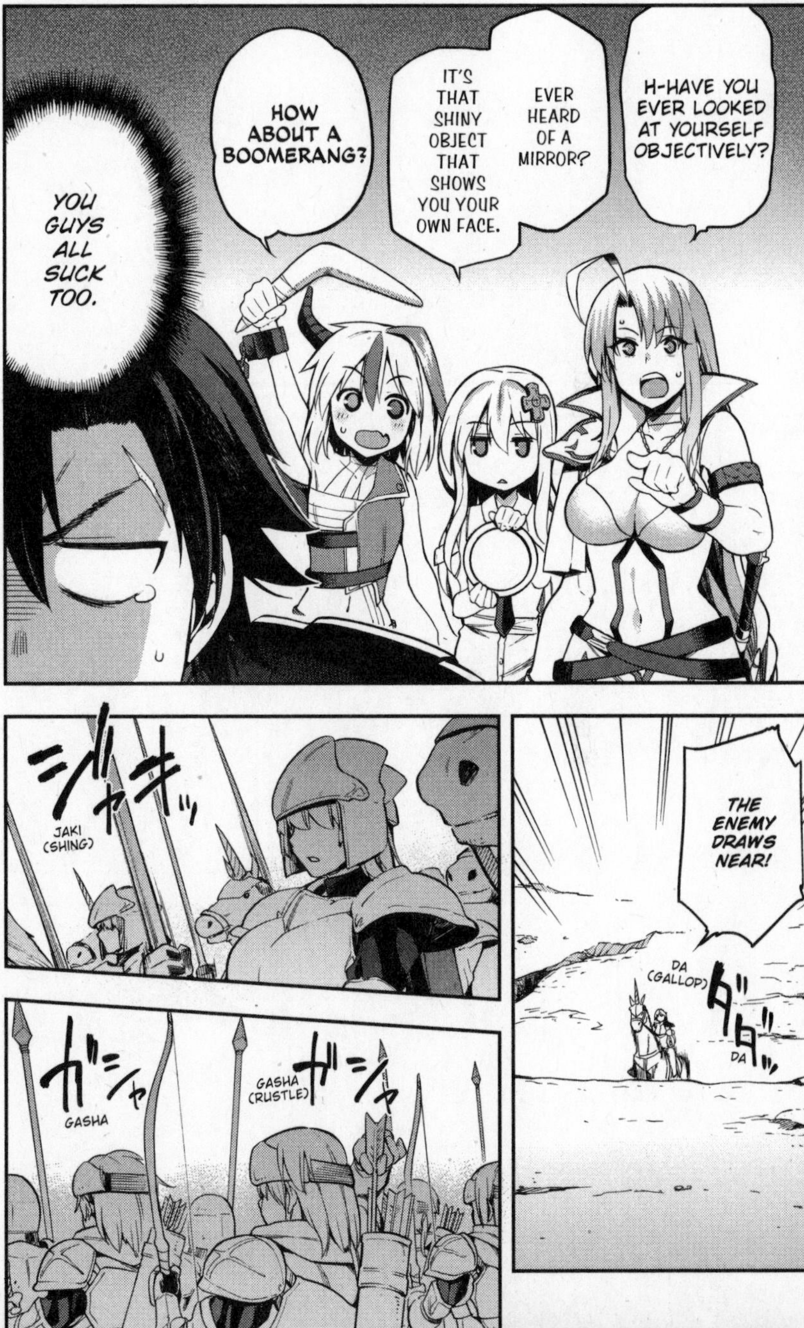
H-HAVE YOU EVER LOOKED AT YOURSELF OBJECTIVELY?
EVER HEARD OF A MIRROR?
IT'S THAT SHINY OBJECT THAT SHOWS YOU YOUR OWN FACE.
HOW ABOUT A BOOMERANG?
YOU GUYS ALL SUCK TOO.
THE ENEMY DRAWS NEAR!
ダダッ
DA (GALLOP)
DA
ジャキッ
JAKI (SHING)
ガシャ
GASHA (RUSTLE)
ガシャ
GASHA

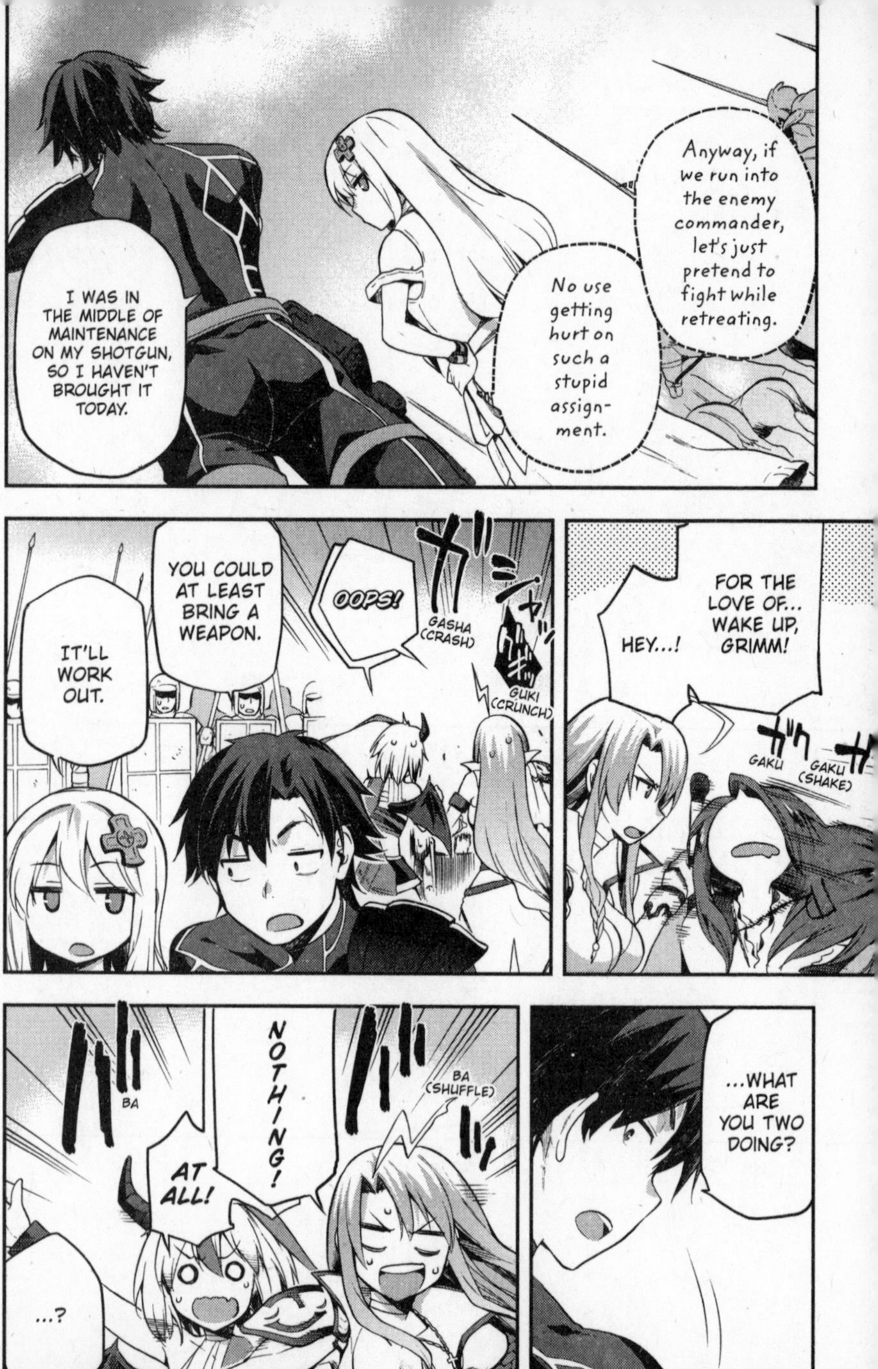
Anyway, if we run into the enemy commander, let's just pretend to fight while retreating.
No use getting hurt on such a stupid assignment.
I WAS IN THE MIDDLE OF MAINTENANCE ON MY SHOTGUN, SO I HAVEN'T BROUGHT IT TODAY.
FOR THE LOVE OF... WAKE UP, GRIMM!
HEY...!
GAKU GAKU (SHAKE)
OOPS!
GASHA (CRASH)
GUKI (CRUNCH)
YOU COULD AT LEAST BRING A WEAPON.
IT'LL WORK OUT.
...WHAT ARE YOU TWO DOING?
BA (SHUFFLE)
NOTHING!
AT ALL!
BA
...?

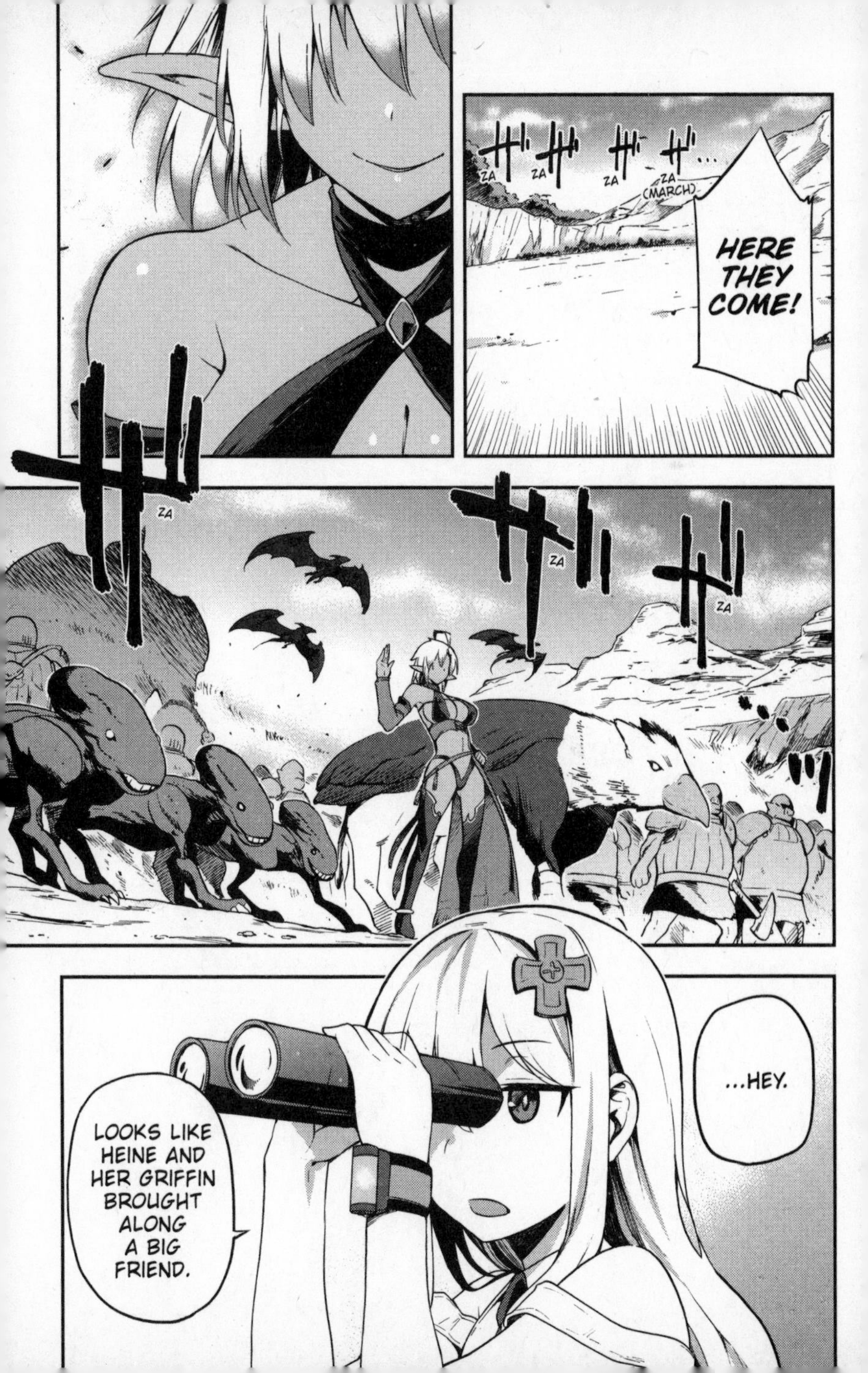
HERE THEY COME!
ZA ZA ZA ZA (MARCH)
ZA
ZA
ZA
...HEY.
LOOKS LIKE HEINE AND HER GRIFFIN BROUGHT ALONG A BIG FRIEND.

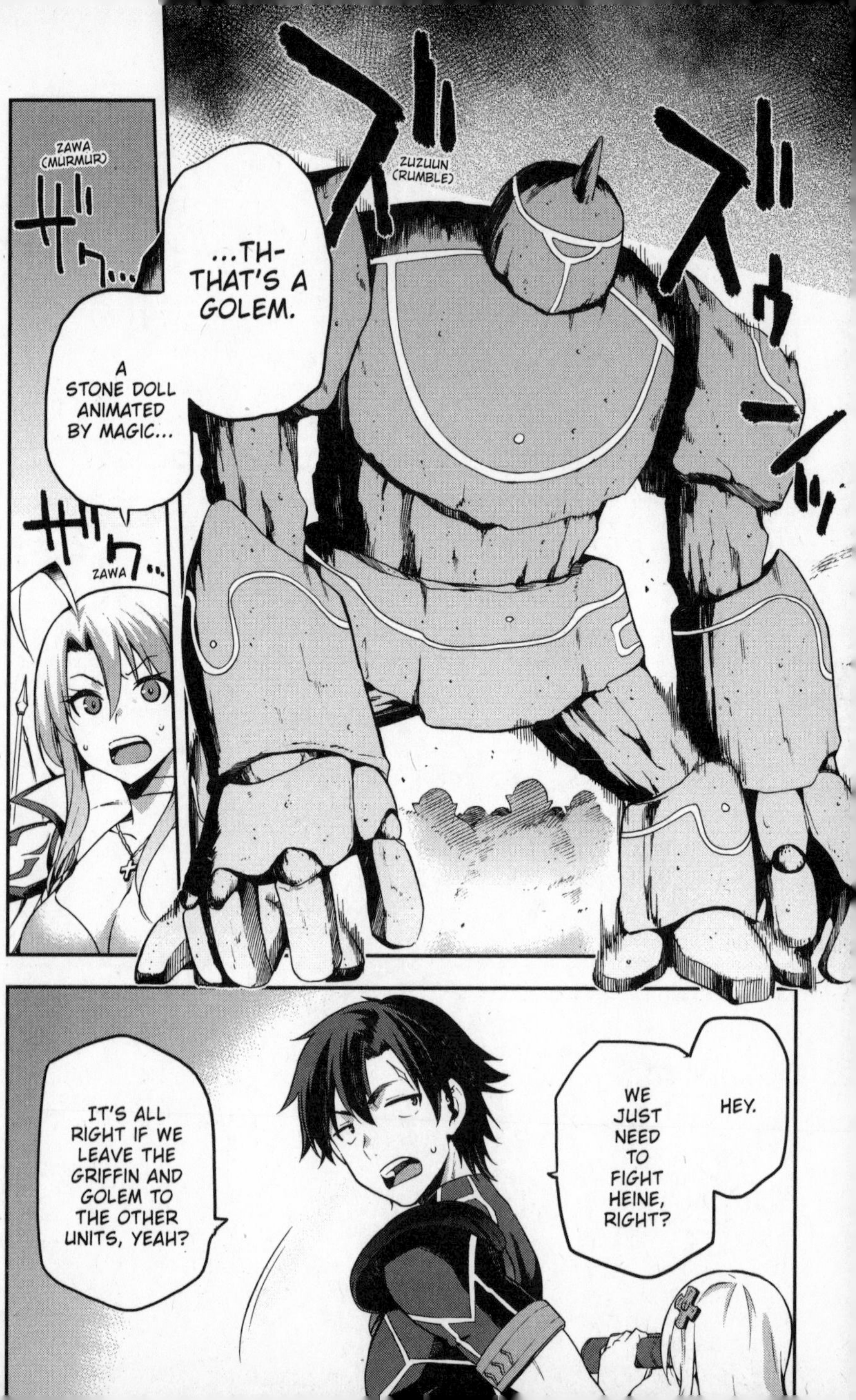
ZUZUUN (RUMBLE)
...TH-THAT'S A GOLEM.
A STONE DOLL ANIMATED BY MAGIC...
ZAWA (MURMUR)
ZAWA
HEY.
WE JUST NEED TO FIGHT HEINE, RIGHT?
IT'S ALL RIGHT IF WE LEAVE THE GRIFFIN AND GOLEM TO THE OTHER UNITS, YEAH?

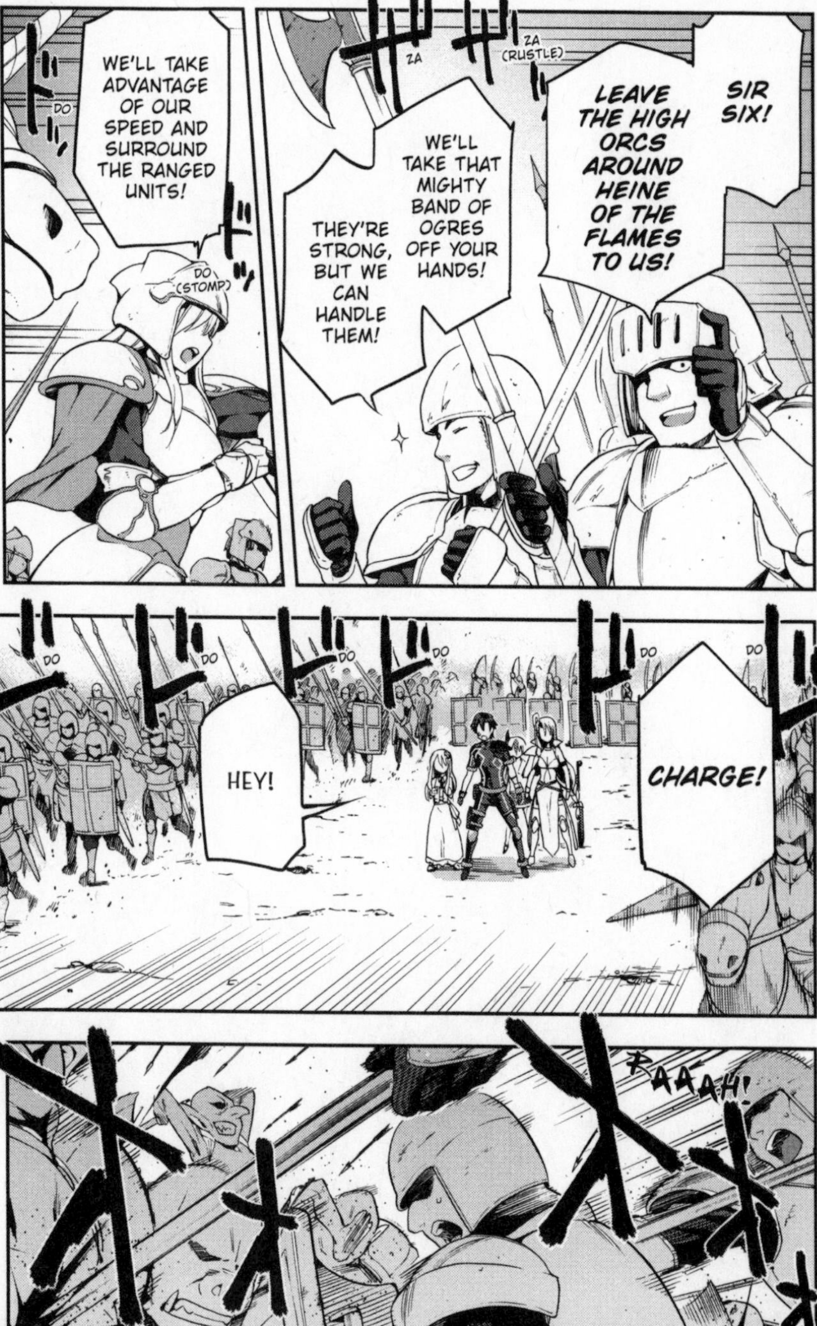
ZA
ZA (RUSTLE)
SIR SIX!
LEAVE THE HIGH ORCS AROUND HEINE OF THE FLAMES TO US!
WE'LL TAKE THAT MIGHTY BAND OF OGRES OFF YOUR HANDS!
THEY'RE STRONG, BUT WE CAN HANDLE THEM!
DO
WE'LL TAKE ADVANTAGE OF OUR SPEED AND SURROUND THE RANGED UNITS!
DO (STOMP)
DO
DO
CHARGE!
DO
DO
HEY!
DO
DO
RAAAH!

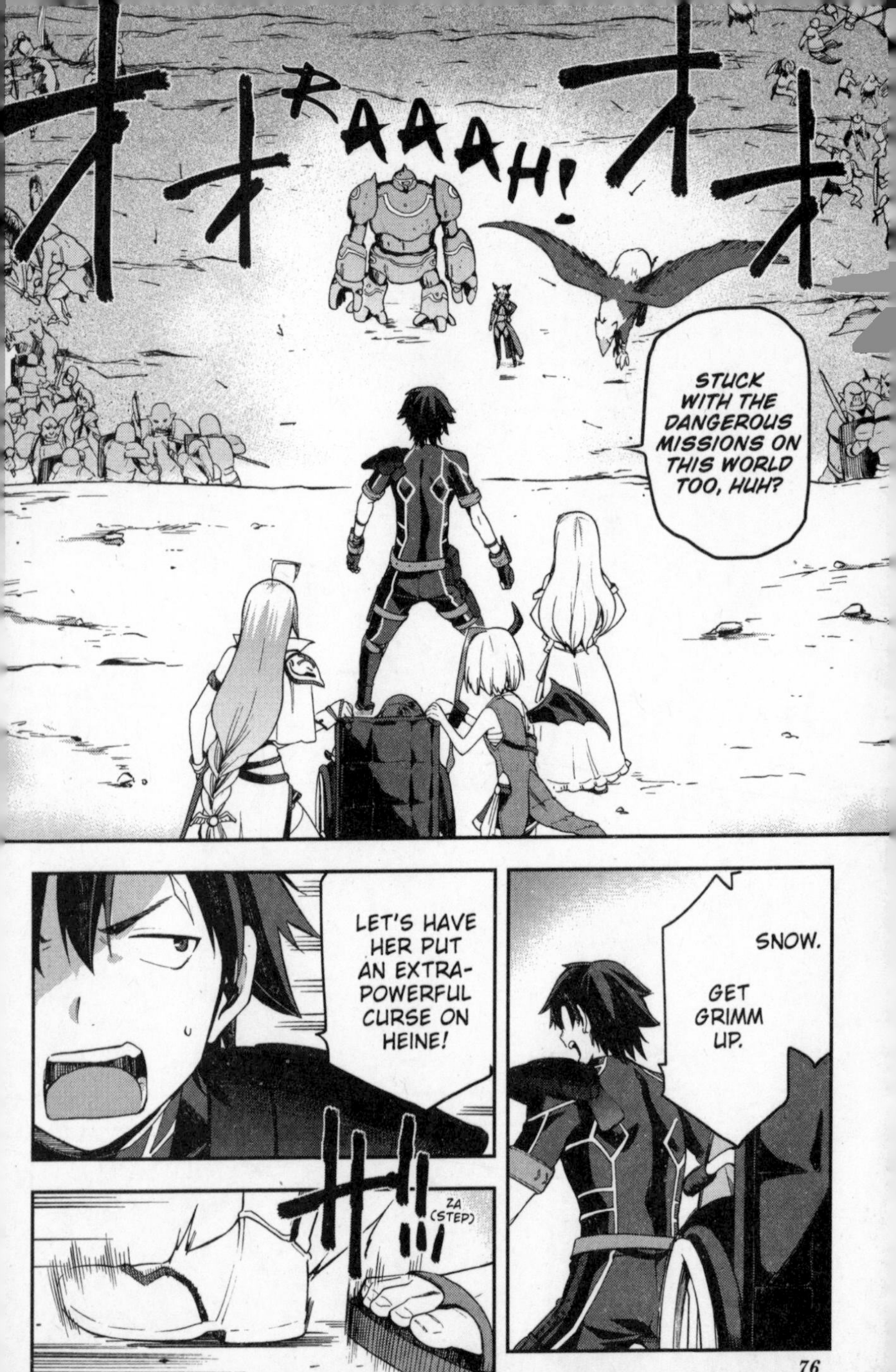
オオ
RAAAAH!
オオ
STUCK WITH THE DANGEROUS MISSIONS ON THIS WORLD TOO, HUH?
SNOW.
GET GRIMM UP.
LET'S HAVE HER PUT AN EXTRA-POWERFUL CURSE ON HEINE!
ZA (STEP)

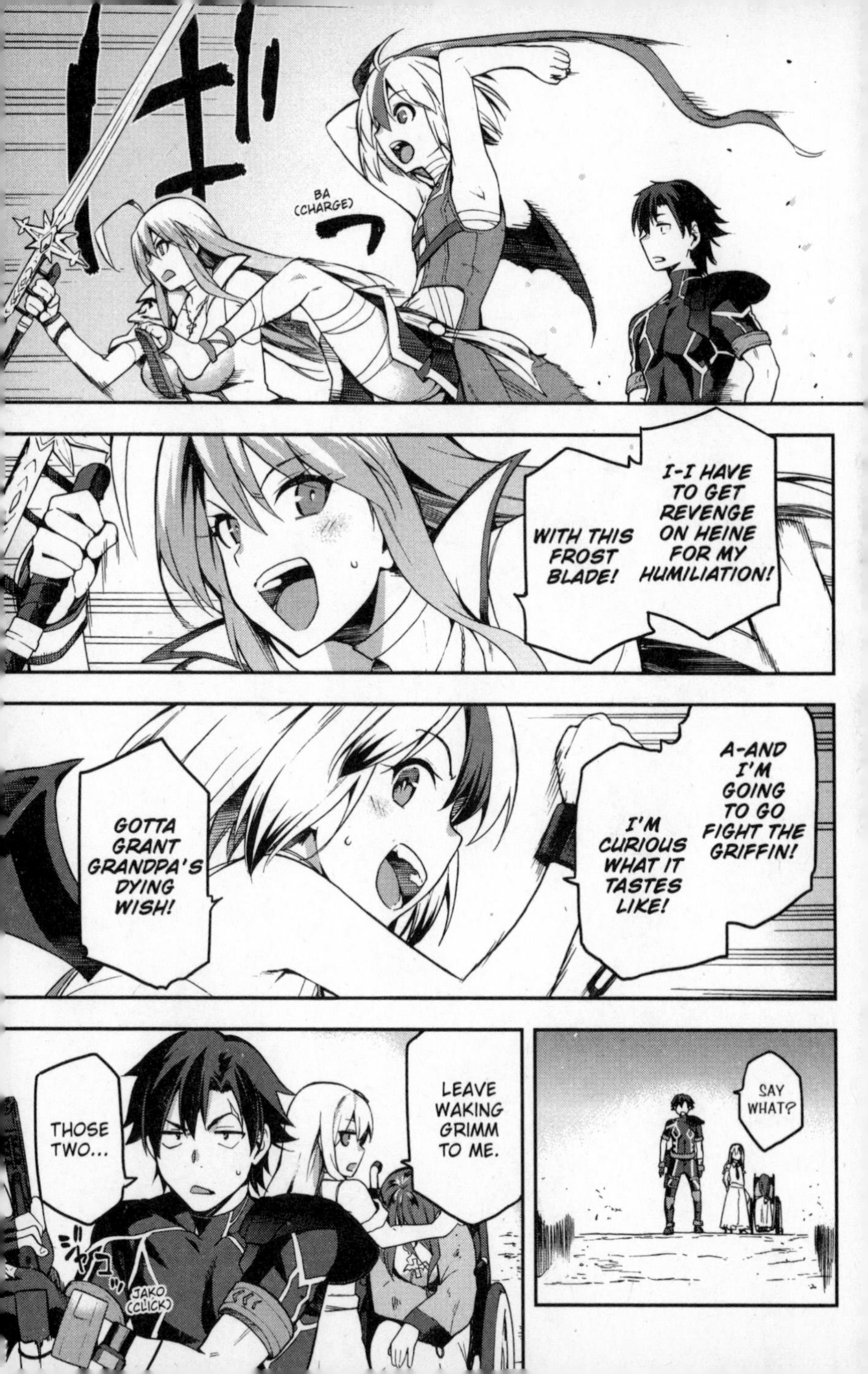
BA (CHARGE)
I-I HAVE TO GET REVENGE ON HEINE FOR MY HUMILIATION!
WITH THIS FROST BLADE!
A-AND I'M GOING TO GO FIGHT THE GRIFFIN!
I'M CURIOUS WHAT IT TASTES LIKE!
GOTTA GRANT GRANDPA'S DYING WISH!
SAY WHAT?
LEAVE WAKING GRIMM TO ME.
THOSE TWO...
JAKO (CLICK)

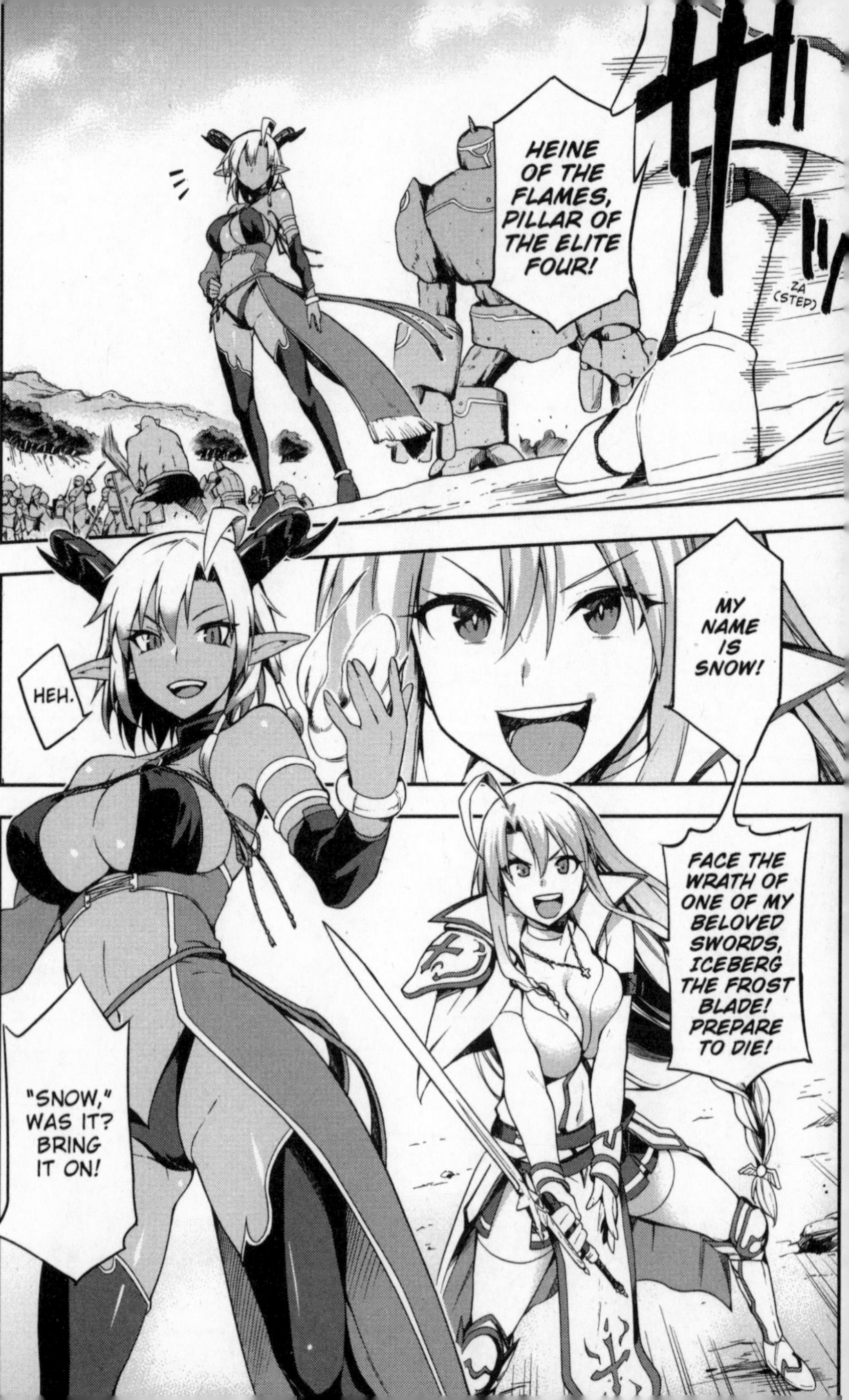
HEINE OF THE FLAMES, PILLAR OF THE ELITE FOUR!
ZA (STEP)
MY NAME IS SNOW!
HEH.
FACE THE WRATH OF ONE OF MY BELOVED SWORDS, ICEBERG THE FROST BLADE! PREPARE TO DIE!
"SNOW," WAS IT? BRING IT ON!

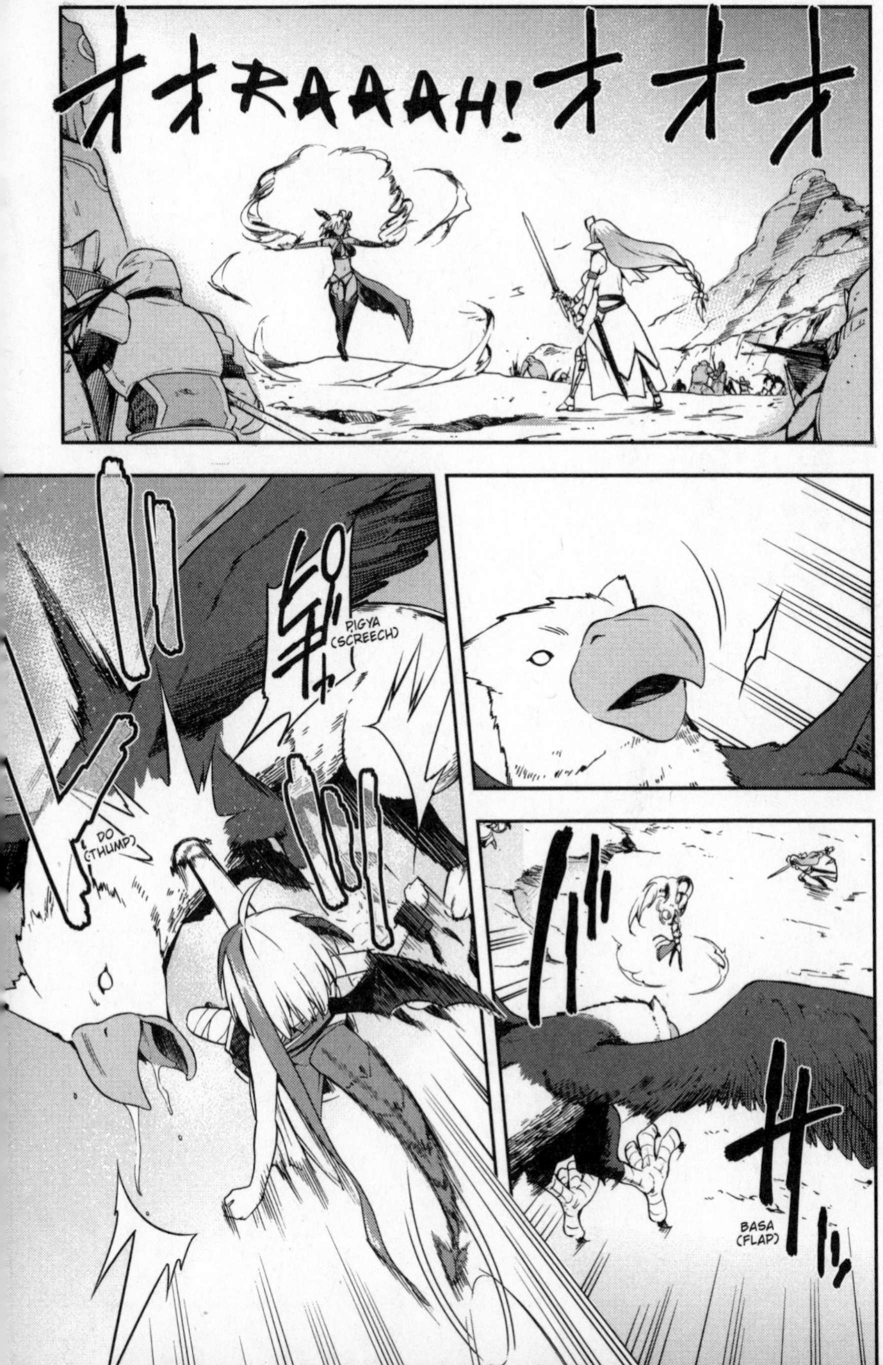

オオRAAAAH!オオオ
BASA (FLAP)
PIGYA (SCREECH)
DO (THUMP)

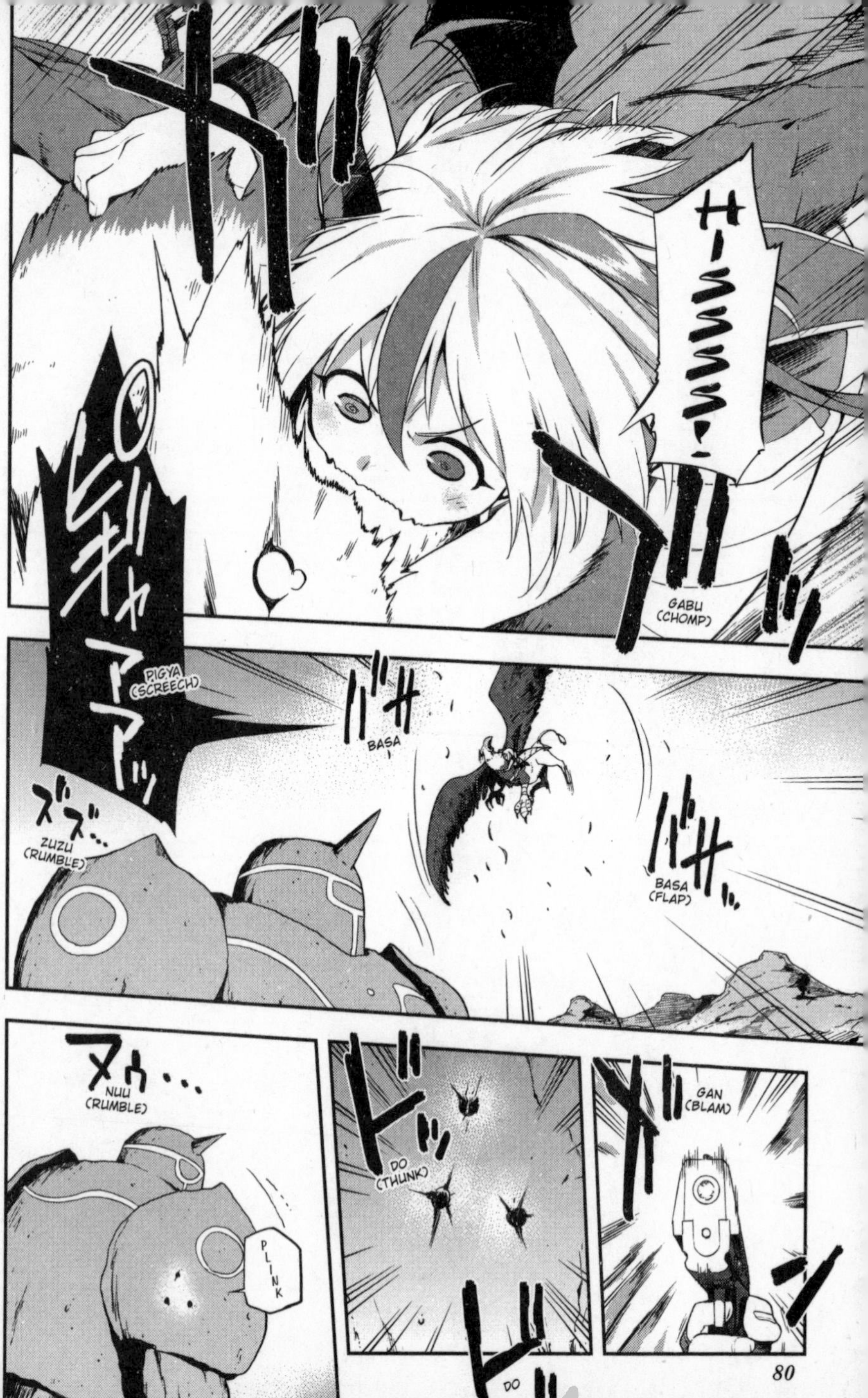
GABU (CHOMP)
BASA (FLAP)
BASA
PIGYA (SCREECH)
ZUZU (RUMBLE)
GAN (BLAM)
DO (THUNK)
DO
NUU (RUMBLE)
PLINK

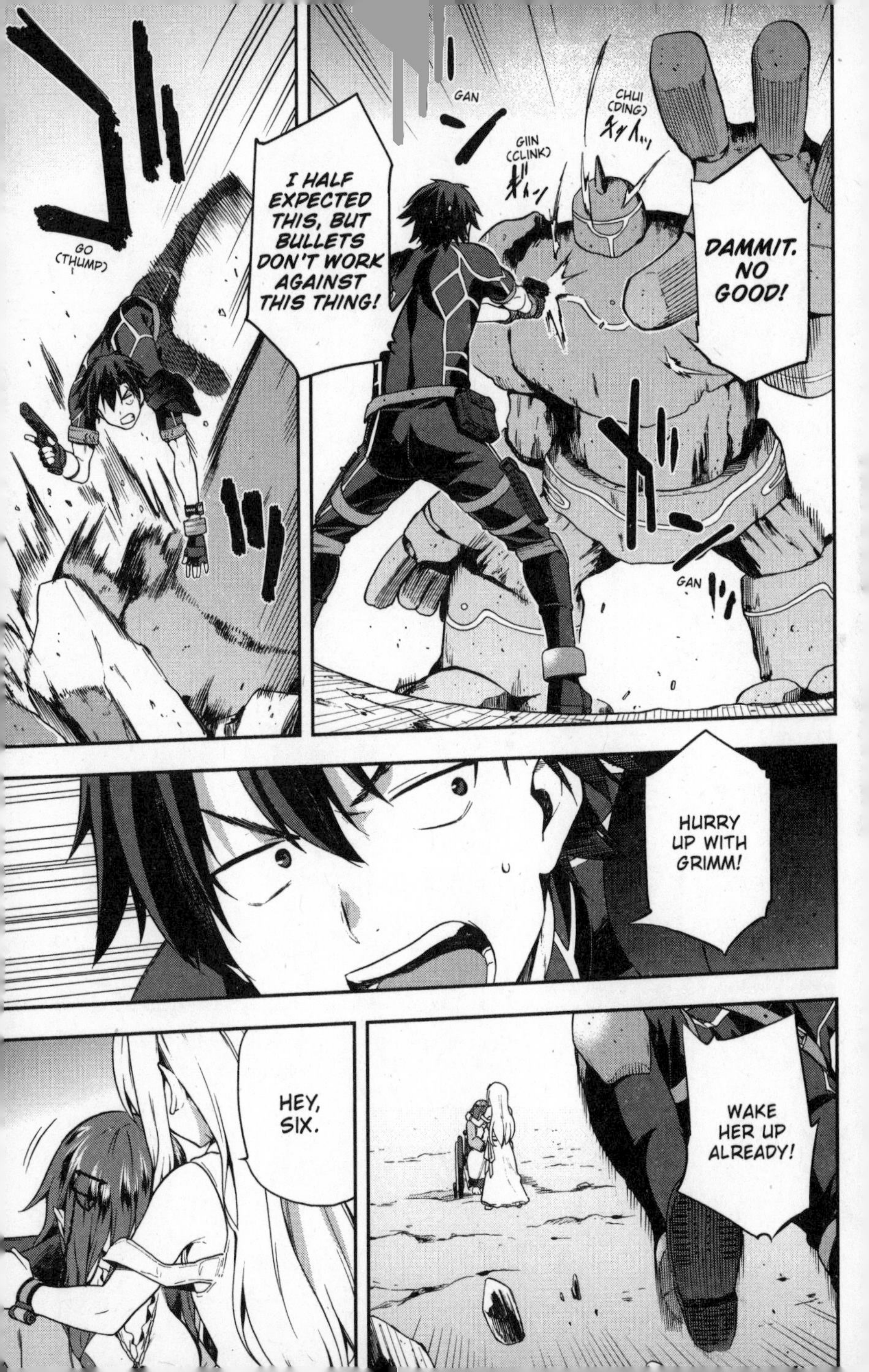
CHUI (DING)
DAMMIT. NO GOOD!
GAN
GIIN (CLINK)
I HALF EXPECTED THIS, BUT BULLETS DON'T WORK AGAINST THIS THING!
GAN
GO (THUMP)
HURRY UP WITH GRIMM!
WAKE HER UP ALREADY!
HEY, SIX.

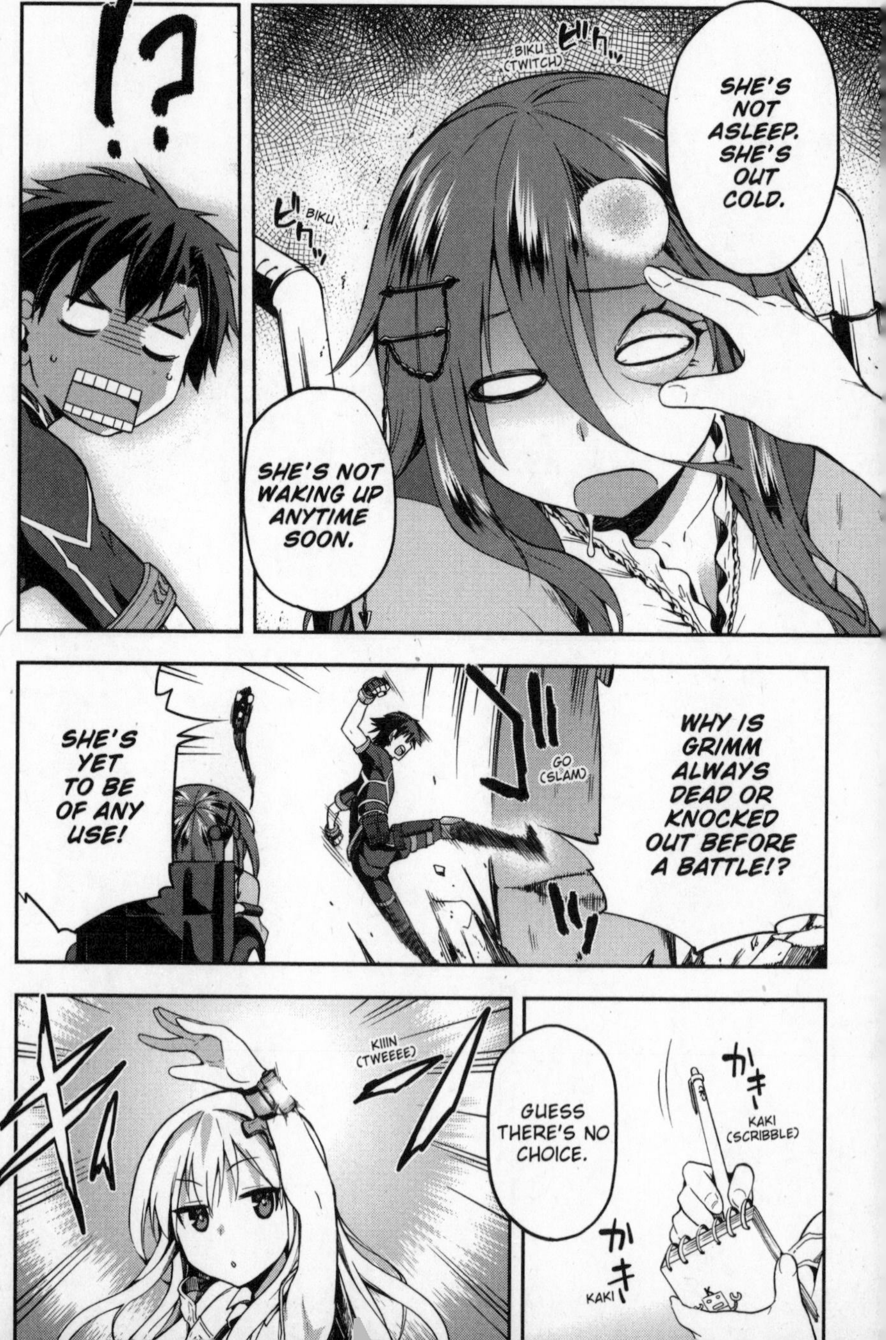
SHE'S NOT ASLEEP. SHE'S OUT COLD.
BIKU (TWITCH)
BIKU
SHE'S NOT WAKING UP ANYTIME SOON.
!?
WHY IS GRIMM ALWAYS DEAD OR KNOCKED OUT BEFORE A BATTLE!?
GO (SLAM)
SHE'S YET TO BE OF ANY USE!
KAKI (SCRIBBLE)
GUESS THERE'S NO CHOICE.
KAKI
KIIIN (TWEEEE)

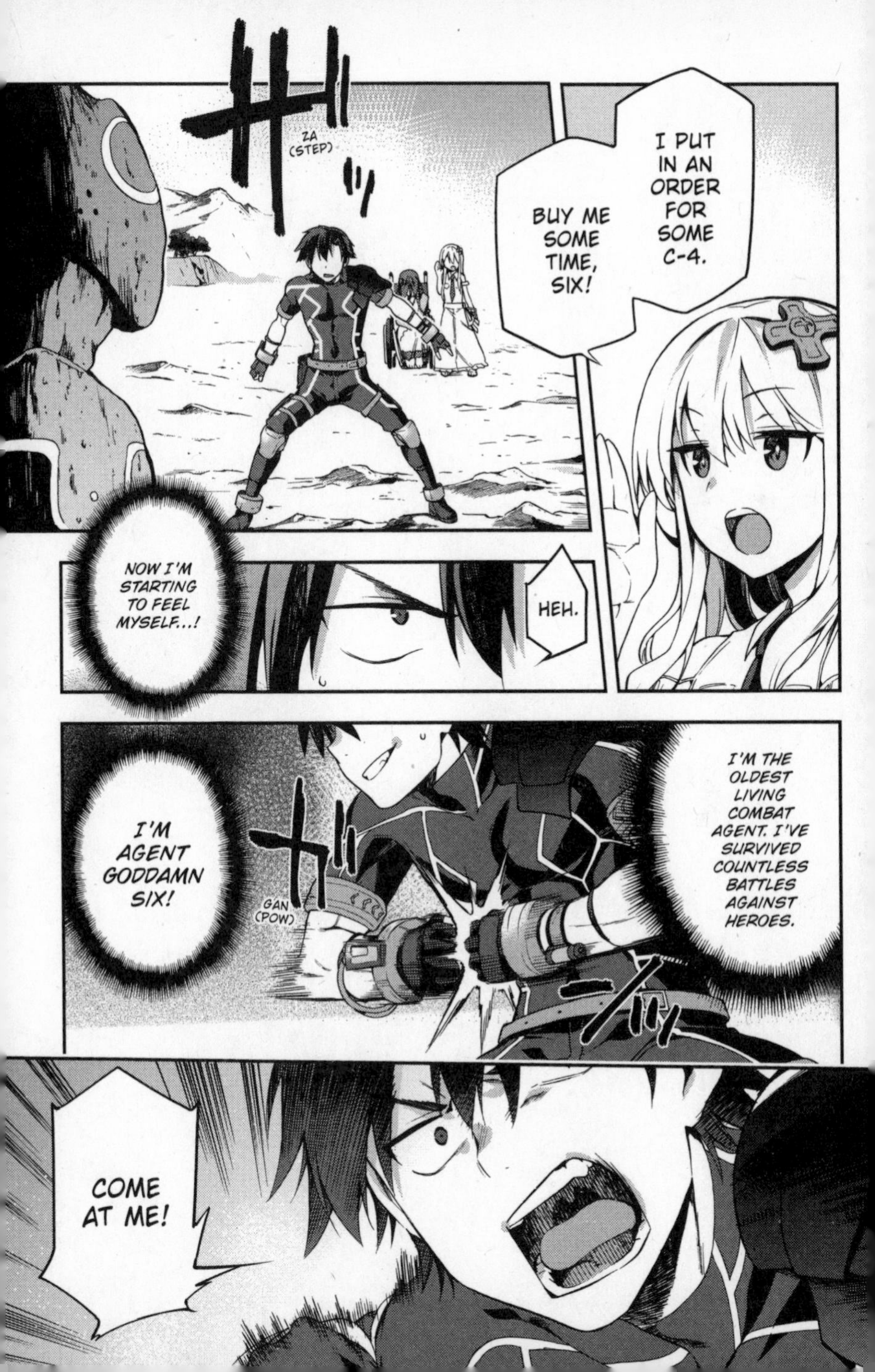
I PUT IN AN ORDER FOR SOME C-4.
BUY ME SOME TIME, SIX!
ZA (STEP)
HEH.
NOW I'M STARTING TO FEEL MYSELF...!
I'M THE OLDEST LIVING COMBAT AGENT. I'VE SURVIVED COUNTLESS BATTLES AGAINST HEROES.
I'M AGENT GODDAMN SIX!
GAN (POW)
COME AT ME!

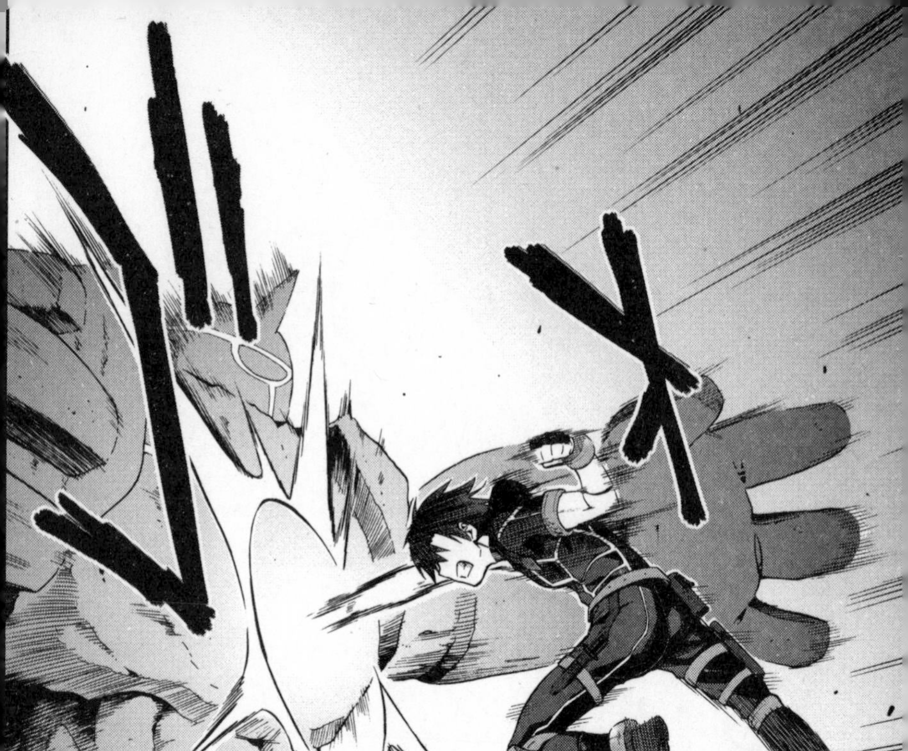
GOON
(POOOW)
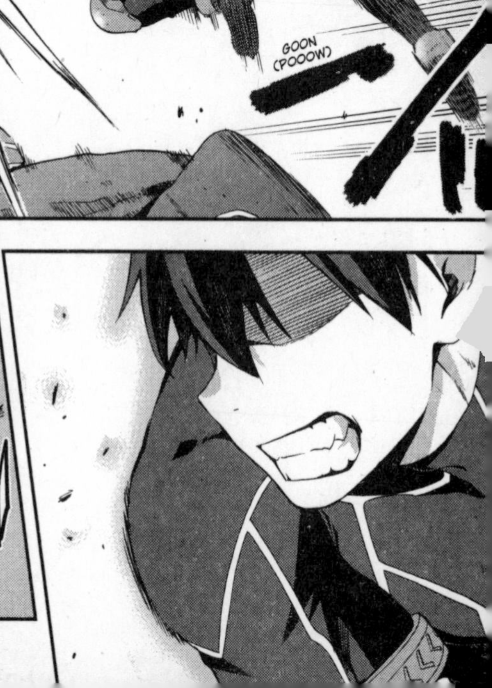
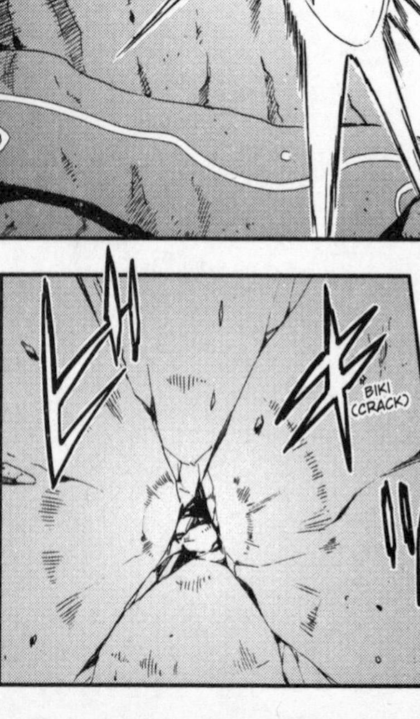
BIKI
(CRACK)

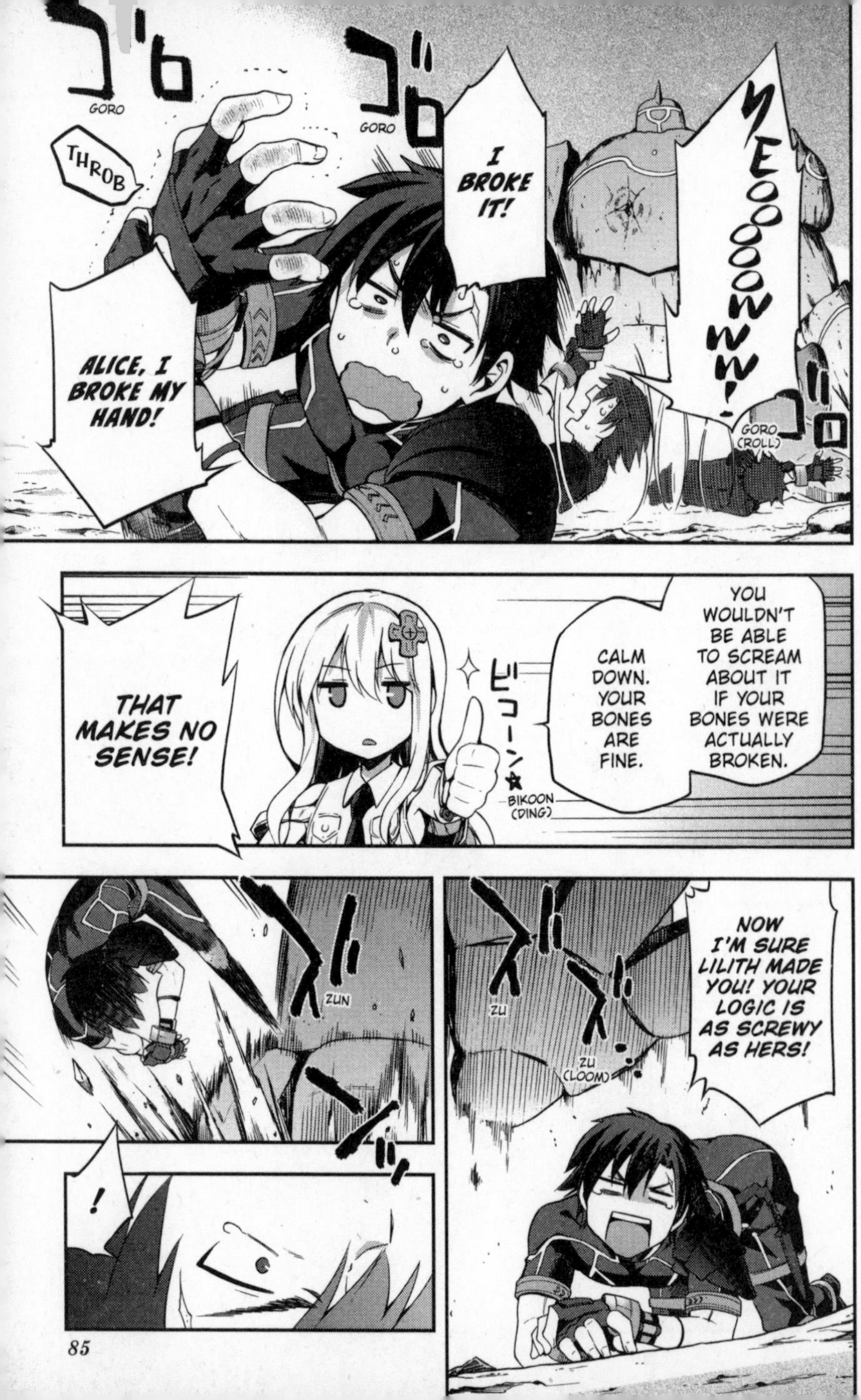
MEOOOOOWWW!
I BROKE IT!
GORO
GORO
THROB
ALICE, I BROKE MY HAND!
GORO (ROLL)
YOU WOULDN'T BE ABLE TO SCREAM ABOUT IT IF YOUR BONES WERE ACTUALLY BROKEN.
CALM DOWN. YOUR BONES ARE FINE.
BIKOON (DING)
THAT MAKES NO SENSE!
NOW I'M SURE LILITH MADE YOU! YOUR LOGIC IS AS SCREWY AS HERS!
ZU
ZU (LOOM)
ZUN
!

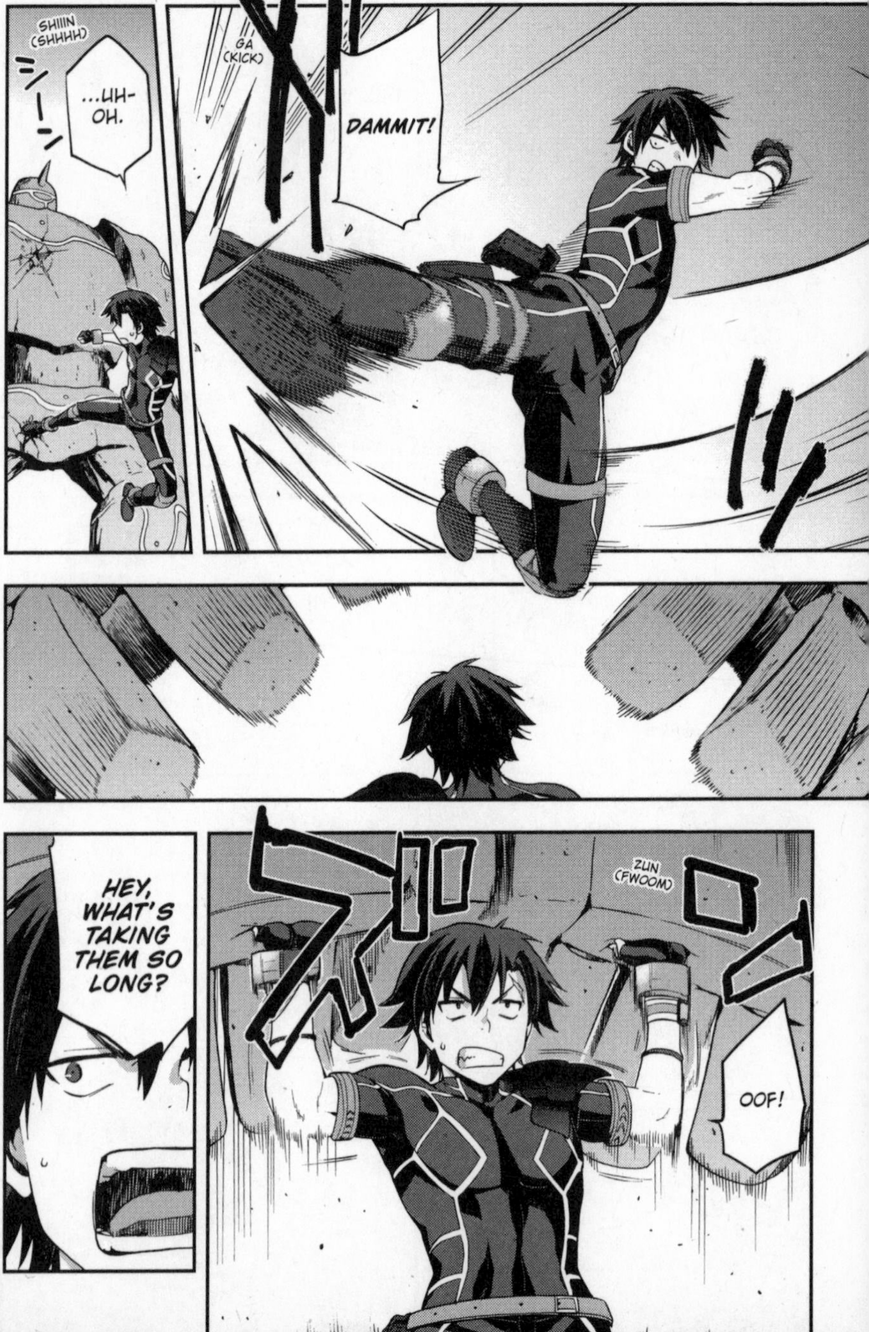
GA (KICK)
DAMMIT!
SHIIIN (SHHHH)
...UH-OH.
ZUN (FWOOM)
OOF!
HEY, WHAT'S TAKING THEM SO LONG?

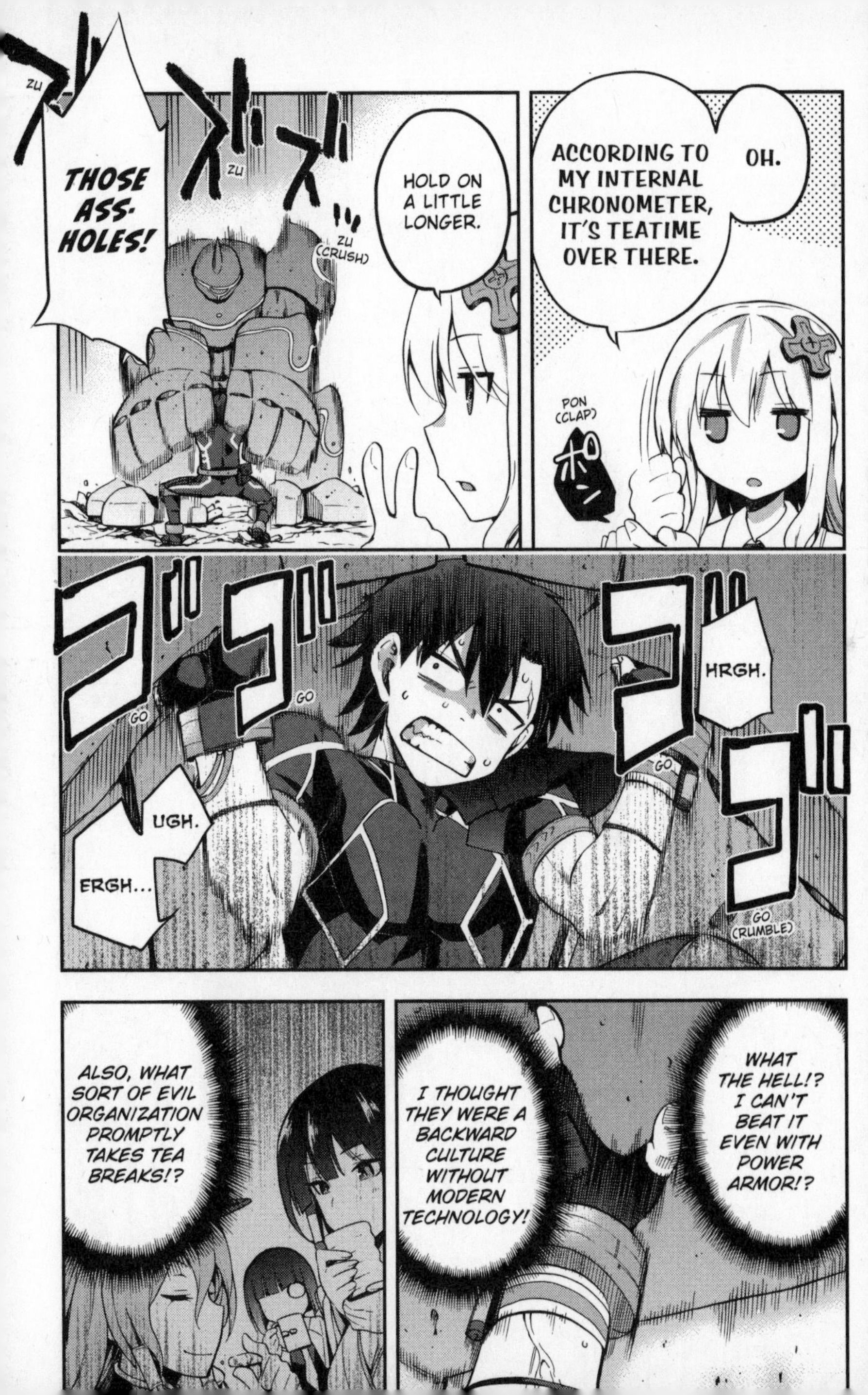
OH.
ACCORDING TO MY INTERNAL CHRONOMETER, IT'S TEATIME OVER THERE.
PON (CLAP)
HOLD ON A LITTLE LONGER.
ZU
ZU
ZU (CRUSH)
THOSE ASS-HOLES!
HRGH.
GO
GO (RUMBLE)
GO
GO
UGH.
ERGH...
WHAT THE HELL!? I CAN'T BEAT IT EVEN WITH POWER ARMOR!?
I THOUGHT THEY WERE A BACKWARD CULTURE WITHOUT MODERN TECHNOLOGY!
ALSO, WHAT SORT OF EVIL ORGANIZATION PROMPTLY TAKES TEA BREAKS!?

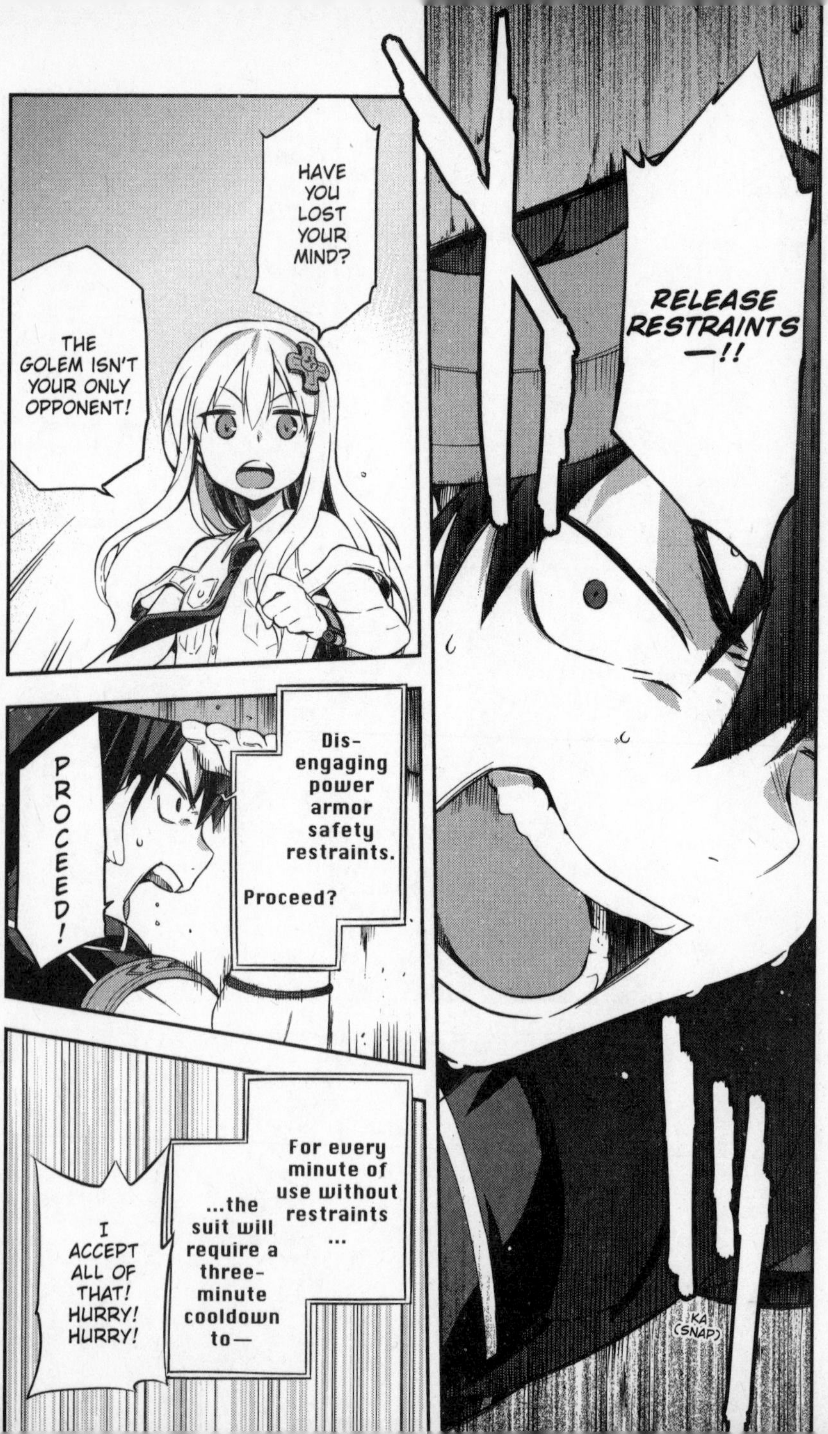
RELEASE RESTRAINTS—!!
KA (SNAP)
HAVE YOU LOST YOUR MIND?
THE GOLEM ISN'T YOUR ONLY OPPONENT!
Dis-engaging power armor safety restraints.
Proceed?
PROCEED!
For every minute of use without restraints...
...the suit will require a three-minute cooldown to—
I ACCEPT ALL OF THAT! HURRY! HURRY!

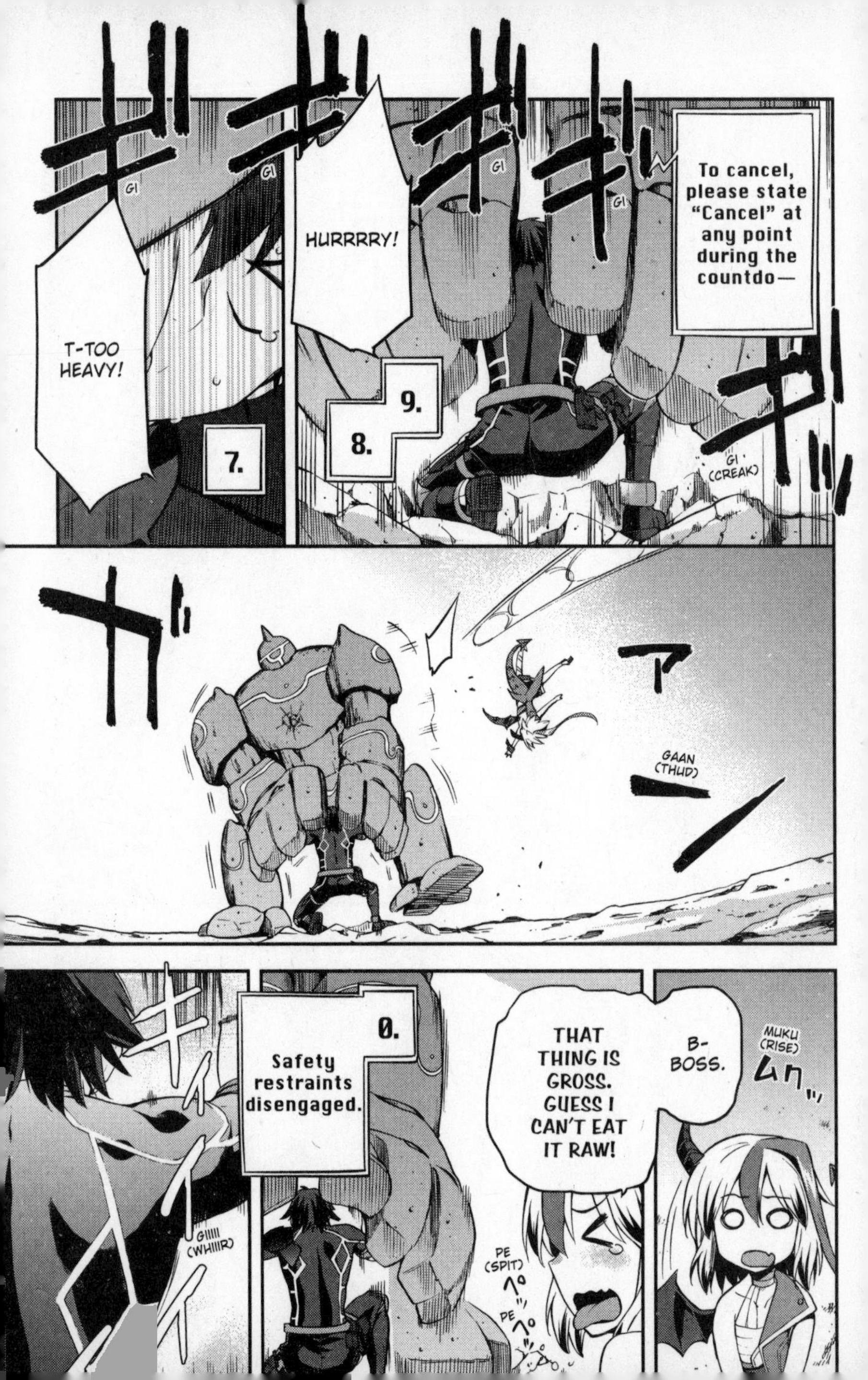
To cancel, please state "Cancel" at any point during the countdo—
GI
GI
GI (CREAK)
HURRRRY!
9.
8.
GI
GI
T-TOO HEAVY!
7.
GAAN (THUD)
MUKU (RISE)
B-BOSS.
THAT THING IS GROSS. GUESS I CAN'T EAT IT RAW!
PE (SPIT)
PE
0.
Safety restraints disengaged.
GIIII (WHIIIR)

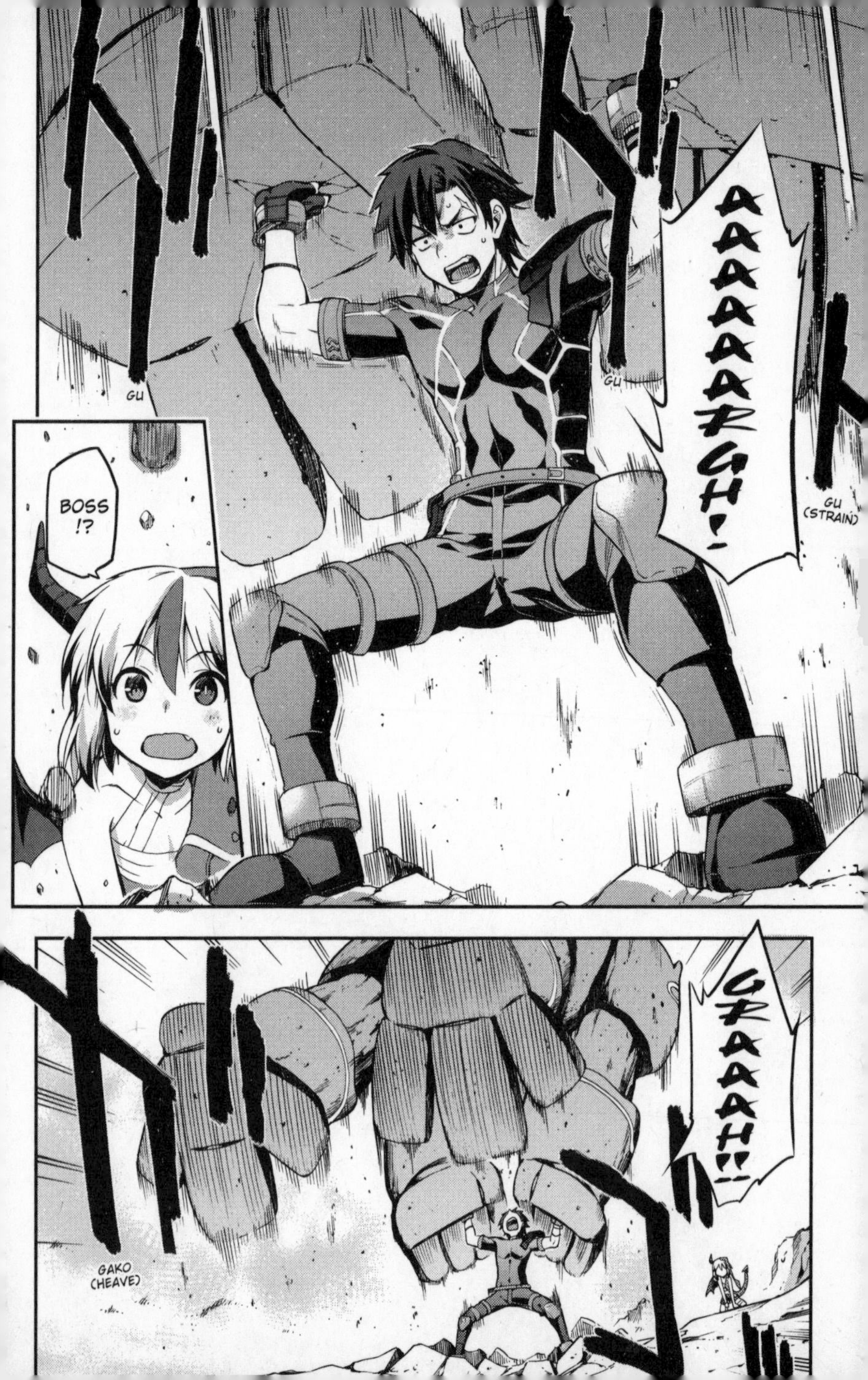
AAAAAAARGH!
GU
GU
GU (STRAIN)
BOSS!?
GRAAAAAH!!
GAKO (HEAVE)

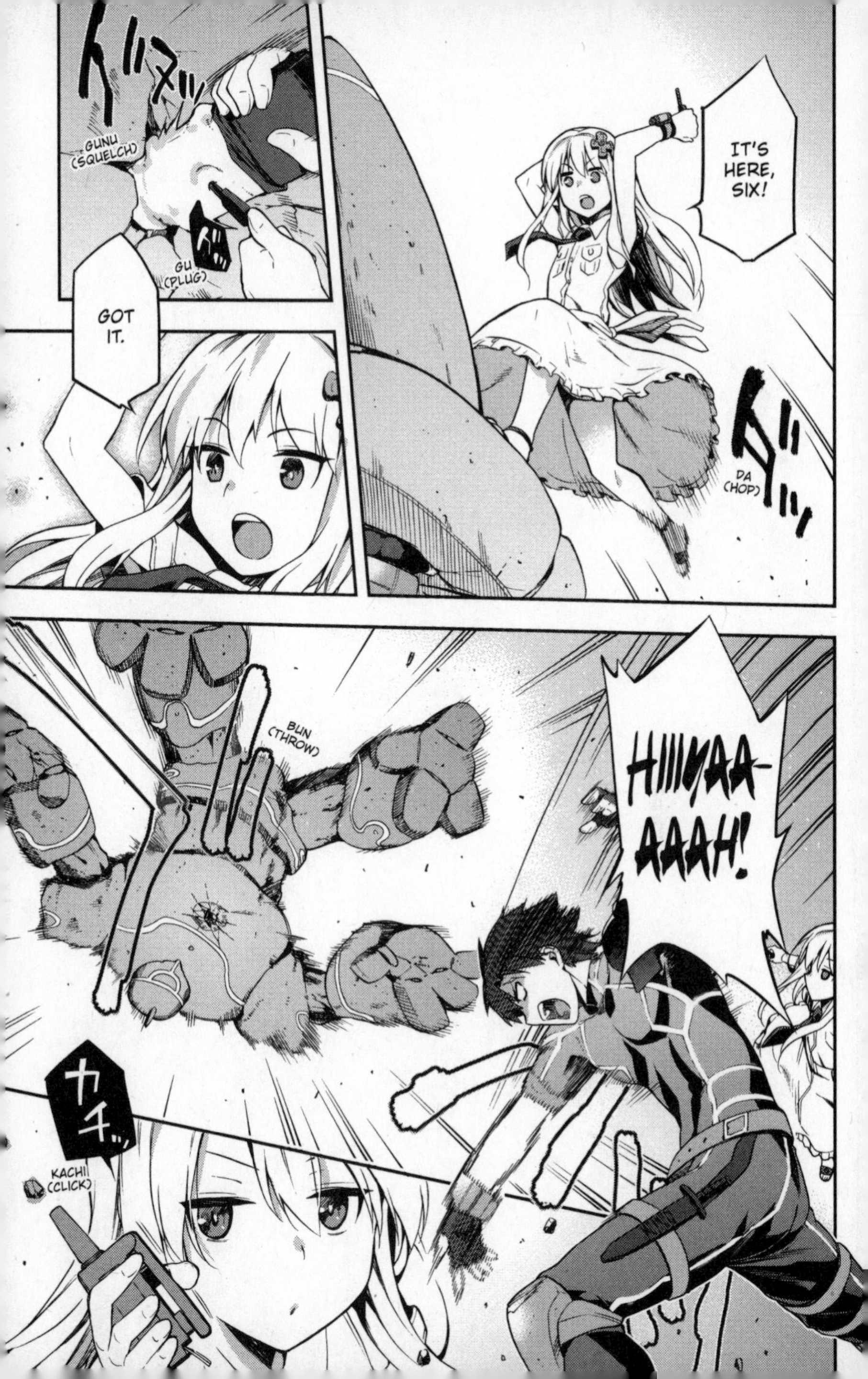
IT'S HERE, SIX!
DA (HOP)
GUNU (SQUELCH)
GU (PLUG)
GOT IT.
HIIIYAA-AAAH!
BUN (THROW)
カチッ
KACHI (CLICK)

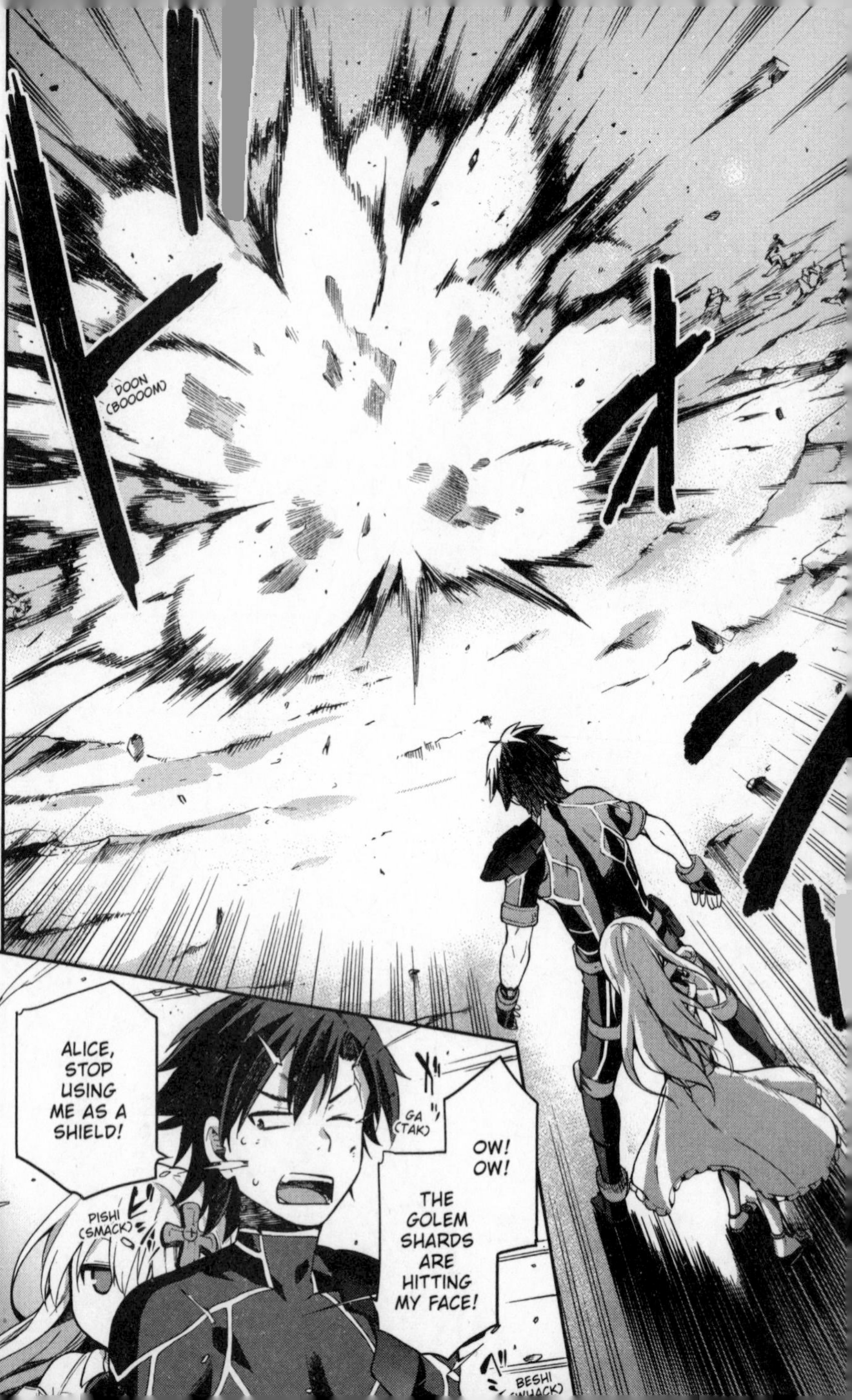
DOON (BOOOOM)
OW! OW!
THE GOLEM SHARDS ARE HITTING MY FACE!
GA (TAK)
ALICE, STOP USING ME AS A SHIELD!
PISHI (SMACK)
BESHI (WHACK)

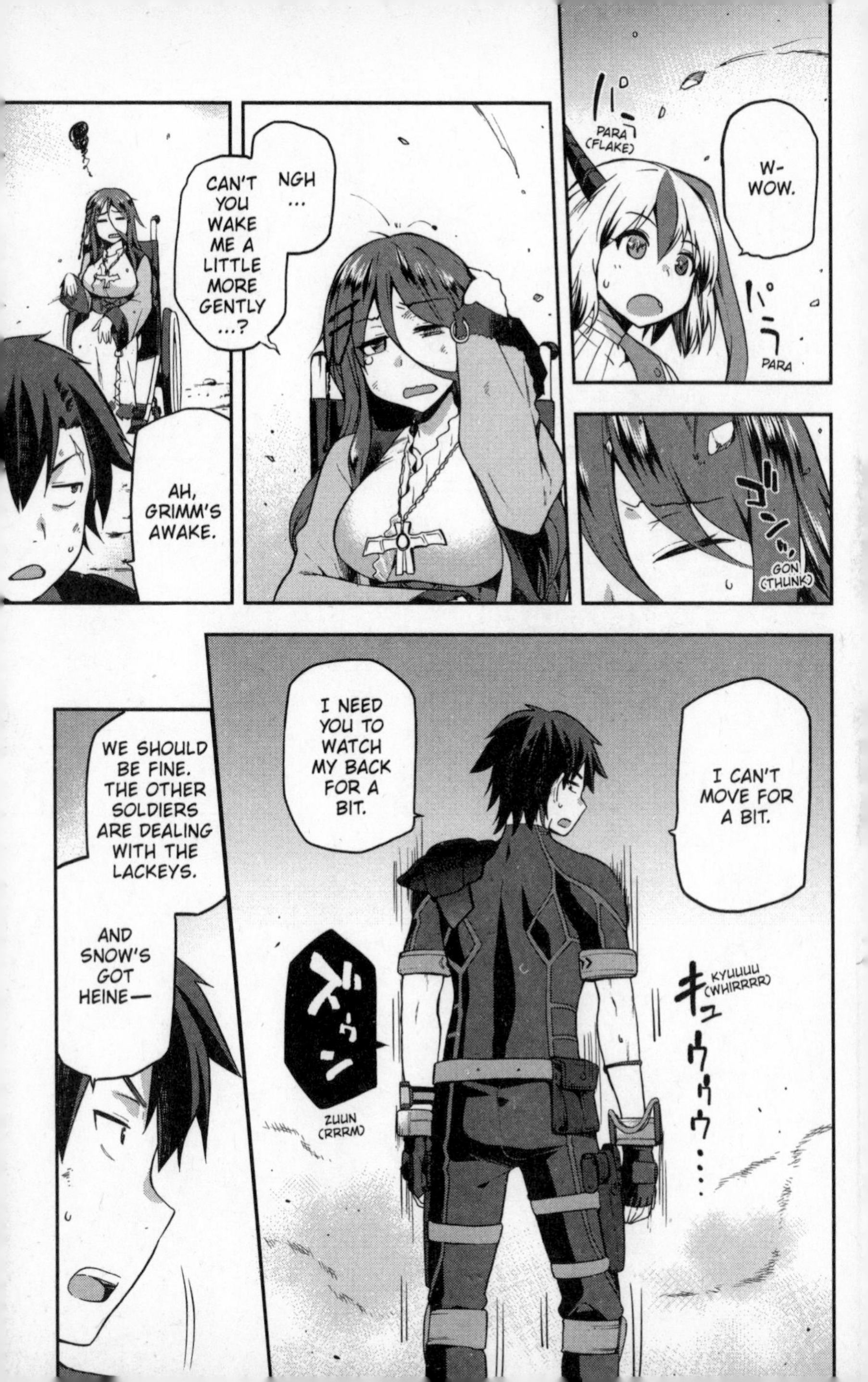

PARA (FLAKE)
W- WOW.
PARA
GON (THUNK)
NGH ...
CAN'T YOU WAKE ME A LITTLE MORE GENTLY ...?
AH, GRIMM'S AWAKE.
I CAN'T MOVE FOR A BIT.
I NEED YOU TO WATCH MY BACK FOR A BIT.
KYUUUUU (WHIRRRR)
ZUUN (RRRM)
WE SHOULD BE FINE. THE OTHER SOLDIERS ARE DEALING WITH THE LACKEYS.
AND SNOW'S GOT HEINE—

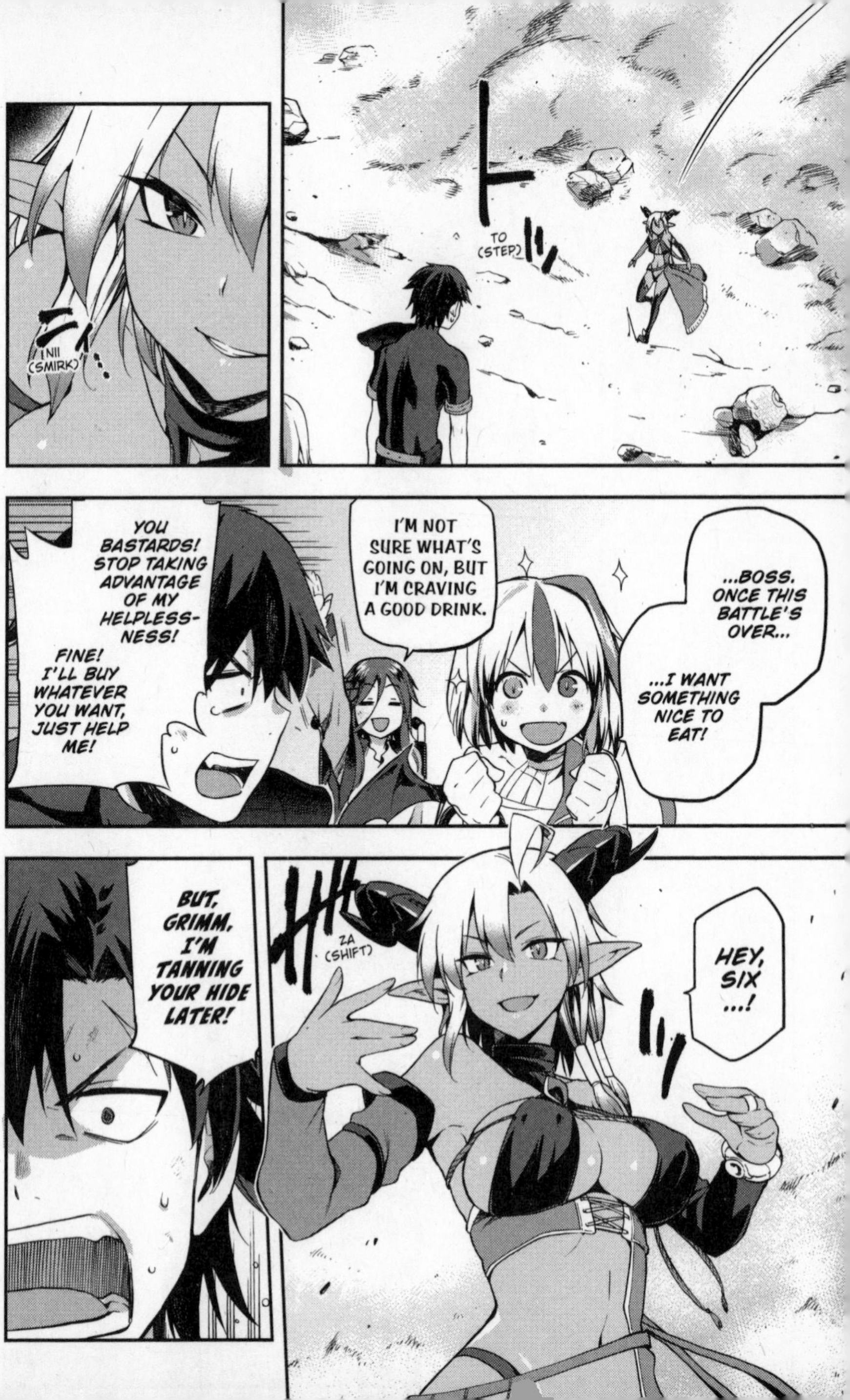
TO
(STEP)
NII
(SMIRK)
...BOSS. ONCE THIS BATTLE'S OVER...
...I WANT SOMETHING NICE TO EAT!
I'M NOT SURE WHAT'S GOING ON, BUT I'M CRAVING A GOOD DRINK.
YOU BASTARDS! STOP TAKING ADVANTAGE OF MY HELPLESS-NESS!
FINE! I'LL BUY WHATEVER YOU WANT, JUST HELP ME!
HEY, SIX ...!
ZA
(SHIFT)
BUT, GRIMM, I'M TANNING YOUR HIDE LATER!

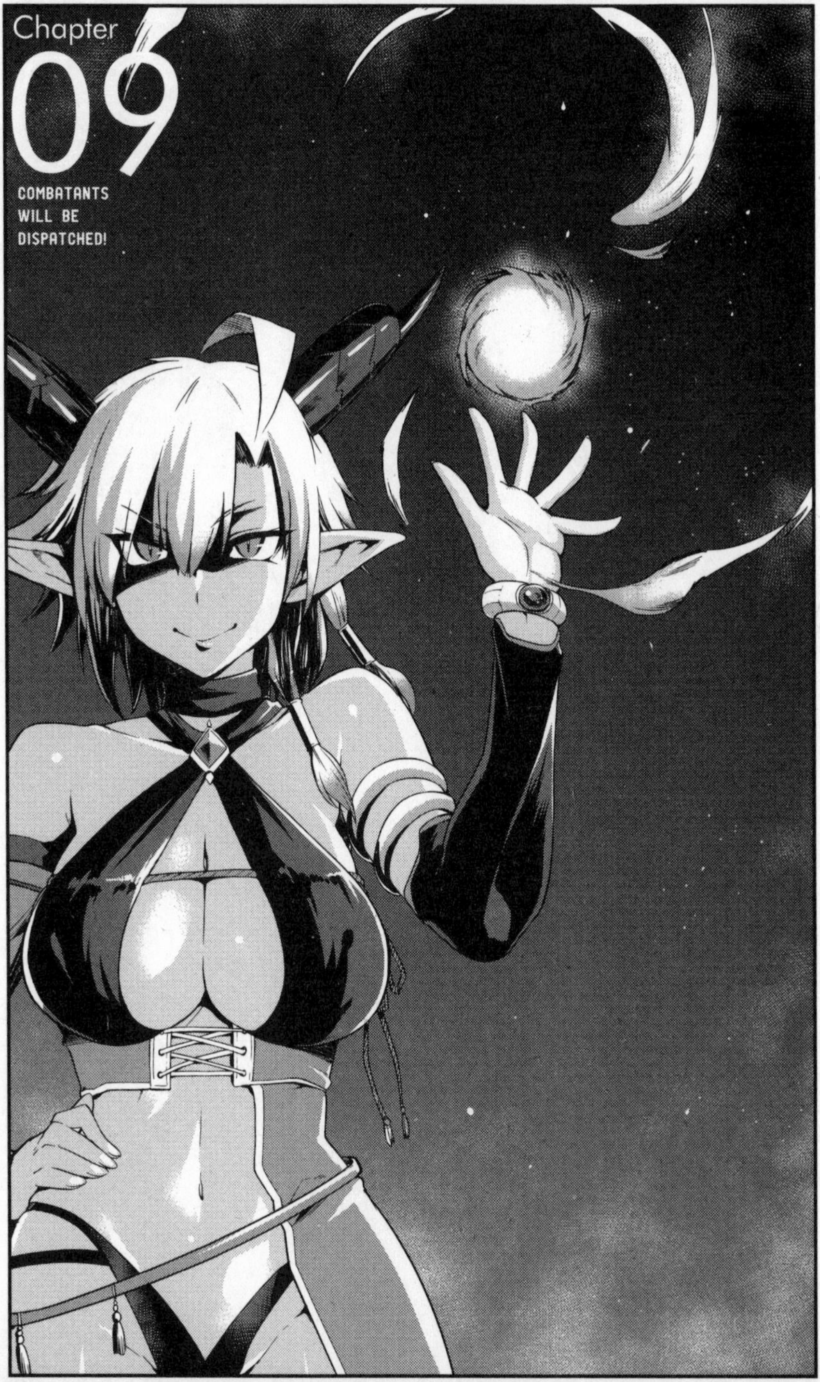
Chapter
09
COMBATANTS
WILL BE
DISPATCHED!

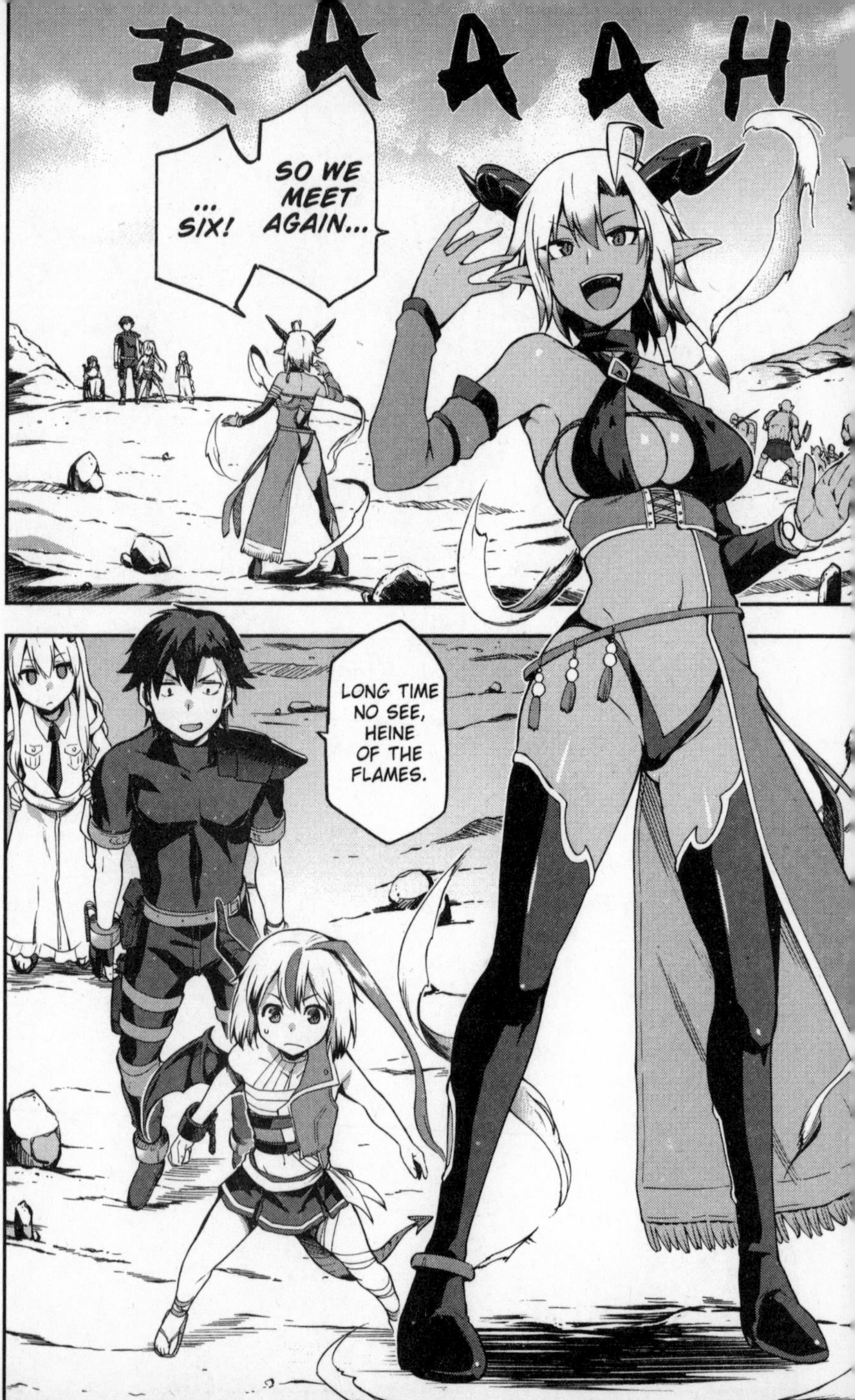
RAAAH
SO WE MEET AGAIN... ...SIX!
LONG TIME NO SEE, HEINE OF THE FLAMES.

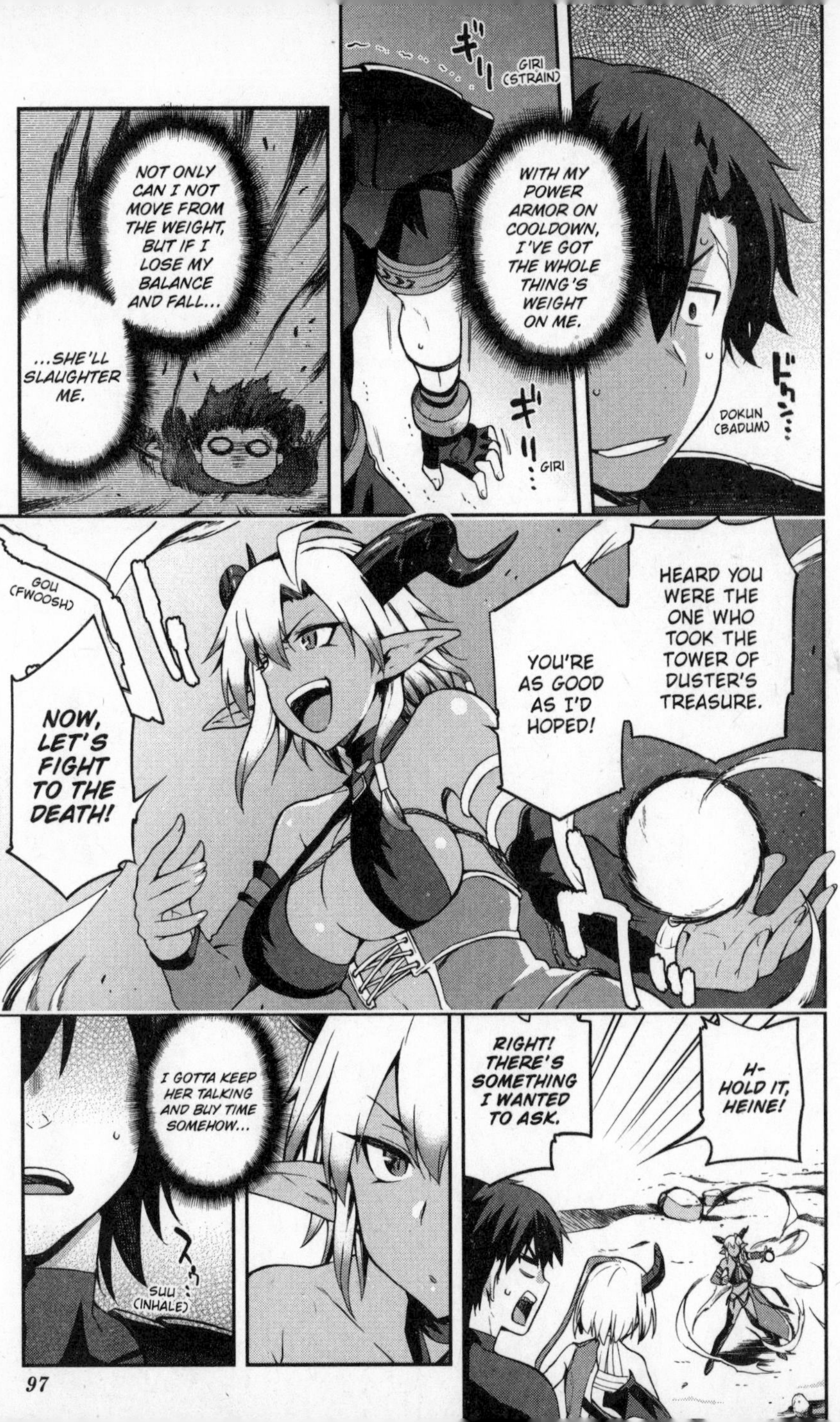

ギリ
GIRI (STRAIN)
WITH MY POWER ARMOR ON COOLDOWN, I'VE GOT THE WHOLE THING'S WEIGHT ON ME.
ドクン…
DOKUN (BADUM)
ギリ…
GIRI
NOT ONLY CAN I NOT MOVE FROM THE WEIGHT, BUT IF I LOSE MY BALANCE AND FALL…
…SHE'LL SLAUGHTER ME.
HEARD YOU WERE THE ONE WHO TOOK THE TOWER OF DUSTER'S TREASURE.
YOU'RE AS GOOD AS I'D HOPED!
GOU (FWOOSH)
NOW, LET'S FIGHT TO THE DEATH!
H-HOLD IT, HEINE!
RIGHT! THERE'S SOMETHING I WANTED TO ASK.
I GOTTA KEEP HER TALKING AND BUY TIME SOMEHOW…
SUU (INHALE)

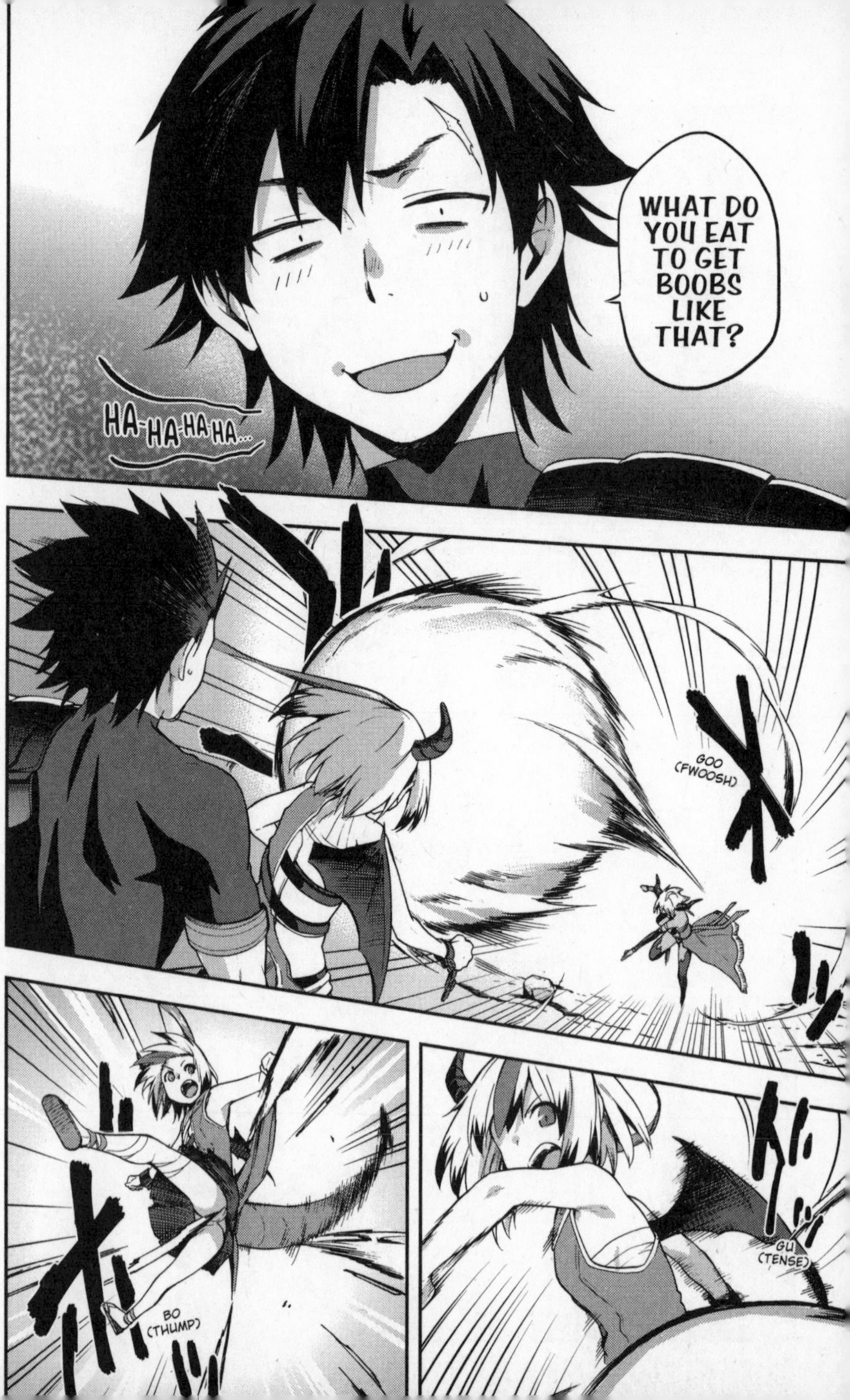
WHAT DO YOU EAT TO GET BOOBS LIKE THAT?
HA-HA-HA-HA...
GOO (FWOOSH)
GU (TENSE)
BO (THUMP)

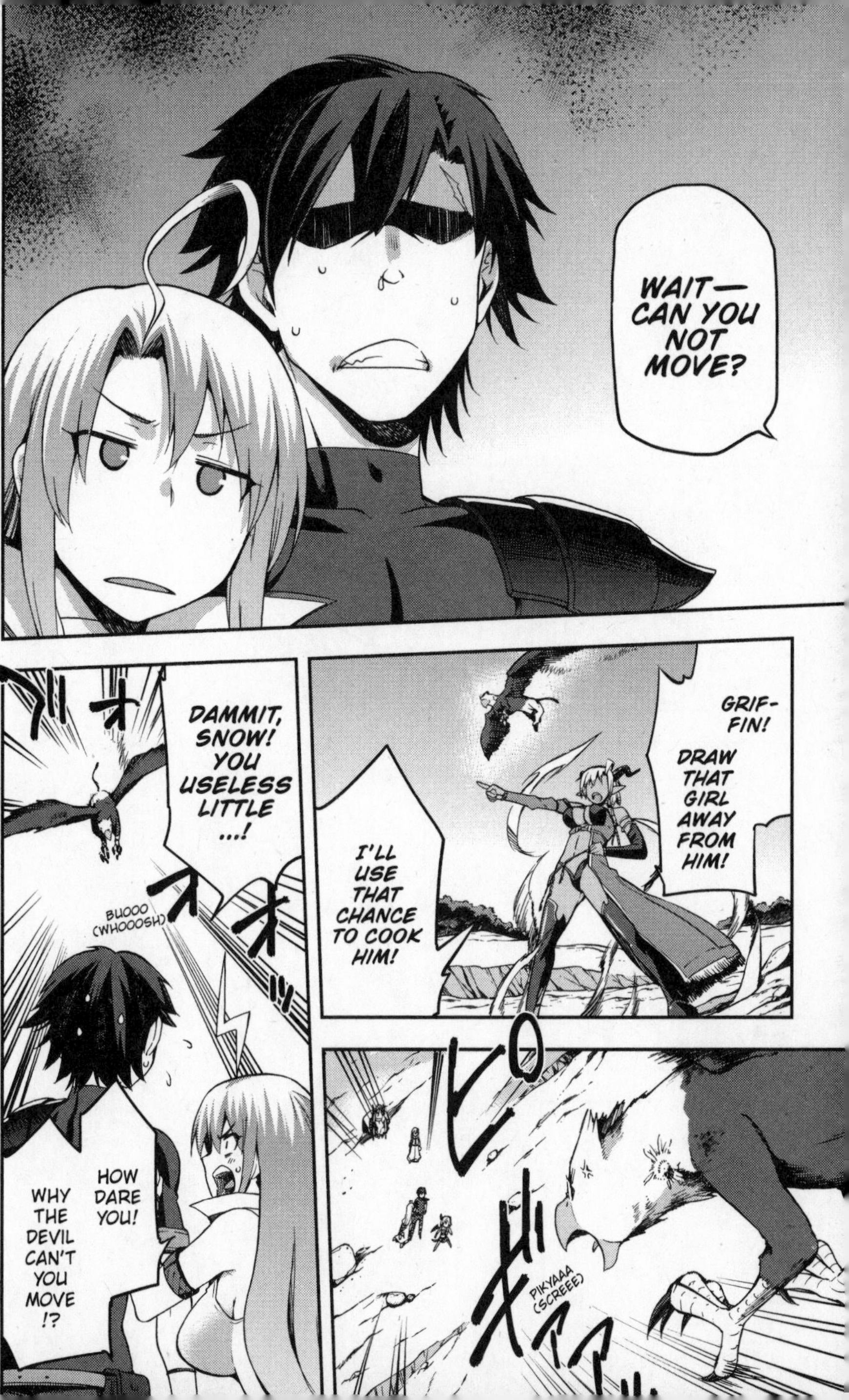
WAIT— CAN YOU NOT MOVE?
GRIF-FIN!
DRAW THAT GIRL AWAY FROM HIM!
I'LL USE THAT CHANCE TO COOK HIM!
PIKYAAA (SCREEE)
DAMMIT, SNOW! YOU USELESS LITTLE ...!
BUOOO (WHOOOSH)
HOW DARE YOU!
WHY THE DEVIL CAN'T YOU MOVE !?

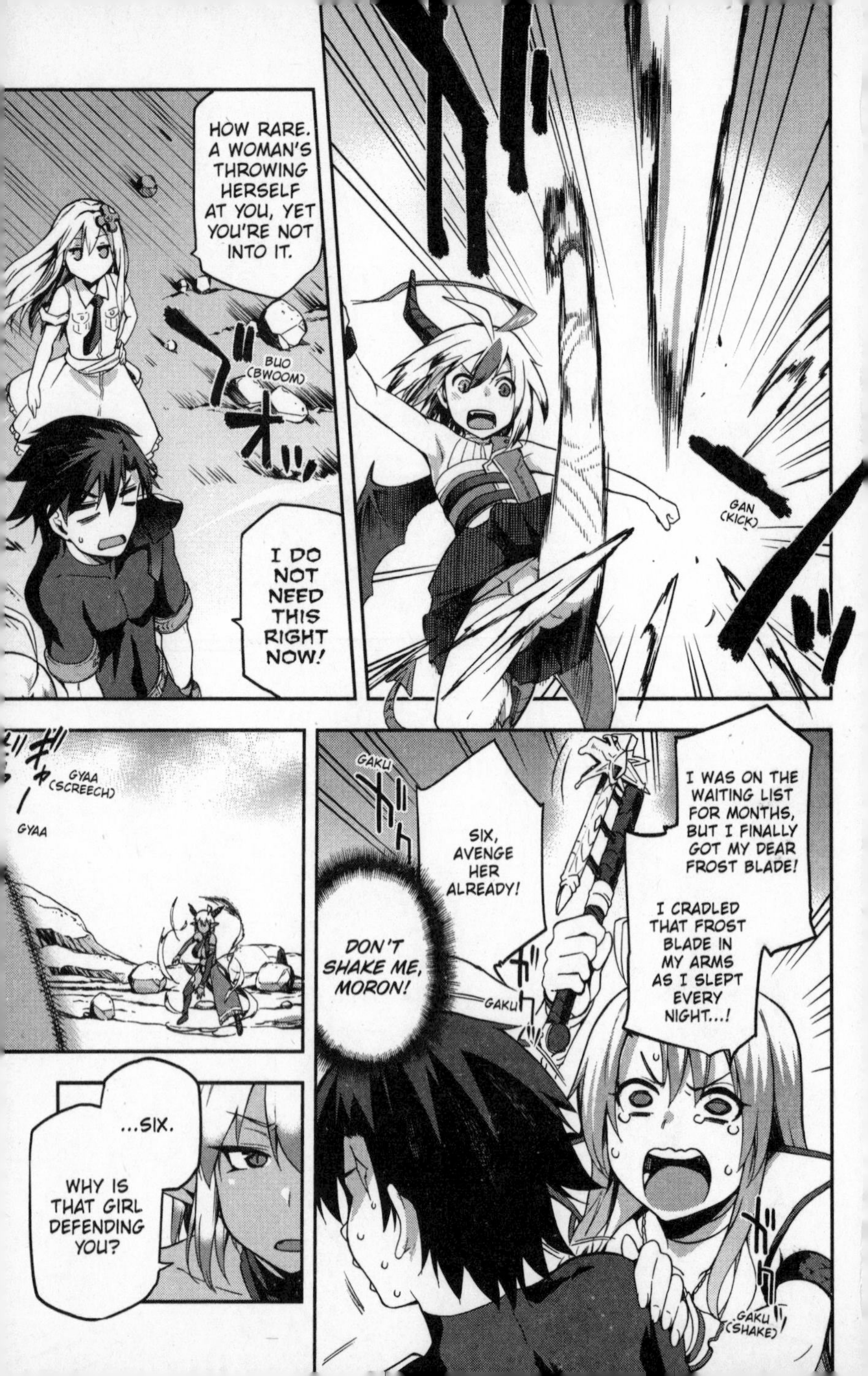
GAN (KICK)
HOW RARE. A WOMAN'S THROWING HERSELF AT YOU, YET YOU'RE NOT INTO IT.
BUO (BWOOM)
I DO NOT NEED THIS RIGHT NOW!
I WAS ON THE WAITING LIST FOR MONTHS, BUT I FINALLY GOT MY DEAR FROST BLADE!
GAKU
SIX, AVENGE HER ALREADY!
I CRADLED THAT FROST BLADE IN MY ARMS AS I SLEPT EVERY NIGHT...!
DON'T SHAKE ME, MORON!
GAKU
GAKU (SHAKE)
GYAA (SCREECH)
GYAA
...SIX.
WHY IS THAT GIRL DEFENDING YOU?

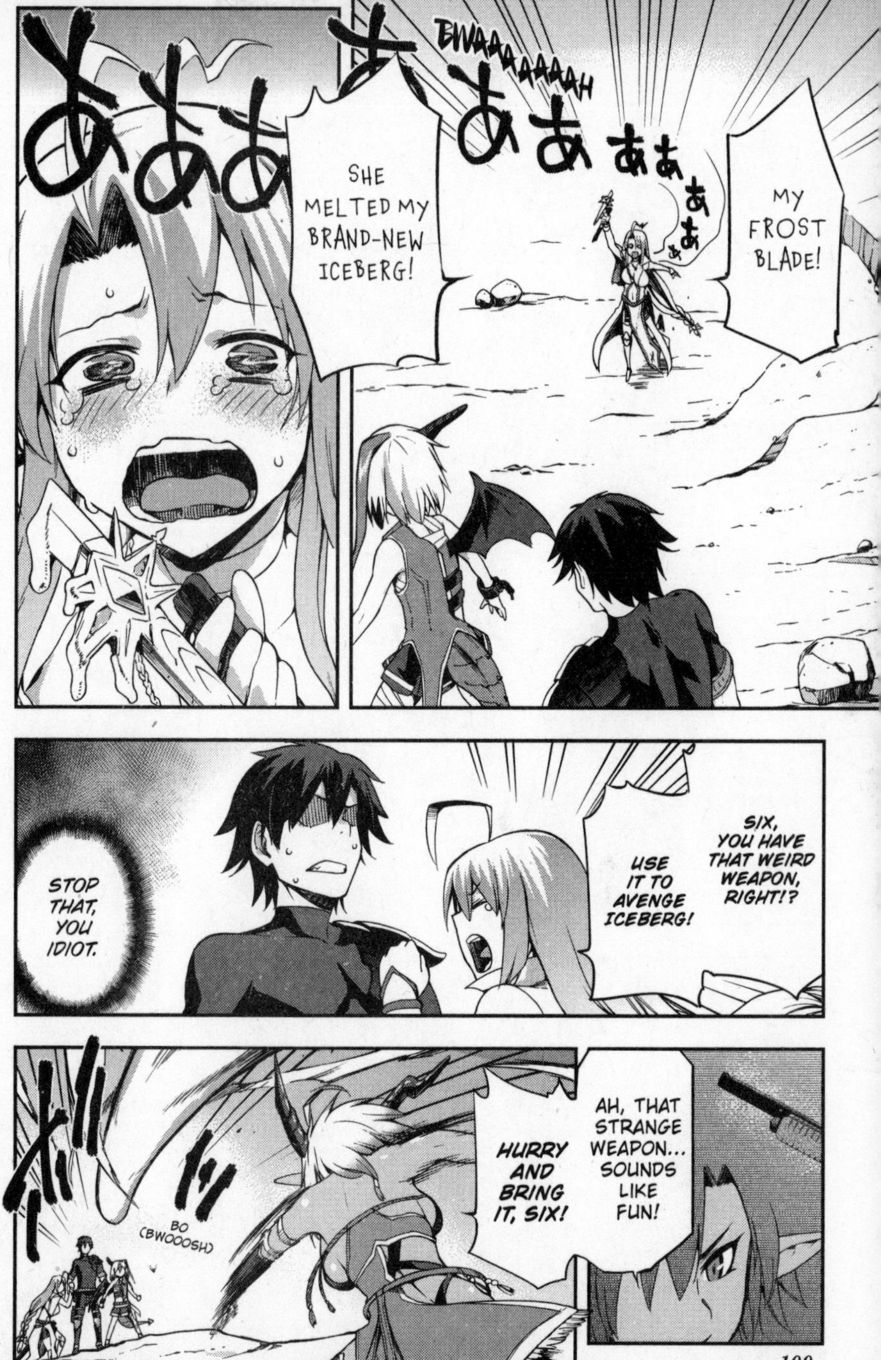
BWAAAAAAAAAH
ああああああああああ
MY FROST BLADE!
SHE MELTED MY BRAND-NEW ICEBERG!
SIX, YOU HAVE THAT WEIRD WEAPON, RIGHT!?
USE IT TO AVENGE ICEBERG!
STOP THAT, YOU IDIOT.
AH, THAT STRANGE WEAPON... SOUNDS LIKE FUN!
HURRY AND BRING IT, SIX!
BO (BWOOOSH)

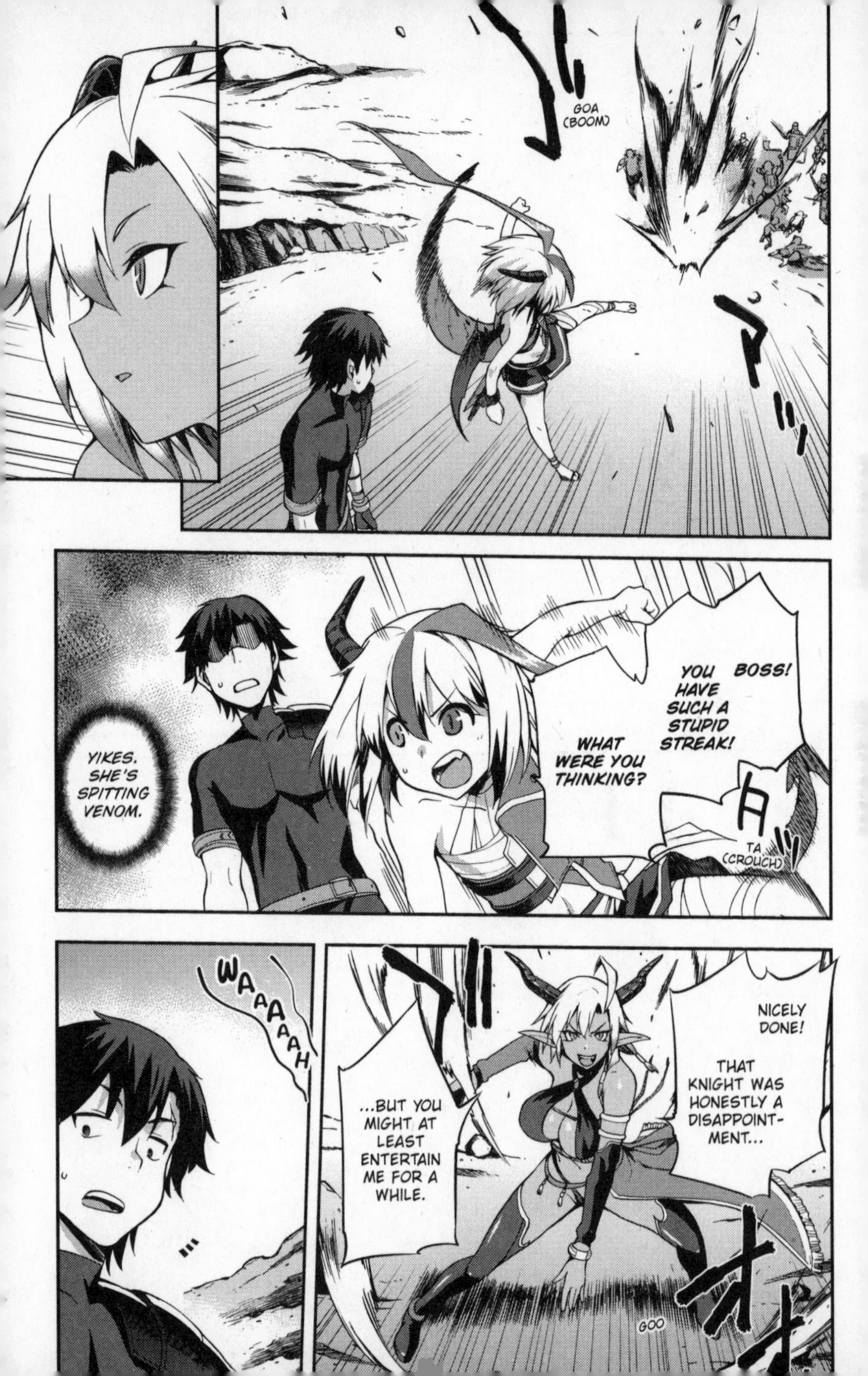
GOA (BOOM)
BOSS!
YOU HAVE SUCH A STUPID STREAK!
WHAT WERE YOU THINKING?
TA (CROUCH)
YIKES. SHE'S SPITTING VENOM.
NICELY DONE!
THAT KNIGHT WAS HONESTLY A DISAPPOINT-MENT...
...BUT YOU MIGHT AT LEAST ENTERTAIN ME FOR A WHILE.
GOO
WAAAAAAH
...

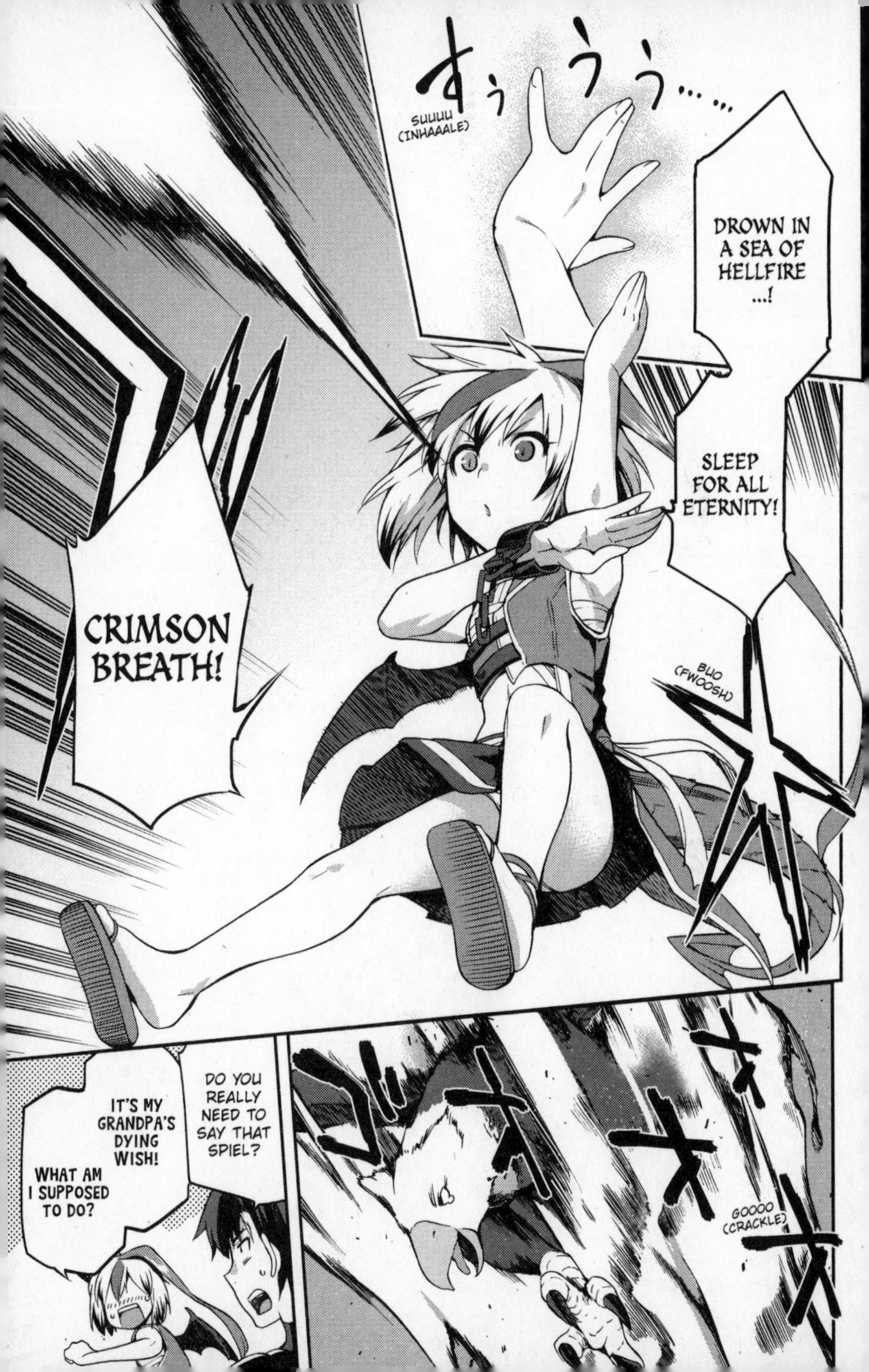
すぅうぅ……
SUUUU (INHAAALE)
DROWN IN A SEA OF HELLFIRE ...!
SLEEP FOR ALL ETERNITY!
CRIMSON BREATH!
BUO (FWOOSH)
GOOOO (CRACKLE)
DO YOU REALLY NEED TO SAY THAT SPIEL?
IT'S MY GRANDPA'S DYING WISH!
WHAT AM I SUPPOSED TO DO?

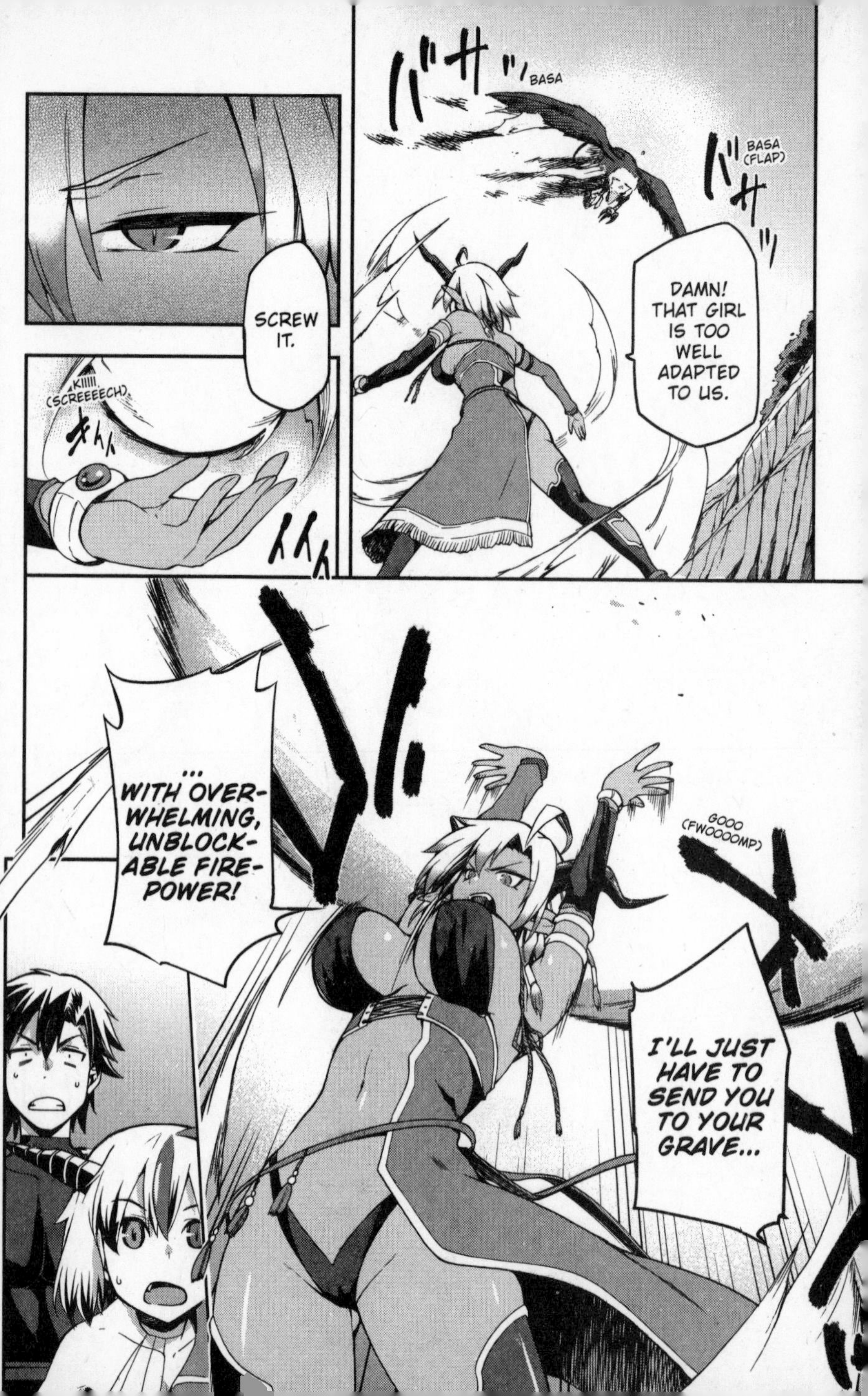
BASA
BASA (FLAP)
DAMN! THAT GIRL IS TOO WELL ADAPTED TO US.
SCREW IT.
KIIII (SCREEEECH)
GOOO (FWOOOOMP)
I'LL JUST HAVE TO SEND YOU TO YOUR GRAVE...
...WITH OVER-WHELMING, UNBLOCK-ABLE FIRE-POWER!

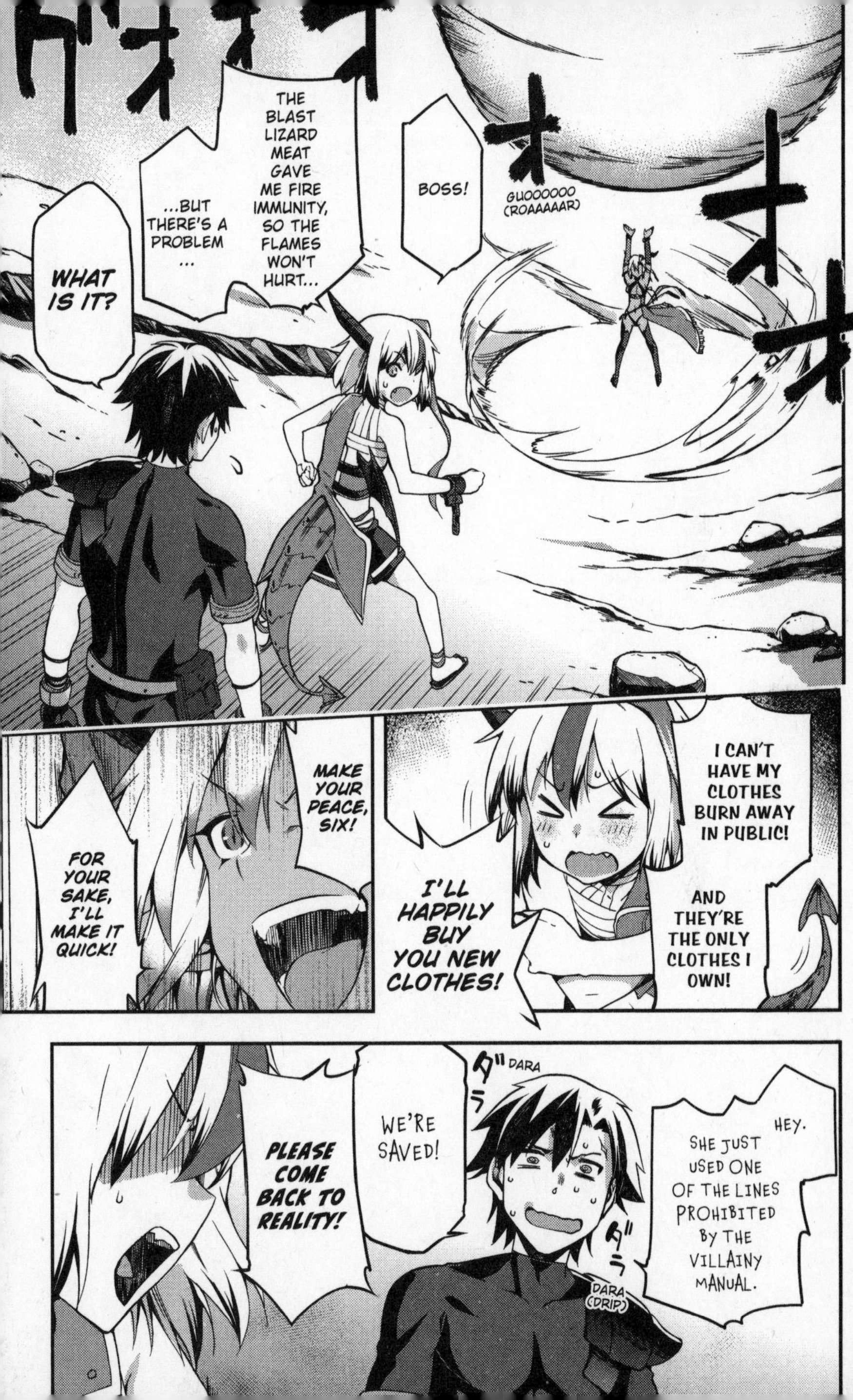
GUOOOOOO (ROAAAAAAR)
BOSS!
THE BLAST LIZARD MEAT GAVE ME FIRE IMMUNITY, SO THE FLAMES WON'T HURT...
...BUT THERE'S A PROBLEM ...
WHAT IS IT?
I CAN'T HAVE MY CLOTHES BURN AWAY IN PUBLIC!
AND THEY'RE THE ONLY CLOTHES I OWN!
I'LL HAPPILY BUY YOU NEW CLOTHES!
MAKE YOUR PEACE, SIX!
FOR YOUR SAKE, I'LL MAKE IT QUICK!
HEY. SHE JUST USED ONE OF THE LINES PROHIBITED BY THE VILLAINY MANUAL.
DARA
DARA (DRIP)
WE'RE SAVED!
PLEASE COME BACK TO REALITY!

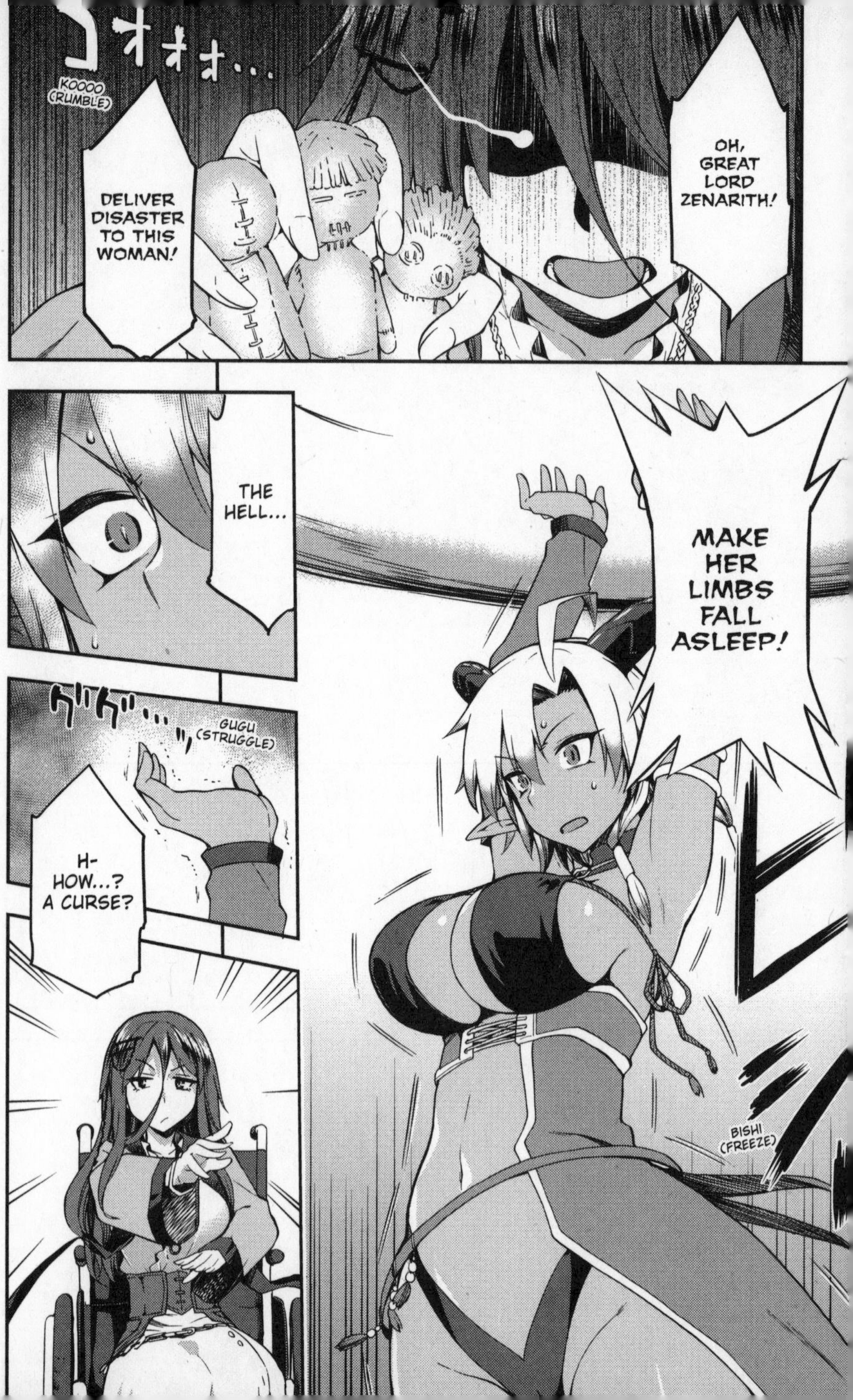
OH, GREAT LORD ZENARITH!
KOOOO (RUMBLE)
DELIVER DISASTER TO THIS WOMAN!
MAKE HER LIMBS FALL ASLEEP!
BISHI (FREEZE)
THE HELL...
GUGU (STRUGGLE)
H- HOW...? A CURSE?

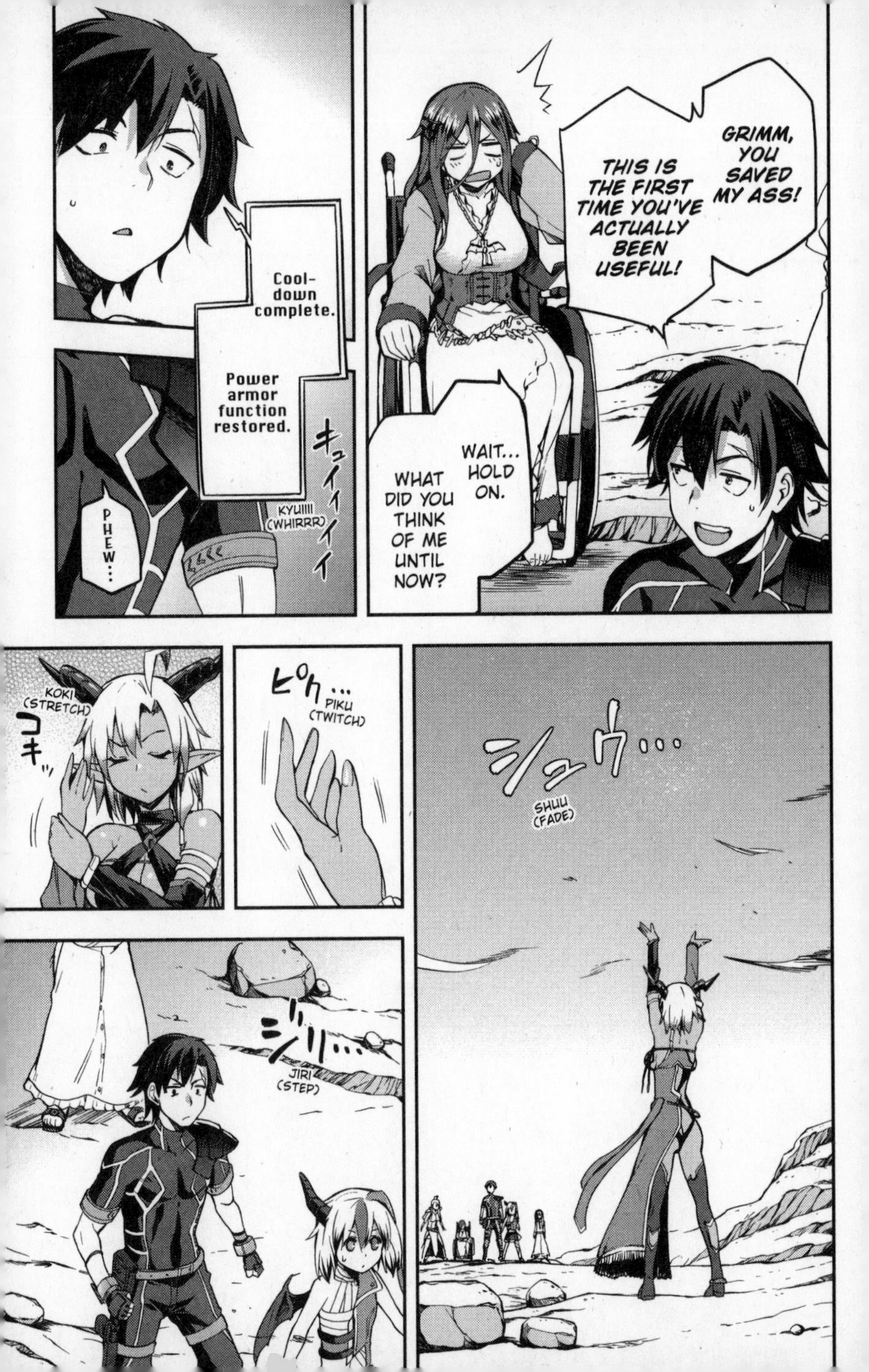
GRIMM, YOU SAVED MY ASS!
THIS IS THE FIRST TIME YOU'VE ACTUALLY BEEN USEFUL!
WAIT... HOLD ON.
WHAT DID YOU THINK OF ME UNTIL NOW?
Cool-down complete.
Power armor function restored.
キュイイイイ
KYUIIII (WHIRRR)
PHEW...
シュウ…
SHUU (FADE)
ピク…
PIKU (TWITCH)
コキッ
KOKI (STRETCH)
ジリ…
JIRI (STEP)

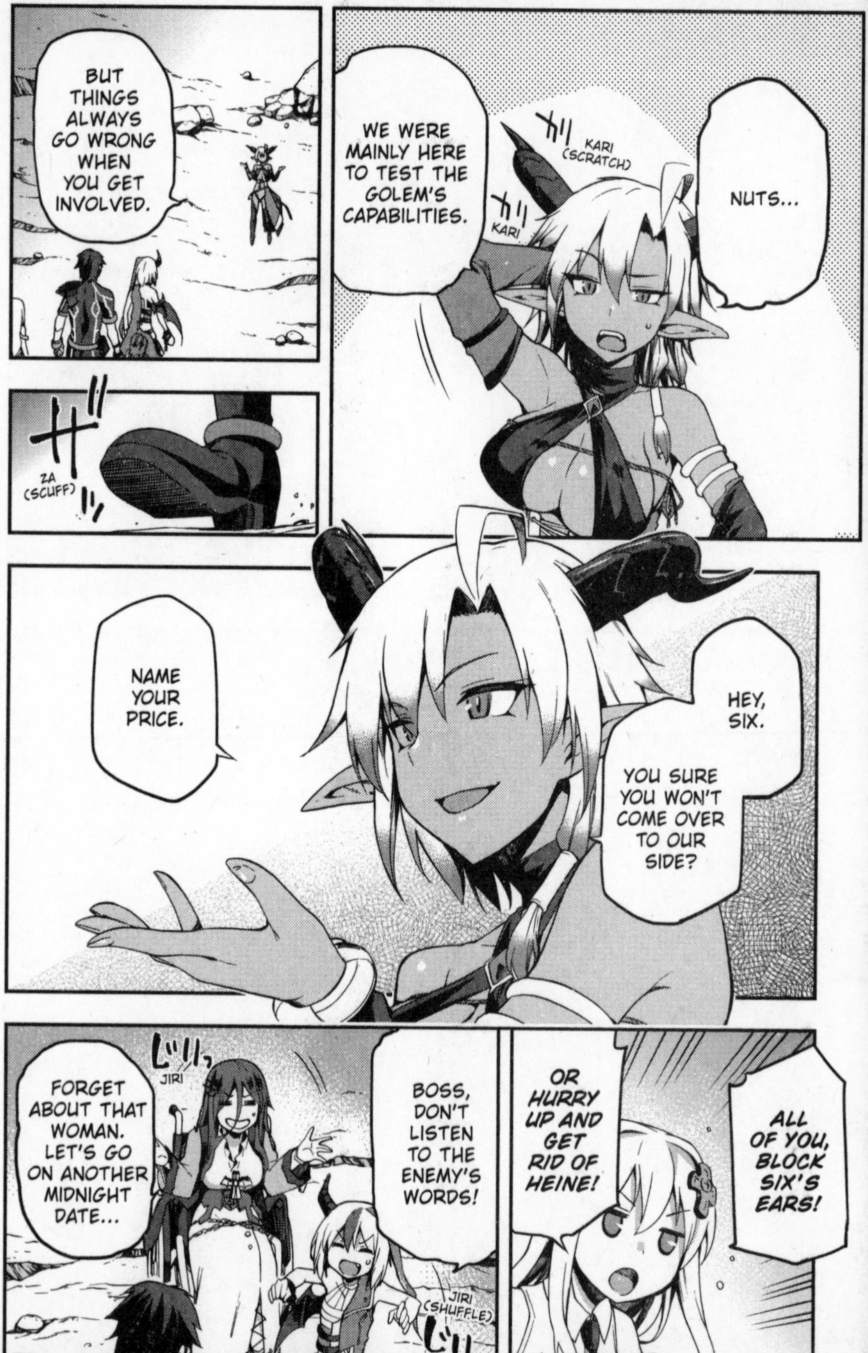
NUTS...
WE WERE MAINLY HERE TO TEST THE GOLEM'S CAPABILITIES.
KARI (SCRATCH)
KARI
BUT THINGS ALWAYS GO WRONG WHEN YOU GET INVOLVED.
ZA (SCUFF)
HEY, SIX.
YOU SURE YOU WON'T COME OVER TO OUR SIDE?
NAME YOUR PRICE.
ALL OF YOU, BLOCK SIX'S EARS!
OR HURRY UP AND GET RID OF HEINE!
BOSS, DON'T LISTEN TO THE ENEMY'S WORDS!
JIRI (SHUFFLE)
FORGET ABOUT THAT WOMAN. LET'S GO ON ANOTHER MIDNIGHT DATE...
JIRI

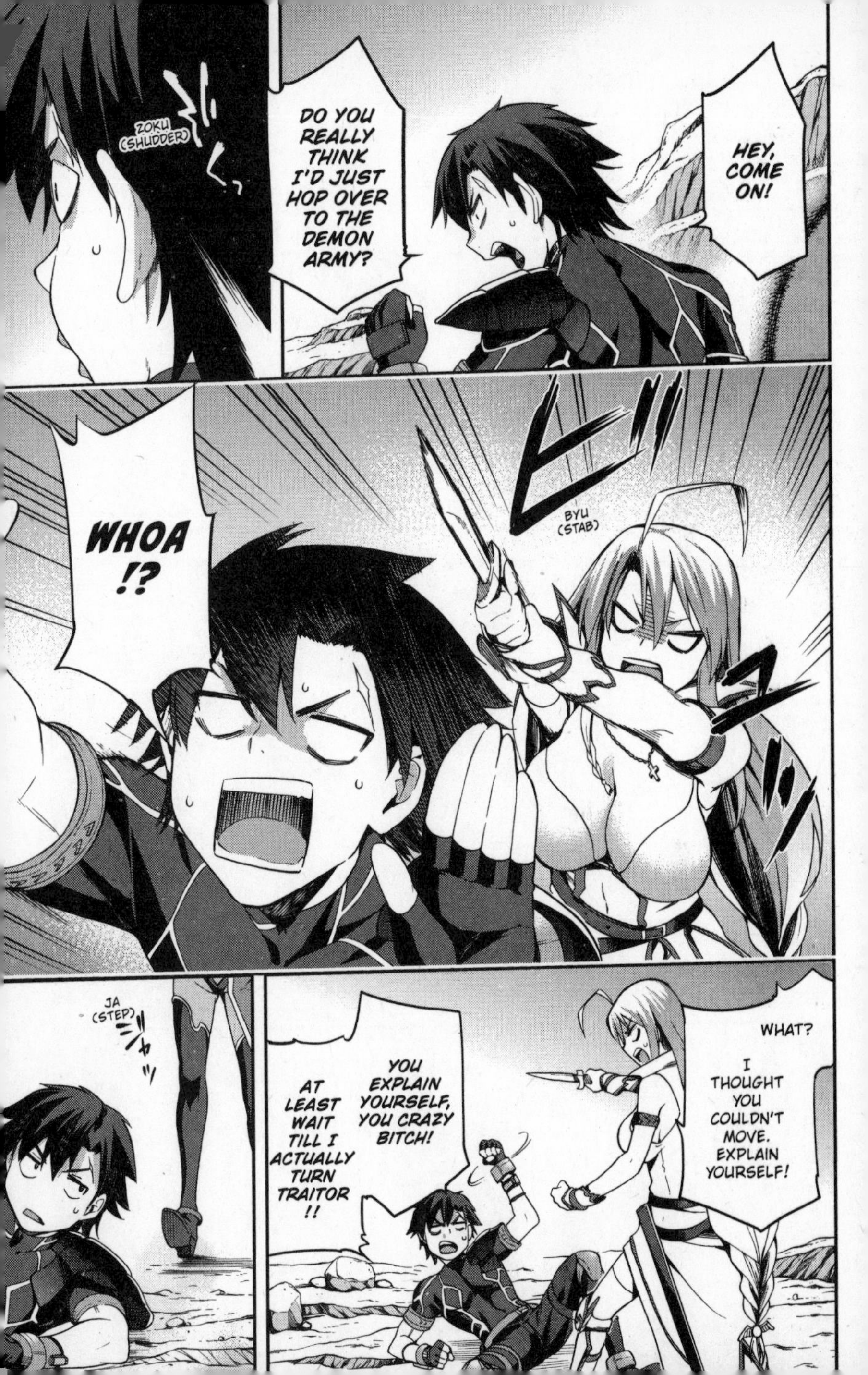
HEY, COME ON!
DO YOU REALLY THINK I'D JUST HOP OVER TO THE DEMON ARMY?
ZOKU (SHUDDER)
BYU (STAB)
WHOA!?
WHAT?
I THOUGHT YOU COULDN'T MOVE. EXPLAIN YOURSELF!
YOU EXPLAIN YOURSELF, YOU CRAZY BITCH!
AT LEAST WAIT TILL I ACTUALLY TURN TRAITOR!!
JA (STEP)

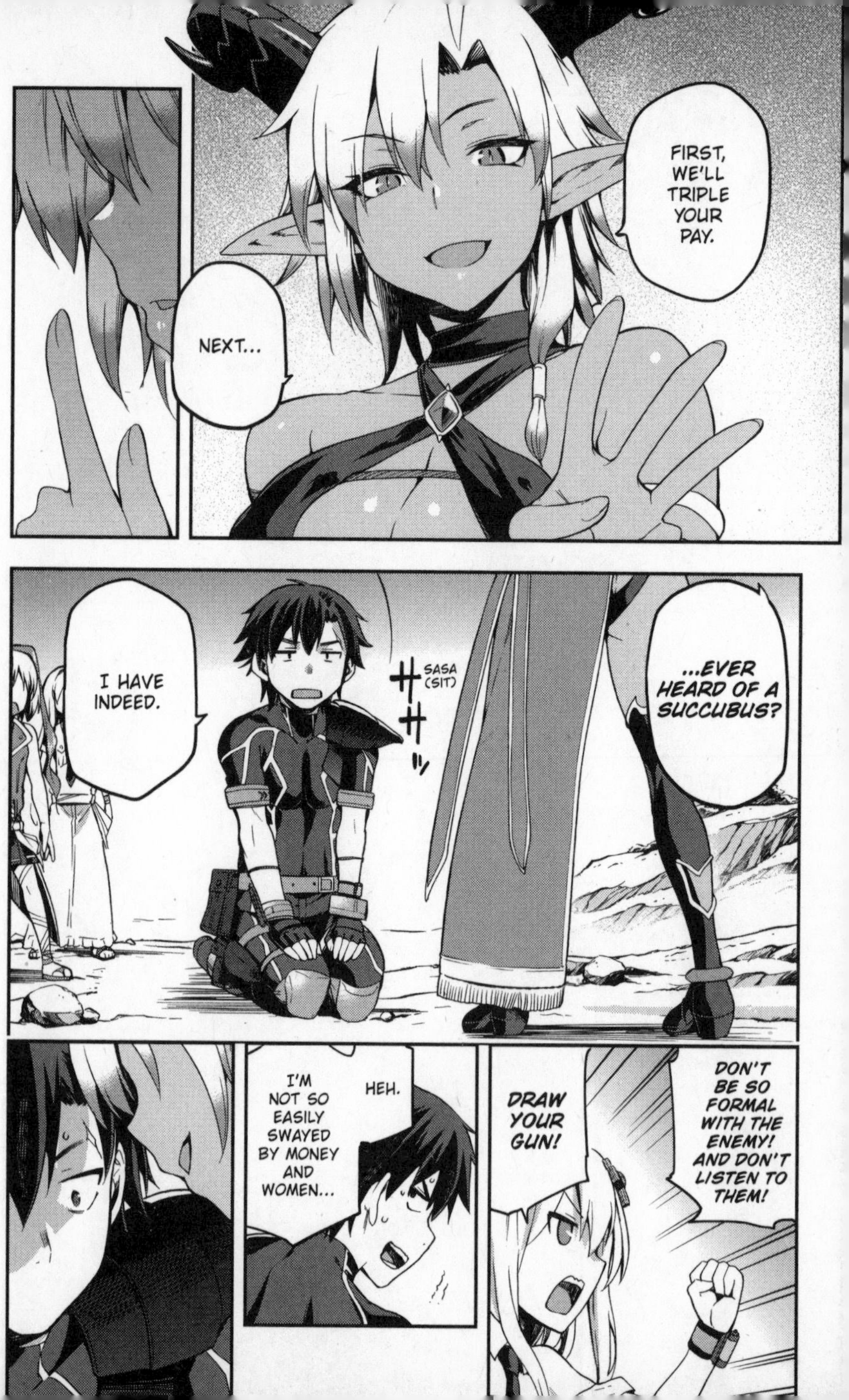
FIRST, WE'LL TRIPLE YOUR PAY.
NEXT...
...EVER HEARD OF A SUCCUBUS?
SASA (SIT)
I HAVE INDEED.
DON'T BE SO FORMAL WITH THE ENEMY! AND DON'T LISTEN TO THEM!
DRAW YOUR GUN!
HEH.
I'M NOT SO EASILY SWAYED BY MONEY AND WOMEN...

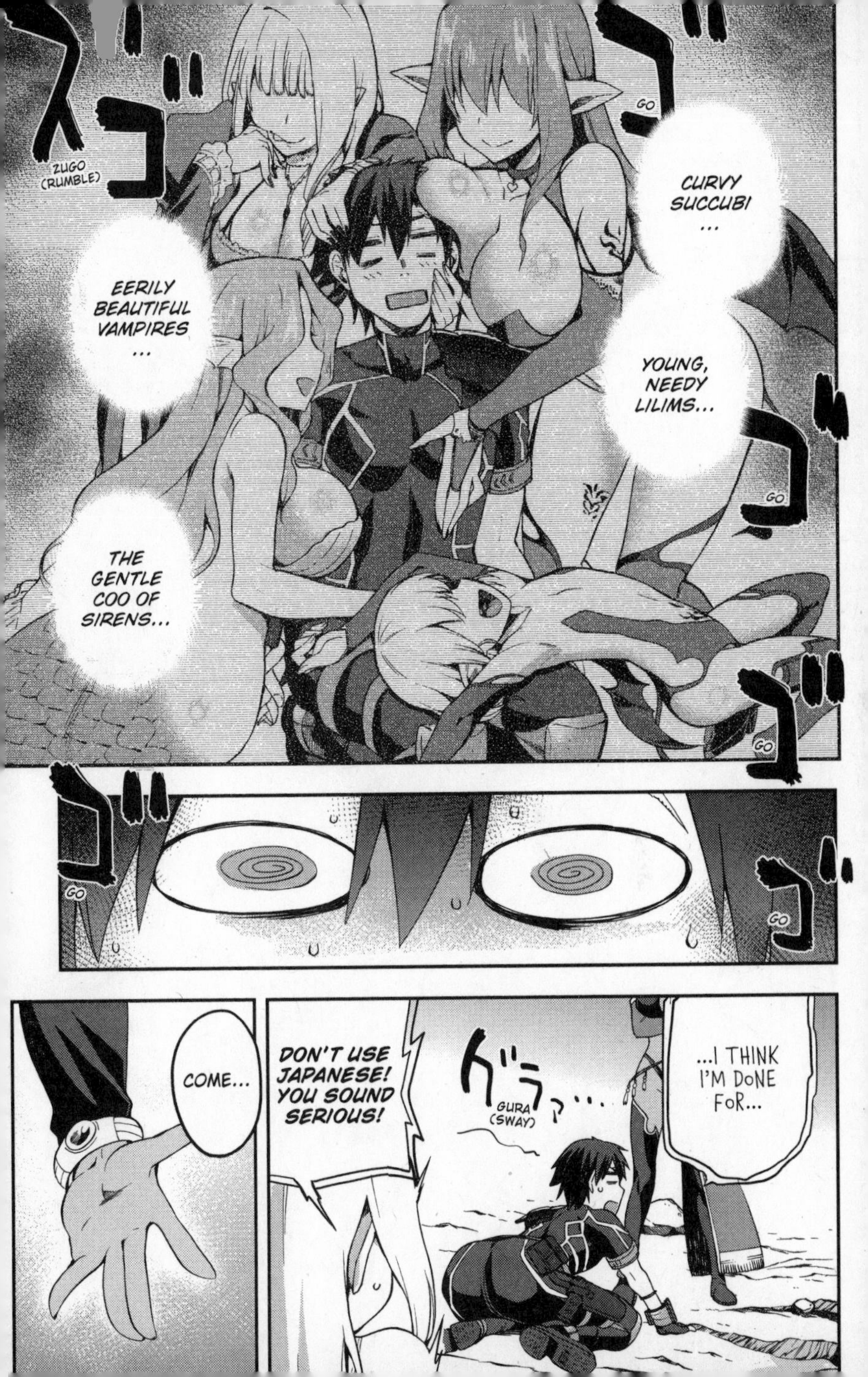
GO
CURVY SUCCUBI ...
ZUGO (RUMBLE)
EERILY BEAUTIFUL VAMPIRES ...
YOUNG, NEEDY LILIMS...
GO
THE GENTLE COO OF SIRENS...
GO
GO
GO
...I THINK I'M DONE FOR...
GURA (SWAY)
DON'T USE JAPANESE! YOU SOUND SERIOUS!
COME...

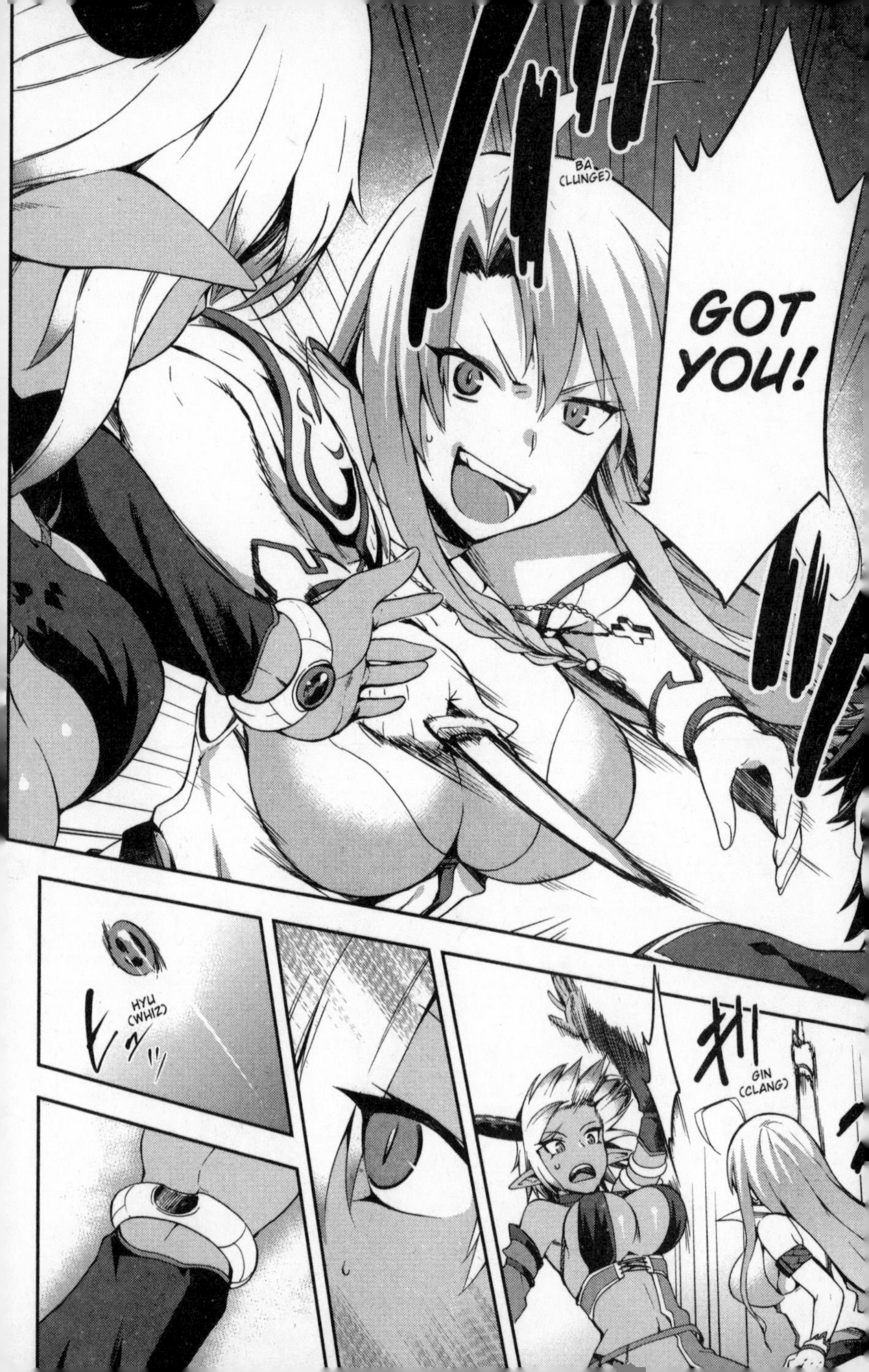
BA (LUNGE)
GOT YOU!
HYU (WHIZ)
GIN (CLANG)

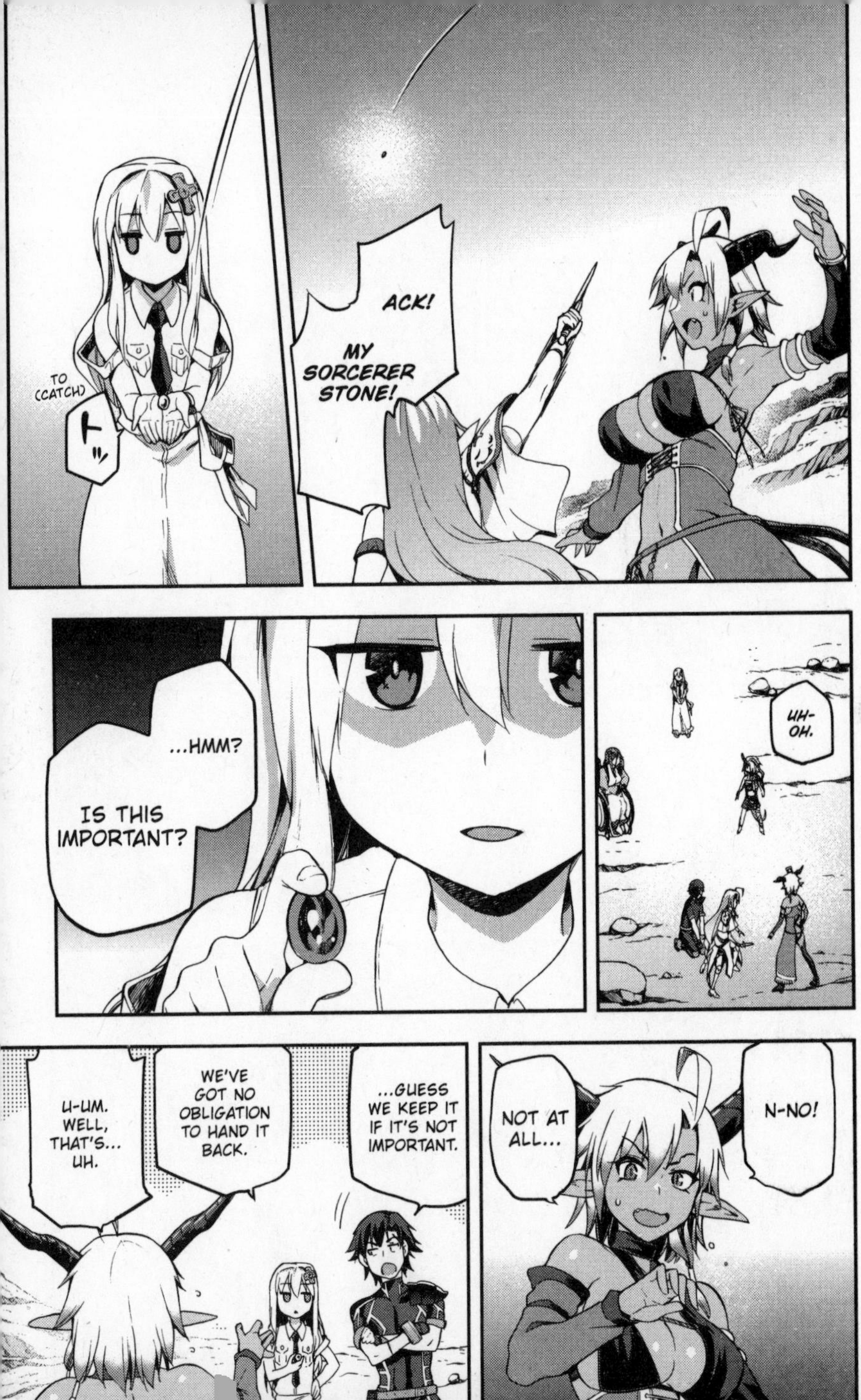
ACK!
MY SORCERER STONE!
TO (CATCH)
トッ
UH-OH.
...HMM?
IS THIS IMPORTANT?
N-NO!
NOT AT ALL...
...GUESS WE KEEP IT IF IT'S NOT IMPORTANT.
WE'VE GOT NO OBLIGATION TO HAND IT BACK.
U-UM. WELL, THAT'S... UH.

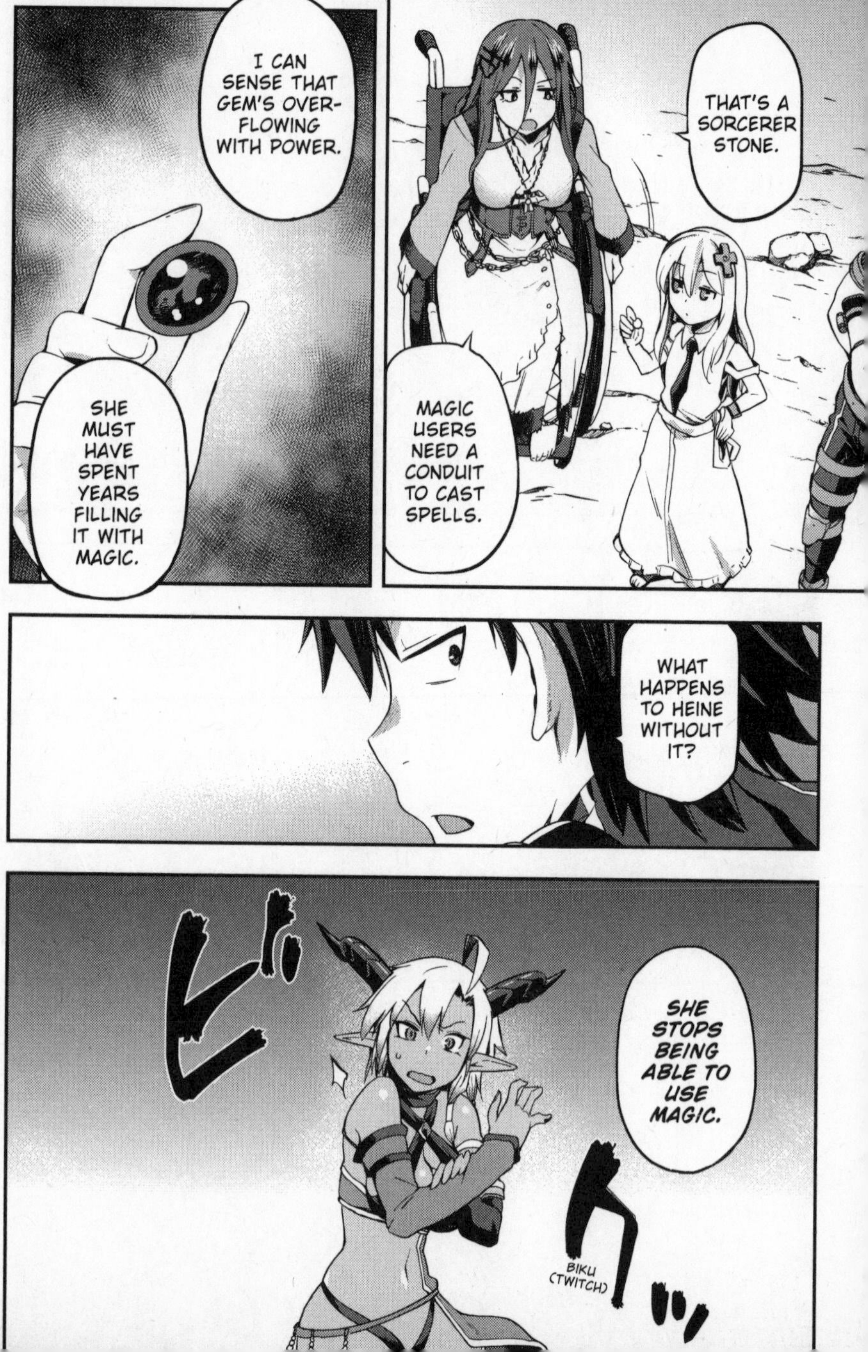
THAT'S A SORCERER STONE.
MAGIC USERS NEED A CONDUIT TO CAST SPELLS.
I CAN SENSE THAT GEM'S OVER-FLOWING WITH POWER.
SHE MUST HAVE SPENT YEARS FILLING IT WITH MAGIC.
WHAT HAPPENS TO HEINE WITHOUT IT?
SHE STOPS BEING ABLE TO USE MAGIC.
BIKU (TWITCH)

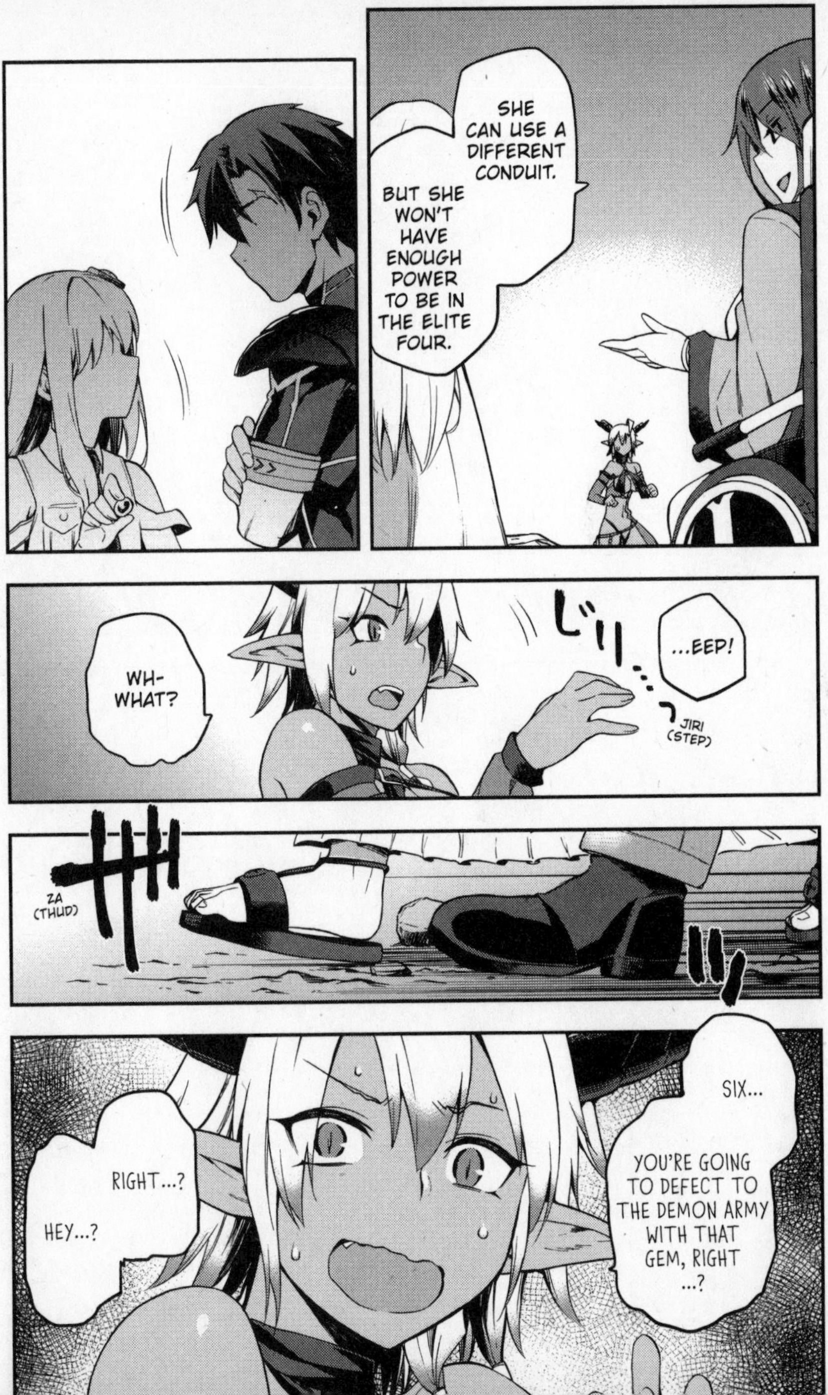
SHE CAN USE A DIFFERENT CONDUIT.
BUT SHE WON'T HAVE ENOUGH POWER TO BE IN THE ELITE FOUR.
...EEP!
じり…っ
JIRI (STEP)
WH-WHAT?
ZA (THUD)
SIX...
YOU'RE GOING TO DEFECT TO THE DEMON ARMY WITH THAT GEM, RIGHT ...?
RIGHT...?
HEY...?

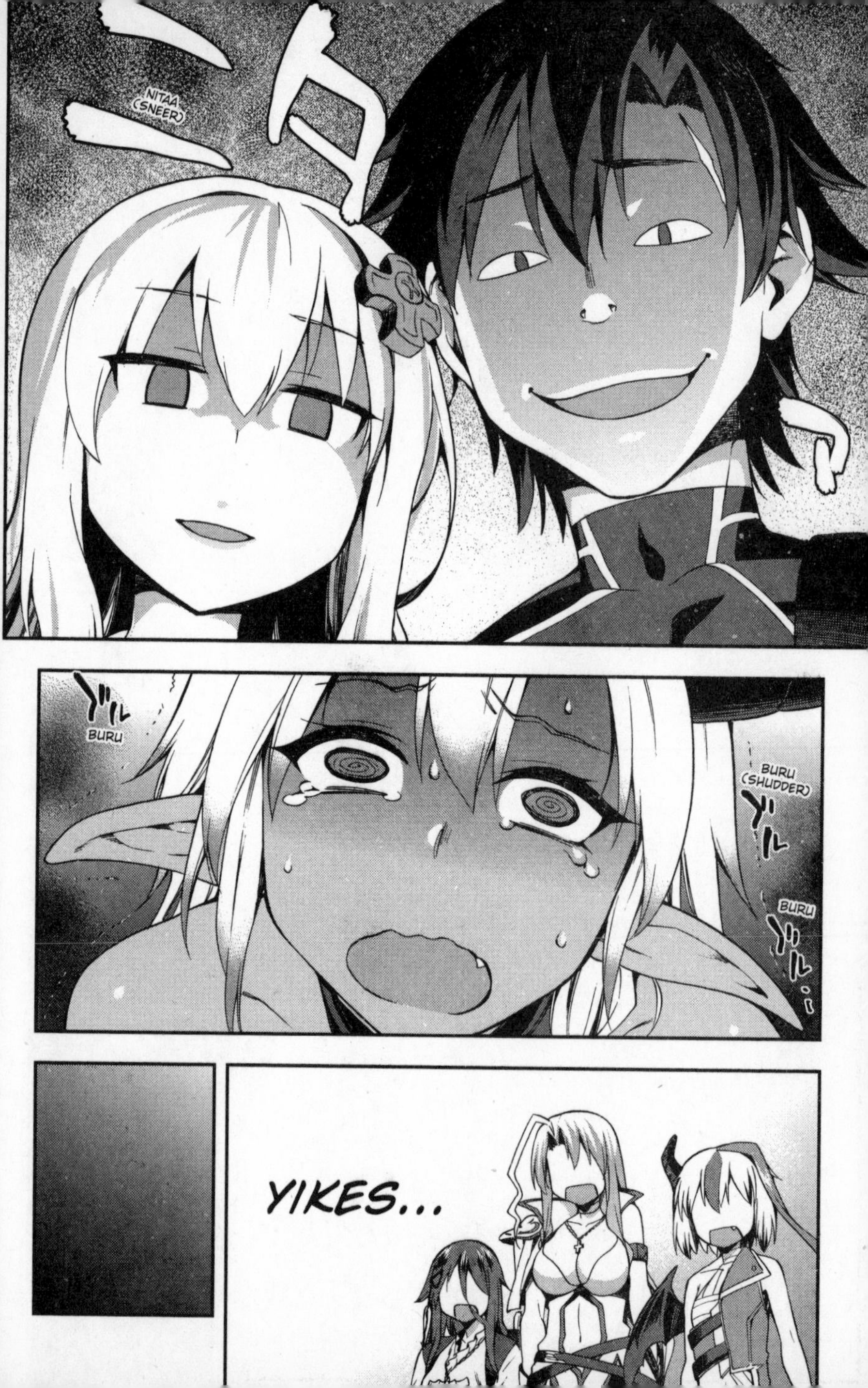
NITAA (SNEER)
BURU
BURU (SHUDDER)
BURU
YIKES...

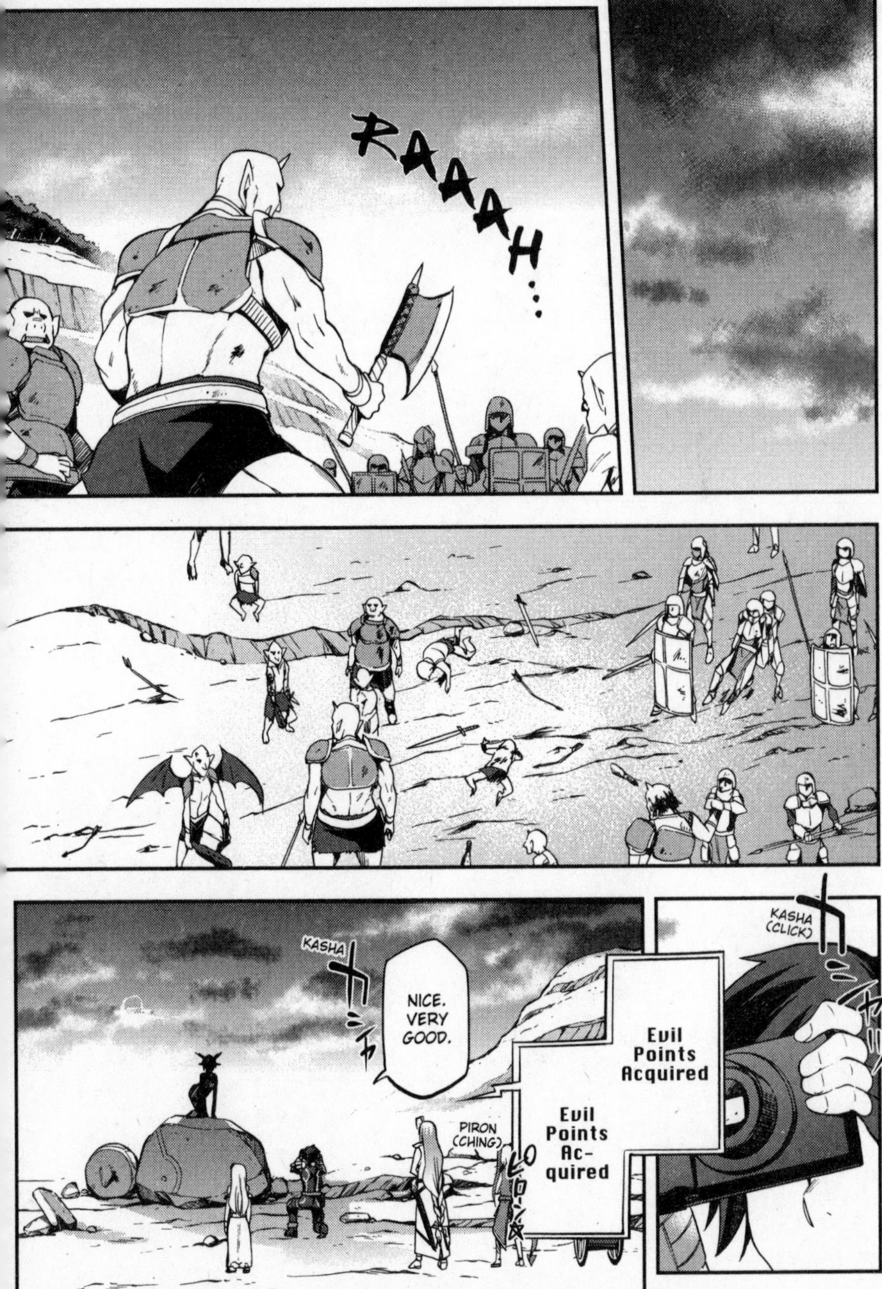
RAAAAH...
KASHA (CLICK)
KASHA
NICE. VERY GOOD.
Evil Points Acquired
PIRON (CHING)
Evil Points Ac-quired

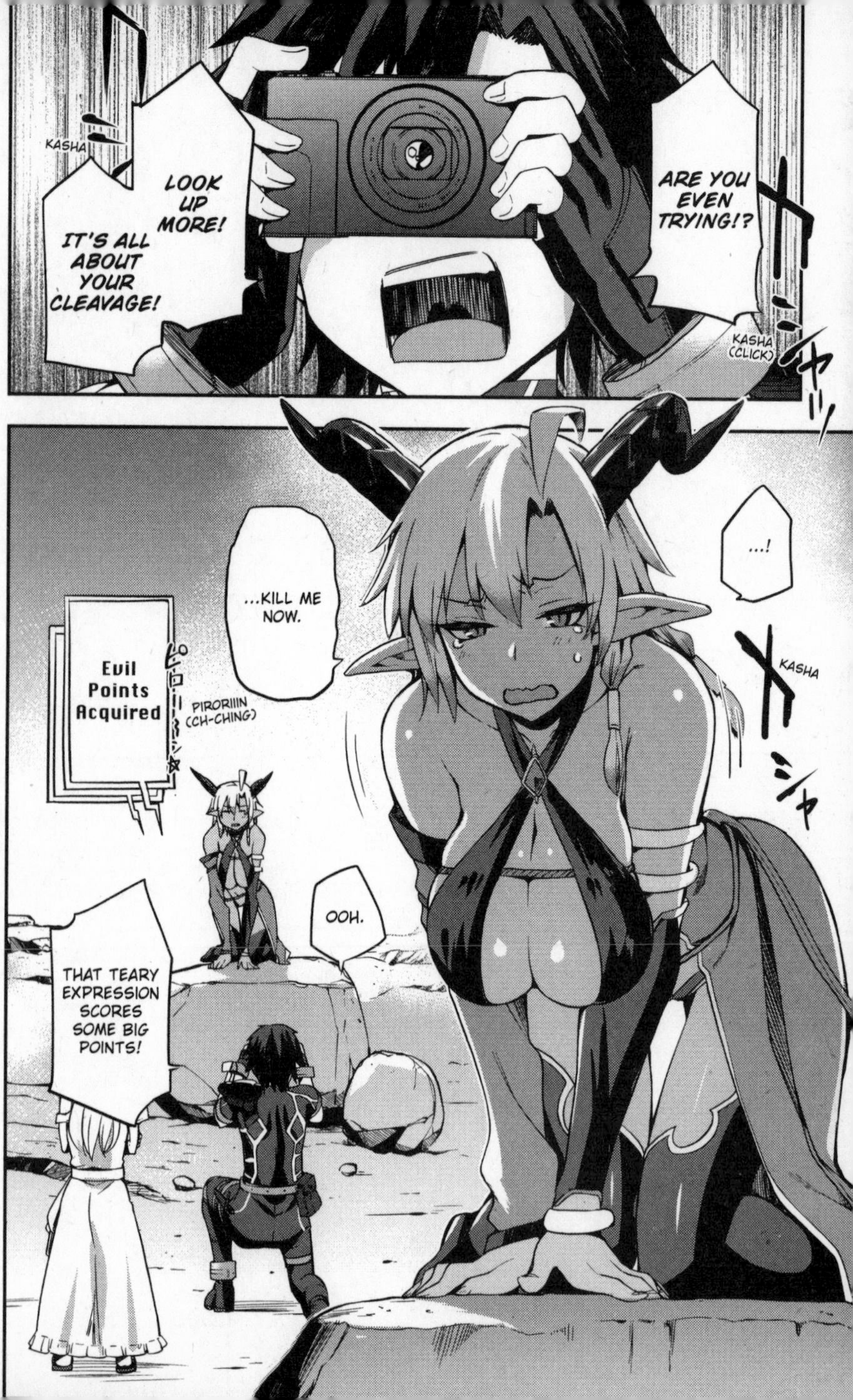
ARE YOU EVEN TRYING!?
KASHA (CLICK)
KASHA
LOOK UP MORE!
IT'S ALL ABOUT YOUR CLEAVAGE!
...!
KASHA
...KILL ME NOW.
PIRORIIIN (CH-CHING)
Evil Points Acquired
OOH.
THAT TEARY EXPRESSION SCORES SOME BIG POINTS!

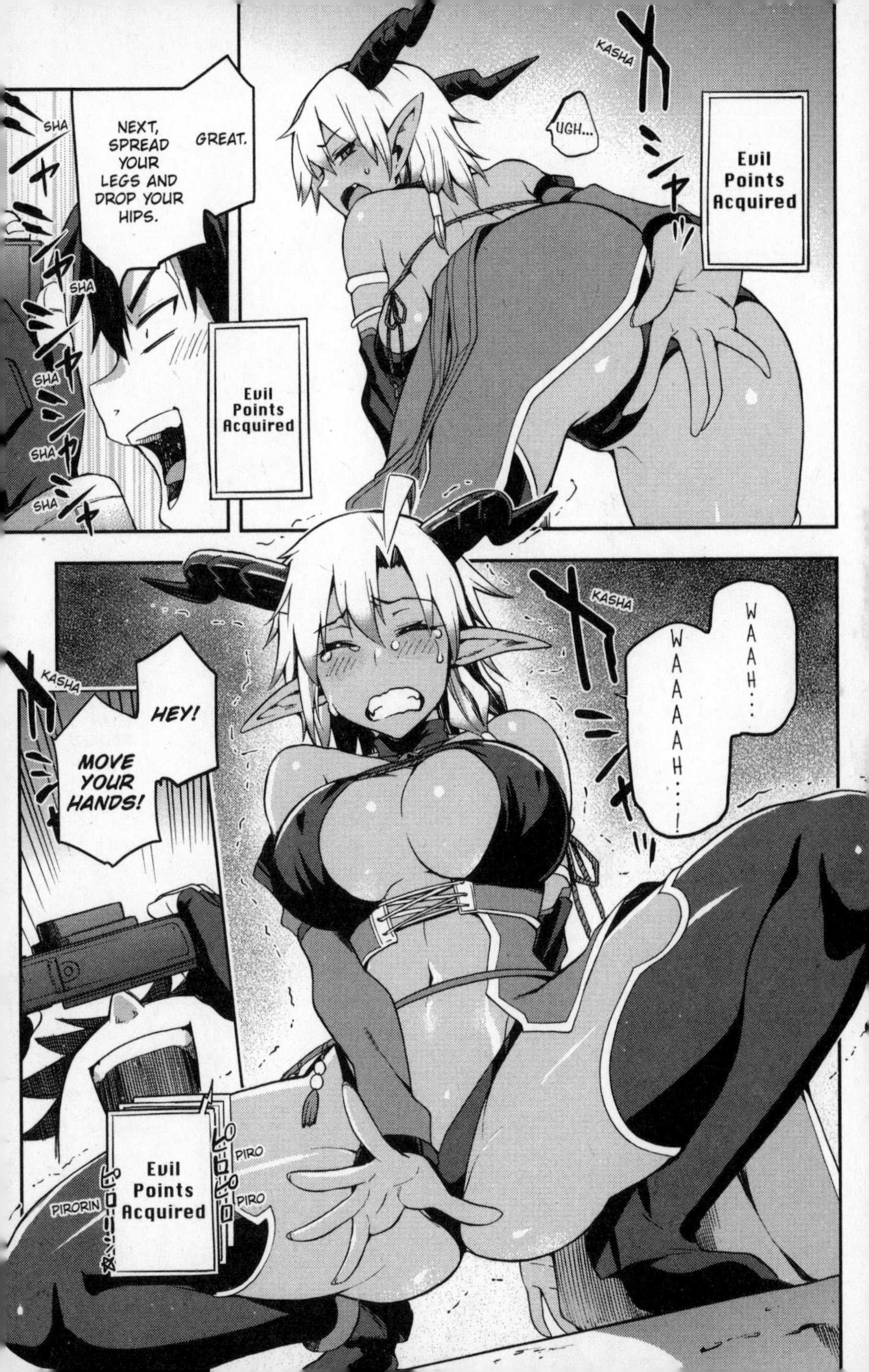
KASHA
UGH...
Evil Points Acquired
Evil Points Acquired
GREAT.
NEXT, SPREAD YOUR LEGS AND DROP YOUR HIPS.
SHA
SHA
SHA
SHA
SHA
KASHA
WAAAH...
WAAAAAAH...!
KASHA
HEY!
MOVE YOUR HANDS!
PIRO
PIRO
Evil Points Acquired
PIRORIN

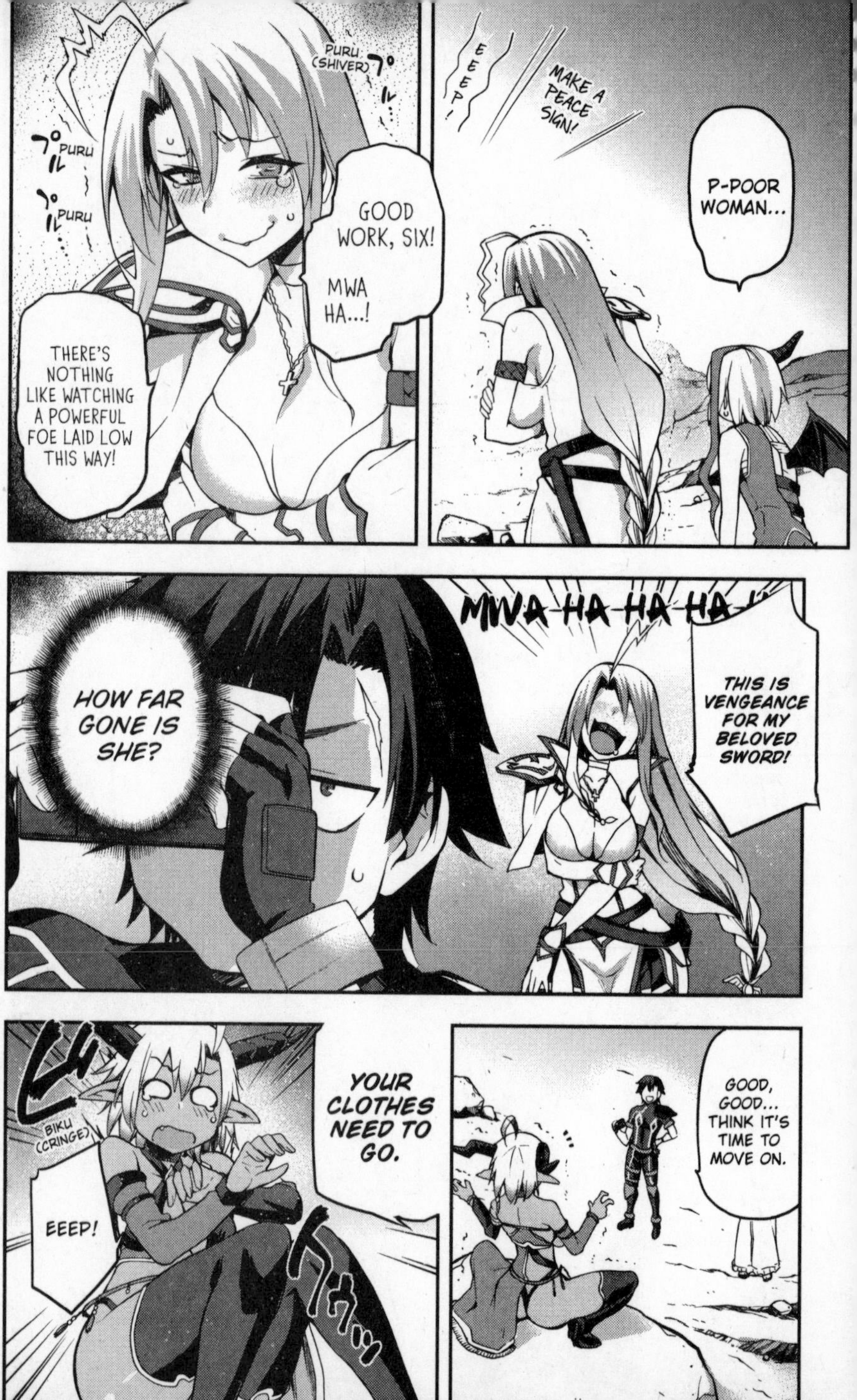
EEEP!
MAKE A PEACE SIGN!
P-POOR WOMAN...
PURU (SHIVER)
PURU
PURU
GOOD WORK, SIX!
MWA HA...!
THERE'S NOTHING LIKE WATCHING A POWERFUL FOE LAID LOW THIS WAY!
MWA HA HA HA
THIS IS VENGEANCE FOR MY BELOVED SWORD!
HOW FAR GONE IS SHE?
GOOD, GOOD... THINK IT'S TIME TO MOVE ON.
YOUR CLOTHES NEED TO GO.
BIKU (CRINGE)
EEEP!

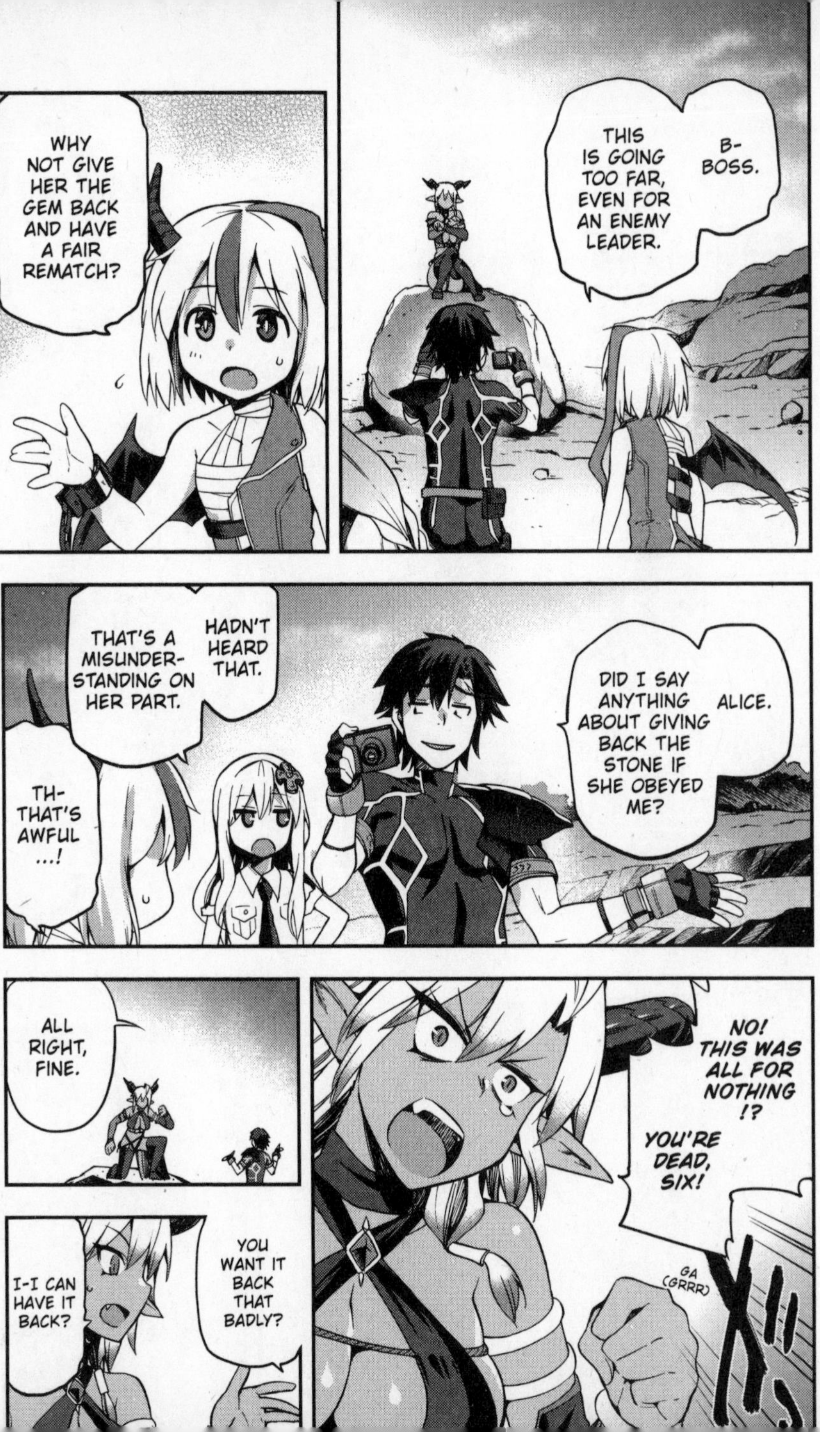
B-BOSS.
THIS IS GOING TOO FAR, EVEN FOR AN ENEMY LEADER.
WHY NOT GIVE HER THE GEM BACK AND HAVE A FAIR REMATCH?
ALICE.
DID I SAY ANYTHING ABOUT GIVING BACK THE STONE IF SHE OBEYED ME?
HADN'T HEARD THAT.
THAT'S A MISUNDER-STANDING ON HER PART.
TH-THAT'S AWFUL ...!
NO! THIS WAS ALL FOR NOTHING !?
YOU'RE DEAD, SIX!
GA (GRRR)
ALL RIGHT, FINE.
YOU WANT IT BACK THAT BADLY?
I-I CAN HAVE IT BACK?

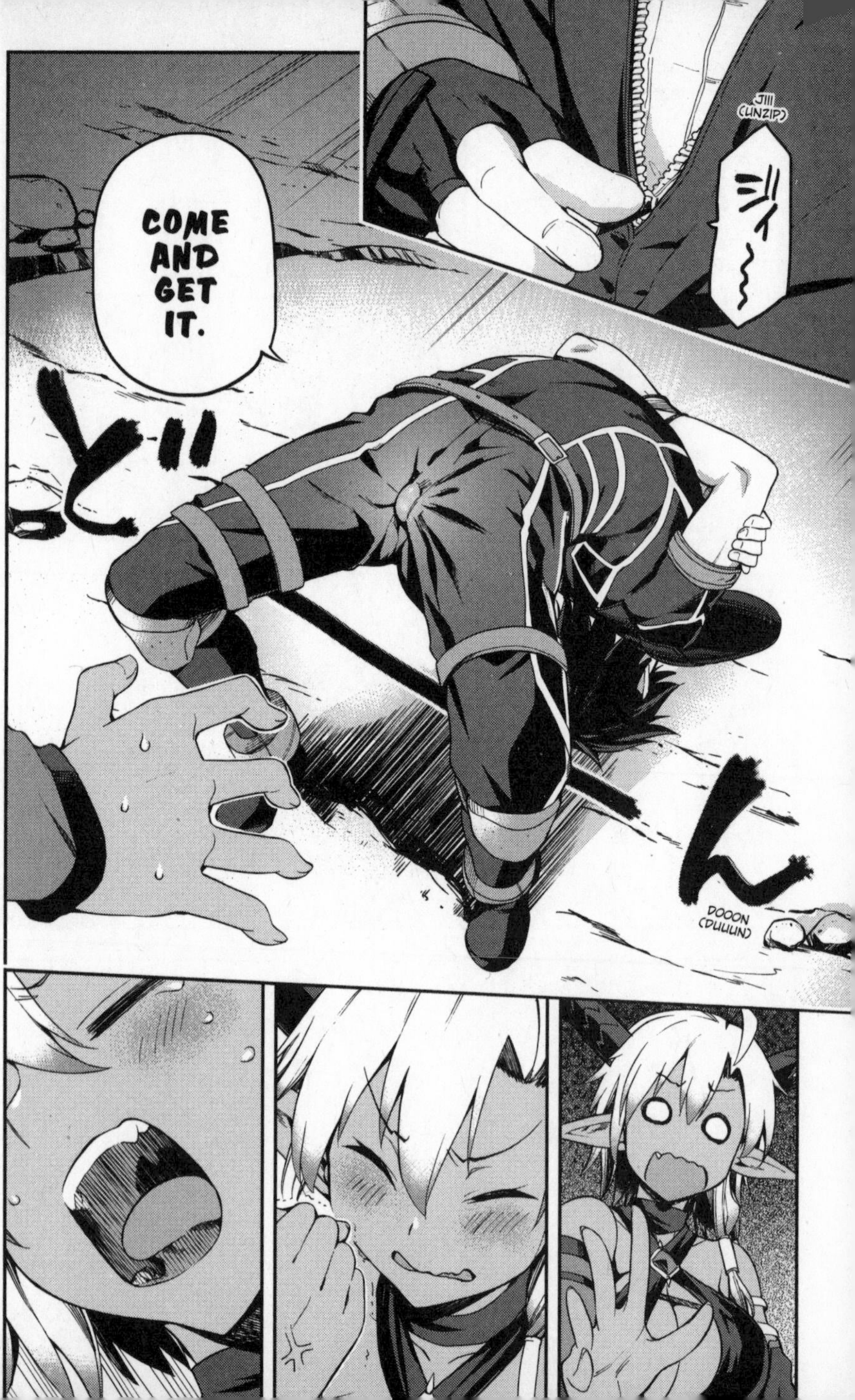
JIII (UNZIP)
COME AND GET IT.
DOOON (DUUUN)

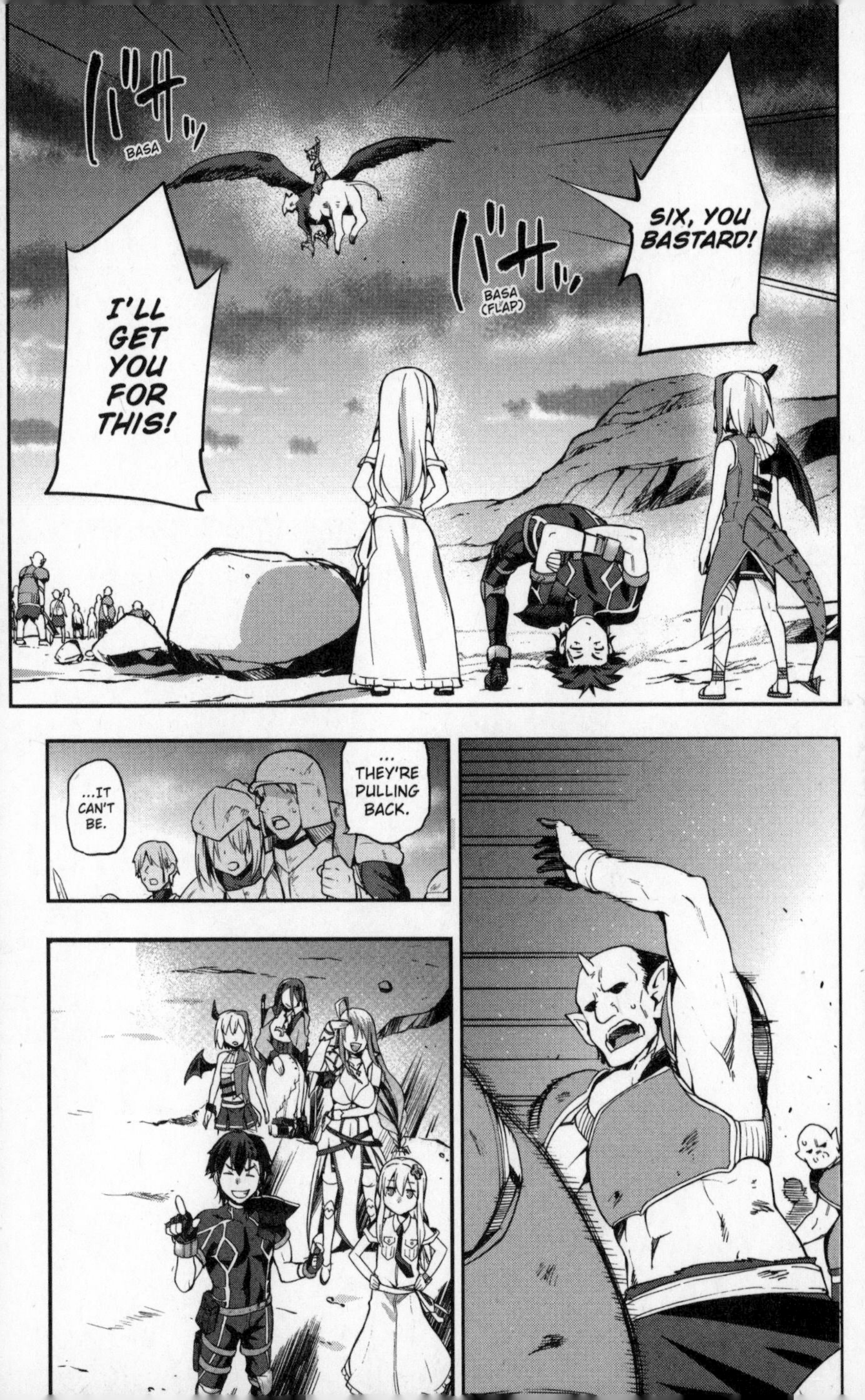
SIX, YOU BASTARD!
バサッ
BASA (FLAP)
バサッ
BASA
I'LL GET YOU FOR THIS!
... THEY'RE PULLING BACK.
...IT CAN'T BE.

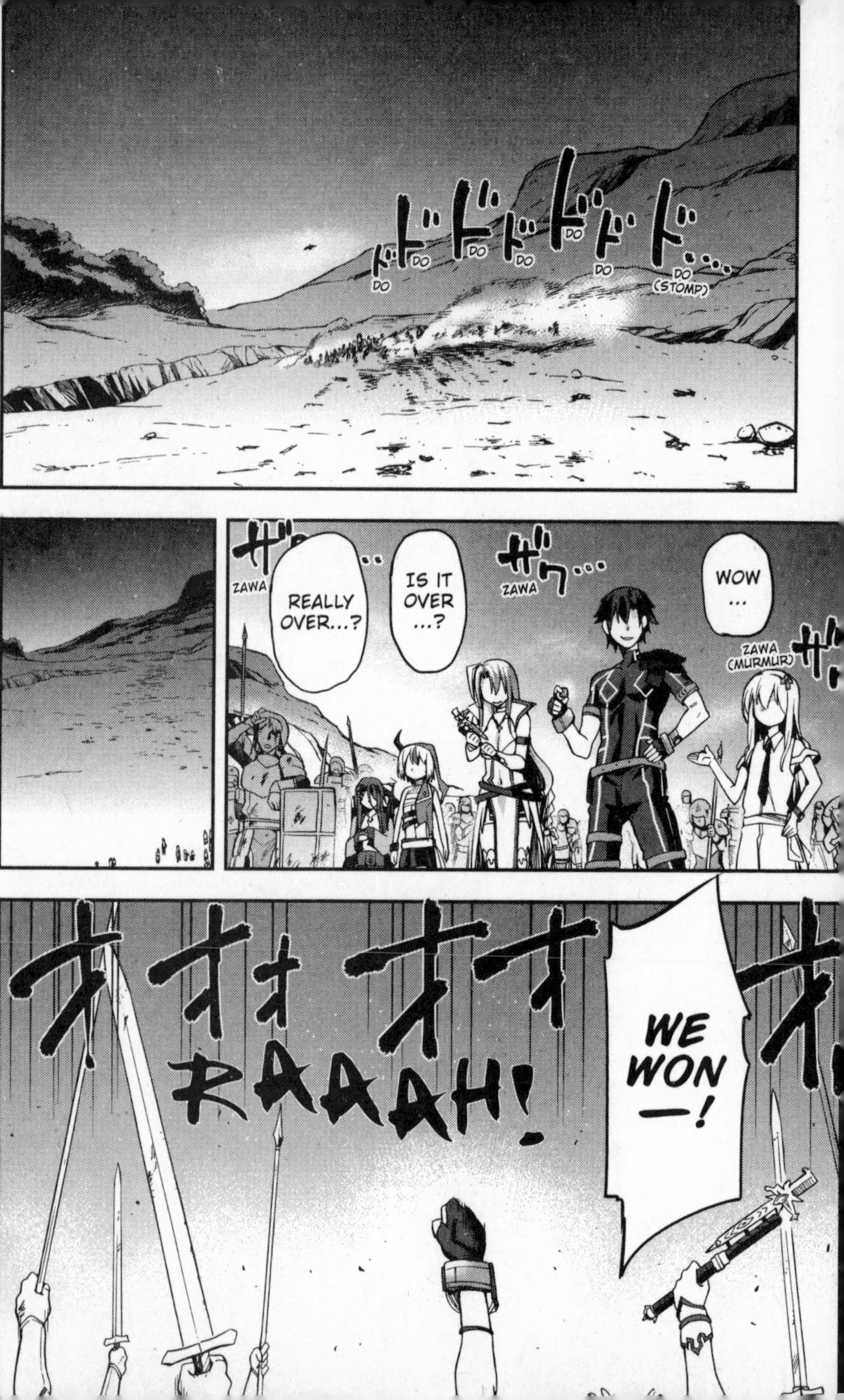
DO DO DO DO DO DO DO DO (STOMP)
ZAWA (MURMUR)
WOW ...
ZAWA
IS IT OVER ...?
REALLY OVER...?
ZAWA
WE WON—!
RAAAH!

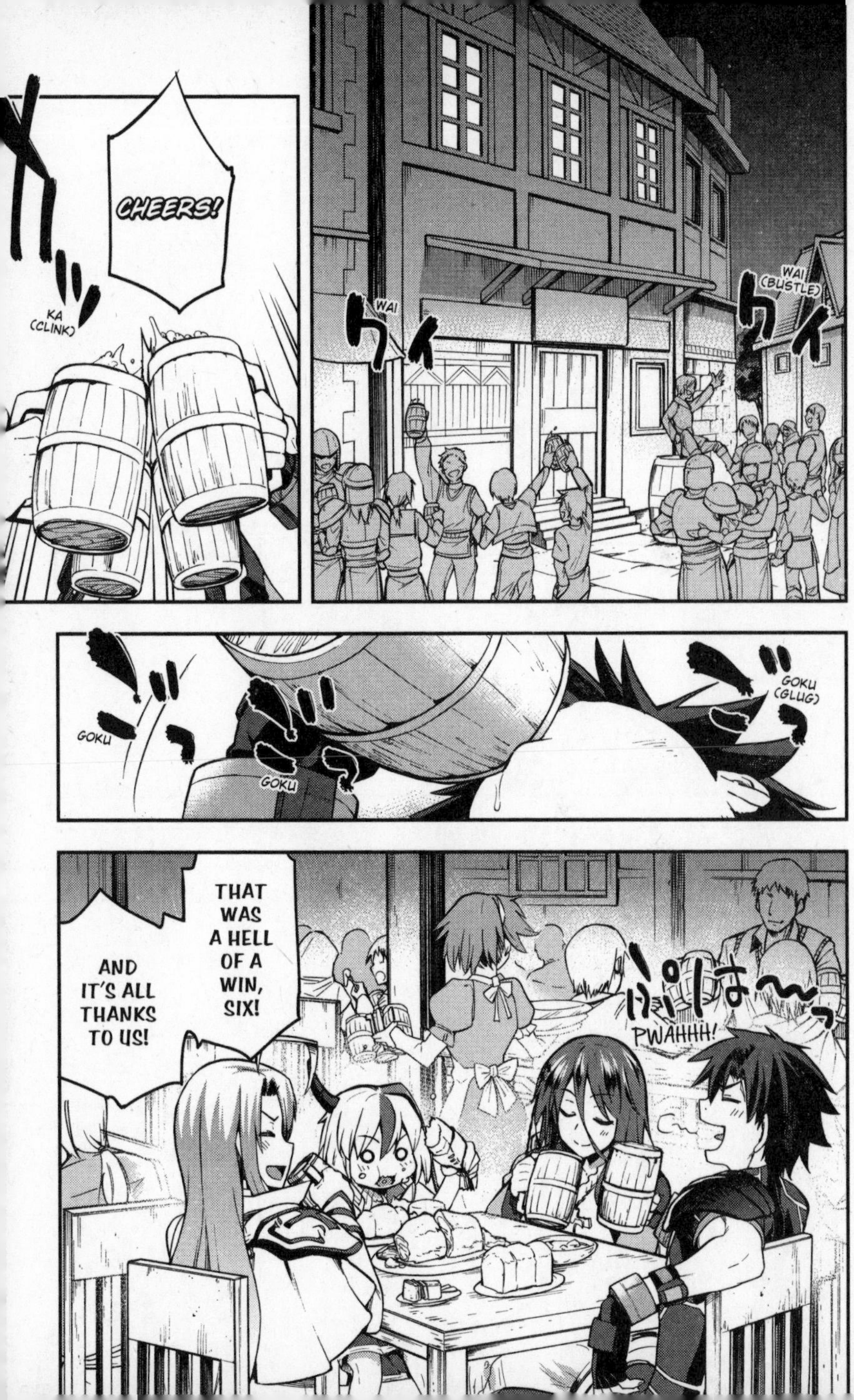
WAI (BUSTLE)
WAI
CHEERS!
KA (CLINK)
GOKU (GLUG)
GOKU
GOKU
PWAHHH!
THAT WAS A HELL OF A WIN, SIX!
AND IT'S ALL THANKS TO US!

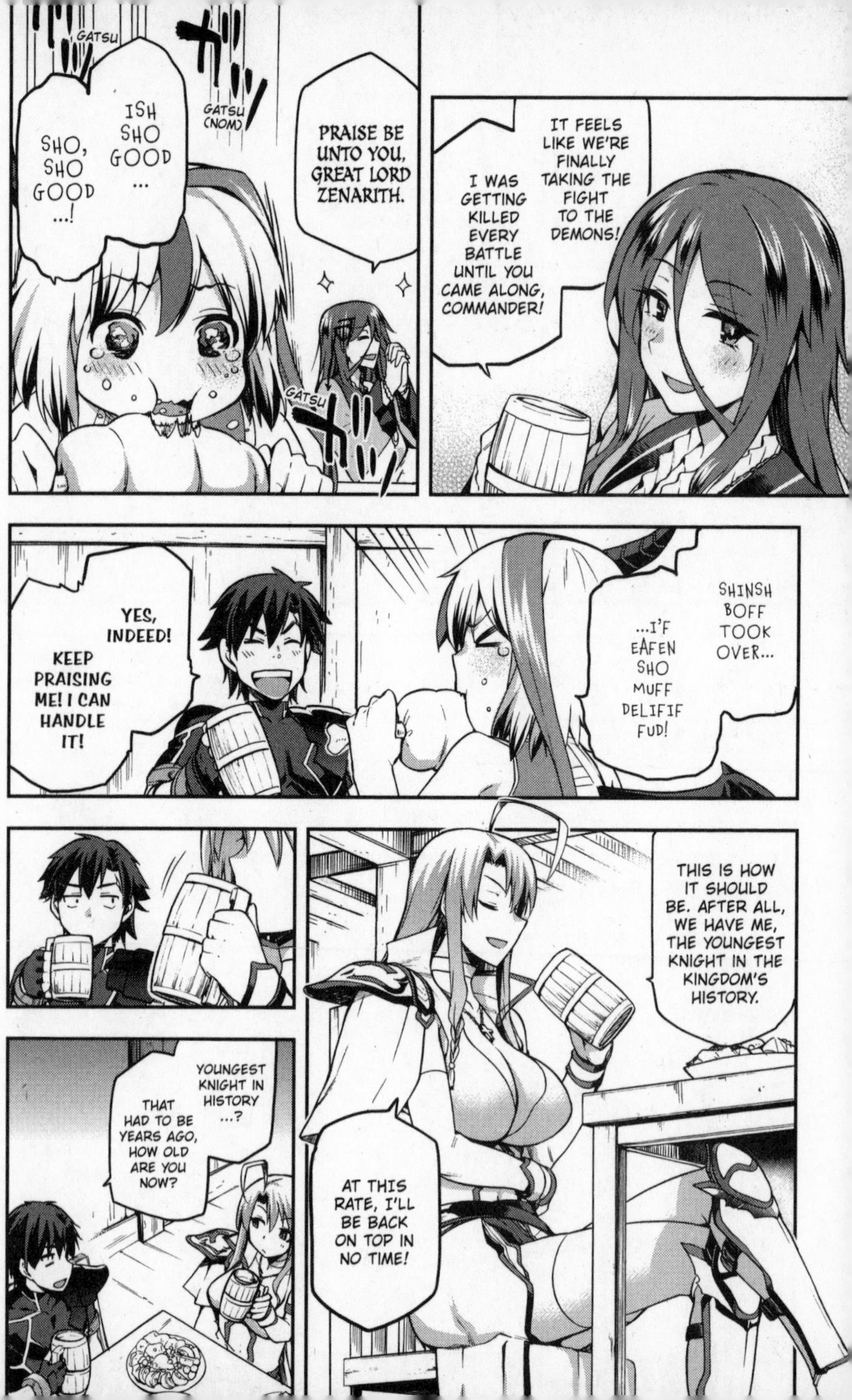
IT FEELS LIKE WE'RE FINALLY TAKING THE FIGHT TO THE DEMONS!
I WAS GETTING KILLED EVERY BATTLE UNTIL YOU CAME ALONG, COMMANDER!
PRAISE BE UNTO YOU, GREAT LORD ZENARITH.
GATSU (NOM)
ISH SHO GOOD...
GATSU
SHO, SHO GOOD...!
GATSU
SHINSH BOFF TOOK OVER...
...I'F EAFEN SHO MUFF DELIFIF FUD!
YES, INDEED!
KEEP PRAISING ME! I CAN HANDLE IT!
THIS IS HOW IT SHOULD BE. AFTER ALL, WE HAVE ME, THE YOUNGEST KNIGHT IN THE KINGDOM'S HISTORY.
AT THIS RATE, I'LL BE BACK ON TOP IN NO TIME!
YOUNGEST KNIGHT IN HISTORY ...?
THAT HAD TO BE YEARS AGO, HOW OLD ARE YOU NOW?

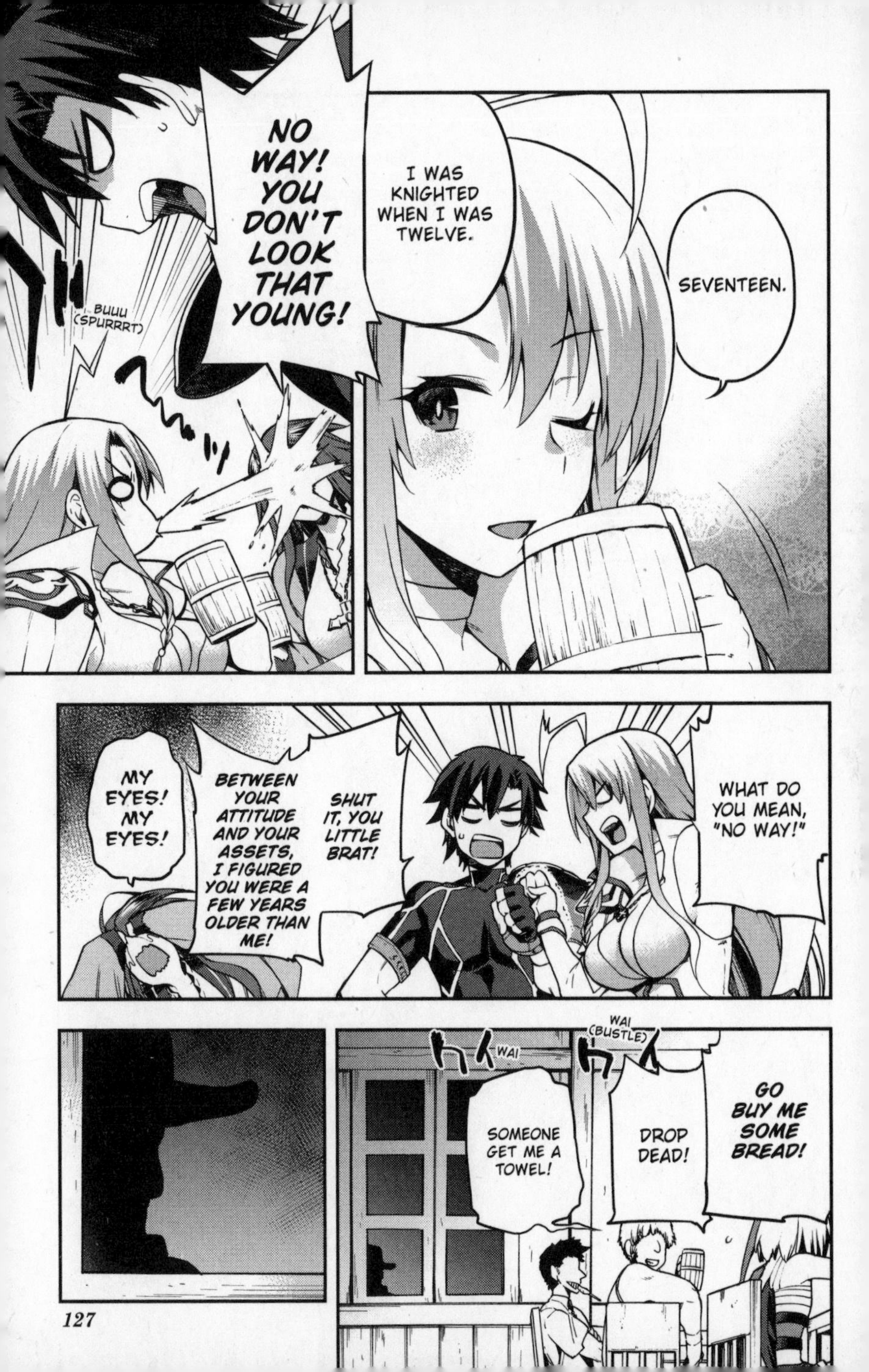
SEVENTEEN.
I WAS KNIGHTED WHEN I WAS TWELVE.
NO WAY! YOU DON'T LOOK THAT YOUNG!
BUUU (SPURRRT)
WHAT DO YOU MEAN, "NO WAY!"
SHUT IT, YOU LITTLE BRAT!
BETWEEN YOUR ATTITUDE AND YOUR ASSETS, I FIGURED YOU WERE A FEW YEARS OLDER THAN ME!
MY EYES! MY EYES!
WAI (BUSTLE)
WAI
GO BUY ME SOME BREAD!
DROP DEAD!
SOMEONE GET ME A TOWEL!

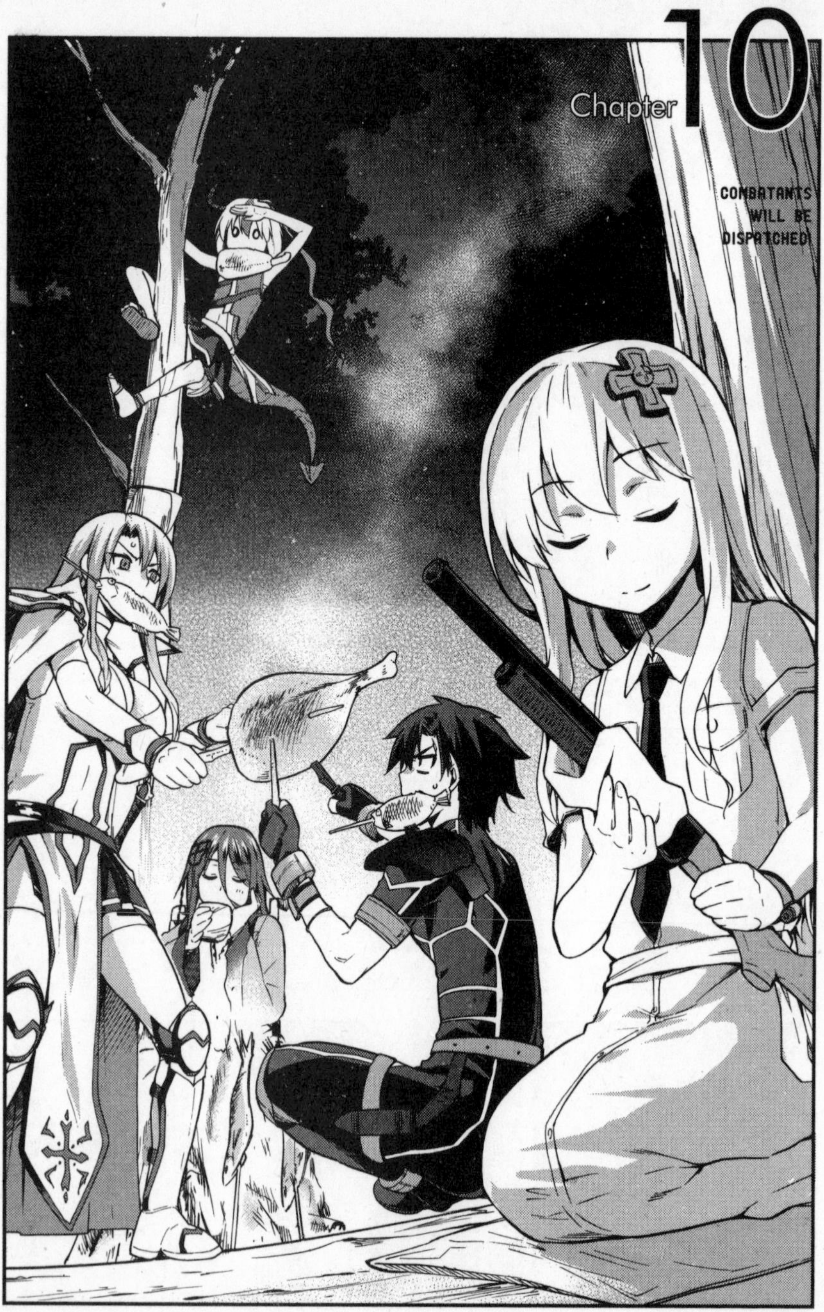
Chapter 10
COMBATANTS WILL BE DISPATCHED!

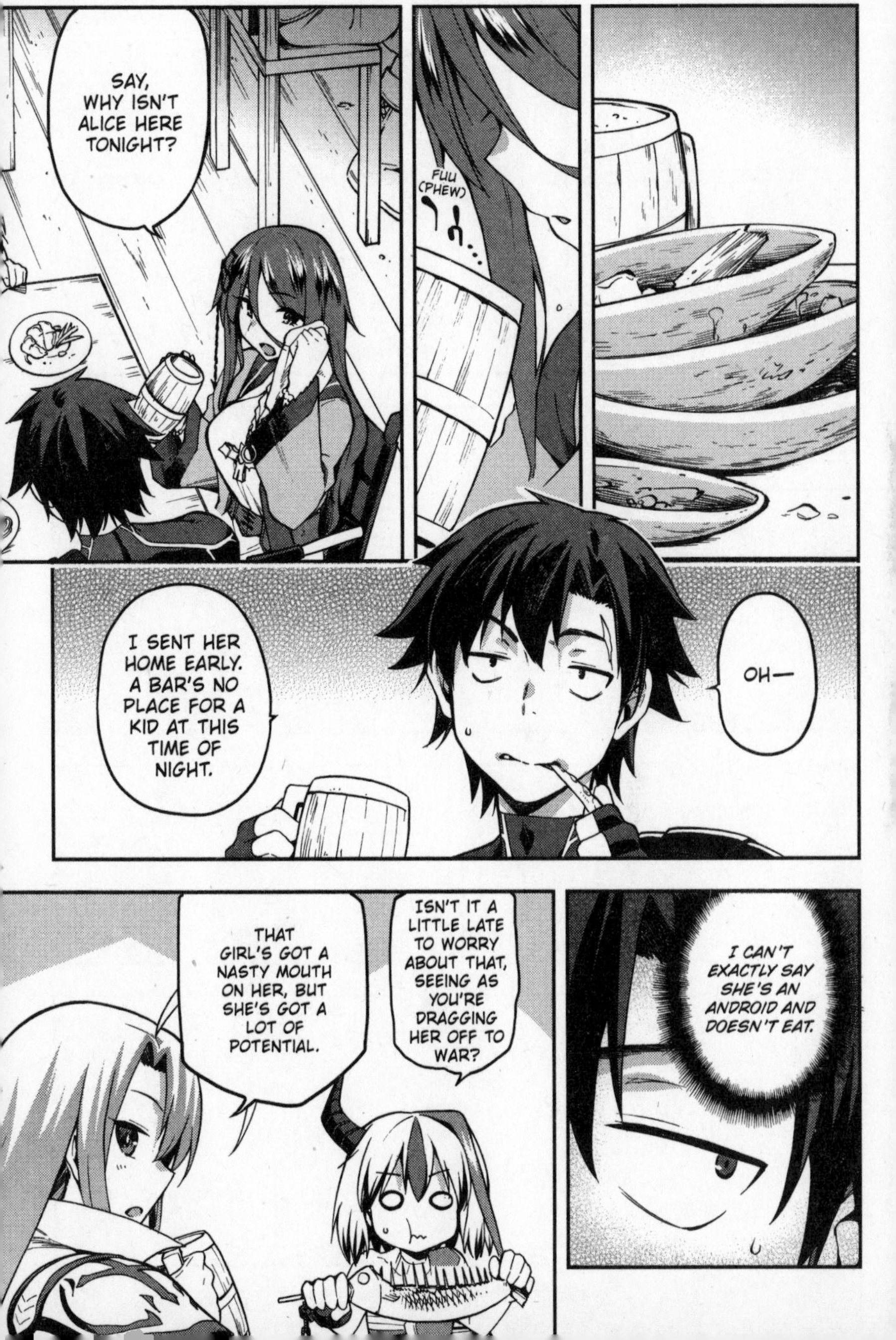

FUU (PHEW)
SAY, WHY ISN'T ALICE HERE TONIGHT?
OH—
I SENT HER HOME EARLY. A BAR'S NO PLACE FOR A KID AT THIS TIME OF NIGHT.
I CAN'T EXACTLY SAY SHE'S AN ANDROID AND DOESN'T EAT.
ISN'T IT A LITTLE LATE TO WORRY ABOUT THAT, SEEING AS YOU'RE DRAGGING HER OFF TO WAR?
THAT GIRL'S GOT A NASTY MOUTH ON HER, BUT SHE'S GOT A LOT OF POTENTIAL.

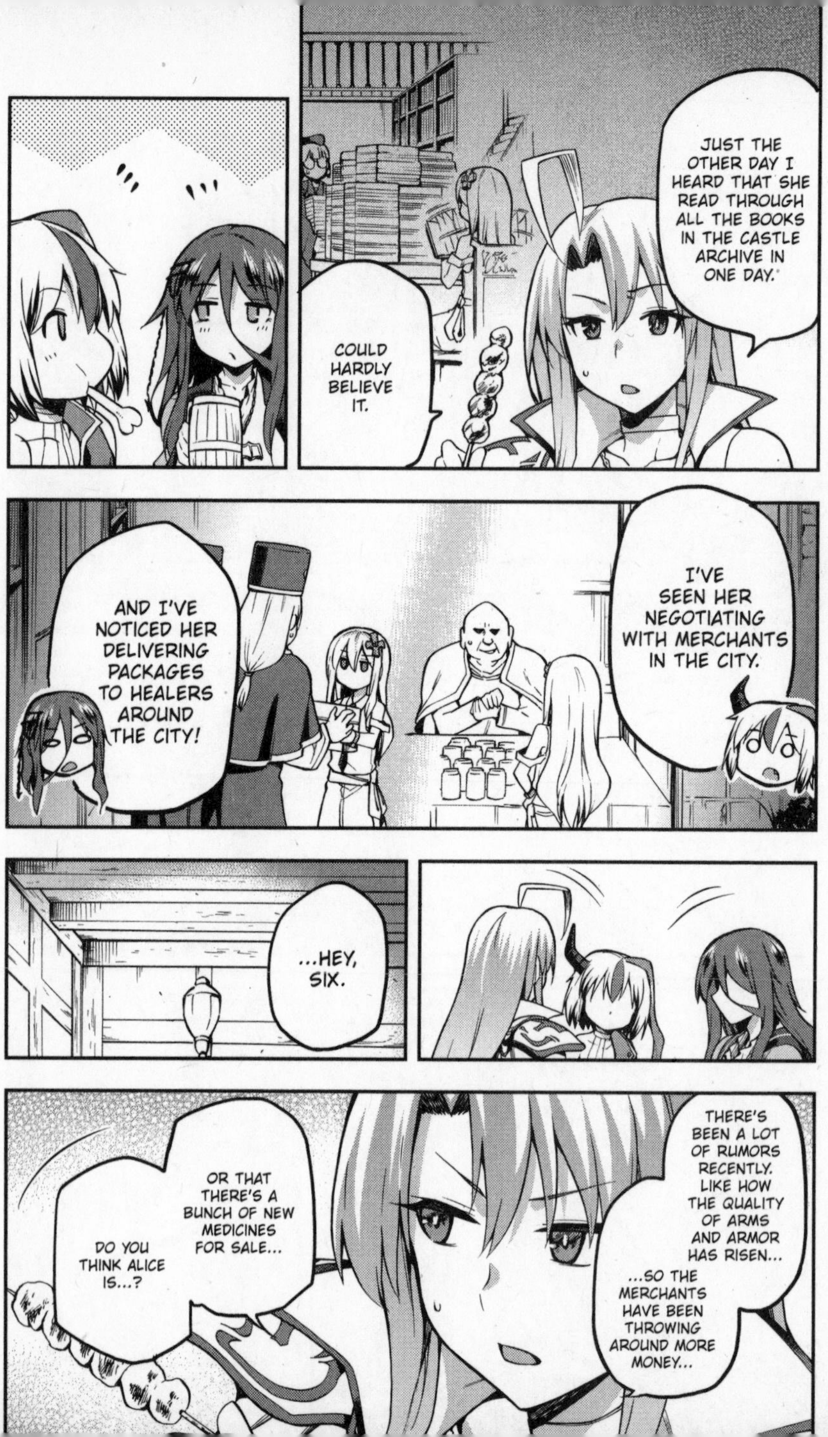
JUST THE OTHER DAY I HEARD THAT SHE READ THROUGH ALL THE BOOKS IN THE CASTLE ARCHIVE IN ONE DAY.
COULD HARDLY BELIEVE IT.
I'VE SEEN HER NEGOTIATING WITH MERCHANTS IN THE CITY.
AND I'VE NOTICED HER DELIVERING PACKAGES TO HEALERS AROUND THE CITY!
...HEY, SIX.
THERE'S BEEN A LOT OF RUMORS RECENTLY. LIKE HOW THE QUALITY OF ARMS AND ARMOR HAS RISEN...
...SO THE MERCHANTS HAVE BEEN THROWING AROUND MORE MONEY...
OR THAT THERE'S A BUNCH OF NEW MEDICINES FOR SALE...
DO YOU THINK ALICE IS...?

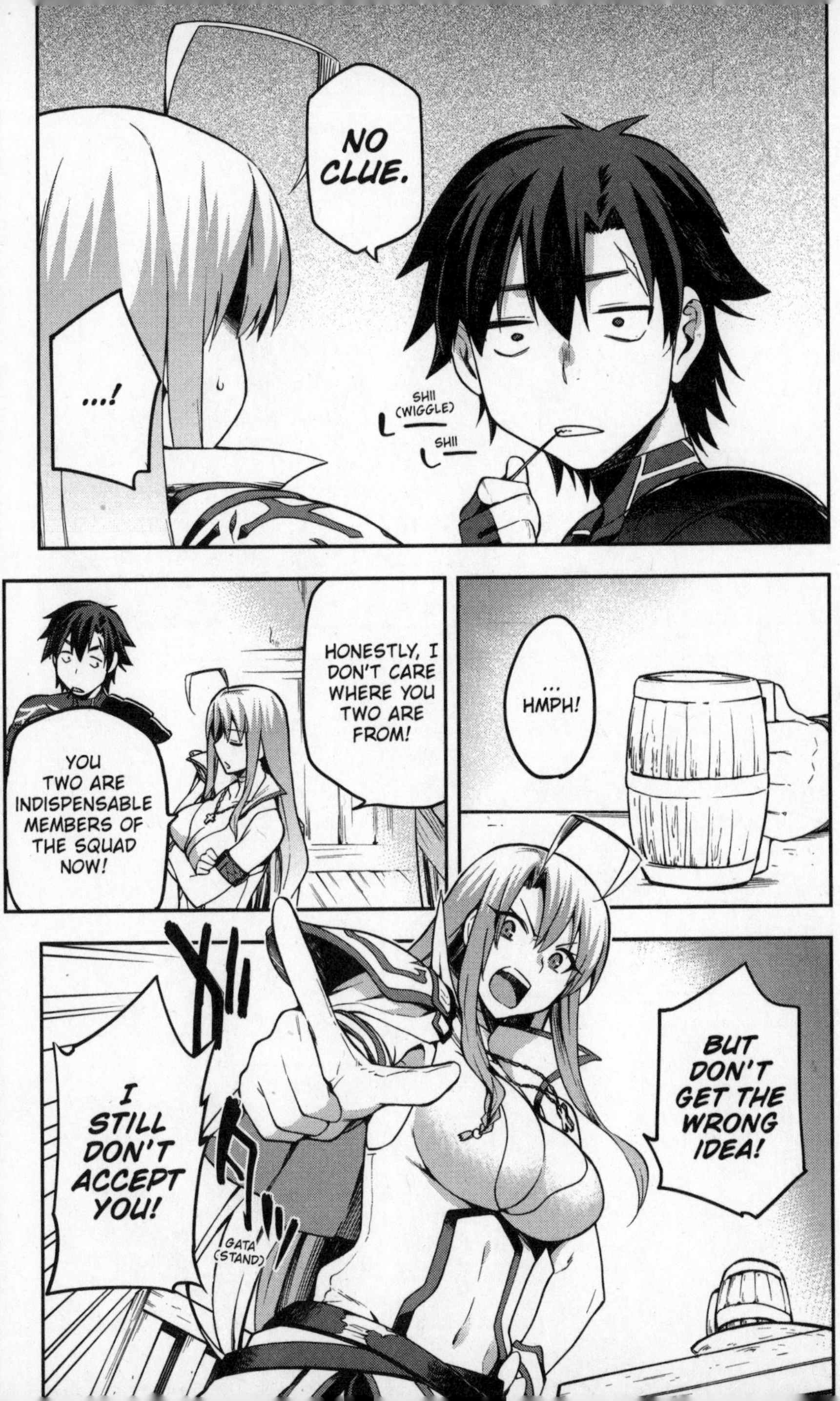
NO CLUE.
SHII (WIGGLE)
SHII
...!
... HMPH!
HONESTLY, I DON'T CARE WHERE YOU TWO ARE FROM!
YOU TWO ARE INDISPENSABLE MEMBERS OF THE SQUAD NOW!
BUT DON'T GET THE WRONG IDEA!
I STILL DON'T ACCEPT YOU!
GATA (STAND)

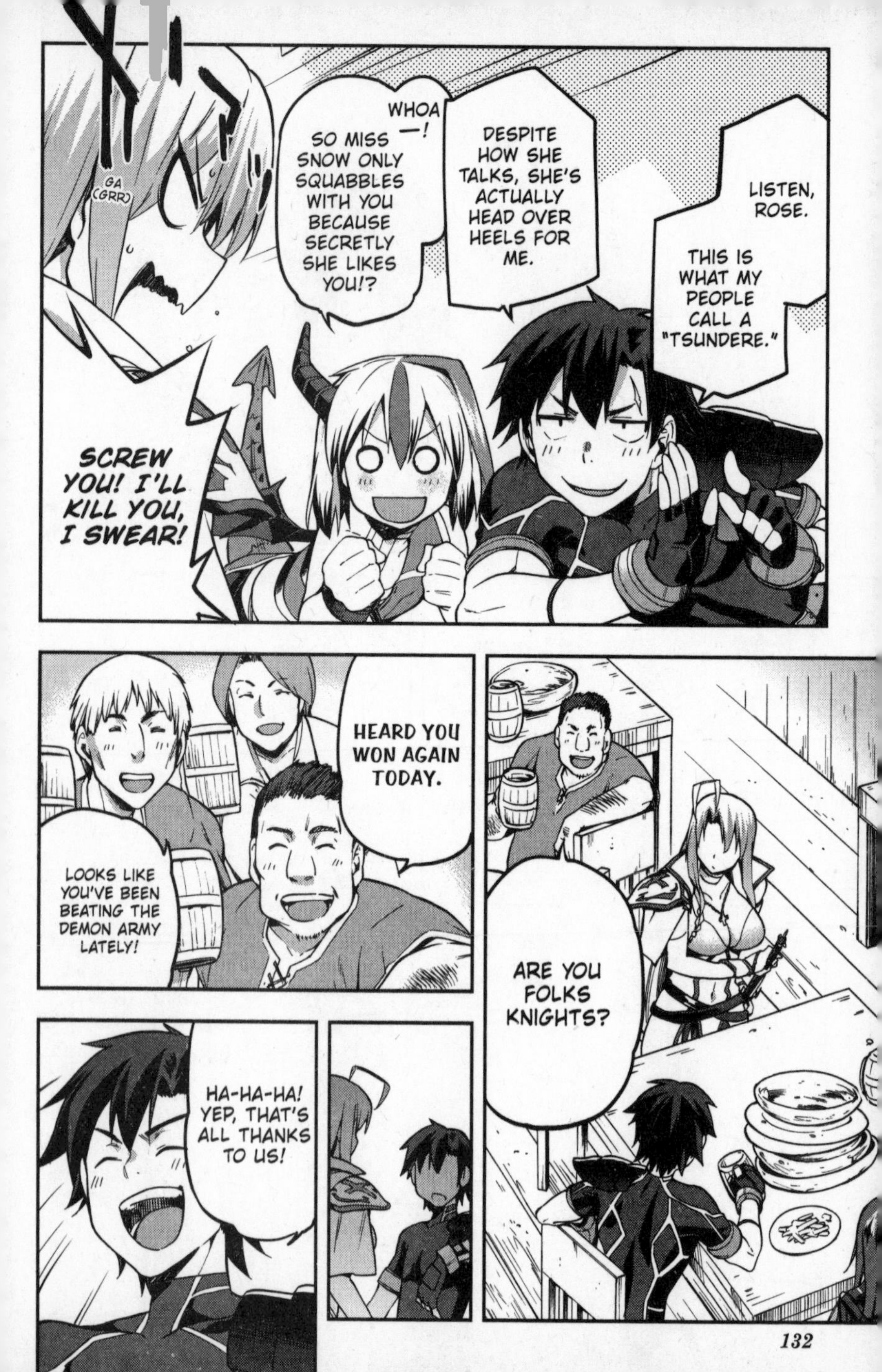
LISTEN, ROSE.
THIS IS WHAT MY PEOPLE CALL A "TSUNDERE."
DESPITE HOW SHE TALKS, SHE'S ACTUALLY HEAD OVER HEELS FOR ME.
WHOA—!
SO MISS SNOW ONLY SQUABBLES WITH YOU BECAUSE SECRETLY SHE LIKES YOU!?
GA (GRR)
SCREW YOU! I'LL KILL YOU, I SWEAR!
ARE YOU FOLKS KNIGHTS?
HEARD YOU WON AGAIN TODAY.
LOOKS LIKE YOU'VE BEEN BEATING THE DEMON ARMY LATELY!
HA-HA-HA! YEP, THAT'S ALL THANKS TO US!

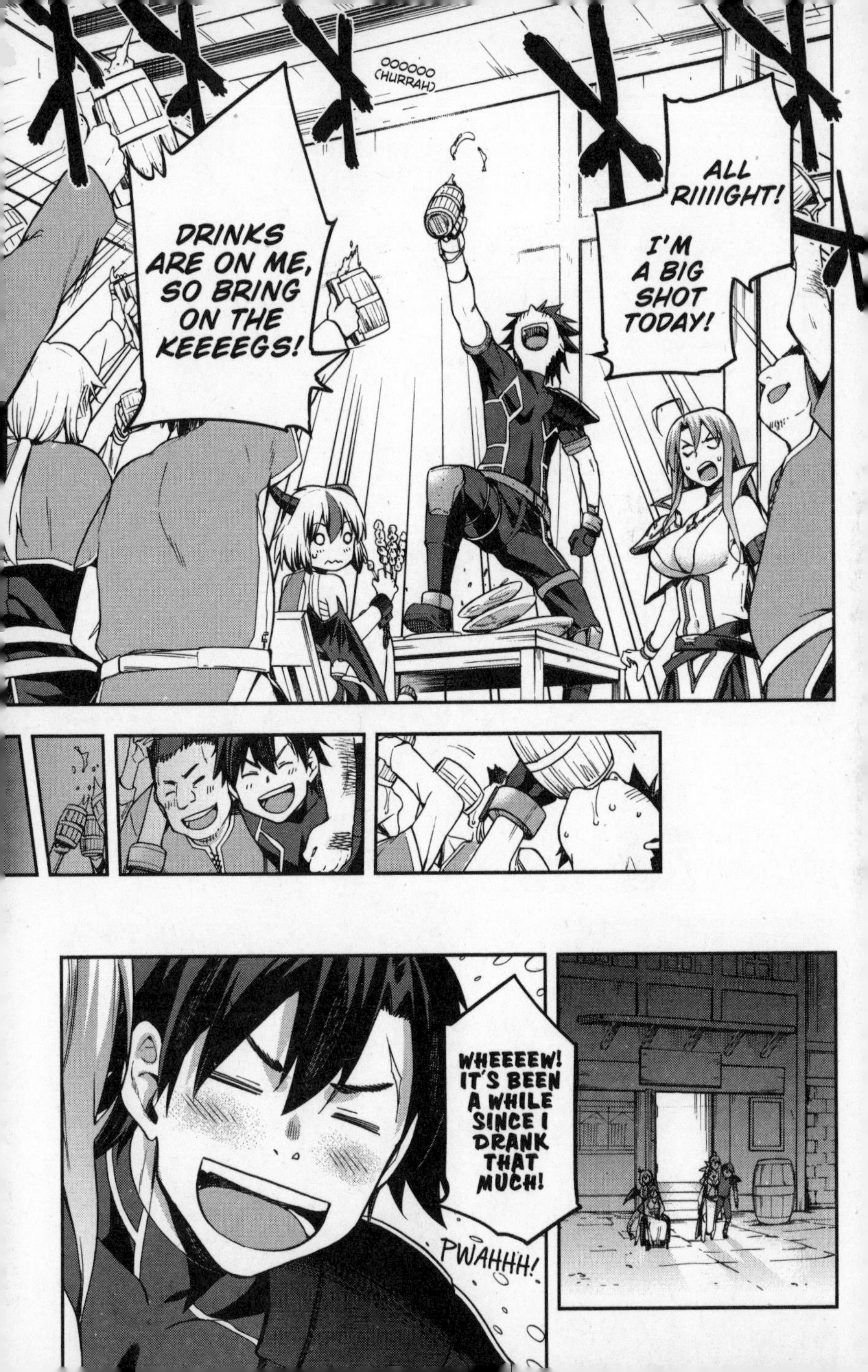
ALL RIIIIGHT!
I'M A BIG SHOT TODAY!
DRINKS ARE ON ME, SO BRING ON THE KEEEEGS!
OOOOOO (HURRAH)
WHEEEEW! IT'S BEEN A WHILE SINCE I DRANK THAT MUCH!
PWAHHH!

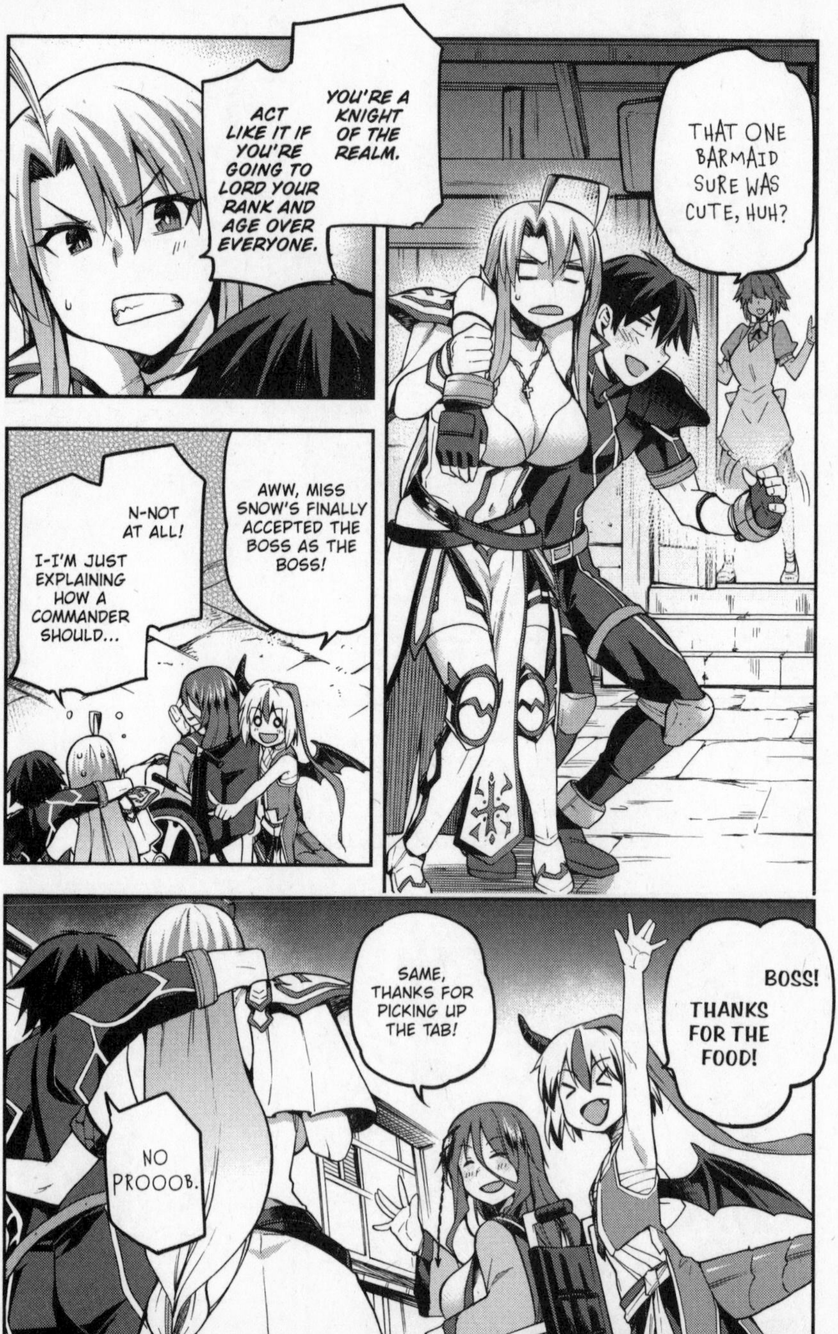
THAT ONE BARMAID SURE WAS CUTE, HUH?
YOU'RE A KNIGHT OF THE REALM.
ACT LIKE IT IF YOU'RE GOING TO LORD YOUR RANK AND AGE OVER EVERYONE.
AWW, MISS SNOW'S FINALLY ACCEPTED THE BOSS AS THE BOSS!
N-NOT AT ALL!
I-I'M JUST EXPLAINING HOW A COMMANDER SHOULD...
BOSS!
THANKS FOR THE FOOD!
SAME, THANKS FOR PICKING UP THE TAB!
NO PROOOB.

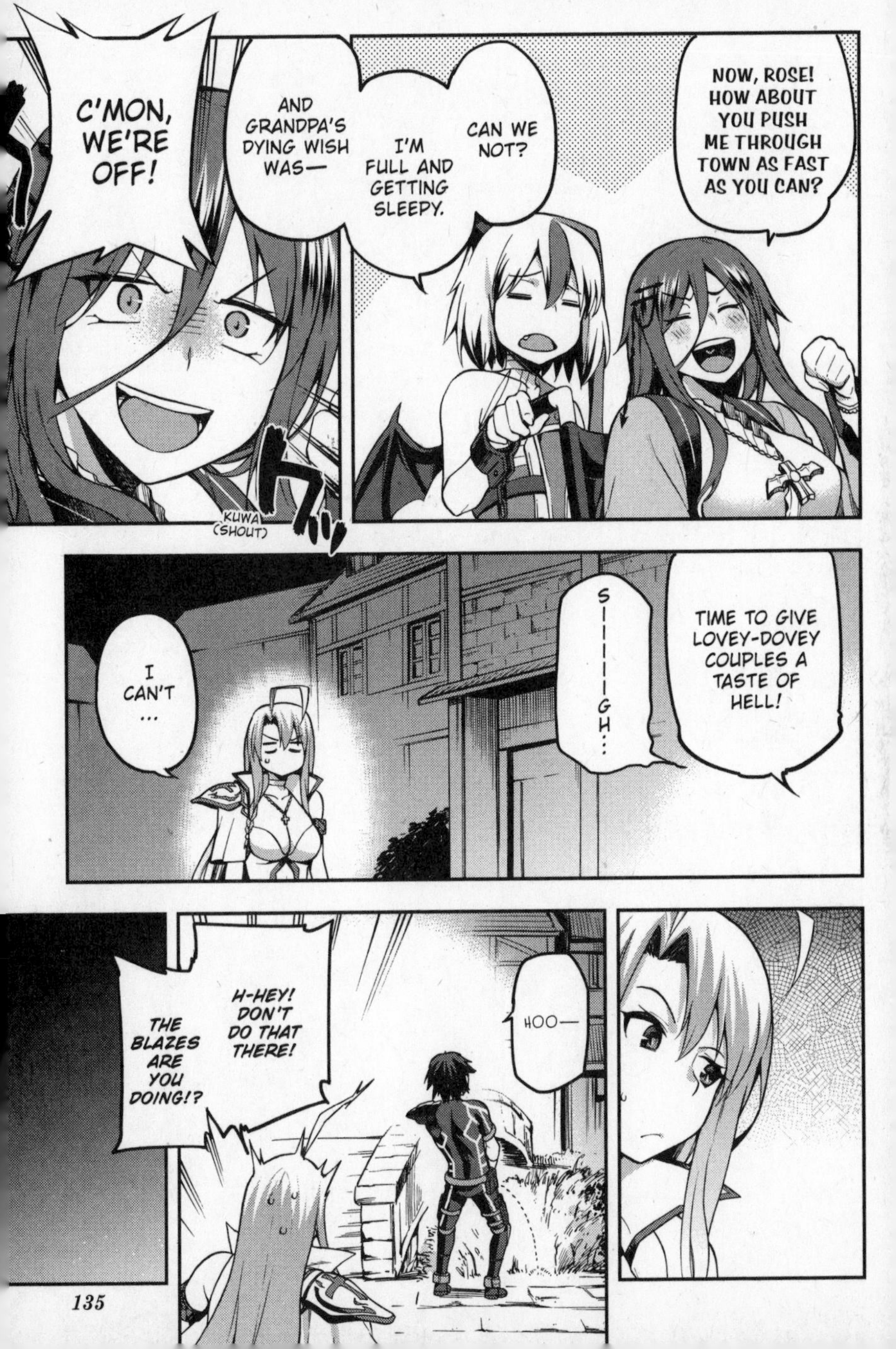
NOW, ROSE! HOW ABOUT YOU PUSH ME THROUGH TOWN AS FAST AS YOU CAN?
CAN WE NOT?
I'M FULL AND GETTING SLEEPY.
AND GRANDPA'S DYING WISH WAS—
C'MON, WE'RE OFF!
KUWA (SHOUT)
TIME TO GIVE LOVEY-DOVEY COUPLES A TASTE OF HELL!
S-I-I-I-G-H...
I CAN'T ...
HOO—
H-HEY! DON'T DO THAT THERE!
THE BLAZES ARE YOU DOING!?

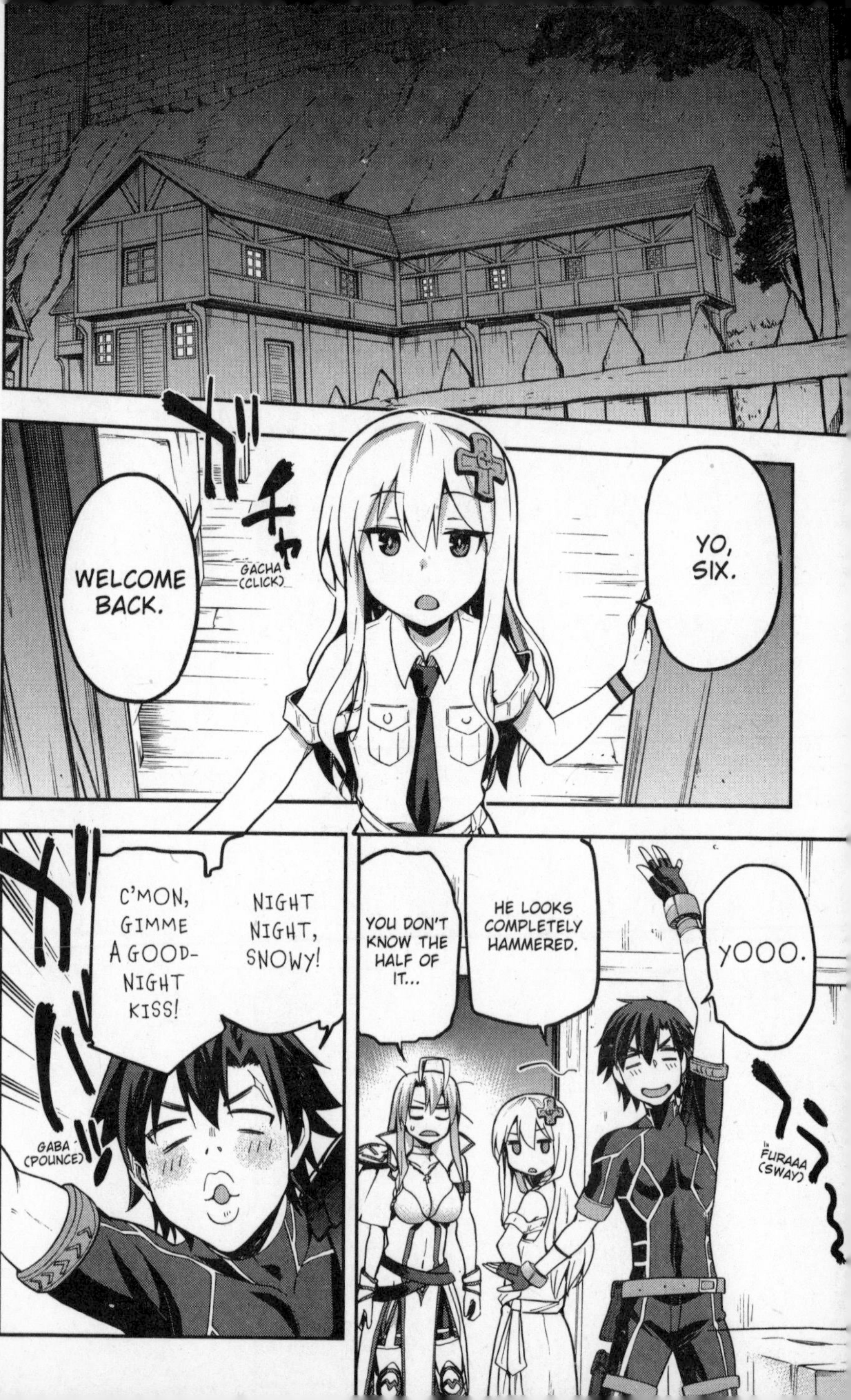
YO, SIX.
GACHA (CLICK)
WELCOME BACK.
YOOO.
FURAAA (SWAY)
HE LOOKS COMPLETELY HAMMERED.
YOU DON'T KNOW THE HALF OF IT...
NIGHT NIGHT, SNOWY!
C'MON, GIMME A GOOD-NIGHT KISS!
GABA (POUNCE)

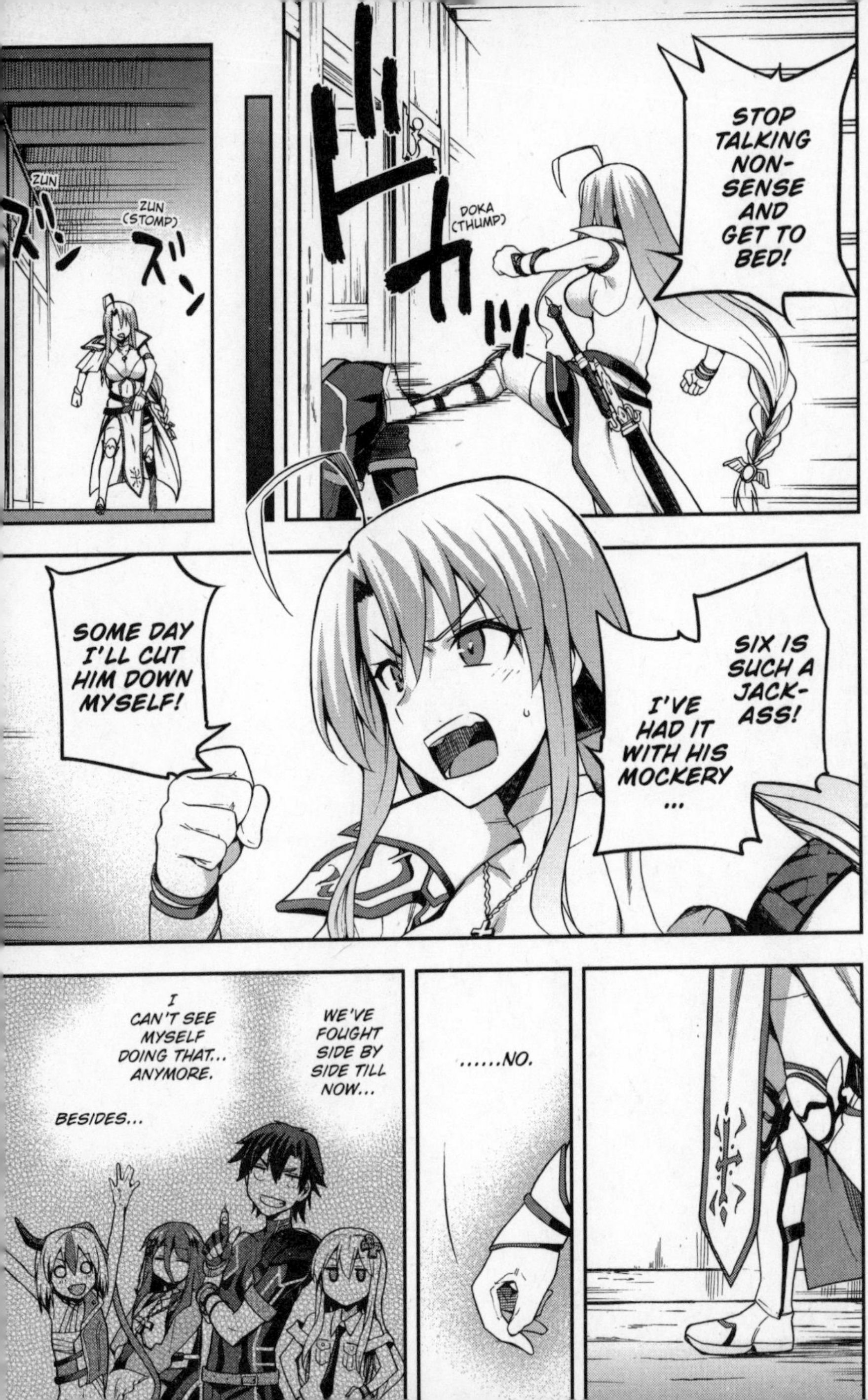
STOP TALKING NON-SENSE AND GET TO BED!
DOKA (THUMP)
ZUN (STOMP)
ZUN
SIX IS SUCH A JACK-ASS!
I'VE HAD IT WITH HIS MOCKERY ...
SOME DAY I'LL CUT HIM DOWN MYSELF!
......NO.
WE'VE FOUGHT SIDE BY SIDE TILL NOW...
I CAN'T SEE MYSELF DOING THAT... ANYMORE.
BESIDES...

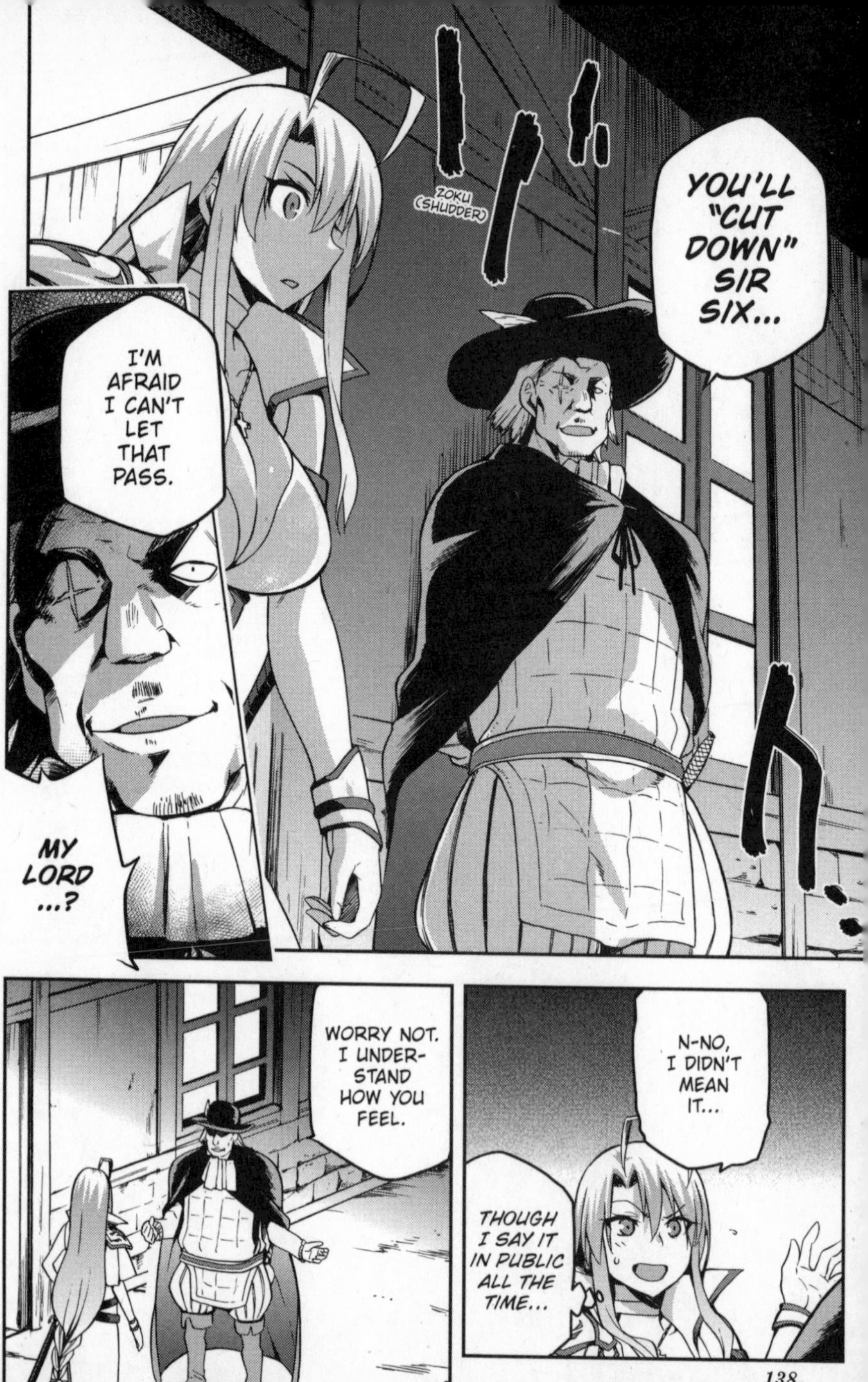

YOU'LL "CUT DOWN" SIR SIX...
ZOKU (SHUDDER)
I'M AFRAID I CAN'T LET THAT PASS.
MY LORD ...?
N-NO, I DIDN'T MEAN IT...
THOUGH I SAY IT IN PUBLIC ALL THE TIME...
WORRY NOT. I UNDER-STAND HOW YOU FEEL.
...

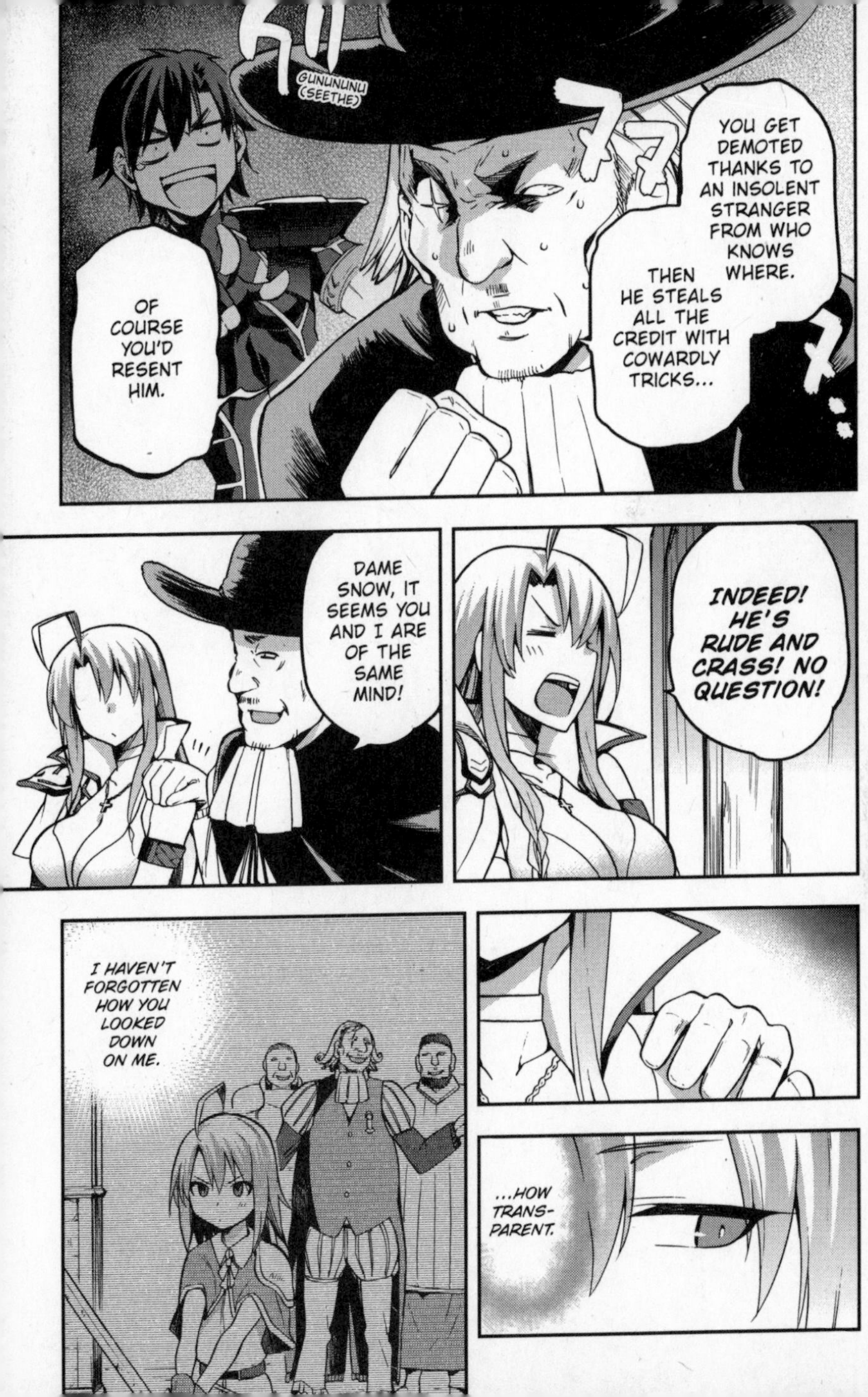
YOU GET DEMOTED THANKS TO AN INSOLENT STRANGER FROM WHO KNOWS WHERE.
THEN HE STEALS ALL THE CREDIT WITH COWARDLY TRICKS...
GUNUNUNU (SEETHE)
OF COURSE YOU'D RESENT HIM.
INDEED! HE'S RUDE AND CRASS! NO QUESTION!
DAME SNOW, IT SEEMS YOU AND I ARE OF THE SAME MIND!
...HOW TRANS-PARENT.
I HAVEN'T FORGOTTEN HOW YOU LOOKED DOWN ON ME.

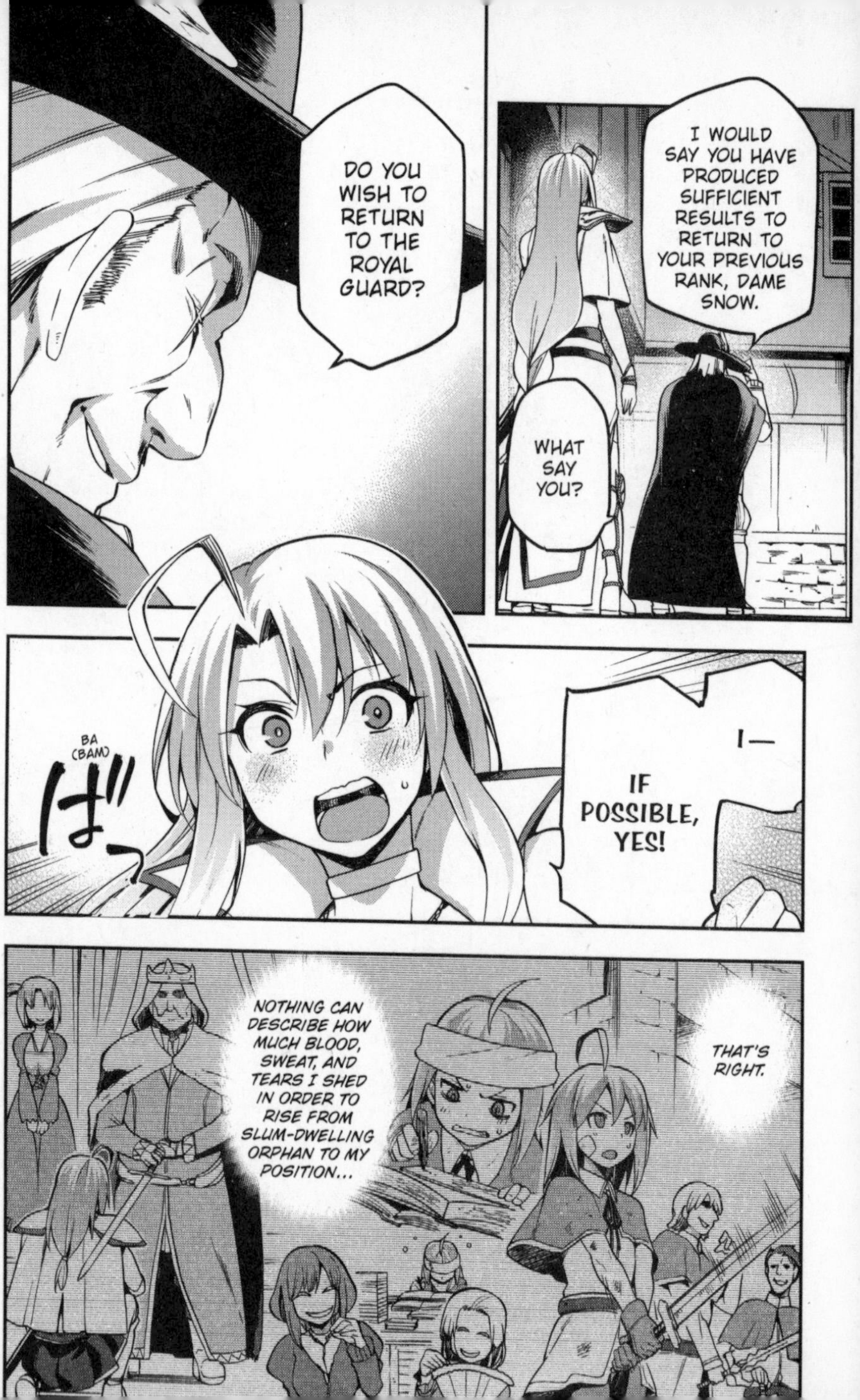
I WOULD SAY YOU HAVE PRODUCED SUFFICIENT RESULTS TO RETURN TO YOUR PREVIOUS RANK, DAME SNOW.
WHAT SAY YOU?
DO YOU WISH TO RETURN TO THE ROYAL GUARD?
I—
IF POSSIBLE, YES!
BA (BAM)
ばっ
THAT'S RIGHT.
NOTHING CAN DESCRIBE HOW MUCH BLOOD, SWEAT, AND TEARS I SHED IN ORDER TO RISE FROM SLUM-DWELLING ORPHAN TO MY POSITION...

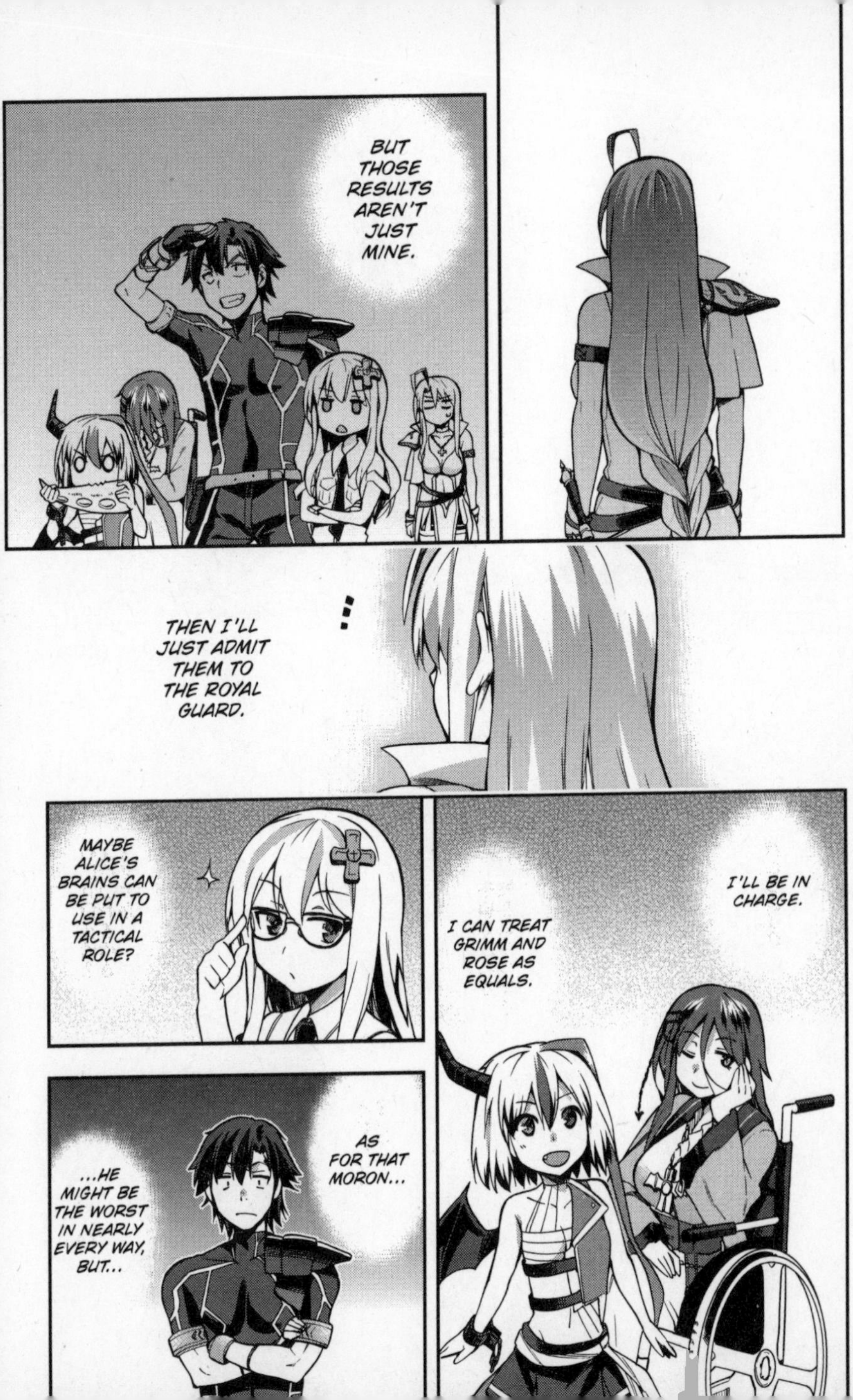
BUT THOSE RESULTS AREN'T JUST MINE.
!
THEN I'LL JUST ADMIT THEM TO THE ROYAL GUARD.
I'LL BE IN CHARGE.
I CAN TREAT GRIMM AND ROSE AS EQUALS.
MAYBE ALICE'S BRAINS CAN BE PUT TO USE IN A TACTICAL ROLE?
AS FOR THAT MORON...
...HE MIGHT BE THE WORST IN NEARLY EVERY WAY, BUT...

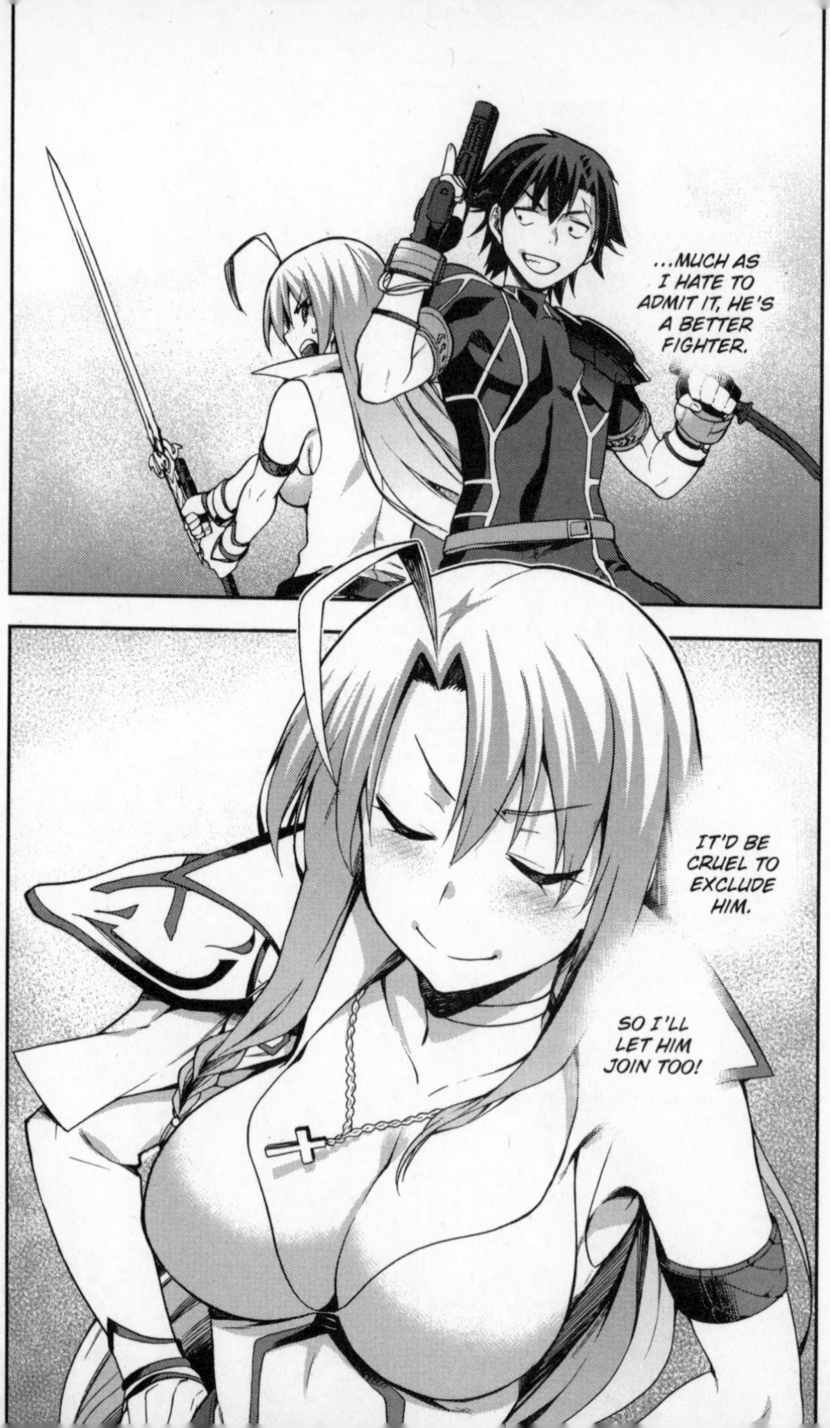
...MUCH AS I HATE TO ADMIT IT, HE'S A BETTER FIGHTER.
IT'D BE CRUEL TO EXCLUDE HIM.
SO I'LL LET HIM JOIN TOO!

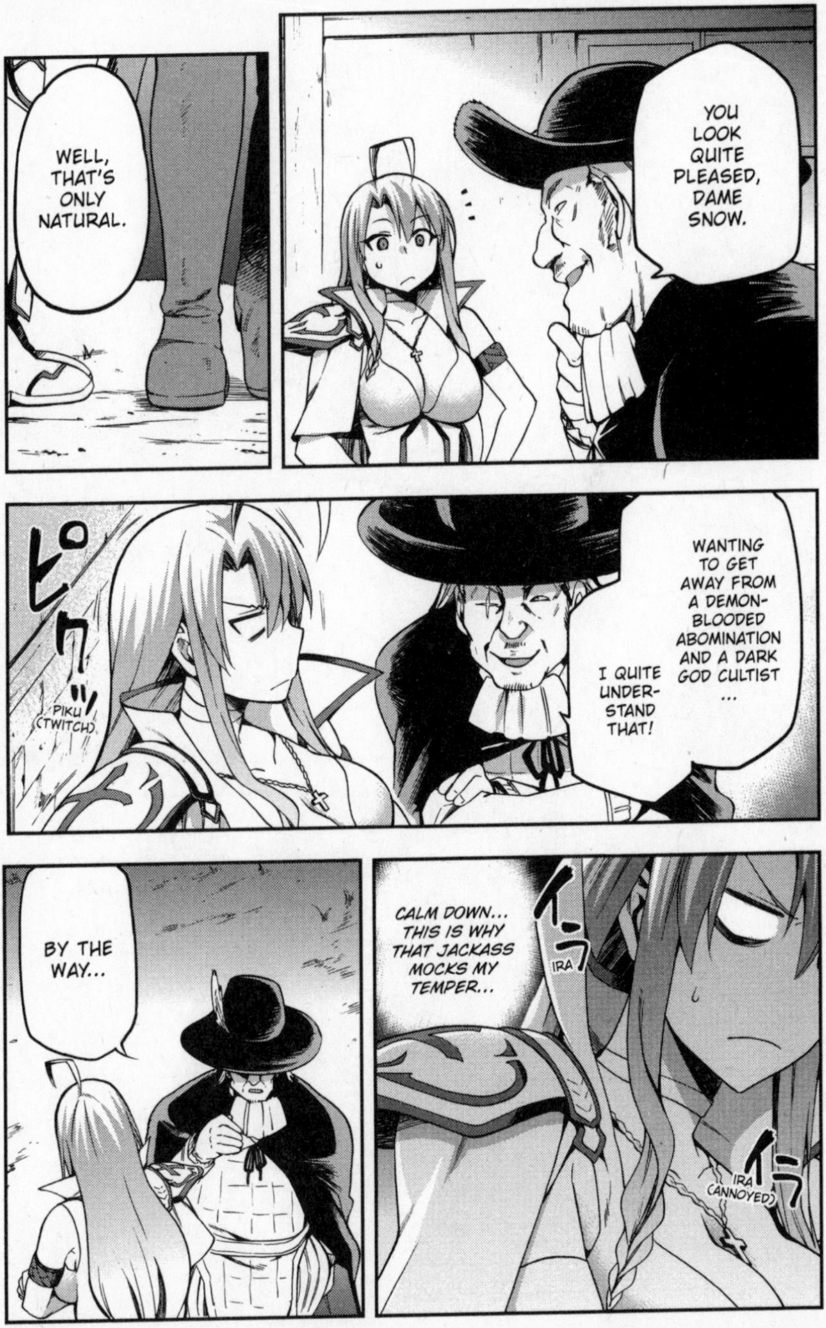
YOU LOOK QUITE PLEASED, DAME SNOW.
WELL, THAT'S ONLY NATURAL.
WANTING TO GET AWAY FROM A DEMON-BLOODED ABOMINATION AND A DARK GOD CULTIST ...
I QUITE UNDER-STAND THAT!
PIKU (TWITCH)
IRA
CALM DOWN... THIS IS WHY THAT JACKASS MOCKS MY TEMPER...
IRA (ANNOYED)
BY THE WAY...

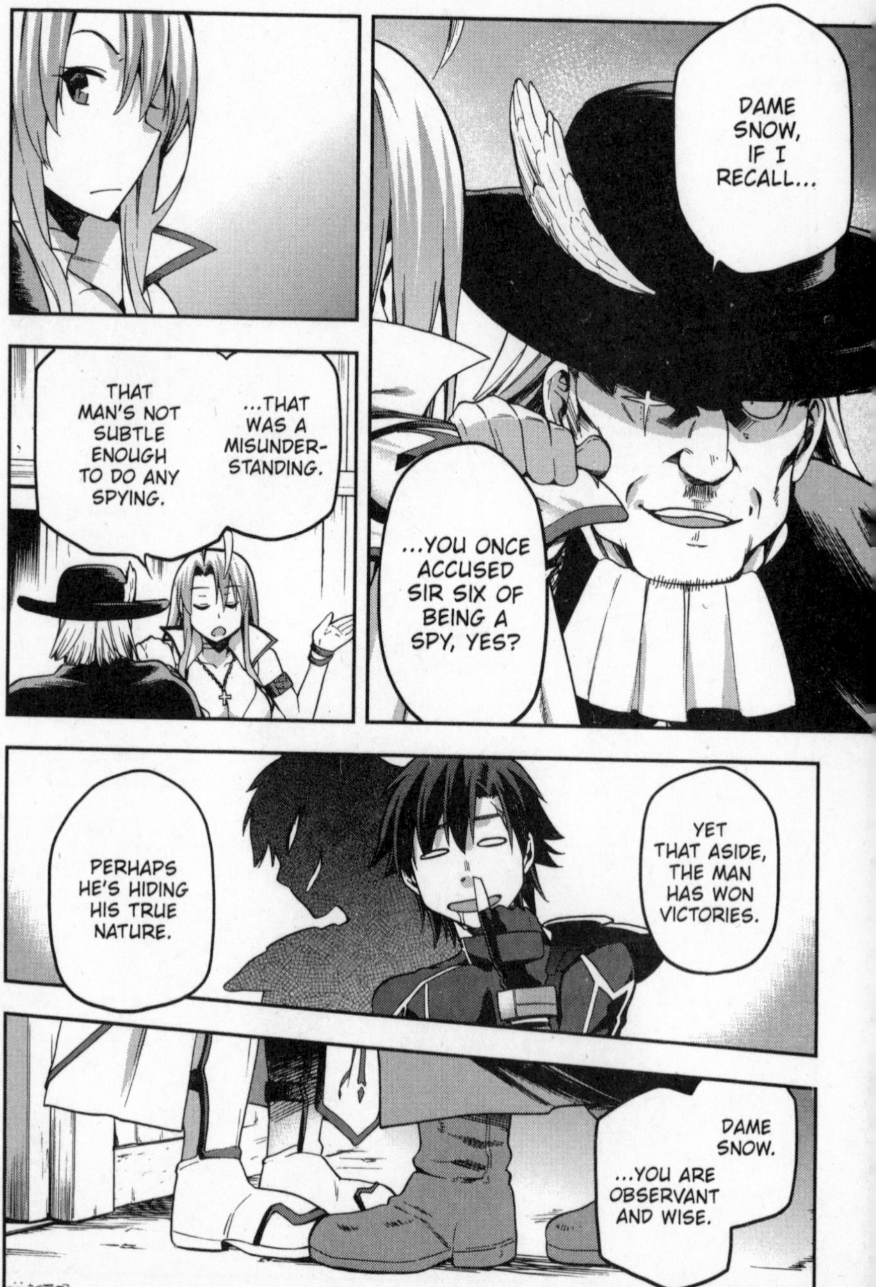
DAME SNOW, IF I RECALL...
...YOU ONCE ACCUSED SIR SIX OF BEING A SPY, YES?
...THAT WAS A MISUNDER-STANDING.
THAT MAN'S NOT SUBTLE ENOUGH TO DO ANY SPYING.
YET THAT ASIDE, THE MAN HAS WON VICTORIES.
PERHAPS HE'S HIDING HIS TRUE NATURE.
DAME SNOW.
...YOU ARE OBSERVANT AND WISE.

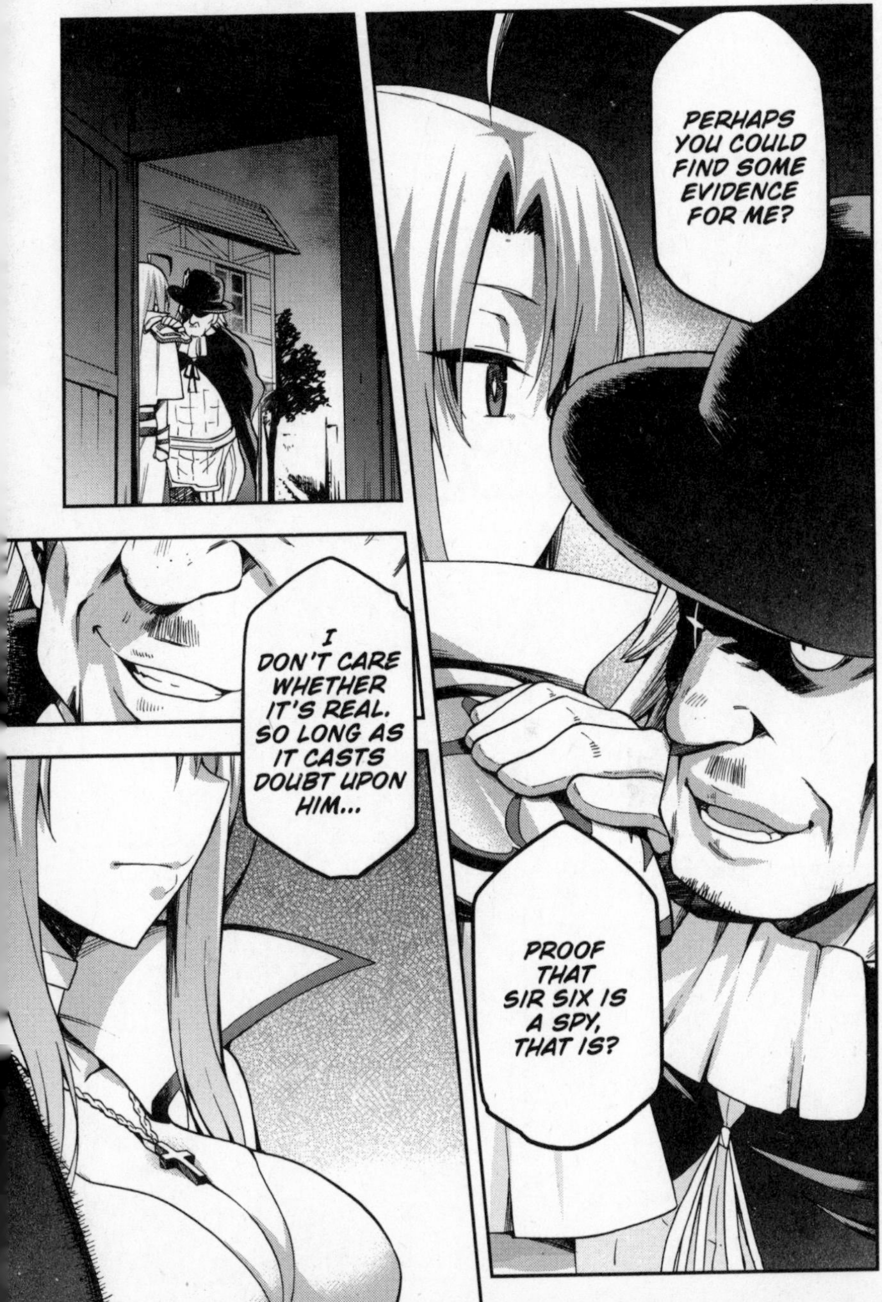
PERHAPS YOU COULD FIND SOME EVIDENCE FOR ME?
PROOF THAT SIR SIX IS A SPY, THAT IS?
I DON'T CARE WHETHER IT'S REAL. SO LONG AS IT CASTS DOUBT UPON HIM...

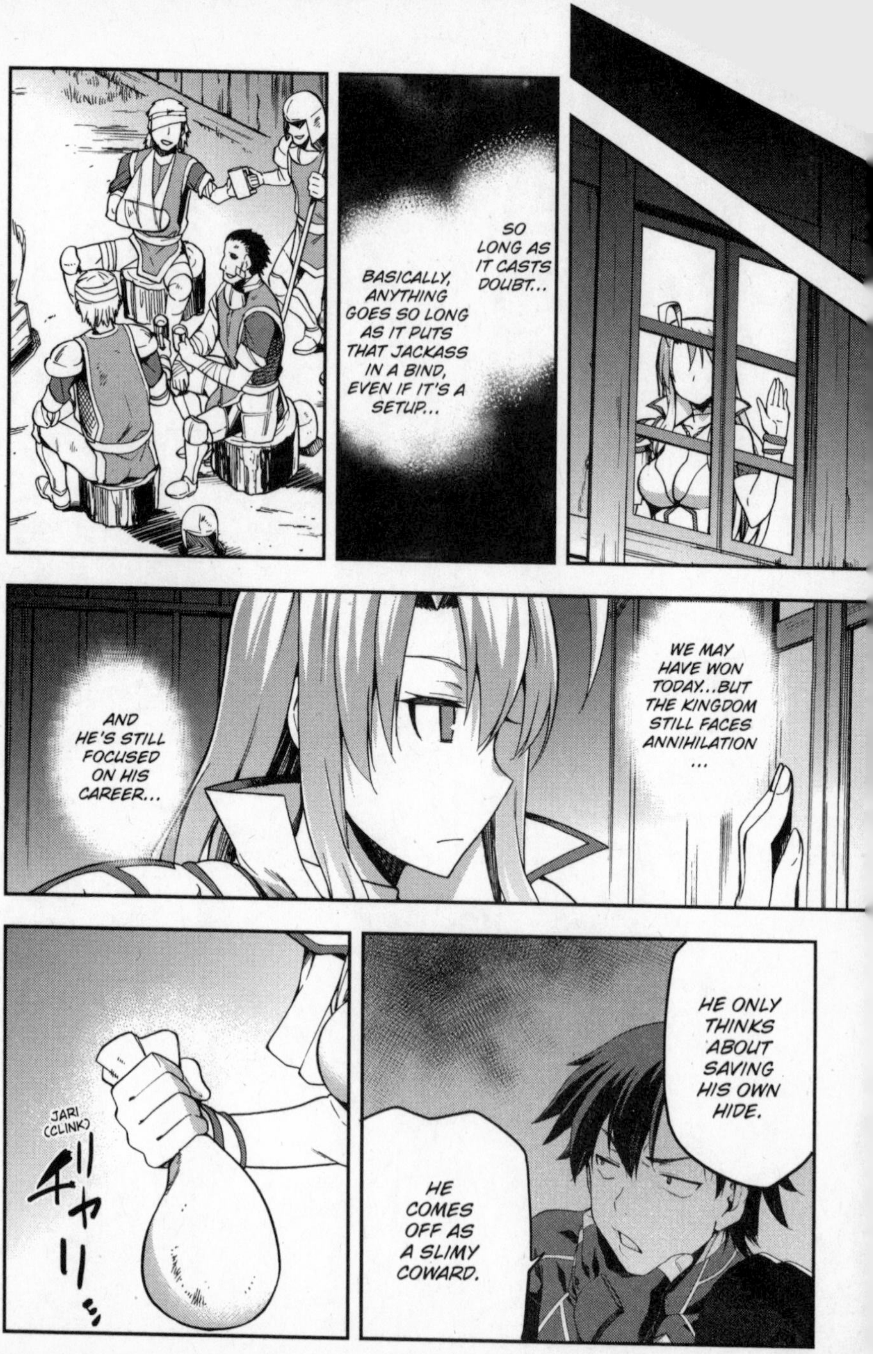
SO LONG AS IT CASTS DOUBT...
BASICALLY, ANYTHING GOES SO LONG AS IT PUTS THAT JACKASS IN A BIND, EVEN IF IT'S A SETUP...
WE MAY HAVE WON TODAY...BUT THE KINGDOM STILL FACES ANNIHILATION...
AND HE'S STILL FOCUSED ON HIS CAREER...
HE ONLY THINKS ABOUT SAVING HIS OWN HIDE.
HE COMES OFF AS A SLIMY COWARD.
JARI (CLINK)
ジャリッ

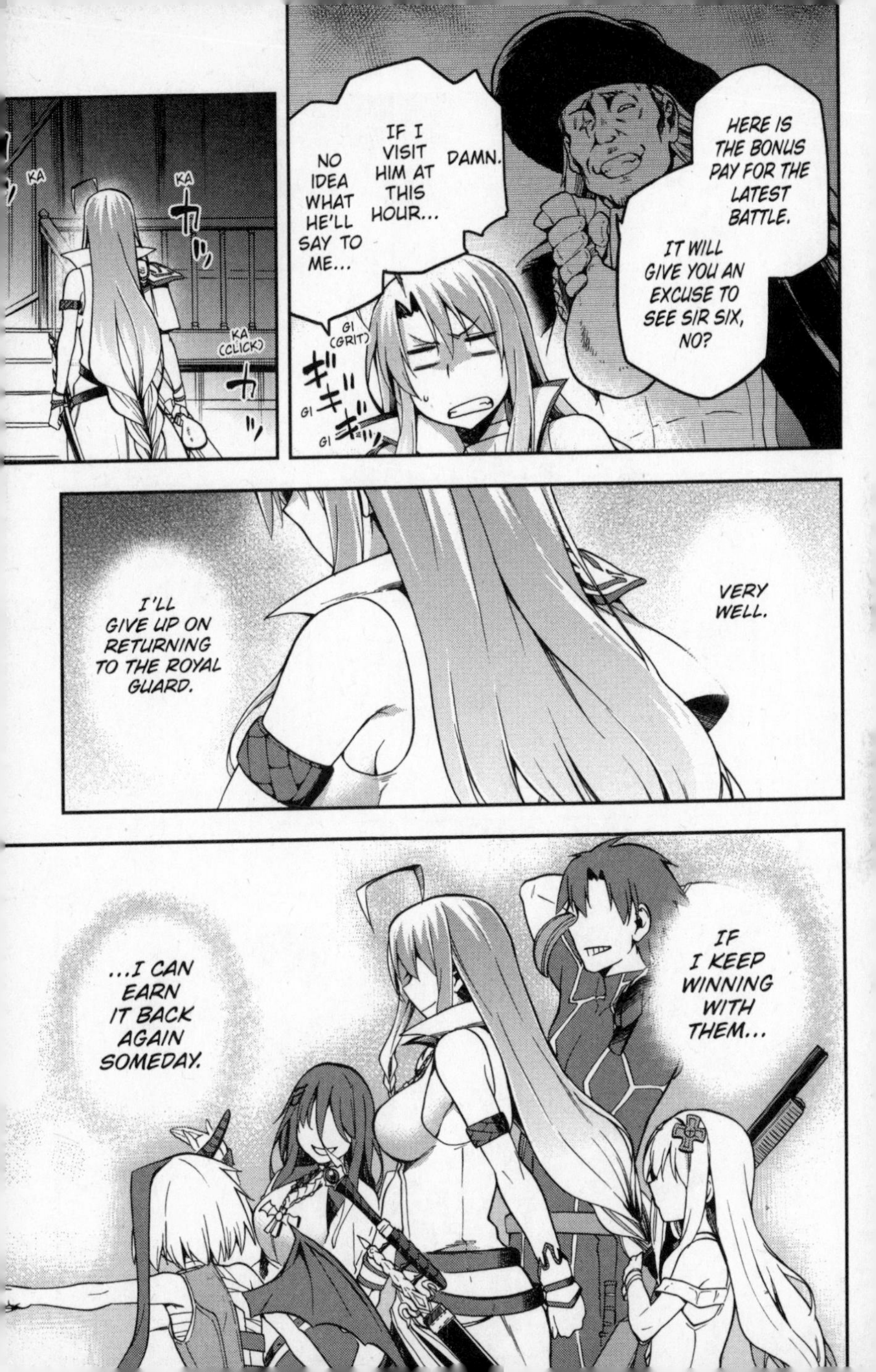
HERE IS THE BONUS PAY FOR THE LATEST BATTLE.
IT WILL GIVE YOU AN EXCUSE TO SEE SIR SIX, NO?
DAMN.
IF I VISIT HIM AT THIS HOUR...
NO IDEA WHAT HE'LL SAY TO ME...
GI (GRIT)
GI
GI
KA
KA
KA (CLICK)
VERY WELL.
I'LL GIVE UP ON RETURNING TO THE ROYAL GUARD.
IF I KEEP WINNING WITH THEM...
...I CAN EARN IT BACK AGAIN SOMEDAY.

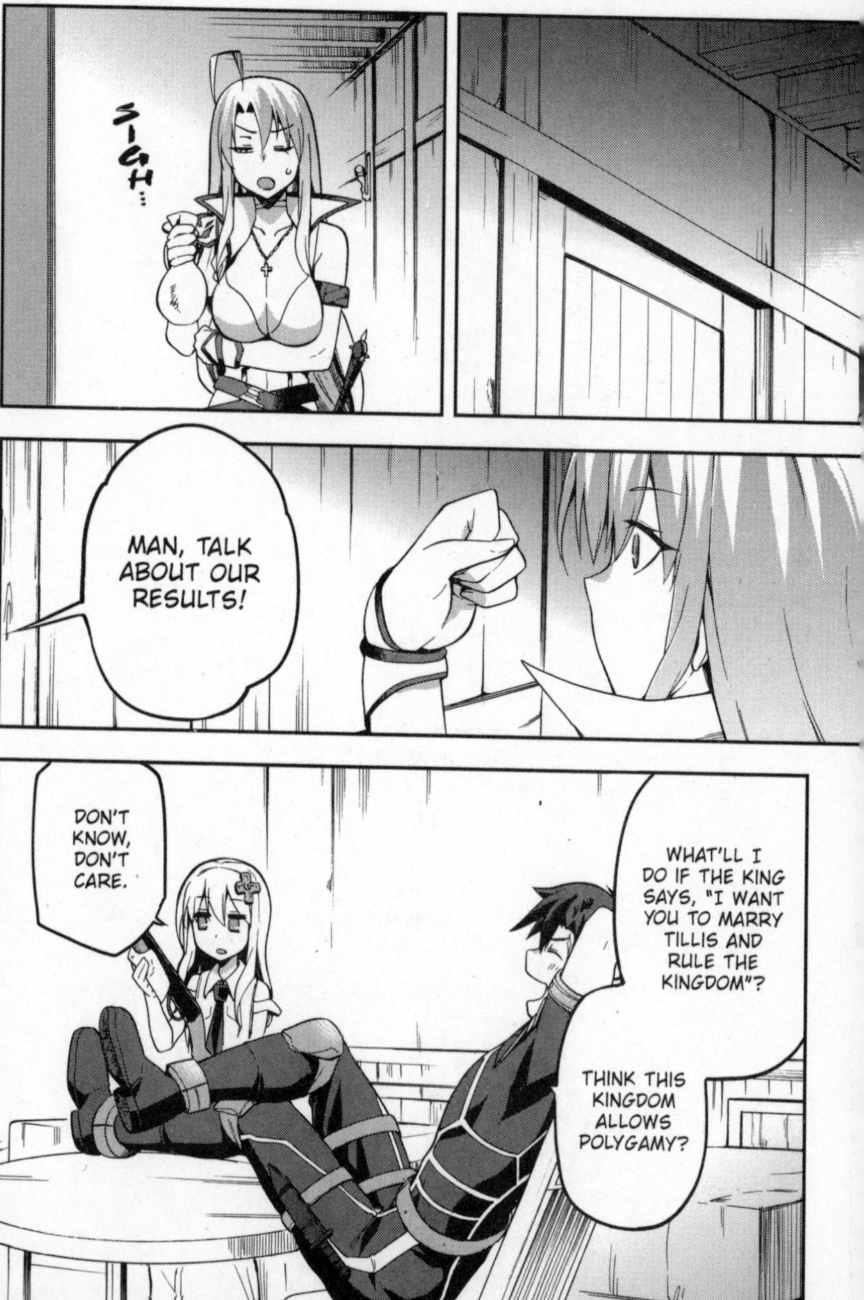
SIGH...
MAN, TALK ABOUT OUR RESULTS!
WHAT'LL I DO IF THE KING SAYS, "I WANT YOU TO MARRY TILLIS AND RULE THE KINGDOM"?
THINK THIS KINGDOM ALLOWS POLYGAMY?
DON'T KNOW, DON'T CARE.

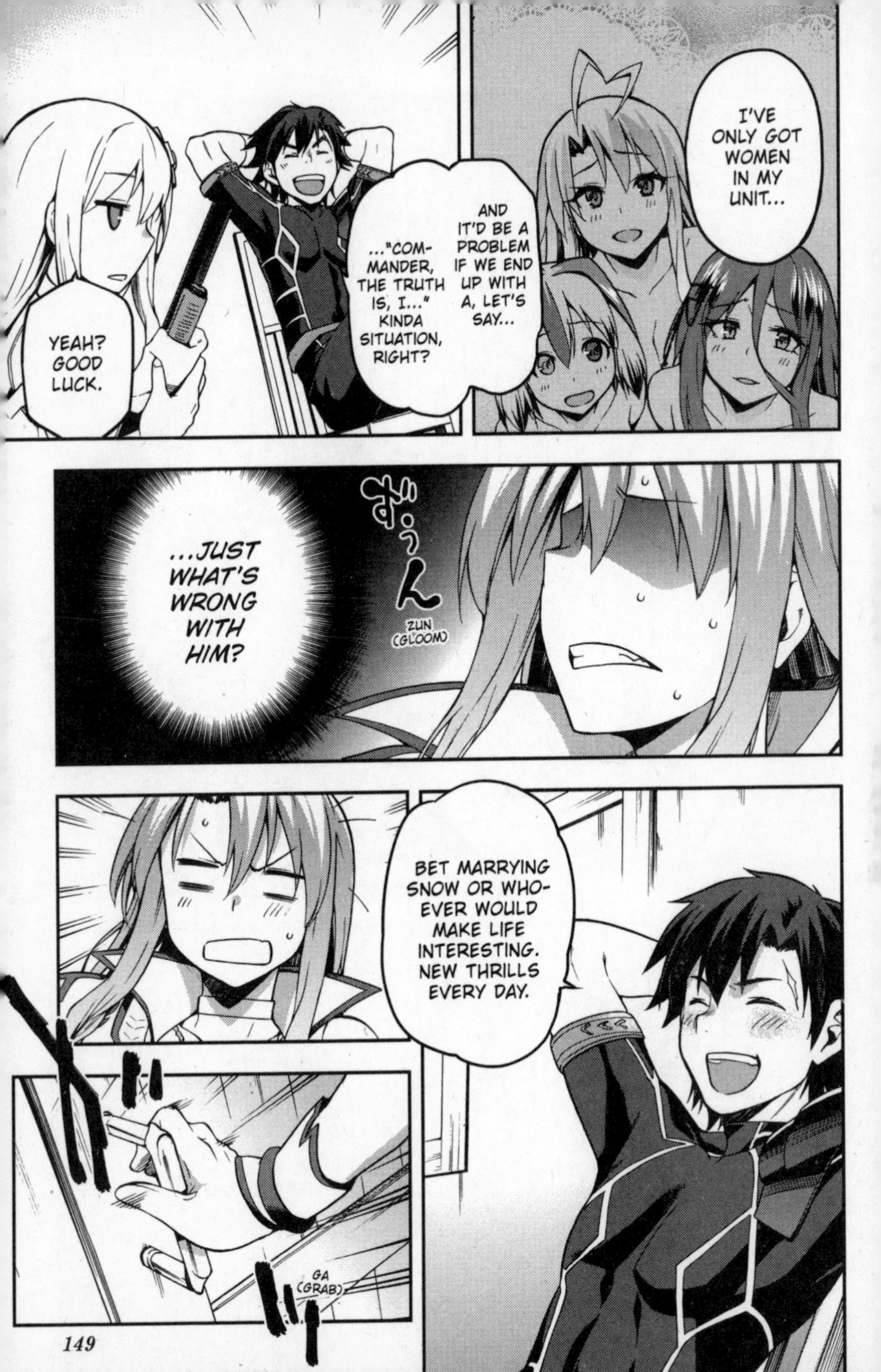
I'VE ONLY GOT WOMEN IN MY UNIT...
AND IT'D BE A PROBLEM IF WE END UP WITH A, LET'S SAY...
..."COMMANDER, THE TRUTH IS, I..." KINDA SITUATION, RIGHT?
YEAH? GOOD LUCK.
ずぅん
ZUN (GLOOM)
...JUST WHAT'S WRONG WITH HIM?
BET MARRYING SNOW OR WHOEVER WOULD MAKE LIFE INTERESTING. NEW THRILLS EVERY DAY.
GA (GRAB)

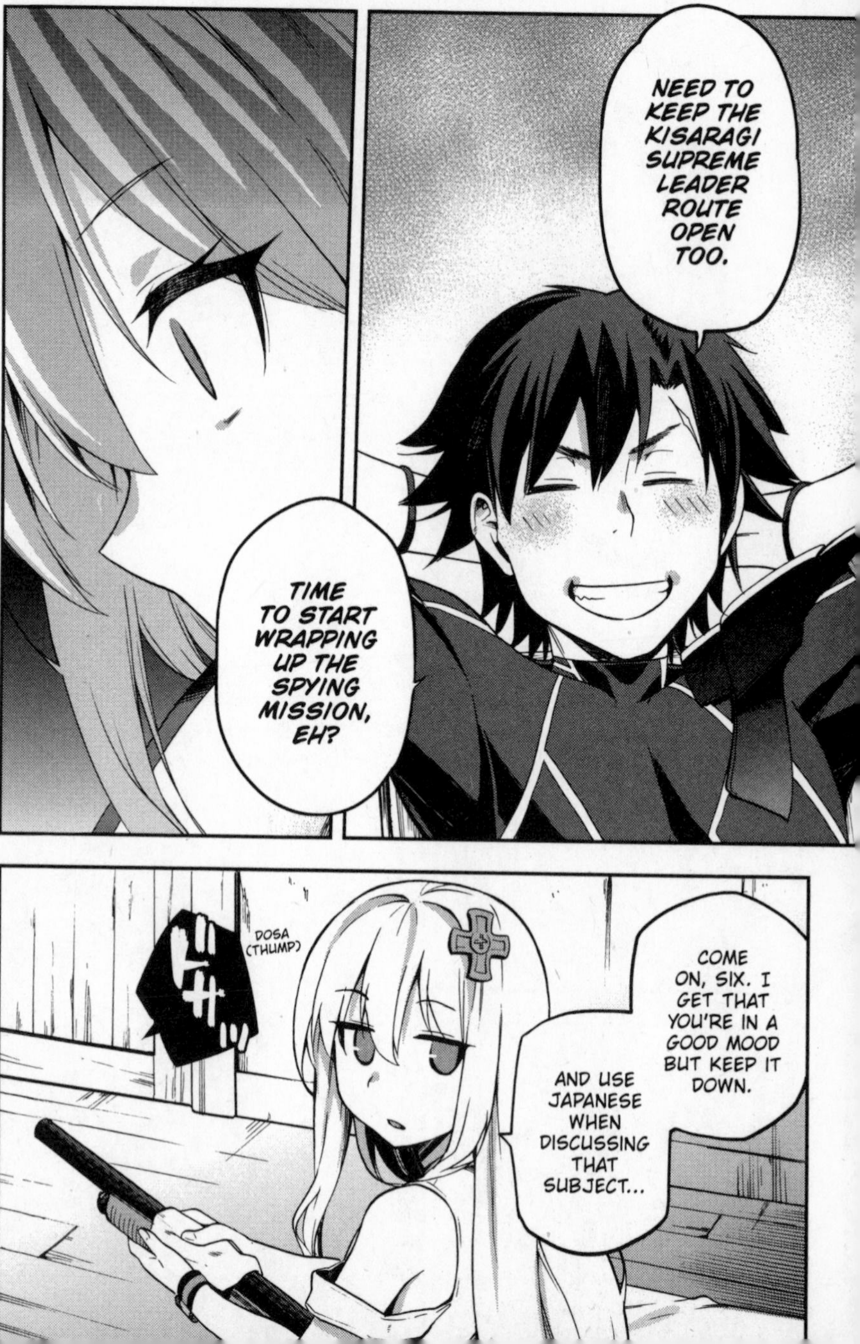
NEED TO KEEP THE KISARAGI SUPREME LEADER ROUTE OPEN TOO.
TIME TO START WRAPPING UP THE SPYING MISSION, EH?
COME ON, SIX. I GET THAT YOU'RE IN A GOOD MOOD BUT KEEP IT DOWN.
AND USE JAPANESE WHEN DISCUSSING THAT SUBJECT...
DOSA (THUMP)

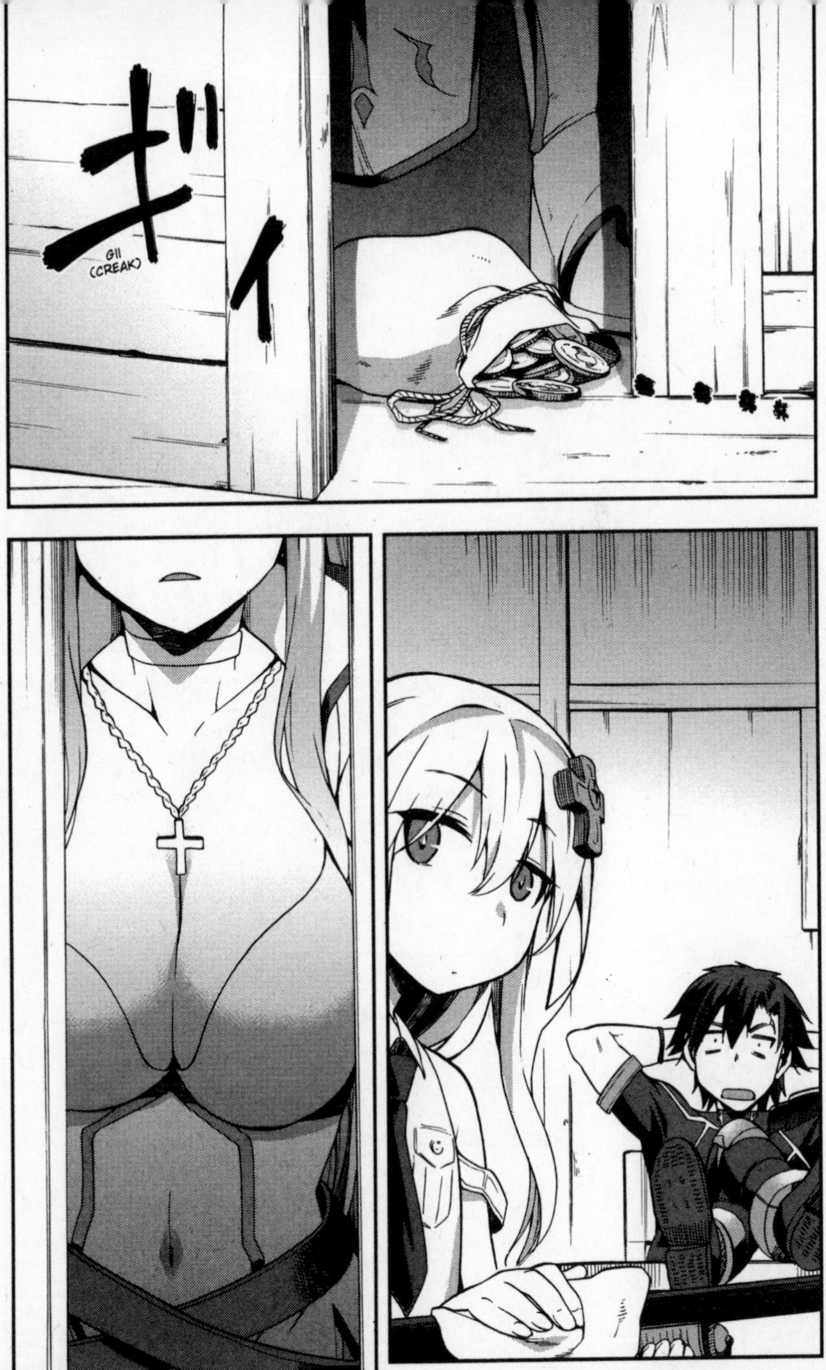
ギイ
GII
(CREAK)

ギィ・・・
(CREEAAK)
GII

STATUS REPORT: SURVEY OF THIS PLANET IS ALMOST COMPLETE.

WILL NOW PRIORITIZE OBTAINING A HIDEOUT TO SERVE AS A BASE FOR OUR INVASION.

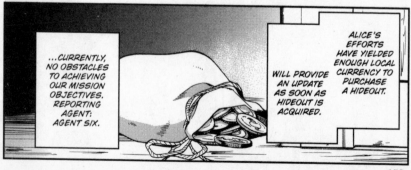

ALICE'S EFFORTS HAVE YIELDED ENOUGH LOCAL CURRENCY TO PURCHASE A HIDEOUT.

WILL PROVIDE AN UPDATE AS SOON AS HIDEOUT IS ACQUIRED.

...CURRENTLY, NO OBSTACLES TO ACHIEVING OUR MISSION OBJECTIVES. REPORTING AGENT: AGENT SIX.

Chapter 10.5

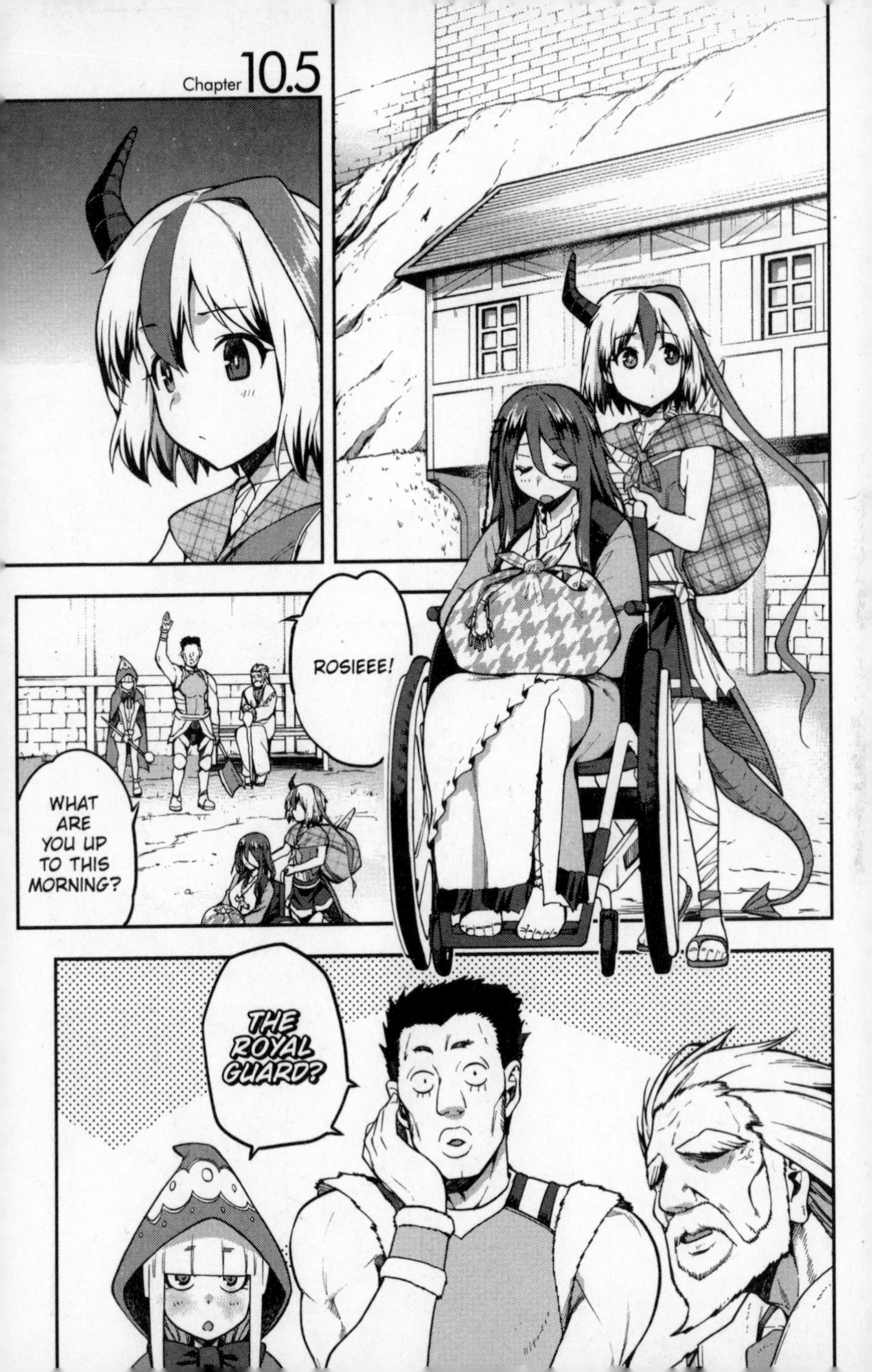
ROSIEEE!
WHAT ARE YOU UP TO THIS MORNING?
THE ROYAL GUARD?

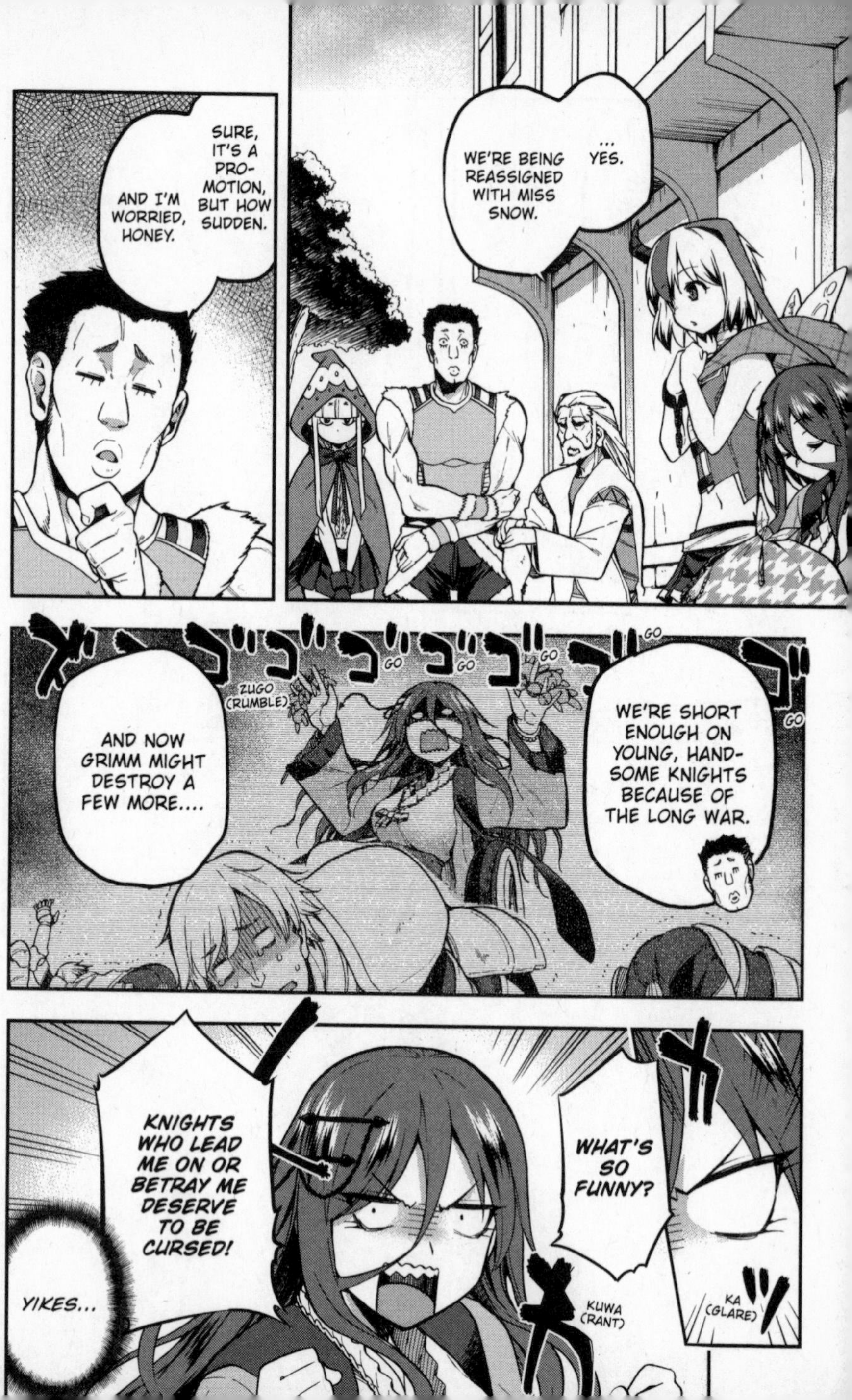
... YES.
WE'RE BEING REASSIGNED WITH MISS SNOW.
SURE, IT'S A PRO-MOTION, BUT HOW SUDDEN.
AND I'M WORRIED, HONEY.
GO GO GO GO GO GO
WE'RE SHORT ENOUGH ON YOUNG, HAND-SOME KNIGHTS BECAUSE OF THE LONG WAR.
ZUGO (RUMBLE)
AND NOW GRIMM MIGHT DESTROY A FEW MORE....
KA (GLARE)
WHAT'S SO FUNNY?
KUWA (RANT)
KNIGHTS WHO LEAD ME ON OR BETRAY ME DESERVE TO BE CURSED!
YIKES...

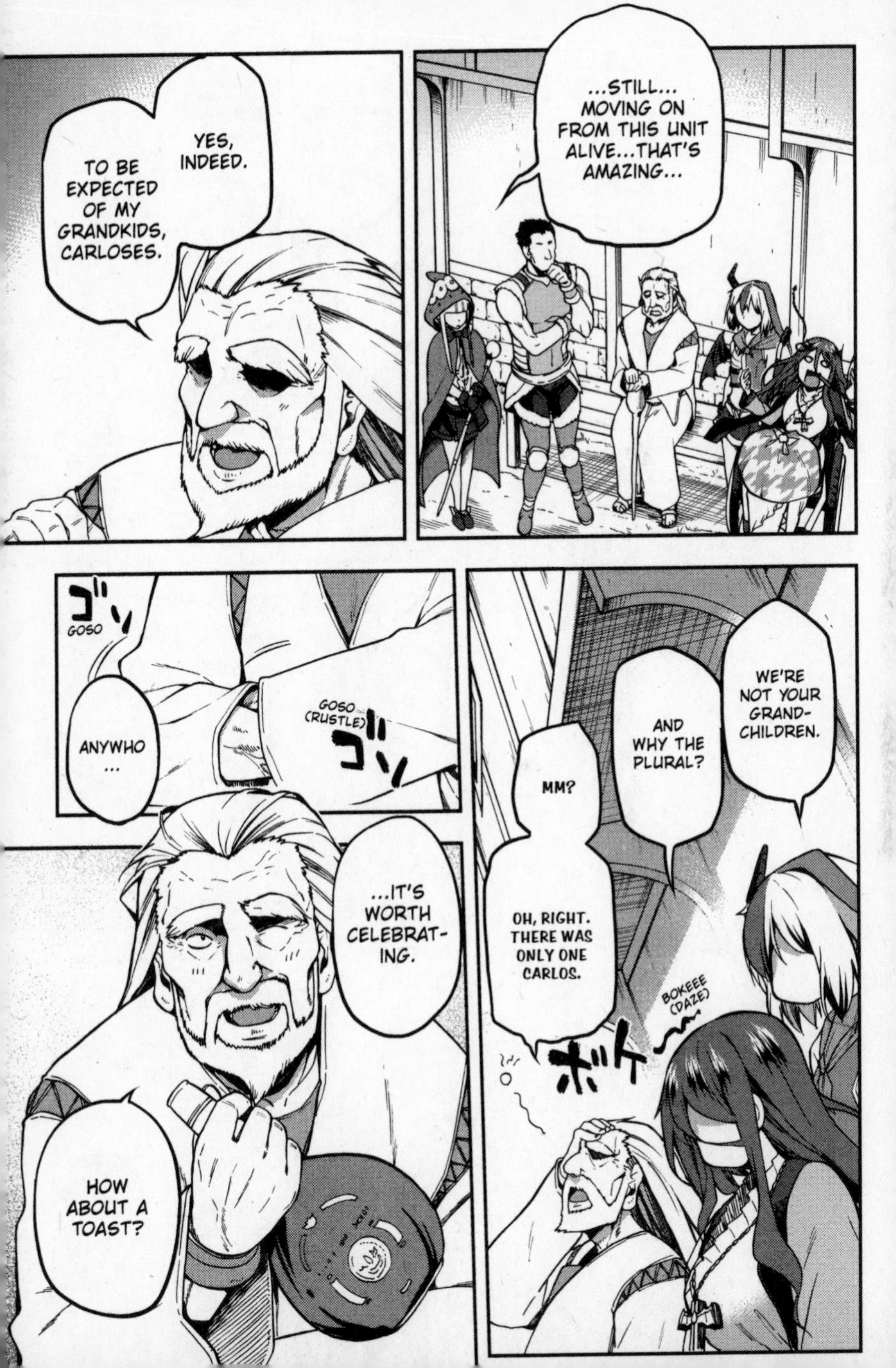
...STILL... MOVING ON FROM THIS UNIT ALIVE...THAT'S AMAZING...
YES, INDEED.
TO BE EXPECTED OF MY GRANDKIDS, CARLOSES.
WE'RE NOT YOUR GRAND-CHILDREN.
AND WHY THE PLURAL?
MM?
OH, RIGHT. THERE WAS ONLY ONE CARLOS.
ボケ~
BOKEEE (DAZE)
ゴソ
GOSO
GOSO (RUSTLE)
ゴソ
ANYWHO...
...IT'S WORTH CELEBRAT-ING.
HOW ABOUT A TOAST?

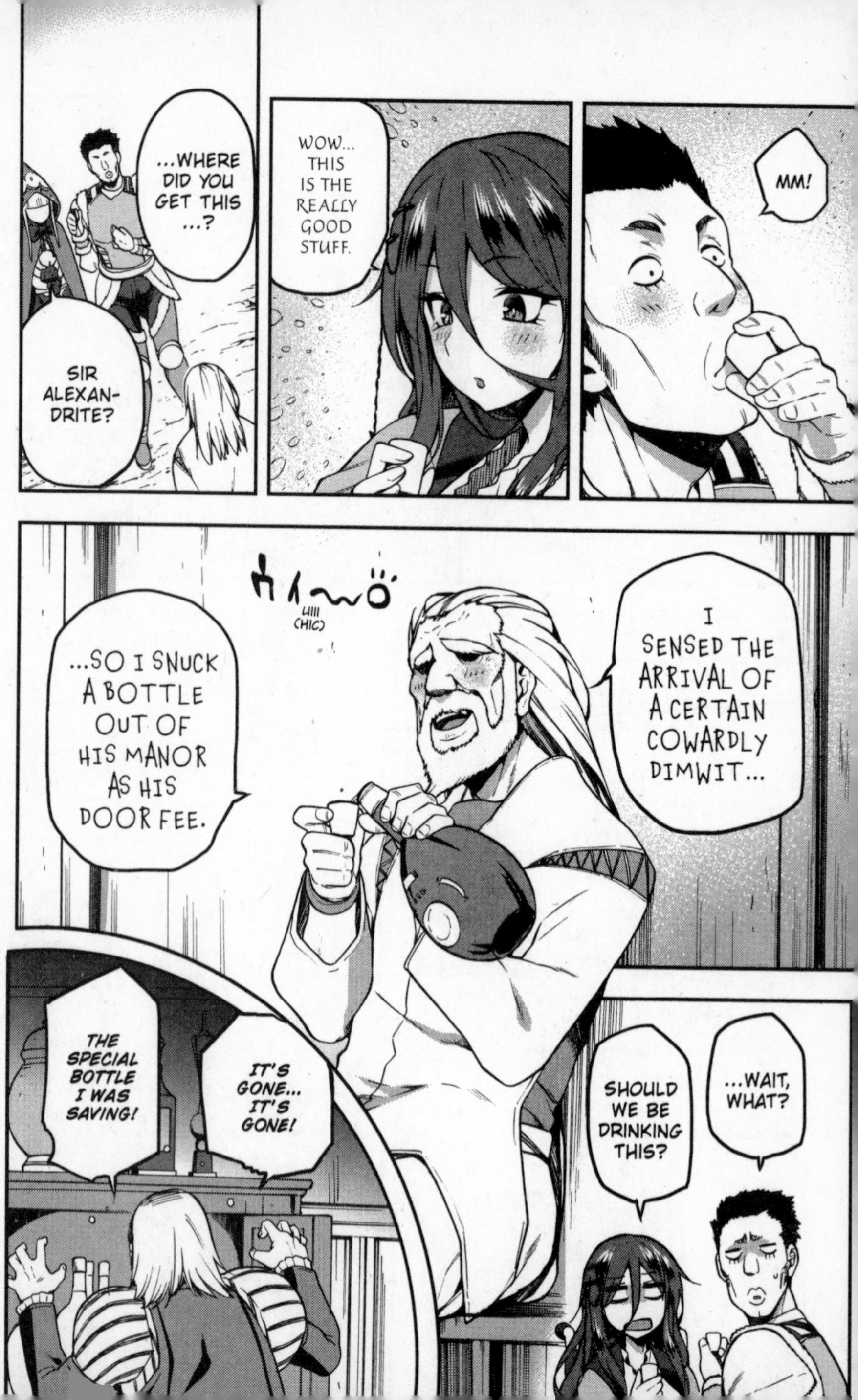
MM!
WOW... THIS IS THE REALLY GOOD STUFF.
...WHERE DID YOU GET THIS ...?
SIR ALEXANDRITE?
I SENSED THE ARRIVAL OF A CERTAIN COWARDLY DIMWIT...
UIII (HIC)
...SO I SNUCK A BOTTLE OUT OF HIS MANOR AS HIS DOOR FEE.
...WAIT, WHAT?
SHOULD WE BE DRINKING THIS?
IT'S GONE... IT'S GONE!
THE SPECIAL BOTTLE I WAS SAVING!

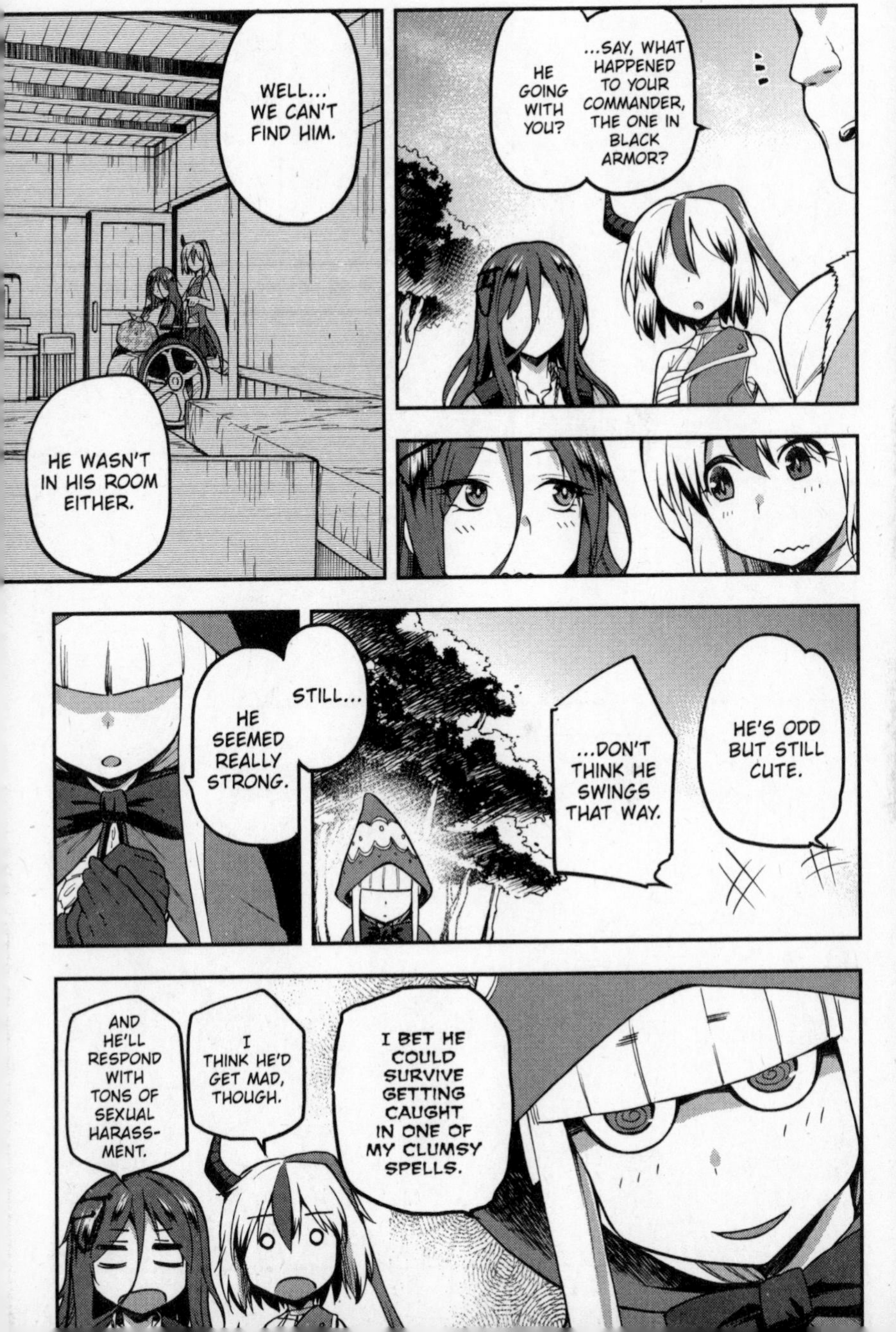
...SAY, WHAT HAPPENED TO YOUR COMMANDER, THE ONE IN BLACK ARMOR?
HE GOING WITH YOU?
WELL... WE CAN'T FIND HIM.
HE WASN'T IN HIS ROOM EITHER.
HE'S ODD BUT STILL CUTE.
...DON'T THINK HE SWINGS THAT WAY.
STILL...
HE SEEMED REALLY STRONG.
I BET HE COULD SURVIVE GETTING CAUGHT IN ONE OF MY CLUMSY SPELLS.
I THINK HE'D GET MAD, THOUGH.
AND HE'LL RESPOND WITH TONS OF SEXUAL HARASS-MENT.

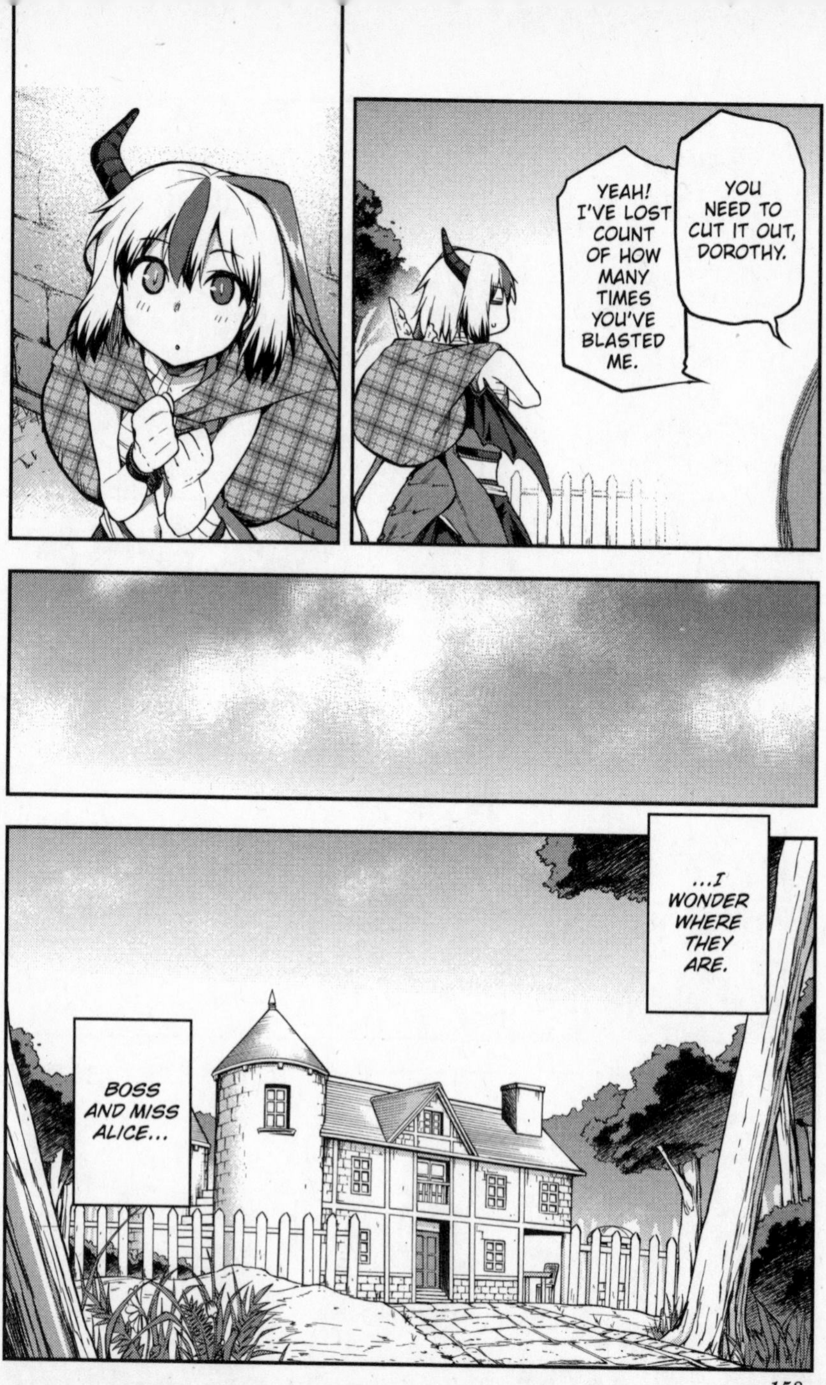
YOU NEED TO CUT IT OUT, DOROTHY.
YEAH! I'VE LOST COUNT OF HOW MANY TIMES YOU'VE BLASTED ME.
...I WONDER WHERE THEY ARE.
BOSS AND MISS ALICE...

—TO BE CONTINUED...

02

Extra Episode

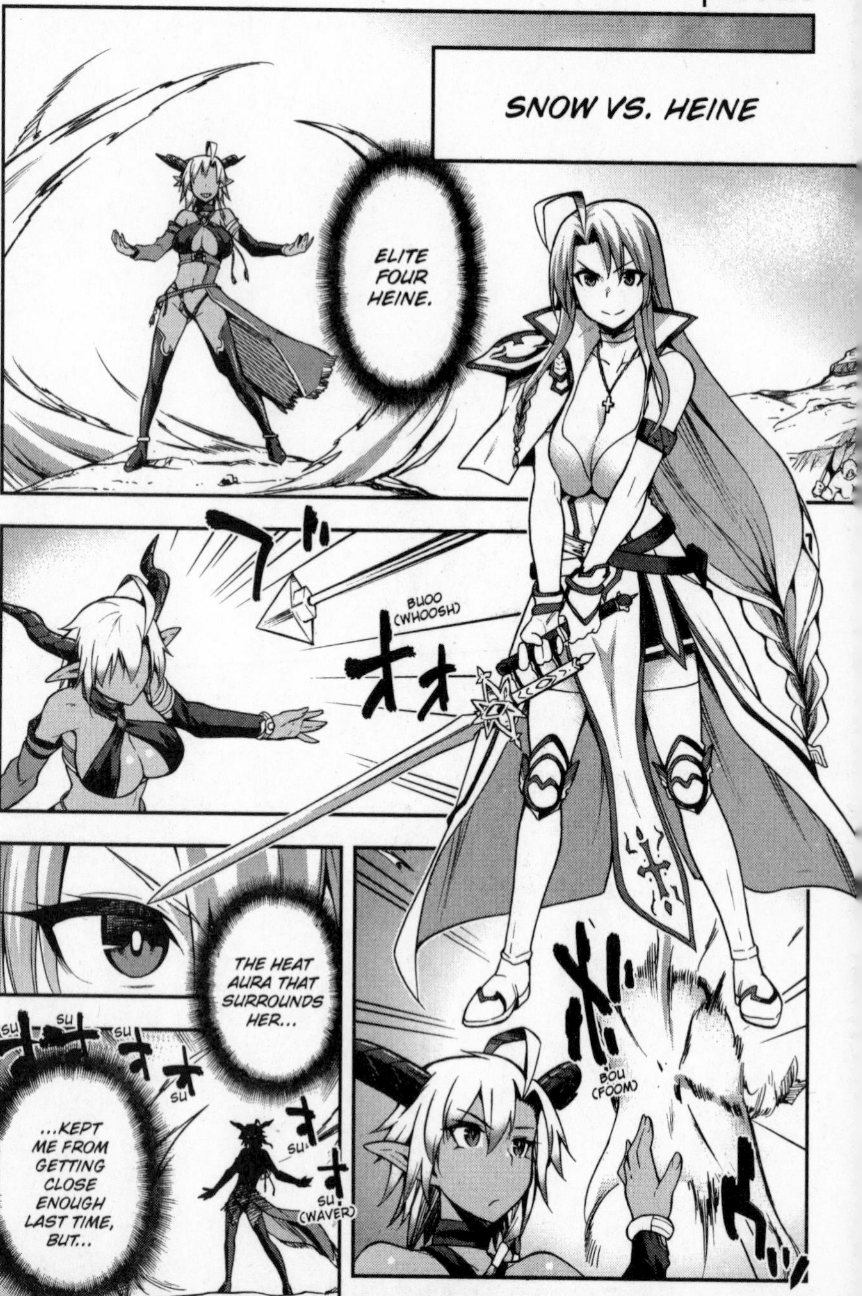

SNOW VS. HEINE
ELITE FOUR HEINE.
BUOO (WHOOSH)
BOU (FOOM)
THE HEAT AURA THAT SURROUNDS HER...
SU SU SU SU SU SU (WAVER)
...KEPT ME FROM GETTING CLOSE ENOUGH LAST TIME, BUT...

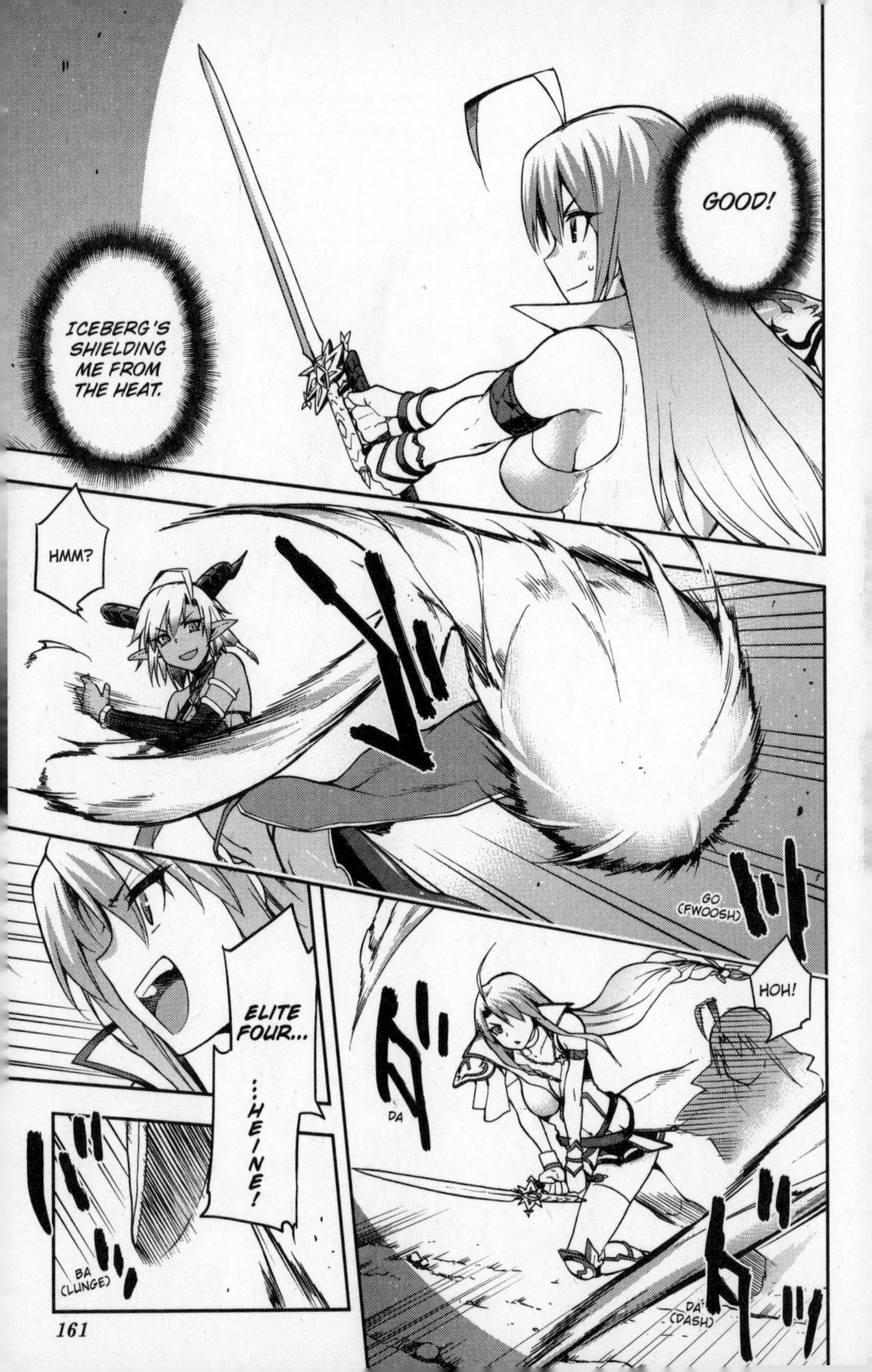
GOOD!
ICEBERG'S SHIELDING ME FROM THE HEAT.
HMM?
GO (FWOOSH)
HOH!
DA
DA (DASH)
ELITE FOUR...
...HEINE!
BA (LUNGE)

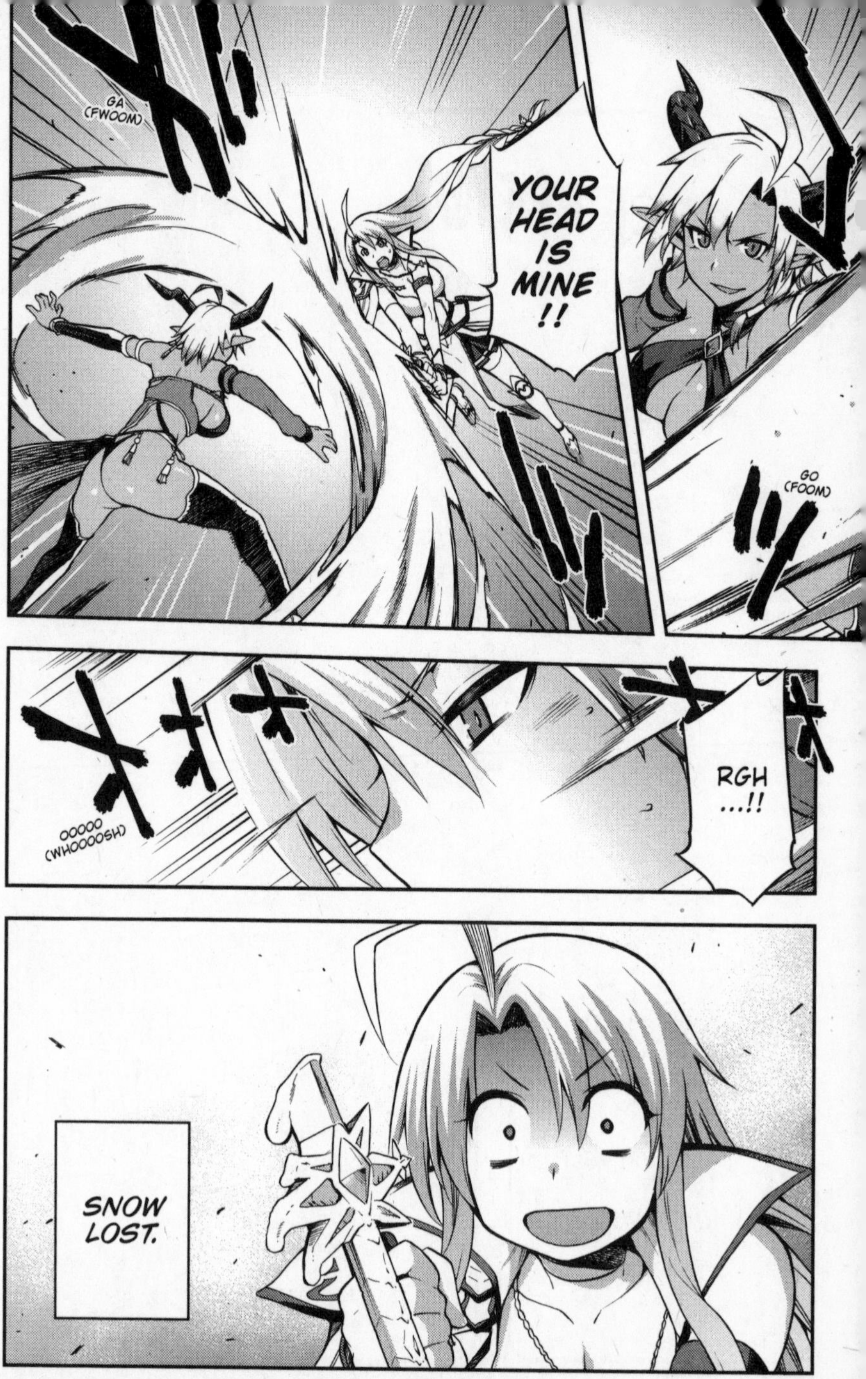
YOUR HEAD IS MINE!!
GO (FOOM)
GA (FWOOM)
RGH ...!!
OOOOO (WHOOOOSH)
SNOW LOST.

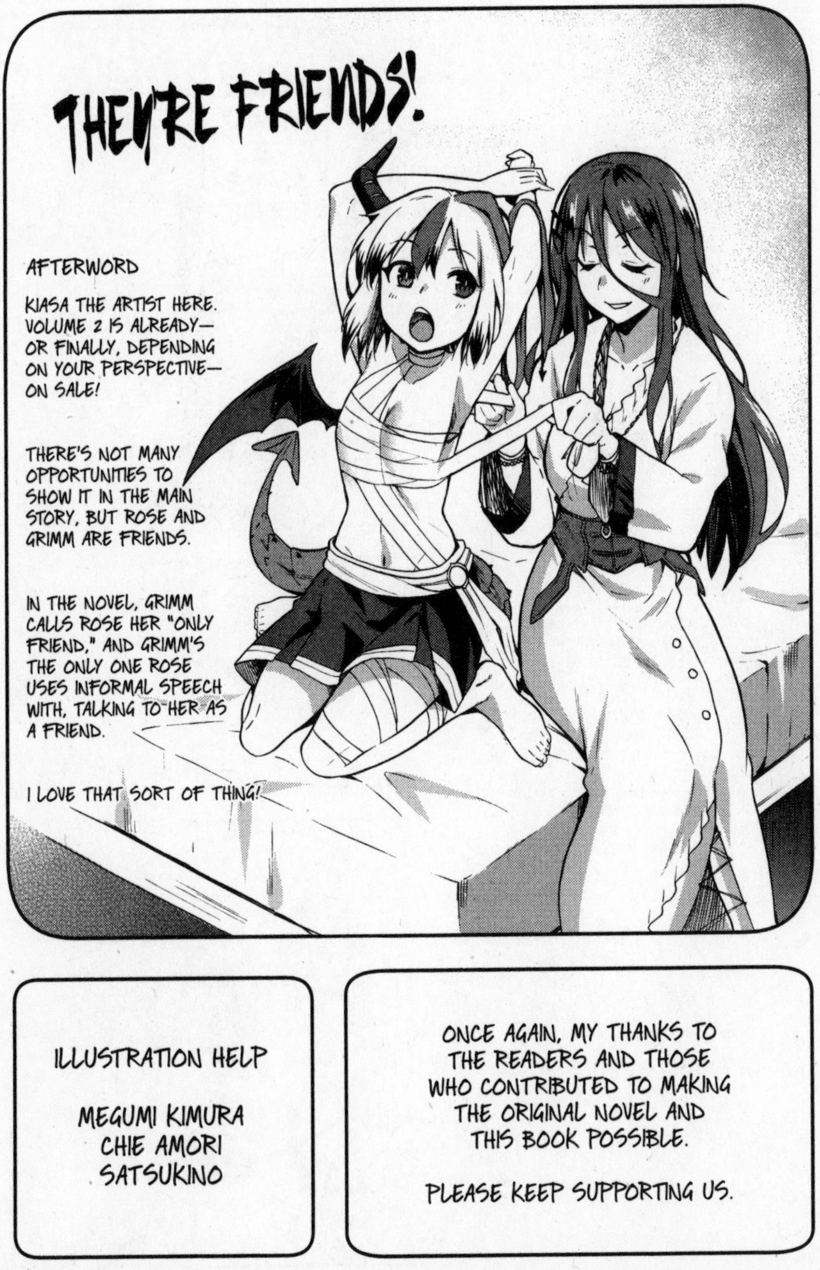
THEY'RE FRIENDS!
AFTERWORD
KIASA THE ARTIST HERE. VOLUME 2 IS ALREADY—OR FINALLY, DEPENDING ON YOUR PERSPECTIVE—ON SALE!
THERE'S NOT MANY OPPORTUNITIES TO SHOW IT IN THE MAIN STORY, BUT ROSE AND GRIMM ARE FRIENDS.
IN THE NOVEL, GRIMM CALLS ROSE HER "ONLY FRIEND," AND GRIMM'S THE ONLY ONE ROSE USES INFORMAL SPEECH WITH, TALKING TO HER AS A FRIEND.
I LOVE THAT SORT OF THING!

ONCE AGAIN, MY THANKS TO THE READERS AND THOSE WHO CONTRIBUTED TO MAKING THE ORIGINAL NOVEL AND THIS BOOK POSSIBLE.

PLEASE KEEP SUPPORTING US.

ILLUSTRATION HELP

MEGUMI KIMURA
CHIE AMORI
SATSUKINO

COMBATANTS WILL BE DISPATCHED!

02

ART: **MASAAKI KIASA**

STORY: **NATSUME AKATSUKI**

CHARACTER DESIGN: **KAKAO LANTHANUM**

Translation: Noboru Akimoto   **Lettering: Brandon Bovia**

SENTOIN, HAKENSHIMASU! Vol. 2
©Masaaki Kiasa 2019
©Natsume Akatsuki, Kakao • Lanthanum 2019
First published in Japan in 2019 by KADOKAWA CORPORATION, Tokyo. English translation rights arranged with KADOKAWA CORPORATION, Tokyo through TUTTLE-MORI AGENCY, INC., Tokyo.

English translation © 2020 by Yen Press, LLC

Yen Press
150 West 30th Street, 19th Floor
New York, NY 10001

Visit us at yenpress.com
facebook.com/yenpress
twitter.com/yenpress
yenpress.tumblr.com
instagram.com/yenpress

First Yen Press Edition: February 2020

Yen Press is an imprint of Yen Press, LLC.
The Yen Press name and logo are trademarks of Yen Press, LLC.

The publisher is not responsible for websites (or their content) that are not owned by the publisher.

Library of Congress Control Number: 2019942967

ISBNs: 978-1-9753-9901-6 (paperback)
        978-1-9753-0861-2 (ebook)

10 9 8 7 6 5 4 3 2 1

WOR

Printed in the United States of America